Download Forms on Nolo.com

To download the forms, go to this book's companion page at:

www.nolo.com/back-of-book/PROBM.html

Checking the companion page is also a good way
to stay informed on topics related to this book.

More Resources
from Nolo.com

Legal Forms, Books, & Software
Hundreds of do-it-yourself products—all written in plain English,
approved, and updated by our in-house legal editors.

Legal Articles
Get informed with thousands of free articles on everyday legal
topics. Our articles are accurate, up to date, and reader friendly.

Find a Lawyer
Want to talk to a lawyer? Use Nolo to find a lawyer who can
help you with your case.

NOLO
LAW for ALL

13th Edition

Dealing With
Problem Employees

How to Manage Performance
& Personality Issues in the Workplace

The Editors of Nolo

NOLO
LAW for ALL

THIRTEENTH EDITION	JANUARY 2026
Editor	ANN O'CONNELL
Cover Design	SUSAN PUTNEY
Book Design	SUSAN PUTNEY
Proofreading	IRENE BARNARD
Printing	SHERIDAN

ISSN: 2169-3862 (print)

ISSN: 2169-3870 (online)

ISBN: 978-1-4133-3309-1 (pbk)

ISBN: 978-1-4133-3310-7 (ebook)

This book covers only United States law, unless it specifically states otherwise.

Please note

Accurate, plain-English legal information can help you solve many of your own legal problems. But this text is not a substitute for personalized advice from a knowledgeable lawyer. If you want the help of a trained professional—and we'll always point out situations in which we think that's a good idea—consult an attorney licensed to practice in your state.

MH Sub I, LLC dba Nolo, 909 N. Pacific Coast Hwy, 11th Fl., El Segundo, CA 90245.

About the Authors

Nolo's editorial department includes more than a dozen legal editors and a full-time legal researcher, who collectively have more than 100 years' experience turning legal jargon into plain English. Most of our editors gave up careers as practicing lawyers in favor of furthering Nolo's mission: Getting legal information into the hands of the people who really need it.

All Nolo legal editors specialize in certain areas of the law, and many are recognized as national experts in their field. They write books, edit books by outside authors, and in their spare time write online articles, develop legal forms, and create the legal content for Nolo software.

Table of Contents

Appendixes

Introduction

No matter how carefully they hire workers, how many incentives they give for strong performance, or how diligently they try to create positive and productive work environments, most businesses ultimately have to deal with a problem employee.

Perhaps you picked up this book because that day has already come for you. Or perhaps an employee has demonstrated attitude or performance problems that won't go away, has sexually harassed other employees, has stolen from the company, or has threatened violence. Or, you might have picked up this book because you're concerned about the bigger picture and frustrated with the number of employee problems that crop up year after year. Instead of simply reacting to each problem as it arises, you've decided it's time to be more proactive.

Employee problems aren't inevitable, nor must they fill you with fear or anxiety. In the chapters that follow, we provide you with the practical and legal information you need to handle employee problems confidently and to create policies and procedures that will reduce the number and degree of problems you face in the future. As an added bonus, the strategies described in this book will make your workplace more collaborative and increase employee morale.

The High Cost of Problem Employees

For many employers, figuring out whether and how to discipline or fire a worker is one of the most stressful parts of the job. And understandably so—ignoring or mishandling worker problems can have costly ramifications.

Lawsuits

Wrongful termination and other employment lawsuits brought by current and former employees are disruptive and often expensive. Depending on the scope of the matter, losing an employment lawsuit could mean your company will have to pay the plaintiff tens or hundreds of thousands of dollars—maybe even millions. And that doesn't even include the cost of paying a lawyer to defend you, win or lose. According to a 2017 report by Hiscox, a business insurance company, the average cost to defend and settle employment discrimination charges that resulted in some payment to the employee was $160,000. Hiscox hasn't released a more recent report, but the costs have almost certainly escalated since 2017. Consider these examples:

- An Ohio jury awarded more than $46 million to a former manager at Republic Services, Inc., who claimed he was fired in retaliation for refusing to fire three older employees, which he believed would have been age discrimination. Jurors were particularly upset by evidence that the company tried to prevent the manager from getting another job after he was fired and that the company manufactured evidence of the manager's poor performance only after the manager sued.

- A California jury awarded $61 million to two drivers for Federal Express, who claimed that they had been harassed and called derogatory names because of their Lebanese heritage. The case later settled (to avoid an appeal by FedEx).

- UBS was ordered to pay more than $29 million to an employee who alleged that she was belittled and denied important accounts because of her sex. UBS also had to pay sanctions for destroying important documents after the plaintiff filed a complaint with the Equal Employment Opportunity Commission (EEOC), and the jury was told to assume that those documents would have hurt the company's case.

- A jury ordered Metris Companies to pay its former CEO $30 million for wrongful termination. The CEO claimed he was fired because he wanted to tell shareholders that the company was for sale and under investigation by the federal government.

Discrimination Charges Filed With the EEOC

The EEOC collects statistics on how many discrimination charges are filed with the agency each year and what those charges allege. (An employee who wants to sue for discrimination must first file a charge with the EEOC or a similar state agency.) More than 88,000 charges were filed in fiscal year 2024. In recent years, there have been more charges alleging disability discrimination than any other type; previously, race discrimination charges were more common. However, as has been true for more than a decade, the most frequently filed charge wasn't for any type of discrimination, but for retaliation.

Employee Turnover

If you ignore problem employees, handle workplace problems ineffectively, or operate in a draconian manner, you will soon have an employee retention problem. The problem employee will receive neither the guidance nor the opportunity necessary to improve, and will, in all likelihood, be fired or quit. In the meantime, your other employees— who have picked up the slack for that problem worker or, even worse, put up with that worker's abuse and mistreatment—will soon look for other opportunities.

So, you'll hire new employees, right?

Well, replacing employees rather than taking steps to retain good ones is an expensive strategy. Many experts estimate that it can cost one-and-a-half times a new hire's salary to replace an employee. The cost of replacing managerial employees can run even higher. Wouldn't it be easier—and less expensive—to hang on to the good employees you already have and help your problem employees turn their performance around?

Poor Workplace Morale

Problem employees can really drag down the spirit of a workplace. Coworkers who see the difficult employee get away with breaking the rules, mistreating others, performing poorly, or being insubordinate, will feel resentful and unappreciated. They might even feel frightened if the troublemaker poses a threat to their safety or well-being.

If you don't take action to stop the downward spiral, you could face any number of associated problems. You'll have trouble recruiting new workers and getting the most out of your remaining employees. You might even find yourself with an epidemic of workers with poor attitudes on your hands.

Workers who believe they're being treated unfairly or taken advantage of are also more likely to resort to small acts of revenge, including theft and fraud.

The Bottom Line

Problem employees ultimately hurt your company's bottom line. Lawsuits, employee turnover, and low morale drain resources and reduce the productivity of your business. All that time problem employees spend harassing coworkers, arguing with you, or scrolling on TikTok is time spent not working. And all the time other employees spend complaining about a problem worker, taking on the unaccomplished work, and laying bets on when you'll finally get up the nerve to terminate is likewise lost to the company.

How This Book Can Help

So what can you do about your problem employees? With the help of this book, plenty. Read on for proven strategies for dealing with the most common employment problems, legal information on your rights and responsibilities as an employer, and practical tips that will help you get the job done.

Learn how to:

- avoid hiring problem employees in the first place
- effectively deal with specific problems that arise in your workplace
- turn problem employees into productive, valuable workers
- safely and legally terminate employees who can't or won't improve
- tap into the potential of every employee

- promote productivity, loyalty, and camaraderie in your workforce, and
- stay out of legal trouble.

Chapter 1 dissects the most common types of employee problems and explains strategies for handling them. Chapter 2 explains the basic legal rules that you must keep in mind when making employment decisions. Chapters 3 through 6 take an in-depth look at management practices—performance evaluations, progressive discipline, investigations, and alternative dispute resolution programs—that will prevent many problems from cropping up. When problems do arise, these same practices will enable you to deal with them effectively and legally.

For those situations in which nothing else works, four full chapters examine how to fire problem employees and include information on:

- how to decide whether you should fire the employee, including whether you've done all you can to protect against lawsuits (Chapter 7)
- how to handle post-termination issues, such as references, unemployment compensation, and continuing health insurance (Chapter 8)
- how to decide whether to offer a severance package (including what to include in the package and whether to ask the employee to sign a release agreeing not to sue you) (Chapter 9), and

- how to legally and safely terminate an employee, step by step (Chapter 10).

Chapter 11 will help you develop sound hiring and personnel policies to weed out problem employees of the future. Chapter 12 explains how to find and select an employment lawyer if you need expert help.

Finally, check out Appendix B for a number of charts showing state-specific laws as well as more details about certain federal laws.

Who Should Use This Book

This book is for anyone who oversees employees, including business owners, human resource professionals, supervisors, and managers. If you're a conscientious, well-intentioned employer who wants to learn about the law, pick up tips and strategies to manage more effectively, and know how to treat your employees fairly, this book is for you.

Who Shouldn't Use This Book

This book isn't for people who work in the state or federal government. Although many of the strategies that we discuss could be applied to government workers, most employment laws operate slightly differently—or not at all—in the public setting. If you are a manager or supervisor of government employees, this book probably isn't for you.

This book also isn't for people who are looking for ways to "get around" workplace laws. If you're looking for a guide that will show you how to skirt the boundaries of the law, this book won't help. Our goal is to help well-meaning employers deal with their employment problems legally and effectively, not to help those who wish to evade their legal responsibilities.

Get Forms and More on Nolo.com

This book includes forms, checklists, and policies you can use in your own company. You can access them in digital form on this book's online companion page at:

www.nolo.com/back-of-book/PROBM.html

What's Your Problem?

n the chapters that follow, we talk extensively about strategies for dealing with problem employees. Before we do that, however, we'd like to turn the spotlight on the problems themselves.

In this chapter, we address how to deal with certain employee problems. As part of this discussion, we refer to the strategies and management techniques that we discuss throughout the rest of the book, including:

- performance evaluations (see Chapter 3)
- progressive discipline (see Chapter 4)
- workplace investigations (see Chapter 5)
- termination (see Chapters 7 through 10), and
- effective hiring practices (Chapter 11).

The chart at the end of this chapter summarizes the typical employee problems you might face and possible strategies for resolving them.

Performance or Productivity Problems

For the most part, your business will only be as good as your employees. This simple fact makes performance and productivity problems a real threat to the success of your business. For this reason, resolving performance problems is one of the most important tasks of an employer or manager.

In some cases, detecting a performance or productivity problem will be as simple as observing and noting the subpar nature of an employee's work. Or you might receive weekly reports of employee productivity and notice that an employee's numbers are low. In other cases, an employee will be able to hide performance or productivity problems. You'll know something is wrong somewhere in the company, but you won't be able to nail down exactly who is working below your standards.

The most effective way to deal with employee performance or productivity problems is through a performance evaluation system. As you'll learn in Chapter 3, such a system will force you to track each employee, so you always know who is doing what. It will also give employees a clear understanding of your expectations so that they can tailor their work performance to meet them.

If an employee fails to live up to your expectations, regular performance reviews will foster the communication and collaboration you need to address the problem. At review time, you'll discuss what help or resources the employee might need to turn their performance around. Then, if the employee doesn't improve, you'll have laid the groundwork for progressive discipline and, if necessary, termination.

When faced with a performance or productivity problem, look beyond the employee's willingness—or lack thereof—to do well. Consider the work environment and any personal issues that could have an impact on the employee's performance. For example, simply telling the employee to do better will accomplish little if the employee's supervisor is the true cause of the problem. Similarly, if the employee doesn't have the necessary skills to do the job or if they're struggling with a personal or family problem, you'll have to take these factors into account.

Healthy Practices for a Healthy Workplace

The following are just a few examples of employment practices that promote positive employee relations, reduce the number of employee problems, and provide protection from lawsuits. We discuss these and others throughout this book:

- **Communicate with your employees.** Make sure they know your expectations, and tell them when they're doing well or poorly.
- **Listen to your employees.** They have valuable insight into your workplace and the solutions to many employee problems.
- **Act consistently.** Apply the same standards of performance and conduct to all of your employees and avoid favoritism. Workers quickly sour on a boss who plays favorites.
- **Follow your own policies.** Why should your employees follow the rules if you're willing to bend them for yourself whenever the mood strikes?
- **Treat employees with respect.** Your workers will treat you as you treat them. And workers will thrive in a workplace where they feel respected and treated fairly.

In addition, workers who must be disciplined, investigated, or fired will take the bad news much better if they feel that you've treated them decently throughout the process.

- **Make merit-based decisions.** Always be guided by criteria related to the job and the worker's ability to do that job, not by an employee's characteristics (race, gender, or disability, for example), personal activities, or your own whims.
- **Take action when necessary.** The sooner you deal with an employee problem, the better your chance of nipping it in the bud.
- **Keep good records.** Good employers keep regular, thorough records of major employment decisions and conclusions, including performance evaluations, discipline, counseling sessions, investigations, and firings. These records provide invaluable evidence that you were driven by sound business reasons, not illegal motivations. Remember, if you end up in court, you'll not only have to explain what you did and why; you'll also have to prove it with evidence.

New Employees

If an employee is new to the job, consider the following questions before you decide how to respond:

- **Did you give the employee adequate training?** For example, did you teach the employee how to use your accounting system, or did you assume that the employee could just figure it out? If you did the latter, it could explain why the employee is taking more time than is reasonable to do the work; perhaps the employee is struggling with a system that's tough to understand.
- **Does the employee have the necessary skills?** For example, the new artist you hired might be very talented but not know how to use the design program your company relies on.
- **Does the employee understand what is expected of them?** For example, the salesperson you hired might not realize that part of the job is to clean the store when business is slow.
- **Have you provided the employee with adequate tools and resources?** For instance, requiring employees to share a necessary piece of equipment might have an impact on productivity that really isn't the fault of individual employees.
- **Are there any rules or systems that make it difficult for the employee to do the job?** For instance, have you asked a supplier to deliver materials by such a late date that your employee doesn't have enough time to produce the goods?

> **TIP**
>
> **Make sure remote employees are ready to succeed.** It can be harder to ensure that remote employees have the information and resources they need to do their jobs well. You can't count on remote employees picking up the office culture or learning how to do their jobs by observing their coworkers. You might not know whether the employee has the necessary resources at home to get the job done. When you bring on a remote employee, you need to be clear about your expectations. Check in regularly—and often—to find out whether the employee needs anything or has any questions. And invest extra time in training and coaching to help the employee understand what good performance looks like to you.

New Problems

If an employee has been in the job for a while, possible causes for the decline in performance might include:

- **Changes in the work environment.** If there have been no performance or productivity problems in the past, does the employee have a new supervisor? New coworkers? New customers? If so, maybe the employee is having trouble working with the new person. Or maybe the new person—and not the employee—is the true cause of the problem.

- **Shifts at home.** Something in the employee's personal life—such as a new child or a divorce—might be affecting their work quality. A little flexibility can go a long way for an otherwise solid employee who lets you know that a life-changing event is making it hard to focus at work.
- **Substance abuse.** Has the employee developed an addiction to drugs or alcohol? (See "Drugs and Alcohol," below, for more about substance abuse.)

Of course, the best way to find the answers to all of these questions is through careful communication with the employee and thoughtful observation of the workplace.

Interpersonal Problems

Interpersonal problems—employees who don't get along with each other, with customers and vendors, or with managers and supervisors—arise in an endless number of contexts. Sometimes the solution is as simple as moving an employee's desk or changing an employee's work group. Other times, the problem is far more complex, with roots in an employee's personal life or psyche. Still other times, the problem is really about stereotypes, prejudice, and illegal discrimination.

We explore some of these scenarios in the subsections below. Regardless of the sort of interpersonal problem you have on your hands, however, know this: It is perfectly legal for you to discipline employees who

are unable or unwilling to get along with coworkers, customers, vendors, managers, and supervisors. It is also legal to fire them if they don't improve. Your performance evaluation and progressive discipline systems (Chapters 3 and 4, respectively) will be invaluable in laying the groundwork for corrective action.

Employees With Contextual Problems

The most common type of interpersonal problem—and the most straightforward— involves an employee who has a problem with a coworker or work situation. Maybe the employee doesn't get along with a particular supervisor, or perhaps the employee's workstation is so noisy that it distracts the employee from concentrating. Usually, employers can easily address such problems by putting the employee in a different work group, for example, or moving the employee's workstation to a quieter part of the office.

If the employee has never had interpersonal problems in the past, find out if something has changed in the employee's work environment. If the problem is with a supervisor, for example, is this the first supervisor with whom the employee has had conflicts? If so, then perhaps the fault lies with the supervisor and not with the employee.

If the problem can't be solved easily, you should impose consequences for inappropriate behavior through your performance evaluation and progressive discipline systems.

Employees With Personal Problems

Some employees have problems that exist independently of the workplace. These problems are usually the result of the employee's own personal issues or personality. Although these problems can be more thorny for you to deal with than the contextual problems described above, they still find their solutions in performance evaluation and progressive discipline.

Difficult Personalities

Sooner or later, every workplace will have someone who is just a bad apple, who can't get along with others, or whom everyone dislikes and for a good reason. An employee might have a hair-trigger temper, for example, or a cruel sense of humor.

This is the employee who undoubtedly has similar problems with other employers, coworkers, friends, and family. No matter what adjustments you might make to this employee's schedule, environment, or other working conditions, you'd still have a problem employee.

In these situations, it's worth intervening; after all, you won't know you have a hopeless case until you've tried. But if all signs point to the door, you should consider termination. If you've conscientiously used your performance evaluation and progressive discipline systems and noted how the employee's comments or behavior have negatively affected job performance (and possibly the performance of coworkers), you should be on solid legal ground when you do so.

EXAMPLE: Ben works at an accounting firm and considers himself quite the comic. He loves teasing his coworkers about everything, from the way they wear their hair to their various personality quirks. As a result, no one likes to work with Ben, and his coworkers have complained to Molly, their supervisor. At his performance evaluation, Molly gives Ben a low ranking on his ability to work with others. Ben is shocked and hurt. He tells Molly that it's part of his personality to tease people; he can't help it. Molly tells him that his comments must stop, because they are hurtful and upsetting to his coworkers. Now it's up to Ben. He can either suppress his jokes and keep his job, or he can continue the comedy routine and find another place to work.

Difficult Personal Situations

It would be nice if employees could leave their personal problems at home, but they often can't. A tough personal life can derail even the most conscientious employee.

For the employer, this is a particularly difficult issue: Your employee isn't obligated to tell you about personal, nonwork difficulties, and even if you know about the situation, you're probably not in a position to offer solutions. The most you can do is be understanding and flexible, which is often just what the employee wants and needs. If that fails, you should resort to your progressive discipline system. No matter how sympathetic you are to an employee's situation, at some point the work needs to get done.

Is Your Company the Problem?

When facing employee issues with performance, productivity, or insubordination, you should ask yourself whether the company could be the real problem—especially if more than one employee is struggling or complaining.

For example, if employees aren't meeting their performance and productivity goals, this might mean their supervisors are setting goals too high. Or, employees might not have the resources they need to perform at peak levels. They also could be dealing with a supervisor who micromanages, plays favorites, bullies employees, or simply doesn't set clear expectations. It could be that you have a problem manager or supervisor on your hands rather than a problem employee.

EXAMPLE: Ever since Ani's teenage son was arrested for drug use, Ani has been useless at work after 3:00 p.m. She worries about what he's doing every day after school. She spends afternoons fretting and distracted until she leaves at 5:00 p.m. Her productivity has dropped off significantly. Her boss, Jose, doesn't want to lose Ani, who is a good worker, but he also can't afford to have her wasting her afternoons in this way. Jose suggests a flexible work schedule to Ani. Rather than working 9:00 a.m. to 5:00 p.m., she can work from 7:00 a.m. to 3:00 p.m. That way, her schedule will coincide with her son's, and she can be home when he gets out of school. Ani accepts the new schedule, and her productivity returns to its former level.

TIP

Refer employees to your employee assistance program. Does your workplace have an employee assistance program (EAP)? If so, it can be a valuable resource for employees who are undergoing personal problems, including addiction, financial troubles, family conflict, and more. In addition to any workplace changes you make to accommodate an employee's situation, you should also refer the employee to your company's EAP for help with the underlying problem.

Discrimination

Some employee interpersonal problems result from ignorance, hate, and prejudice. For example, an employee might not get along with a Black supervisor because the employee harbors racial prejudices. Or a Jewish employee might not get along with coworkers who are anti-Semitic. If what appears at first glance to be an interpersonal problem is really a discrimination problem, you've got a serious situation on your hands—one that carries potential legal liability. (See Chapter 2 for a discussion of antidiscrimination laws.) Whether the employee is the perpetrator or the victim, this sort of problem requires a swift and effective response from you.

Be on the lookout for this situation if the problem employee is of a different race or gender from coworkers or has another protected characteristic (for example, the employee has a disability or is pregnant). Investigate the problem to see how serious it is, then discipline any coworkers or managers who've harassed or discriminated against the employee based on race, gender, or any other trait that's protected by law. Employees who are the targets of discrimination might push back against the aggressor(s) or have performance or productivity problems stemming from their mistreatment. If you focus on the reaction instead of the cause, you'll miss the opportunity to correct the situation at its roots.

If you learn that an employee is harassing or discriminating against others, you must take action. Figure out what happened and who was involved by conducting an effective investigation. No matter how good their performance is, be prepared to discipline or terminate any employees who discriminate against or harass others.

TIP

If discrimination and harassment issues occur in your workplace frequently, it might be time to be more proactive. Consider using diversity training to deal with a workplace culture that is hostile toward women or toward people of a certain race or religion, for example.

You can find strategies for preventing and dealing with harassment and discrimination, including information on diversity and antiharassment training, in *The Essential Guide to Handling Workplace Harassment & Discrimination*, by Deborah C. England (Nolo).

Insubordination

An employee is "insubordinate" when refusing to follow a direct order or a workplace rule. Don't confuse insubordination with a negative attitude or foot-dragging. Those responses reflect interpersonal problems and are not as serious as flat-out refusals.

Like the interpersonal problems discussed above, insubordination occurs in varying contexts. A refusal without good reason, legally or practically, is the easiest to deal with: Discipline or terminate the employee. But if certain reasons underlie the refusal— such as an employee's concern that something in the workplace is unsafe or illegal— you'll need to take other corrective measures. In such a situation, you're dealing with a problem, not a problem employee.

Unjustifiable Insubordination

Sometimes employees don't follow rules or orders because they just don't like them (or the person who gave them). When refusals are based on whim, laziness, or a bad attitude, you are free to respond with appropriate discipline.

Of course, the trick here is knowing whether insubordination is truly unjustified. If an employee didn't know about the order or rule or thought the rule was unreasonable or unfair, you might want to take a step back, give the employee another chance, and consider whether the rule or order should be adjusted.

If you think that the employee's refusal to follow an order or rule is unjustified, you should use progressive discipline. For employees who refuse to follow less important work rules and orders, you might respond with coaching, which is often the first step of progressive discipline. For refusals involving more important issues, you could discipline a first offense with a verbal or written warning. For work rules that relate directly to physical safety or to serious business issues (such as keeping trade secrets confidential), termination might be appropriate.

Insubordination issues often arise in the context of safety rules. For example, an employee might refuse to wear a hardhat or fail to follow safety requirements in using particular types of machinery. The need for action in these cases is particularly strong: Not only is the employee flouting the rules, but that misconduct is endangering the employee and others.

Failure to enforce could lead to employee illness, serious morale problems, OSHA violations, and more.

When Employees Have Safety Concerns

If an employee refuses to follow a rule or an order out of concern that it's unsafe, you must investigate those concerns. The employee's complaint has put you on notice that something in your workplace might be dangerous or hazardous. If you ignore the employee's concern—for example, if you think it's unfounded or that the employee is lying—and your workplace is indeed unsafe, you will violate state or federal workplace safety laws. Willful violation of such laws can carry heavy penalties and fines. In addition, if one of your employees gets hurt because of the unsafe condition, that employee might be able to sue you outside of the workers' compensation system, because you knew about the unsafe condition and failed to fix it. This means your business could be liable for the employee's injuries and could be on the hook for a variety of damages that won't be covered by your workers' compensation insurance policy, including punitive damages, emotional distress damages, and lost wages.

You must also refrain from disciplining the employee. State and federal workplace safety laws give employees the right to complain without fear of retaliation—and sometimes even to refuse to work—if they think a workplace is unsafe. And they prohibit you from penalizing an employee who refuses to work in unsafe conditions or who complains about a violation of these laws. Even though you might think that you're disciplining the employee for insubordination, not for complaining about health and safety issues, third parties—such as your state labor board or a judge or jury—will probably see it differently.

> **EXAMPLE:** Lily works at an oil refinery where there has recently been a fire that killed 10 of her coworkers. Although the owner shut the plant down for several days after the fire, he's now ordering employees back to work. Lily believes that the plant still poses a fire hazard, and she tells the owner this. She refuses to return to work on this basis. Not only must the owner investigate Lily's concerns, but he also can't terminate her for insubordination. If he fails to investigate her concerns and another fire breaks out, injured workers or their families could sue him for large amounts of damages. He could even go to prison for forcing people to work in deadly conditions of which he was aware.

If you investigate an employee's concerns and determine that they're meritless, inform the employee of your findings. If the employee continues to refuse to follow the order or rule, you can resort to progressive discipline, secure in the knowledge that you have a documented investigation to support any decisions you make.

RESOURCE
Want to know more about health and safety rules? The federal workplace health and safety law is the Occupational Safety and Health Act, or the OSH Act (29 U.S.C. §§ 651 to 678). This law is enforced by the federal Occupational Safety and Health Administration (OSHA), in conjunction with state health and safety offices. To learn about the OSH Act, go to OSHA's website at www.osha.gov. Contact your state labor department for information about your state's health and safety law. In addition, you'll find an entire chapter devoted to the OSH Act in *The Essential Guide to Federal Employment Laws*, by Sachi Clements (Nolo).

Concerns About Illegality

Concerns about illegal conduct in the workplace arise in a variety of circumstances. The most obvious occurs when an employee is ordered to commit an actual crime—for example, to steal money from a customer or to sell pharmaceutical drugs on the black market—but such events are relatively rare.

Illegality problems more commonly arise when an employer asks an employee to do something that arguably violates a workplace law or regulation. For example, an employee might refuse to work through lunch breaks, believing that your order violates state wage and hour laws. Similarly, an employee might refuse to send certain types of waste to a landfill because the contents appear to exceed limits set by state regulations.

If an employee refuses to follow a rule or an order for legal reasons like these, you must investigate the employee's concerns. The employee's refusal puts you on notice that illegal conduct or practices could be happening in your workplace. If you ignore the concern and a government agency later finds out about the practices, it will consider your violations of the law to be willful and knowledgeable. This could mean heavier penalties and fines for your company.

In addition, you shouldn't discipline an employee for refusing to engage in conduct that the employee believes to be illegal. Many states explicitly prohibit employers from penalizing employees who refuse to engage in illegal conduct.

If you investigate an employee's concerns and conclude that they are unwarranted, document your investigation and inform the employee of your findings. If the employee continues to refuse to follow the order or rule, you can resort to progressive discipline, knowing you have proof to back up your decisions.

Excessive Absenteeism

Even a model employee occasionally misses a day of work or is laid low with a bout of the flu or a more serious illness. This person isn't a problem employee; in fact, they could be an especially conscientious employee who doesn't want to infect others.

Some employees, however, miss so many workdays that their absences become a problem. Even if the employee has a legitimate reason for missing work, frequent absences can be hard to manage. The consequences of excessive absenteeism for companies commonly include:

- **Increased wage costs.** When employees call in sick, you might still have to pay them for the day. In addition, you might have to hire temporary help or pay other employees overtime to cover these absences.
- **Decreased productivity.** An employee who has a high number of absences is a less productive employee. That employee must spend time catching up after returning and might require assistance from other workers to get back up to speed.
- **Low morale.** If other employees have to work harder to make up for the absent employee, they might feel stressed and overworked.

Sometimes employees are indeed sick when they use sick leave; other times, however, they use the leave to extend their vacations, take a break from work, or deal with personal problems (such as taking the car to the mechanic or caring for a child on a school holiday). As with other issues we've discussed in this chapter, it's important for employers to understand the reasons behind the absenteeism before deciding on a course of action. The subsections below cover some common situations and provide you with practical, legal responses.

Family Absences

Employees often need to take time off from work to care for family members who are sick or recuperating. Under federal law and many state laws, you might have to give employees leave from work to deal with these sorts of issues. These laws are called family and medical leave laws. If the employee's absences are covered by one of these family and medical leave laws, the employee has a protected right to time off, and you cannot impose discipline.

Employees Who Have Disabilities

An employee who is missing a lot of work might be suffering from a medical condition that qualifies as a disability under state or federal law. In that case, you might have a duty to accommodate the employee's disability. Such an accommodation can include time off work or a reduced work schedule, depending on the circumstances.

Using Sick Leave as a Pretense

Unfortunately, some employees use sick leave as a way to extend vacations or take personal days. These aren't legitimate uses of sick time

and—assuming there are no medical leave or disability issues in the background—you're legally free to respond with appropriate steps. Usually, employers start at the bottom of the progressive discipline ladder and use coaching or a verbal warning for the first offense. Repeated abuse of sick leave merits sterner measures.

One way to discourage this type of behavior is to require all employees who call in sick to personally speak to their supervisors rather than just emailing, texting, or leaving a voicemail. It's just human nature: Most of us feel less comfortable bending the truth when talking to a real live human being. Employees who know they'll have to talk to supervisors in person might be more reluctant to lie about being ill.

Some employers require a doctor's note verifying illness. If you choose this approach, be sure that you tell employees, via your employee handbook, that you will ask for this type of verification. You'll want to be sure that no employee can claim to have been singled out for more onerous treatment.

Some employers deal with the problem by not paying employees for time they miss as a result of being sick. This might not be a good response, for a number of reasons. For example, employees might come in to work when sick because they don't want to lose the pay. They could infect other employees and customers. Also, you might have trouble recruiting people to come work for you when you tell them that you don't provide paid sick leave.

○! CAUTION
You might be legally required to provide paid sick leave, family leave, or other paid time off. In recent years, state and local governments have started to pass laws that require employers to provide paid sick time. As of 2025, 17 states (Alaska, Arizona, California, Colorado, Connecticut, Maryland, Massachusetts, Michigan, Minnesota, Nebraska, New Jersey, New Mexico, New York, Oregon, Rhode Island, Vermont, and Washington) and the District of Columbia have paid sick leave laws on the books; many city and county governments have passed such laws as well. In addition, Illinois, Maine, and Nevada have passed laws requiring employers to provide paid time off (PTO), which employees can use for illness or any other reason. If you do business in one of these locations, you might need to pay for a certain number of accrued sick or PTO days or hours per year. Some paid sick leave laws also include other rules, such as limiting how or when an employer can ask for a doctor's note. Learn more about these state laws (and local laws as well) at the website of A Better Balance, www.abetterbalance. org/paid-sick-time-laws.

Another approach is to combine vacation leave and sick leave into a single allotment of PTO. That way, employees know that when they call in sick, they're reducing the amount of time that they can take for vacation. On the plus side for employees, they feel free to take time when they need it and don't have to lie to you about their reasons.

Employees Who Really Are Sick—A Lot

You might have an employee who is frequently and genuinely ill. Once such employees use all their allotted paid sick leave and any rights to unpaid leave under family and medical leave laws, you could have a tough situation on your hands.

If the employee is suffering from a medical condition that qualifies as a disability under state or federal disability laws, you might have a duty to accommodate that disability—and one possible accommodation might be offering more unpaid leave.

If the employee doesn't have a disability, however, you might have to put your sympathies aside and discipline—or even terminate—the employee for excessive absences. After all, you can't run a business by paying employees who are at home sick a great deal of the time. You must be able to rely on your employees to show up to work with reasonable regularity.

Drugs and Alcohol

Employees who abuse alcohol and drugs (including illegal drugs, prescription drugs, and over-the-counter drugs)—either on their own time or at work—can pose significant and wide-ranging problems for their employers, managers, and coworkers. These problems can include diminished job performance, lowered productivity, absenteeism, tardiness, high turnover, and increased medical and workers' compensation bills. These employees can also make your workplace more volatile and dangerous and subject you to legal liability.

Alcohol Use at Work

Your employee handbook or other workplace policies should make it clear to employees that drinking on the job is not allowed. If you catch an employee actually using alcohol at work, you can deal with it through your standard progressive discipline procedures. Depending on the circumstances, you can do anything from coaching the employee to immediately suspending or terminating the employee.

CAUTION
If you serve alcohol at social gatherings during working hours, proceed with caution. If you serve wine at a company lunch, for example, you're taking the risk that some employees will drink a little too much and return to their workstations intoxicated. Similarly, employees might bring alcohol back to their workstations and continue drinking even after the gathering has ended. Obviously, either situation is bad for business and can pose a safety risk depending on the employee's job. The best course of action is to not serve alcohol at gatherings that take place during working hours. If you feel you must, however, make it clear to your employees that it's unacceptable to drink to the point of intoxication and that they can't bring alcohol back to their workstations. If you have employees who drive for work or perform dangerous jobs—such as welders or truck drivers—you shouldn't allow them to drink alcohol at events during the workday.

Alcohol Use Off Hours, Off Site

Most employers aren't concerned about an employee's alcohol consumption as long as it doesn't affect the employee's work performance. But when off-site, off-hours drinking takes its toll on a worker's ability to do the job, you'll have to address the problem.

Alcoholics are protected by the federal Americans with Disabilities Act. This means that you can't make an employment decision based solely on an employee's alcoholism (for example, because the employee attends AA meetings or takes prescription medication to curb the urge to drink). You can, however, make a decision—including a decision to discipline or terminate—based on the employee's inability to meet the same performance and productivity standards that you set for all of your employees, even if the employee's problems stem from alcohol addiction.

You will be responding to the effects of the employee's drinking on performance, not the underlying addiction. Maintaining this distinction will help avoid claims that you're discriminating against an employee based on a disability—alcoholism—or that you're inappropriately intruding into the employee's private life.

Put another way, your concern isn't that the employee drinks after hours or even that the employee has a drinking problem. Instead, you're concerned with the employee's poor work performance.

EXAMPLE: Dre runs a coffee shop in the business district of her city. Her business brings in the most money between 6:00 a.m. and 9:00 a.m., when customers come rushing in to grab a cup of coffee on their way to work. Lately, she has been having trouble with one of her counter workers. Steve arrives to work tired and distracted and has been mixing up customers' orders. Steve has a reputation for being quite a drinker, and he stays up late drinking with his friends.

Sometimes, he doesn't even go home before he shows up to work at 5:30 a.m. Dre doesn't care that Steve drinks, but she does care that he makes customers irate when he mixes up their orders. She disciplines him for his inattention—first coaching him, then giving verbal and written warnings. When he doesn't improve after these measures, she fires him.

A few months after she fires Steve, Dre hires another counter worker named Irene. Soon, Dre realizes she has another problem on her hands. Irene has trouble handling the hectic and fast-paced atmosphere of the coffee shop. She can't handle more than one order at a time, and she often mixes up orders when there are a lot of customers in the shop. Although Irene doesn't drink, she poses essentially the same problem for Dre that Steve did, and Dre responds by taking the same disciplinary measures against Irene that she took against Steve.

Drug Use and Possession

The law makes a big distinction between the legal and illegal use of drugs. You need to pay careful attention to these distinctions when dealing with your employees.

As we explain more fully below, your ability to govern legal drug use by your employees might be limited by disability laws. The legal use of drugs includes the proper use of prescription and over-the-counter drugs. By contrast, the law gives you a great deal of leeway in combating the illegal use of drugs in your workplace. This includes the use of illegal drugs and the misuse or abuse of legal drugs, such as prescription or over-the-counter drugs.

Legal Drug Use

Many employees properly use prescription or over-the-counter drugs. Most employers sensibly believe that it's none of their business, as long as the employee's job performance isn't impaired.

Things get trickier, however, when legal drug use affects an employee's performance. For example, medications that cause drowsiness might make it downright dangerous for a worker to do a job that requires dexterity and alertness. Medication could also impair a person's judgment and abilities.

If an employee's performance is affected by proper use of prescription or over-the-counter drugs, your response options might be limited by state and federal disability laws. Depending on the way the drug affects the employee and on whether the employee suffers from a disability within the meaning of these laws, you might have to accommodate the employee's use of the drugs.

Illegal Drug Use

If an employee appears at work under the influence of illegal drugs, or is abusing prescription or over-the-counter drugs, you aren't limited by disability rights laws. Deal with the employee through your standard progressive discipline procedures. If the employee hasn't created a safety threat or isn't in a highly sensitive position in your company, a written warning might be appropriate for a first offense, depending on the culture of your company.

However, if the employee has endangered the physical safety of others—for example, drove the company van while impaired—something more drastic is called for. If the employee has a substance abuse problem, one option is suspension until the employee successfully completes a treatment program. Some employers, however, choose a zero tolerance policy under these circumstances and immediately suspend and terminate such employees.

Because the use, sale, or possession of illegal drugs is a crime, most employers immediately suspend and then terminate

employees who engage in this type of behavior at work.

Medical and Recreational Marijuana

As of February 2024, 47 states and the District of Columbia allow medical use of marijuana. And, a number of states without medical marijuana laws allow the medical use of products with low levels of THC (which is responsible for the psychoactive effects of marijuana). Although the details vary, the purpose of these laws is generally to allow people to use marijuana to alleviate the symptoms of serious conditions, such as epilepsy, glaucoma, cancer, and multiple sclerosis. Twenty-four states and the District of Columbia have also passed "adult use" or "recreational" marijuana laws, which legalize the possession and personal use of small amounts of marijuana for recreational purposes.

If you do business in a state where marijuana is legal for medicinal or recreational purposes, how should you treat marijuana use by employees? The answer is tricky, because marijuana use, for any reason and in any amount, is still a crime under federal law. If you fire an employee for failing a drug test because of marijuana use, for example, is the firing valid? If your state prohibits employers from discriminating against employees for their legal off-duty activities (as a number of states do), may you discipline or terminate an employee for using marijuana legally on weekends or evenings? If an employee has a disability and uses marijuana as legally prescribed in your state to alleviate pain, must you accommodate that use?

Some states with medical marijuana laws have addressed these issues by prohibiting employers from firing or refusing to hire an employee simply because that employee has a medical marijuana card. Some states also prohibit employers from firing an employee who tests positive for marijuana use, if that employee has a medical marijuana card and didn't use marijuana while at work. However, in other states, marijuana laws don't include specific protections for employees. In these states, some courts have been siding with employers.

The laws in this area are not completely settled. If your state has a medical or recreational marijuana law, you'll need to talk to an attorney to find out how it affects your right to test for marijuana or prohibit off-duty use. (As is true of alcohol, you are likely free to prohibit recreational use of marijuana at work, for safety and productivity reasons.)

Investigating Substance Use

If you suspect an employee is under the influence of illegal drugs or alcohol at work, your most difficult task might be finding proof of your suspicions. Circumstantial evidence can be important. If the employee has slurred speech, has bloodshot eyes, and can't walk a straight line, be sure to note these things in writing.

Never reach a conclusion without talking to the employee. There might be a reasonable explanation for the behavior that will influence whether and how you discipline the employee. For example, the employee might have just started taking a prescription allergy medicine that had an unexpected side effect. As noted above, if problems arise because an employee is properly using prescription drugs, your options could be limited by disability laws.

If there are no acceptable reasons for the employee's condition, discipline might be appropriate. Some employers choose to test employees for alcohol and drugs before lowering the boom, especially if they plan to terminate. Before taking this step, get familiar with the legal limitations on your rights to test.

CAUTION

Don't give them something to talk about. Although you should always keep employee problems as confidential as possible, it's particularly important when dealing with suspected drug and alcohol abuse. If you publicly accuse an employee of drug or alcohol abuse or allow your suspicions to become known, you leave yourself vulnerable to a defamation lawsuit from the employee.

Theft and Dishonesty

Security experts tell us that businesses lose billions of dollars each year from internal theft and fraud. According to a 2018 survey by business insurer Hiscox, companies where embezzlement took place lost more than $350,000, on average, to the theft.

Of course, not all thefts and lies are equally serious. An employee who takes a pen for personal use is quite different from an employee who steals money from customers. Similarly, an employee who lies so that he can leave early to watch a football game is different from an employee who lies about safety standards or product quality.

Develop a Substance Use Policy

Employers can proactively address substance use by developing formal substance abuse policies. By educating managers and workers about substance abuse, you'll avoid some problems before they begin. And providing rehabilitation services to employees who have problems gives these employees a chance to shape up. In fact, you might be legally required to allow employees to take time off for drug or alcohol rehabilitation under the Family and Medical Leave Act, the Americans with Disabilities Act, and some state laws, depending on the circumstances.

Any policy you create should begin with a firm statement describing why the policy is necessary. Explain how substance abuse affects your business, using concrete examples of the impact of such abuse. Include a description of how substance abuse affects employees as individuals, including the impact on their health, their families, and their chances for job advancement. Stress that one purpose of the policy is to help employees overcome their problems.

Your policy should also describe how you plan to detect substance abuse. You have three options:

- The least intrusive and least expensive way is to simply rely on managers and supervisors to observe their workers.
- A more intrusive and more legally complicated method is to search employees and their property at the company.
- The most intrusive, most expensive, and most legally complicated method is to test employees for drugs.

The policy should also explain what role, if any, managers and supervisors have in enforcing the policy. And your policy should explain how you plan to respond to proof of substance abuse. It should clearly set forth the disciplinary or rehabilitative actions you will take.

To find out more about creating your own substance abuse policy and education program, go to the website of the Substance Abuse and Mental Health Services Administration, www.samhsa.gov.

For minor transgressions—such as taking office supplies home for personal use or using the photocopier to make personal copies—you can start the employee on the lowest rung of the progressive discipline ladder. Before disciplining an employee for theft, however, make sure that the company hasn't implicitly condoned the practice. Do you use the photocopier to make personal copies? If so, your employees might have inferred—even if incorrectly—that they were allowed to do so as well.

When faced with significant losses—such as an employee's stealing trade secrets or embezzling from the company—dispense with progressive discipline and suspend or terminate the employee immediately. In some cases, you might even consider calling the authorities.

Violence

Violence in the workplace comes in many forms, from horseplay among coworkers to an employee who brings a gun into the building. How you respond will depend in large part on how serious the violence is.

Your employee handbook should include firm and explicit policies against horseplay, threats, fighting, and weapons in the workplace. Using your progressive discipline system, choose appropriate responses for employees who engage in such behavior. It's

common for employers to give written warnings for first offenses of horseplay and fighting and to immediately terminate someone who attacks a coworker, makes a serious threat of physical harm, or brings a weapon to work.

State Laws on Gun Bans

Many employers adopt the eminently sensible policy of banning all weapons at work. But if you have this type of policy and extend it to all company property, you might have a problem: A growing number of states reserve employees' rights to have a gun in their vehicle, even if that vehicle is parked in a company parking lot during work hours. For example, Florida law explicitly gives employees the right to keep a gun in their cars on employer property, as long as they have a permit to carry it and the car is locked. (Fla. Stat. § 790.251.) If you plan to adopt a comprehensive weapons ban, make sure your state allows it.

It's very important to thoroughly investigate instances of fighting. You'll need to know whether the incident was really a fight between two equals or an attack by one employee on another. Clearly, if it's a one-sided attack, you'll respond differently to the victim than to the attacker.

! **CAUTION**
You could be liable to victims. If you don't respond firmly and swiftly to violent behavior, you leave yourself vulnerable to a lawsuit if the violent employee physically harms a coworker, vendor, or customer. The argument against you is that by not removing the violent employee from your workplace, you allowed a potentially violent situation to develop.

When Technology Is the Problem

The internet, email, social networking, instant messaging platforms, virtual meetings, and other innovations allow instant communication and access to information, increasing efficiency and productivity. These technologies have also made it possible for many businesses to stay open—and productive—while employees work from home.

Special Rules for Federal Contractors and Grantees

The federal Drug-Free Workplace Act of 1988 (41 U.S.C. §§ 701–707) requires all federal grantees and some federal contractors to certify that they maintain a drug-free workplace. The law applies to all companies that receive grants of any size from the federal government.

As part of this certification process, the contractor or grantee must:

- post a statement notifying employees that it prohibits the possession and use of drugs in the workplace
- post a statement that informs employees of the sanctions for violating the policy
- distribute the policy statement to all employees who will be working on the government project
- inform all employees who will be working on the government project that they must abide by the policy statement

- establish a drug-free awareness program that includes information about the dangers of drug use and the availability of drug counseling programs
- require employees to report any criminal drug conviction for a violation occurring in the workplace no later than five days after the conviction
- inform the federal agency with which it is working about the conviction
- sanction the employee for the violation, and
- strive in good faith to maintain a drug-free workplace.

The act neither authorizes nor prohibits drug testing in the workplace. In the wake of this federal law, many states passed their own drug-free workplace laws. To learn if your state is one of them, contact your state labor department. (Find contact information at www.dol.gov/agencies/whd/state/contacts.)

Unfortunately, these advances have also created new ways for employees to get into trouble, whether inadvertently or intentionally, at the speed of light.

Some employees find it difficult to devote their full attention to work when they could be posting comments on Facebook, checking personal email, or texting with friends; this can lead to performance and productivity problems. Other employees use technological tools to bring age-old forms of misconduct into the digital age, whether by emailing sexist or racist jokes, revealing the company's trade secrets on a social networking site, or viewing pornography online. In these situations, technology mostly speeds up (and often exacerbates the harm caused by) misconduct that employers have faced for decades.

An employer's first line of defense against these problems is the employee handbook. Every company that has employees and computers needs to carefully draft policies on appropriate use of email and the internet, including instant messaging and posting to social media pages, blogs, and other websites. Policies are especially important in this area because many people use these tools in both their personal and professional lives, leading to a lot of confusion about what's appropriate in a work setting. And, it's doubly important to have clear rules for employees using technology from home—not just to lay down the law about appropriate use of these technologies, but also to protect the security of your company's information. Although most courts to consider the issue have found that employees have no right to privacy in email sent using a company system or the sites they visit using an employer internet connection, many employees continue to regard these communications as private.

TIP

Define expectations for remote employees who use video conferencing. One of the benefits of working from home is flexibility. Your employees can read reports in their pajamas, walk the dog at lunchtime, and call clients from the comfort of their living rooms. However, video conferencing technology changes this equation. An employee's appearance, dress, and workspace are no longer matters of personal choice when they're visible to coworkers, partners, and clients.

We've all heard the stories of inappropriate comments when an employee thought they were muted, loud toddlers (and louder pets) joining the meeting, that lawyer in Texas who turned himself into a kitten, and more than one employee whose idea of professional video conferencing attire didn't include pants. Your company culture will determine how much formality you'll require of employees during internal video meetings (as long as you prohibit anything that could constitute harassment). When dealing with clients, customers, and other outside parties, however, you'll want to see more professional attire and conduct. Let employees know exactly what you expect by putting it in your remote work policy.

Drafting policies that clearly state your company's expectations—and telling employees in no uncertain terms that the company reserves the right to read all employee communications sent on its equipment—can go a long way toward shaping employee behavior to avoid problems in the first place.

Once you have clear policies in place, you've set the stage to use your progressive discipline system when employees break the rules. For relatively minor transgressions that don't cause harm to others (such as spending too much time surfing the web or using the email system for too many personal messages), coaching is probably appropriate for a first offense. For more serious misconduct, a written warning or even termination might be in order. If, for example, an employee emails company trade secrets to a competitor or harasses other employees by email, a more serious intervention is called for.

As you determine how to handle employee problems involving technology, keep in mind that your legal obligations as an employer apply with equal force in the virtual world. For example, just as you may not retaliate against an employee who complains about discrimination or safety hazards, you also may not retaliate against an employee who expresses these concerns online. Similarly, courts have generally held that employees don't have a right to privacy in communications on employer equipment, whether made by phone, fax, email, or text, as long as the employer has put employees on notice that it may monitor communications. However, just as this doesn't give an employer the right to monitor an employee's home phone, it also doesn't give an employer the right to hack into an employee's personal email account or password-restricted website.

CAUTION
Don't punish employees for discussing working conditions, online or offline. Employees have a legal right to talk to each other and work together to try to improve or change their working conditions. This right was first recognized in the context of face-to-face conversations; it was then extended to email communications. And now, the National Labor Relations Board has found that this right extends to other online communications. If you fire or discipline employees for talking about their jobs on each other's social media pages or other online forums, you might be breaking the law. This is true even if the employees are harshly critical of the company or engage in name-calling. As long as the topic of discussion is workplace rules, conditions, terms (such as pay or hours), or management, you generally can't discipline the employees for this conduct. See "Unfair Labor Practices," in Chapter 2, for more information.

Summary of Problems and Strategies for Resolving Them

This chart lists a number of common employment problems and the strategies you can use to handle them. Each of these strategies is described in more detail in later chapters.

Problem	Main Strategies	Issues to Consider
Poor performance/ productivity (new hire)	• Use performance evaluations. • If that doesn't work, use progressive discipline. • If that doesn't work, terminate the employee.	• Does the employee know what's expected? • Does the employee need more training? • Does the employee have the proper skills? • Does the employee feel free to ask for assistance? • Is the employee a slow starter? • Does the employee need additional resources? • Are you providing incentives for the employee to do well? • Is anything happening in the employee's work environment that's preventing them from performing well?
Sudden drop in performance/ productivity	• Use performance evaluations. • If that doesn't work, use progressive discipline. • If that doesn't work, terminate the employee.	• Has anything changed in the employee's work environment? • Has the employee been put in a new work group? • Has the employee been assigned to a new manager or supervisor? • Does the employee know what's expected? • Does the employee need more training? • Has the employee told you about personal issues that are affecting work performance?
Coworker complains that the employee has made sexually or racially inappropriate comments and gestures	• Investigate to see if the employee really did engage in this conduct. • If the employee did engage in the conduct, use progressive discipline in minor cases, terminate the employee in egregious cases.	• Is the employee guilty of the conduct? • How serious is the conduct? • How many times has the employee done this? • Has the employee done this to anyone else?

Summary of Problems and Strategies for Resolving Them (continued)		
Problem	**Main Strategies**	**Issues to Consider**
Coworkers dislike employee	• Find out why coworkers dislike the employee through a formal or informal investigation. • If it's a simple personality conflict, consider changing the employee's shift or department. • Use performance evaluations. • If the employee is at fault, consider progressive discipline. • If coworkers are at fault, consider progressive discipline for them.	• Why don't they like the employee? • Does the employee act inappropriately? • Is racism, sexism, or other discrimination behind the coworkers' feelings? If so, don't change the employee's shift or workplace. Take care of the employee and stop any harassment and intimidation that might be taking place. • Do they dislike the employee because the employee is racist, sexist, or otherwise discriminatory? If so, investigate immediately and use progressive discipline to stop the offensive behavior.
Employee refuses to follow a direct order	• Find out why the employee refused to follow the order. • If the employee doesn't have a legitimate reason, use progressive discipline. • If the employee refused based on safety concerns, don't discipline the employee. Investigate the concerns. • If the employee refused based on legality concerns, don't discipline the employee. Investigate the concerns.	• Why did the employee refuse to follow the order? • Did the employee understand the order? • Was the order reasonable? • Did the employee have legitimate concerns about the order?

Summary of Problems and Strategies for Resolving Them (continued)

Problem	Main Strategies	Issues to Consider
Employee refuses to follow a work rule	• Find out why the employee refused to follow the rule. • If the employee doesn't have a legitimate reason, use progressive discipline. • If the employee refused based on safety concerns, don't discipline the employee. Investigate the concerns. • If the employee refused based on legality concerns, don't discipline the employee. Investigate the concerns.	• Why did the employee refuse to follow the rule? • Did the employee know about the rule? • Did the employee understand the rule? • Is the rule reasonable? • Did the employee have legitimate concerns about the rule?
Employee uses excessive sick leave	• Communicate with the employee to determine whether the use of the leave is legitimate. • Consider whether the employee has a right to use leave under state or federal family and medical leave laws. • Consider whether the employee needs an accommodation for a disability under state or federal disability rights laws. • If the employee's use of leave isn't legitimate, use progressive discipline. • If that doesn't work, consider termination.	• What is happening in the employee's work environment? • Is the employee's workspace safe and comfortable? • Has the employee informed you of personal issues that are affecting attendance? • Is the employee covered under state or federal family and medical leave laws? • Are you subject to state or federal disability rights laws? • Are you subject to paid sick leave laws?

Summary of Problems and Strategies for Resolving Them (continued)		
Problem	**Main Strategies**	**Issues to Consider**
Employee fails to show up for work and fails to notify you	• Use progressive discipline.	• What is happening in the employee's work environment? • Is the employee's workspace safe and comfortable? • Has the employee informed you of personal issues that are affecting attendance?
Employee wants to take unpaid leave for a family problem	• Consider the employee's request. Don't discipline the employee.	• Are you subject to federal or state leave laws? • Is the employee eligible for unpaid leave under state and family leave laws? • Is the employee's family problem something that qualifies for leave?
Employee wants to take unpaid leave for a medical condition	• Consider the employee's request. Don't discipline the employee.	• Are you subject to federal or state leave laws? • Is the employee eligible for unpaid leave under state and family leave laws? • Are you subject to state or federal disability rights laws? • Does the employee's medical condition qualify as a disability?
Employee is at work under the influence of illegal drugs or alcohol	• Investigate. Make sure the employee is actually guilty of the conduct. • Use progressive discipline or terminate the employee, depending on the circumstances.	• Has the employee threatened the health and safety of coworkers, customers, or the public? • Does the employee have a substance abuse problem? • Would a treatment program help the employee?

Summary of Problems and Strategies for Resolving Them (continued)		
Problem	**Main Strategies**	**Issues to Consider**
Employee drinks alcohol at work	• Investigate. Make sure the employee is actually guilty of the conduct. • Use progressive discipline or terminate the employee, depending on the circumstances.	• Have you implicitly condoned the use? • Has the employee threatened the health and safety of coworkers, customers, or the public? • Does the employee have a substance abuse problem? • Would a treatment program help the employee?
Employee sells illegal drugs at work	• Investigate. Make sure the employee is in fact guilty of the conduct. • Terminate the employee. In some circumstances, call the authorities.	• Because this is a serious criminal offense, termination is normally the only option once you're certain the employee did it.
Illegal drug use or alcohol affects employee's performance	• Use performance evaluations. • Use progressive discipline.	• Does the employee have a substance abuse problem? • Would a treatment program help the employee?
Employee's legal drug use is affecting work performance	• Use performance evaluations.	• The employee might be protected by the federal Americans with Disabilities Act or by a state disability rights law. • You might have to reasonably accommodate the employee.
Employee steals from the workplace	• Investigate. Make sure the employee is actually guilty of the conduct. • In minor cases, use progressive discipline. • In egregious cases, terminate the employee. • When circumstances warrant, contact the authorities.	• Did the employee think it was okay to take the property? • Did you implicitly approve the employee's use of the property?

Summary of Problems and Strategies for Resolving Them (continued)		
Problem	**Main Strategies**	**Issues to Consider**
Employee engages in or threatens fighting or violence	• Investigate. Make sure the employee did make threats or cause harm. • In minor cases of horseplay or fighting, use progressive discipline. • For serious threats or acts of violence, terminate the employee.	• In cases of horseplay or fighting, was the incident mutual or one-sided? • For threats or violence, termination is ordinarily the only option once you're certain the employee did it. • See Chapter 10 for information on handling the termination meeting in cases of violence and threats.
Employee is misusing technology	• Investigate. Make sure the employee is actually guilty of the conduct. • Use progressive discipline.	• Are the rules for use of technology clear? • Are the rules for use of technology consistently enforced? • Make sure you aren't imposing discipline for protected activity, such as discussing terms and conditions of employment or complaining about discrimination, safety violations, or other legal violations.

Employment Law Basics

No matter what type of employment problem you face—from how to investigate a complaint to whether to discipline or even fire a worker—you must start with a working knowledge of the law. Employment law provides the basic framework for many decisions you will make. It dictates what you can and can't do and how you must treat employees.

If you don't know the law, you can't follow it. And failing to follow workplace laws can be costly. If you act illegally, you might face lawsuits from employees or investigations by government agencies. You will certainly see a decline in productivity, morale, and team spirit. You might even see your reputation in the business community suffer.

The first step to avoiding these problems is to learn your basic legal rights and obligations as an employer. In this chapter, we explain the legal rules. Throughout the rest of the book, we show you how to implement policies and make employment decisions that will pass legal muster. Along the way, we explain not only what the law requires, but also what practical steps you can take to reduce your chances of ending up in court.

Also, it's important to note that each state has its own employment laws. In Appendix B you'll find a number of charts on various employment-related topics containing the specific laws of each state.

RESOURCE

Want more information on employment law? This chapter explains employment law as it relates to the issues most likely to come up with problem employees: firing and discipline. But your legal obligations as an employer don't end there, of course. For detailed information on your other responsibilities to employees—on everything from wage and hour issues and benefits to work-place safety and paperwork requirements—see *The Employer's Legal Handbook*, by Aaron Hotfelder (Nolo).

Employment at Will

As a private employer in the United States, you start with the law on your side when dealing with employees. Although workers have specified rights in some situations, employers tend to have plenty of latitude to make the employment decisions they feel are right for their businesses. This latitude is protected by an age-old legal doctrine called "employment at will."

Unlike many legal terms, employment at will means what it sounds like: At-will employees are free to quit at any time and for any reason, and you are free to fire them at any time and for any reason, as long as the reason isn't illegal. We cover the illegal reasons to fire, including discrimination, retaliation, and public policy violations, below.

⚠ CAUTION

Different rules apply in Big Sky Country. The state of Montana limits the doctrine of at-will employment. In Montana, an employee works at will only during the employer's probationary period or, if the employer has no probationary period, during the first six months of employment. After that time, an employee may be fired only for good cause. An employee who has been wrongfully discharged can sue for lost wages and benefits, and for punitive damages (damages intended to punish the employer) if the firing was fraudulent or malicious. (Mont. Code § 39-2-904.) If you do business in Montana, make sure you always have good cause (as described in this chapter) to fire a worker after the probationary period.

Broadly speaking, you may fire an at-will employee for even the most whimsical or idiosyncratic reasons: because you don't like their style of dress or the sound of their voice, or simply because you want to hire someone else as a replacement. You're also free to change the terms of employment—job duties, compensation, or hours, for example—for any reason that isn't illegal. Your workers can agree to these changes and continue working, or they can reject the changes and quit. In other words, the employment relationship is voluntary: You can't force your employees to stay forever, and they can't require you to employ them indefinitely.

Employment at will (and your corollary right to fire at will) must be understood in light of its opposite, which is acting "for cause" (sometimes called "good cause" or "just cause"). An employment decision made for cause has a sound business reason behind it. For example, a demotion based on an employee's consistently late work would be "for cause," but a demotion based on an annoying personal characteristic (such as the way a worker eats lunch in the company cafeteria) would not.

Layoffs and Downsizing

Because this book covers only those management challenges presented by problem employees, we don't get into all of the reasons why you might need to demote or fire workers who pose no problems in the workplace. However, good cause to fire encompasses more than an individual worker's poor performance or misconduct. Any legitimate, business-related reason for firing—including business troubles and financial downturns—qualifies. If you're forced to downsize, cut back, close a facility, or shut down some of your operations, you'll almost certainly have to lay workers off, and you'll have good cause to do so.

Legal Limitations on Employment at Will

Employing workers at will gives you broad legal protection when making employment decisions. But this protection is limited in two ways:

- **Employment contracts.** First, employment at will doesn't apply to any employee who has an employment contract—whether written, oral, or implied—that puts some limits on the employer's right to fire. For these employees, the language or nature of the contract usually spells out the terms of employment, including when and for what reasons the employees can be fired. For more information, see "Employment Contracts," below.
- **State or federal laws.** Second, Congress, state legislatures, and judges have carved out some exceptions to the doctrine of employment at will. Generally, these exceptions prevent you from taking any negative action against an employee (including disciplining, demoting, or firing) in bad faith, in violation of public policy, or for a discriminatory or retaliatory reason. These restrictions are also discussed below.

Practical Limitations on Employment at Will

Another limitation on your ability to fire at will has more to do with human nature than with the law. Although the law gives you the right to fire or discipline an at-will employee for any reason, no matter how frivolous, in reality, employers who lack a sensible basis for their employment decisions run both legal and practical risks. These risks include:

- **Productivity and morale problems.** If you fire or discipline a worker without a good reason, the rest of your workforce will be confused and uneasy. Other workers will fear that their jobs could also be at risk. Employees who believe they might be fired or demoted even if they're doing a good job have less incentive to follow performance standards and other rules of the workplace. Conversely, if you set clear rules for performance and follow them consistently, your employees will know what is expected of them and will be encouraged to excel in order to keep their jobs and earn rewards.
- **Recruiting and hiring difficulties.** Once word gets out that an employer fires or disciplines employees without good reason, new employees will be harder to come by. After all, why should an employee take a job that can be lost at any time if another employer will offer a measure of job security or at least a fair shake? An employer that has a reputation for fairness and good employee relations has an advantage in hiring and recruiting.
- **Lawsuits.** An employee who has been treated unfairly has a stronger motivation to sue. And, despite the doctrine of

employment at will, jurors sometimes find ways to punish an employer they perceive to be unfair, arbitrary, or callous. Even if the employee ultimately loses the lawsuit, the employer will spend precious time and money fighting it out in court.

The Real Value of Employment at Will

As you can see, despite the theoretical protection extended by employment at will, there are both legal and practical limitations on an employer's unfettered power to make employment decisions. You might well be wondering: In view of these limitations, what is the at-will doctrine really worth? If you can be sued regardless of the legal realities and can demoralize your workforce by acting at will, why would you ever want to fire (or demote or discipline) without cause?

The candid answer is that, most of the time, you wouldn't. The best way to maintain a good relationship with your employees and promote efficient operations is to make sure that you have a solid business reason for every employment decision. Making decisions based on arbitrary or personal motives rather than objective business-related reasons can only hurt your company's bottom line in the long run.

The real value of employment at will comes not in the workplace, but in the lawyer's office and the courtroom. Lawyers, judges, and juries can always quibble with your reasons for firing: Did you give

the employee enough warnings? Was the employee's behavior really so bad that firing was warranted? Once you have to prove that you really did have good cause to fire, anything can happen. But you won't have to prove that you had good cause as long as you reserve your right to fire at will. Faced with strong at-will provisions *and* documented cause for termination, few lawyers will be willing to represent any employee you believe you have to fire. And if you somehow end up in court, chances are good that the judge will agree to throw out any contract claims against you, as long as you have protected your at-will rights.

Employment Contracts

People sign contracts in order to make their dealings more predictable by binding each other to certain obligations. For example, a manufacturing company can look for a buyer every time it has goods ready to sell, and it can charge whatever price the market will bear. Or it can enter into a contract that obliges a particular buyer to purchase a certain amount of goods at a set price on a regular basis (and obliges the manufacturer to produce those goods and sell them to the buyer for the agreed-upon price).

As you can see from this example, a contract offers the benefit of predictability at the expense of flexibility. If the manufacturing company discovers a new buyer who would pay much more for its goods, it can't just back out of its contract with the first buyer. The same is true of an employment contract: The parties are required to fulfill their contractual obligations to each other, even if they might want to change or abandon their agreement later.

Employees who have employment contracts often aren't subject to the general rule of employment at will. If, as one of its contractual obligations, the employer has limited its right to fire the employee at will, or has promised the employee a job for a set period of time, that contractual promise trumps the at-will rules discussed above. Employment contracts often spell out the length and terms of the worker's employment and specify how and when the employment relationship can end. Sometimes, these contracts require good cause for termination or detail the types of employee misconduct or business troubles that would allow either party to end the contract.

Not all employment contracts limit an employer's right to fire at will, however. Some contracts expressly reserve this right to the employer, while setting forth other agreed-upon terms of the employment relationship (pay, position, job duties, and hours, for example). These are often called "at-will agreements." We explain how and when you might use either a contract limiting your right to fire or a contract preserving your at-will rights in the sections that follow.

There are three types of contracts that might crop up in an employment relationship:

- **A written contract.** Here, you and the employee sit down and negotiate (or at least review) a document with the intent to create an employment contract. For example, you and your employee might sign a document outlining the details of the work to be performed and how much the employee will be paid.
- **An oral contract.** An oral contract has the same features as a written one, but without paper and signatures. For example, if you make certain promises or statements to an employee about the employment relationship and the employee agrees to accept the job on those terms, the two of you might have made an oral contract.
- **An implied contract.** These are contracts that are neither written nor explicitly stated, but come into existence because of your words and actions. For example, if you convey to an employee, through some combination of statements, written policies, and conduct, that the employee will be fired only for cause, the employee might be able to convince a judge or jury that you should be held to that implied promise.

Written Contracts

A written employment contract typically details the terms of the employment relationship. There aren't any legal requirements about what must go into an employment contract; that's up to you and the employee. Typical contract provisions include information on the start date and length of employment, a description of job duties, details about compensation, clauses protecting trade secrets and other confidential information, and termination provisions.

Written employment contracts can serve two very different purposes. Some employers enter into written contracts with their employees in order to preserve their at-will rights. Once an employee has agreed, in writing, that the job is at will, that employee will find it very difficult (if not impossible) to later make any kind of claim to the contrary against the employer. Most courts will not allow an employee to claim that there was an oral or implied contract limiting the employer's right to fire if the employee has signed a written at-will agreement. These contracts (or in some cases, an offer letter signed by the employee) simply provide a little extra at-will insurance for employers.

On the other hand, if an employer wishes to attract or retain a particularly stellar employee, the employer might offer a written contract that binds the employee to work for a set period of time and promises that the employment will last until that term is up, absent particular types of misconduct. This prevents the employer from firing at will and instead binds the employer to whatever the contract requires. It also prevents the employee from quitting during the life of the contract, except for reasons set out in the agreement. In these contracts, both employer and employee give up their at-will rights. If either breaks the contract, the other can sue for damages.

EXAMPLE 1: James was hired by Funco to work in its online commerce division. After James interviewed for the position, Funco sent him an offer letter detailing his start date, job responsibilities, and salary. The letter stated that James would be employed at will. Funco asked James to sign the offer letter to seal the deal, which James did. Because the letter doesn't limit Funco's right to fire him or change the terms of his employment at any time, for any reason, James is an at-will employee.

EXAMPLE 2: Funco hired Carlos as its chief financial officer. Because Carlos had a number of other job offers, Funco worried that he might be wooed away shortly after starting work. Carlos was also concerned that Funco might decide to change its executive team if its profits didn't meet expectations. To allay these fears, Funco and Carlos entered into a two-year employment contract. Both agreed that Carlos would work as Funco's CFO for two years at a specified salary; during that time, he could be fired only for good cause and could quit only for specified reasons. Carlos is not an at-will employee. If Funco fires him without cause or reduces his compensation during those two years, Carlos can bring a lawsuit for breach of contract.

Written Contracts That Preserve Your Right to Fire at Will

To write an employment contract that preserves your right to fire at will, you must:

- state that employment is at will
- avoid restricting your right to fire, and
- get your employee to sign the agreement (and also sign it yourself).

Instead of a formal contract, many employers choose to use an offer letter for these purposes.

Explicit language. The document you and the employee sign must include a clear and explicit statement that the employment is at will. The sample offer letter we provide in this chapter includes such language.

Restrictions. If the contract or letter contains any restrictions on your right to fire, you might lose your ability to terminate at will. Examples of contract language that could limit your right to fire include:

- **Statements about how long the employment relationship or contract will last.** If the contract says that the employment will continue for a measurable period of time (a year, for example, or the duration of a particular project), the employee generally can't be fired during that period without good cause.
- **Guarantees of continued employment.** If the employee is told, "You'll always have a job here," the employer could be legally obligated to keep that commitment unless the employee breaches the contract in some way.
- **Promises of progressive discipline.** If the contract requires the employer to follow certain disciplinary steps before firing an employee, the employee is entitled to those protections.
- **Provisions limiting the employer's right to terminate.** Many written employment contracts detail exactly how and when the employment relationship can end. In some contracts, either the employer or the employee has the right to end the relationship by providing a certain amount of notice (90 days, for example). Other contracts state that the employee can be fired only for good cause or for reasons specifically detailed in the contract. Some of the more common contractual grounds for termination include commission of a crime, gross incompetence, and financial wrongdoing.

Signatures. Many employers include a statement in their handbook or employee manual that employment is at will. This language will work in the employer's favor when faced with an employee's contract claim. However, the best way to protect your at-will rights is to get the employee's signature on an at-will agreement or an offer letter. This prevents the employee from later claiming not to have read the handbook.

If you decide to use a written contract or signed offer letter, provide two copies signed on behalf of the company and ask the employee to sign and return one of them. Put the signed letter into the employee's

Sample Offer Letter Preserving At-Will Employment

May 5, 20xx

Cameron Norman

3333 Nolo Drive

Berkeley, CA 12345

Dear Cameron,

I am pleased to offer you the position of Customer Service Representative for Sportgirl, Inc. We will give you a copy of our Employee Handbook, which explains our personnel policies, on your first day of work, September 1, 20xx. The purpose of this letter is to set forth the terms of your employment.

You will work in the Customer Service department at our main office in Menlo Park. You will receive an annual salary of $75,000, plus the benefits described in our handbook. You have been assigned to the opening shift, from 6 a.m. through 2 p.m., Tuesday through Saturday. However, the company reserves the right to change employee hours and shift assignments as necessary to meet the needs of the business.

I look forward to working with you, as does the Customer Service team. We sincerely hope that you are happy as an employee at Sportgirl, Inc. We value teamwork and strive to make work fun for our employees. However, we cannot make any guarantees about your continued employment here. Your employment with Sportgirl, Inc., is at will. While we hope things work out, you are free to quit at any time, for any reason, just as Sportgirl, Inc., is free to terminate your employment at any time, for any reason.

If you agree to the terms set forth in this letter, please print, sign, and email back your acceptance of employment at Sportgirl, Inc. Welcome aboard!

Marion Hopkins

Marion Hopkins

Human Resources Manager

My signature reflects that I have read and understood this letter. I understand that my employment is at will. No other representations regarding the terms and conditions of my employment have been made to me other than those recited in this letter.

_____

Cameron Norman

_____

Date

personnel file. If you have to fire an employee who later claims that you breached an employment contract, you'll have the signed agreement as proof that you preserved your at-will rights.

Written Contracts Requiring Good Cause to Fire

Because of the substantial benefits of employing workers at will, many businesses refuse to enter into any employment contract that limits their right to fire. However, if you really need to retain a particular employee or you want to sweeten your offer to that perfect applicant, you might consider giving up your at-will rights. A written contract requiring cause to fire might make sense when dealing with the following employees:

- **Highly marketable employees.** If you're recruiting an employee with valuable skills or credentials, a written employment contract promising some job security might be enough to seal the deal. And if the contract obligates the employee to work for you for a set period of time, you're less likely to lose the employee to another suitor.

- **Employees who are key to your company's success.** It's a lesson from Business 101: Keep those employees on whom your business depends. If the employee you're hiring is that important to your company, consider using a written employment contract to make sure the relationship lasts.

- **Employees who will have access to your trade secrets.** If your trade secrets are vital to your company's success, you might consider entering into a written contract with employees who will have regular access to them. A guarantee of job security could also help convince these employees to sign a noncompete or nondisclosure agreement. And they might feel more loyal to the company—and less likely to go work for a competitor—if you make a commitment to keep them on board.

- **Employees who will have to make a sacrifice to work for you.** At some point, you might want to hire an employee who will have to give something up to take the job. You might want to hire an employee away from a secure position at another company, for example, or hire someone who will have to relocate to accept the position. Or you might want someone to come work for you even though it would mean taking a pay cut. In these situations, a written employment contract promising some job security might convince a person to sacrifice something else to come work for you.

Remember that any time you enter into this type of employment contract, you are limiting your right to fire the employee. Even if circumstances warrant offering a contract, do so only if you have good reason to believe that the worker will fit in with your business.

If unsure, consider using a probationary period, during which you and the worker can decide whether the employment relationship will work, before limiting your right to fire in an employment contract.

Oral Contracts

Often, no document memorializes the start of an employment relationship. The employer simply offers the employee a job to perform particular duties for a specified salary, and the employee agrees and shows up for work. Although these informal arrangements are rudimentary contracts, they aren't the types of agreements that restrict an employer's right to fire.

There's nothing to stop an employer and employee from discussing other employment issues like wages, hours, and responsibilities. But if you announce limits on your right to terminate by, for example, promising that the employee will be fired only for good cause or for financial reasons, you've probably destroyed the at-will freedom that you would otherwise have. An employee who can prove that you violated an oral agreement by terminating them without a good reason or by changing other agreed-upon terms of employment can sue you for breach of contract.

Here are examples of the kinds of statements that might create an oral contract restricting an employer's right to fire at will:

- **Promises of job security.** Few employers would promise lifelong employment. However, if you tell prospective or current employees that they'll have a job as long as they perform well or that the company doesn't fire employees without good cause, you'll have to live up to these promises or risk a lawsuit.
- **Assurances of raises, promotions, or bonuses.** If you promise rewards to employees who perform well, a court might interpret that as a guarantee that employees will receive the benefits you promise and will not be fired as long as they are performing reasonably well.
- **Statements about termination.** Of course, if you explicitly promise that an employee will be fired only for certain reasons, you have restricted your right to terminate.

EXAMPLE 1: Jun interviews for a position as a bookstore clerk. At the close of the interview, the manager offers him a job working 40 hours a week at $20 per hour. Jun agrees to take the job and shows up for work as promised the following week. Because the bookstore hasn't made any promises to Jun about the length of his employment or the security of his job, Jun is an at-will employee. The bookstore can fire him, demote him, or change the terms of his employment at any time.

EXAMPLE 2: Julia is recruited to manage a local chain of grocery stores in California. Although she's interested in the job, she's heard rumors that the company might merge with a national grocery chain and is worried that her job might not survive the merger. When she raises this concern during her interviews, the CEO assures her that she is part of the company's long-term plans and that she will keep her position even if the merger goes through. These statements are probably enough to create an oral employment contract limiting the company's right to fire Julia.

Detailed oral contracts are rare, in the employment field and elsewhere. An agreement that isn't reduced to writing is more likely to be forgotten, misconstrued, or disputed later. Usually, both sides will want the agreement written down to avoid confusion in the future.

Implied Contracts

An implied employment contract is an enforceable agreement that hasn't been put into a formal written contract, or even stated explicitly, but is instead implied from a combination of the employer's oral and written statements and actions. Many, but not all, states recognize implied employment contracts.

To prove an implied contract, an employee has to show that you created an expectation that they wouldn't be fired without a good reason. The employee doesn't have to prove that you wrote or said those words, however. Instead, the employee must show that your statements, personnel policies, and actions all led the employee to the reasonable belief that the job was secure.

Creating an Implied Contract

Implied contracts are usually created over time, out of language in employee handbooks, performance evaluations, conversations with employees, and the way you treat workers. When determining whether an implied employment contract was created with a former employee, a judge or jury will consider a number of factors, including whether you:

- gave the employee regular promotions, raises, and positive performance reviews
- assured the worker that the employment was secure or would continue as long as they performed well
- promised, explicitly or implicitly, that the employee's position would be permanent
- employed the worker for a long period of time, or
- adopted policies that place some limits on your right to fire workers at will, such as mandatory progressive discipline policies that don't give you leeway to depart from the stated procedure, policies providing that new employees will become permanent after serving a probationary period, and policies promising regular promotions and raises if performance meets a certain standard.

RESOURCE

Need help writing policies that won't create an implied contract? See *Create Your Own Employee Handbook,* by Sachi Clements (Nolo). This book is packed with sample policy language and comes with digital copies that you can use to put your handbook together.

EXAMPLE: Marguerite worked as an accountant with EZ Ink Printing. EZ Ink's employee manual stated that employees weren't considered permanent until they completed a 90-day probationary period. The manual also contained a long list of offenses for which employees could be terminated and stated that other types of misconduct would be handled through its progressive discipline policy.

For more than 20 years, Marguerite built her life around EZ Ink. She received regular raises and promotions, and her supervisor often spoke of her bright future at the company. But she was fired after 22 years of service. EZ Ink had no beef with Marguerite's job performance; instead, the head of the company wanted to offer the position to a friend.

Marguerite might be able to win a lawsuit against EZ Ink based on breach of an implied contract. By its conduct, the company led Marguerite to believe that she wouldn't be fired once she became a permanent employee unless she did something to warrant a termination. When the company fired Marguerite without good cause, it exposed itself to legal trouble.

CAUTION

State laws differ on what an employee must show to prove an implied contract. Some states don't consider all of the factors listed above. If you're concerned that you might have created an implied contract you won't be able to honor, talk to an attorney.

How to Avoid Creating Implied Contracts

Employers should try to avoid creating implied employment contracts, for good reason: These contracts limit your right to fire workers without giving you anything in return. Unlike a written or oral contract, which can bind employer and employee equally, an implied contract typically works only one way: against the employer.

Steps you can take to make it harder for an employee to fit together bits and pieces of your conversations and policies into the mosaic of an implied contract include:

- **Making it clear that employment is at will.** In your written employment policies, including your employee handbook or personnel manual, state clearly that employment at your company is at will and explain what this means.
- **Asking employees to sign an at-will agreement.** Most courts find that an employee who has agreed, in writing, that employment is at will can't later claim to have had an implied employment contract limiting the employer's right to fire. Consider asking employees to sign a simple form acknowledging that their employment is at will. (If you used a written offer letter as explained above, you've already done this.)
- **Refraining from making promises of continued employment.** If you tell your employees that their jobs are secure, that they won't be fired without good

cause, or even that the company has never had to fire a worker, you risk creating an expectation that they won't be fired. Avoid these types of comments, which are particularly common in job interviews and performance reviews.

- **Training all managers.** With few exceptions, managers' actions and statements will be legally attributable to the company, just as if the company owner or president had said or done them. Managers must understand company policies and procedures, especially regarding discipline, performance reviews, and employment at will. If a manager makes any statements or takes any actions contrary to these policies, your company could be facing an implied contract claim.

- **Keeping your disciplinary options open.** If you adopt a progressive discipline policy, make sure to include clear language preserving your right to fire employees at will. If you list offenses for which firing is appropriate, state that the list isn't exhaustive and that you reserve the right to fire for any reason.

- **Not referring to employees as "permanent."** Many employers have an initial probationary or temporary period for new hires, during which the company is free to fire them. After the probationary period is up, the worker becomes a permanent employee entitled to benefits and so forth. To some courts, this language implies that a "permanent" employee can be fired only for good cause. If you choose to use a probationary period, be clear that you retain the right to fire at will once that period is over.

Breaches of Good Faith and Fair Dealing

Employers have a duty to treat their employees fairly and in good faith. What this duty amounts to, as a practical matter, varies from state to state. Simply firing or disciplining a worker is not enough to breach this duty; an employer that treats employees honestly and with respect, even those employees who must be disciplined or fired, runs no risk. However, an employer that treats an employee in a particularly callous way or fires an employee for a malevolent reason—especially if the firing was intended to deprive the employee of benefits that would otherwise be due, such as retirement benefits—might lose a lawsuit for violating this basic principle.

Courts have held that employers breached the duty of good faith and fair dealing by:

- firing or transferring employees to prevent them from collecting sales commissions or vesting retirement benefits

- intentionally misleading employees about their chances for future promotions and raises
- downplaying the bad aspects of a particular job, such as the need to travel through dangerous neighborhoods late at night, and
- transferring an employee to remote, dangerous, or otherwise undesirable assignments to force the employee to quit in order to avoid having to provide severance pay and other benefits.

CAUTION
Not every state allows employees to sue an employer for violating the duty of good faith and fair dealing. And some states allow only employees with employment contracts to bring these claims. Because of this variation in state law, you might want to consult with a lawyer if you're concerned about good-faith and fair-dealing claims.

Violations of Public Policy and Retaliation

An employer violates public policy when it fires or disciplines an employee for reasons most people would find morally or ethically wrong. If an employer takes any negative action against an employee that a judge or jury would find contrary to public policy,

that employee could end up winning a lawsuit in which the employer is ordered to reinstate the employee, rescind the discipline, or pay money damages.

How Employment Laws Apply to Remote Employees

Despite not being in the workplace, remote workers still enjoy all of the protections of the employment laws addressed in this chapter. For example, they're entitled to be paid for every hour worked, including overtime (if applicable), under wage and hour laws. You must provide them with a safe workplace, free from known hazards, under OSHA. Remote employees are protected from discrimination and retaliation.

If your company has employees who live and work in a different state from their usual workplace, the employment laws of the employee's home state might apply. As a practical matter, this might mean your company has become a multistate employer. Depending on where your employees live, this can have serious repercussions when it comes to wage and hour laws, prohibitions on discrimination, entitlement to time off work, and more. You'll need to make sure your policies and practices reflect these variations.

You could be violating public policy if you fire or demote an employee for:

- exercising a legal right, such as voting, joining a union, filing a workers' compensation claim, taking family medical leave, or refusing to take a lie detector test
- refusing to do something illegal, such as submit false tax returns, defraud customers or service providers, sell faulty equipment, or lie on government reports; or
- reporting illegal conduct or wrongdoing by filing a complaint with a government agency (whistleblowing) or, in some states, reporting misconduct of public concern to higher management within the company—for example, complaints that employees are lying to government officials or endangering the public by selling products that don't meet safety standards.

Many federal and state laws specifically prohibit employers from firing employees for exercising their rights under certain laws or complaining about violations of those laws. The purpose of these provisions is simple: These laws are enforced almost solely through employee complaints. If employers were free to discipline or fire employees for taking advantage of their rights (for example, to take medical leave), few employees would use these laws in the first place. And, if employers were free to retaliate against employees who reported these types of legal violations, employees would be too frightened of losing their jobs to come forward with complaints.

Wage and Hour Claims

The federal Fair Labor Standards Act (FLSA) and similar state and local laws govern wage and hour issues, including overtime and minimum wage. These laws come into play in employee discipline and termination in a couple of ways.

First, employees are protected from retaliation for exercising their rights under these laws, including their right to complain of violations within the company (for example, to their HR representatives), to file a complaint with a government enforcement agency (such as the federal or state labor department), or to file a lawsuit alleging improper payment practices. Employers may not discipline or fire employees for asserting their rights under these laws.

Second, a company that takes a lax approach to wage and hour issues might face a very unpleasant surprise when it later fires an employee. The unhappy employee might consult with a lawyer to find out whether they were fired illegally. If you had good cause for the firing, you might assume you're off the hook: No lawyer will take up a wrongful termination case if you crossed all of your t's and dotted your i's, right? Well, even if the termination was absolutely legal and justified, you could run into trouble if the employee's wage and hour rights were violated during the employment relationship.

While there might not be a case for wrongful termination, the employee could have a sizable unpaid wage claim. And, if you followed the same faulty practices with other employees, you could be looking at a class action lawsuit.

Here are a few key issues to watch out for:

- **Minimum wage violations.** Employees must be paid at least the minimum wage for every hour they work. If your state or local government has adopted a higher minimum wage than the federal standard (currently $7.25 an hour), which many have, you must pay the higher amount. Employers can get into trouble here if they require employees to work uncompensated time (for example, by making them do some work before "clocking in") or simply pay less than the required minimum per hour.

- **Overtime violations.** Under federal law, many employees are entitled to overtime—time and a half—when they work more than 40 hours in a week. A few states also have a daily overtime standard, entitling employees to overtime if they work more than eight hours in a day. Employers might violate these rules by incorrectly classifying employees as exempt, salaried employees, when they're actually hourly employees entitled to overtime. Or, employers might not count all hours worked by an employee or might not be aware that employees are working overtime (for example, because employees are working at home before or after work hours).

- **Meals and rest breaks.** Although federal law doesn't require employers to provide employees with time off for meal or rest breaks during the workday, it does set boundaries for employers that choose to offer such breaks. In general, employees must be paid for breaks of 20 minutes or less. Bona fide meal breaks, typically 30 minutes or more, need not be paid. However, employers must fully relieve employees of all job duties during this unpaid meal break. If your company gives employees an unpaid half hour for lunch, for example, it may not require them to do any work during that time. Otherwise, they must be paid. Some states require employers to provide unpaid meal breaks, and a handful of states require employers to provide paid rest breaks. If you fail to provide legally required breaks, if you ask or expect employees to work through their breaks, or if you fail to pay employees for shorter breaks, you could get into trouble.

- **Misclassifying employees as independent contractors.** In recent years, the federal government has been cracking down on companies that call workers "independent contractors" when they really are employees. The incentive for employers to misclassify this way is mainly financial: Employers don't have payroll tax obligations for independent contractors, who must pay all of their own Social Security and Medicare taxes. Employers also don't need to comply with minimum wage, overtime, and other wage and hour rules for independent contractors. Independent contractors also aren't entitled to certain benefits, including unemployment and workers' compensation.

However, simply calling a worker an independent contractor doesn't make it so. Government agencies (including the IRS, Department of Labor, and state unemployment offices) will look at the economic realities of the relationship to determine a worker's proper classification. A worker who's truly running an independent business, deciding how and when to do the work, and providing a discrete service that's outside your company's field, is more likely to be a contractor. On the other hand, a worker is likely to be classified as an employee if your company has the right to direct when, where, and how the job is done, if the worker works only for your company, and/or if the worker performs services that are integral to your company's operations.

RESOURCE

Need more information on wage and hour issues? You can find loads of free articles, including information on state laws, at Nolo.com. Under "Legal Issues Explained," select "Employment Law," then "Human Resources," then "Compensation & Benefits for Your Employees." You can also get detailed information on wage and hour obligations in *The Employer's Legal Handbook,* by Aaron Hotfelder (Nolo).

Workers' Compensation Claims

Workers' compensation laws provide for payment of lost wages and medical bills for workers who are injured on the job or become ill because of their work. These laws are a mandatory alternative to the court system in nearly every state. (Texas is the only state that makes workers' compensation insurance optional for all employers.) If an employee suffers an injury that falls within the scope of these laws, that employee may not file a lawsuit against the employer. Instead, the employee must go through the workers' compensation system to get compensated for injuries. In exchange for this protection from lawsuits, the employer must pay the claim regardless of fault, ordinarily through workers' compensation insurance purchased through the state or a private insurer. Insurance rates are typically based on the size of your payroll and the hazards of your industry. However, the number and size of the claims against you might also be a factor in determining your premiums.

An employer may not fire or punish a worker for bringing a workers' compensation claim. Contact your state workers' compensation office for more information about your state's coverage and insurance requirements and state antiretaliation protections.

Family and Medical Leave

The federal Family and Medical Leave Act, or "FMLA" (29 U.S.C. §§ 2601 and following), and some state laws require employers to let their employees take time off work to deal with certain family and medical problems. Employers may not fire or discipline workers for taking leave covered by these laws.

Employers are covered by the FMLA if they have at least 50 employees. An employee is eligible for FMLA leave if all of the following are true:

- Your company has 50 or more employees who work within a 75-mile radius of the employee's work site (for remote employees, this is the office where the employee's work is assigned, not the employee's actual home). All employees on your payroll—including those who work part time and those on leave—must be counted in this total.
- The employee seeking leave has worked for you for at least 12 months.
- The employee has worked at least 1,250 hours for you (about 25 hours a week) during the 12 months immediately preceding the leave.

Employees may take up to 12 weeks of leave per year to: bond with a new child; care for a seriously ill spouse, child, or parent; recuperate from their own serious health conditions; or deal with "qualifying exigencies" stemming from a family member's call to active duty in the military. Employees may take up to 26 weeks of leave to care for

a family member who has suffered a serious illness or injury while on active military duty. This 26-week leave provision is available once per servicemember, per injury: It doesn't renew every year, like other types of FMLA leave.

When the employee's leave is over, you must reinstate the employee to the same position or an equivalent one. It's illegal to fire or discipline an employee for taking FMLA leave, to discourage an employee from taking FMLA leave, or to deny an eligible employee FMLA leave.

Some states have laws that are more protective than the FMLA. Some provide for longer periods of leave, some cover smaller businesses, some allow employees to take leave for a larger variety of family issues (including attending children's school conferences and dealing with domestic violence), and some allow employees to take leave to care for a wider circle of family members (such as grandparents, in-laws, and domestic partners). About a dozen states have laws on the books that provide paid leave for family and/or medical reasons; some have not yet gone into effect, but will roll out in the next few years.

To find out the laws in your state, see the State Family and Medical Leave Laws chart in Appendix B. If you're subject to the FMLA and a similar state law, you'll have to follow whichever law gives your workers more protection in any given situation.

RESOURCE

Want more information on the FMLA?
Take a look at *The Essential Guide to Family & Medical Leave*, by Lisa Guerin and Deborah C. England (Nolo). It provides step-by-step instructions for fulfilling your responsibilities under the FMLA, along with practical advice for managing employee leaves successfully. The book also includes sample letters and forms, a sample FMLA policy, information on state leave laws, and much more.

Health and Safety Complaints

Federal law and the laws of most states prohibit employers from firing or disciplining a worker for complaining about health and safety violations. The main federal law covering workplace safety is the Occupational Safety and Health Act, or the OSH Act. (29 U.S.C. §§ 651 to 678.) The OSH Act broadly requires employers to provide a safe workplace, free of dangers that could physically harm their employees.

The law also prohibits employers from firing or disciplining a worker for filing a safety complaint.

Many states have similar laws, most of which protect workers who complain about health and safety violations.

These laws give workers the right to refuse to follow a workplace rule or order that creates a safety hazard and to refuse to work at all if the workplace is unsafe

(if certain conditions are met). Employers faced with these types of complaints should promptly investigate the allegedly unsafe condition and take immediate action to remedy the danger.

RESOURCE

For more about the OSH Act.
You can find a comprehensive discussion of the OSH Act and other federal employment laws in *The Essential Guide to Federal Employment Laws*, by Sachi Clements (Nolo). For factsheets, compliance information, industry-specific rules, and more, check out the website of the Occupational Safety and Health Administration at www.osha.gov.

Other Public Policy Claims

Even if no law explicitly prohibits employers from retaliating against an employee for complaining about or refusing to participate in certain illegal conduct, the employee might still be able to sue for wrongful termination in violation of public policy. State rules differ significantly in this area. In some states, employees may sue only if they were fired for refusing to violate a criminal law or for exercising a clearly stated legal right, such as the right to vote. Other states are more inclusive, allowing claims by employees who were fired for reporting violations of health and safety regulations or for exercising rights set out in prior court cases.

Because of this variation, employers should tread carefully. The best practice is to consult with an attorney when considering discipline against an employee who has recently exercised a civic or legal right, refused to engage in questionable activity, or blown the whistle on workplace problems.

Discrimination

Perhaps the most common complaint employees take to court is that they were fired or disciplined for discriminatory reasons. These claims can be tough to combat. They are intensely personal and upsetting for all involved, which increases the danger that emotions rather than reason will hold sway. And there are strong legal prohibitions against discriminating in the workplace. Even when you're sure that you fired or disciplined a worker for a valid, nondiscriminatory reason, there's always the chance that an administrative agency, judge, or jury will disagree. Your first line of defense is to familiarize yourself with the laws that might be invoked against you.

CAUTION
State laws might be broader. Although the discussion below focuses on federal law, each state also has a set of laws governing employment

discrimination. These laws are often broader than their federal counterparts, which means that you might be covered by your state's law even if you aren't covered by federal law. Your state's law might also protect more classes of people than federal law. See the chart titled "State Laws Prohibiting Discrimination in Employment" in Appendix B.

Title VII

Since 1964, the federal Civil Rights Act, also known as Title VII (42 U.S.C. §§ 2000 and following), has prohibited discrimination in the workplace. Title VII is enforced by the federal Equal Employment Opportunity Commission (EEOC) and applies to all companies and labor unions with 15 or more employees. It also governs employment agencies, state and local governments, and apprenticeship programs. Title VII doesn't apply to federal government employees (who are protected by other antidiscrimination laws) or independent contractors.

Under Title VII, employers may not use race, color, gender (a category that includes pregnancy, sexual orientation, and gender identity), religion, or national origin as the basis for workplace decisions, including promotion, pay, discipline, and termination. Title VII covers every aspect of the employment relationship, including prehiring ads, working conditions, performance reviews, firing, and postemployment references.

Guarding Against Discrimination Claims

Unfortunately, there's no surefire way to guarantee that you'll never face a claim of discrimination. However, you can take steps to protect yourself from legal liability, including:

- **Keep careful records.** If you can prove that you fired a worker for legitimate business reasons, you'll defeat a discrimination claim. This makes documentation very important. Keep written records of discipline, performance problems, counseling sessions, or misconduct by the employee as they occur. If you're later faced with a charge of discrimination, you will be able to show that you had a sound basis for your decision.

- **Be fair and consistent.** If you can show that you treated the fired worker the same as your other employees, a discrimination claim will falter. Conversely, if a jury is convinced that you're harder on workers of a certain race or gender, you'll be in trouble.

- **Examine your workplace demographics.** If the complaining worker is a distinct minority in your business, a lawsuit could be more likely. For example, if firing a female employee will leave you with no women in a particular department or job category, the worker could argue that you fired her because you do not want women in that

position. In this situation, your reason for taking action will have to be especially strong—and you'll need to make sure that you haven't let unconscious bias play a role. We suggest consulting a lawyer before taking any significant disciplinary measures.

- **Don't make biased comments.** It should go without saying that any statement you or any manager makes about an employee will come back to haunt you if that employee is later fired or demoted. Even if you had a valid reason for your decision, any prejudicial statements that you made will make a jury believe that you were motivated by prejudice, not sound judgment.

- **Examine your motives.** Unfortunately, some employers act on discriminatory motives—sometimes unconsciously. Perhaps you do hold certain workers to a higher standard or are more likely to suspect certain workers of misconduct. Do you act on the basis of personal beliefs about, for example, whether new mothers should work or older workers are capable of learning new skills? Guard against letting these beliefs influence employment decisions by applying your policies consistently to all workers, and by judging all workers according to objective, performance-based goals.

CAUTION
Anyone can be discriminated against.
Some employers mistakenly believe that only employees belonging to a group that has faced historical mistreatment and disadvantage can claim discrimination in the workplace. Quite the contrary: Even white men can make successful discrimination charges if they can prove that they were treated differently because of their race or gender. If you decide to terminate a few white men so as to make your workforce more diverse, you could end up facing a discrimination lawsuit. Whenever you make an employment decision based on race, gender, or another protected characteristic, you risk a discrimination charge.

If a court finds that you've discriminated against an employee in violation of Title VII, it can order you to do any or all of the following:

- Rehire, promote, or reassign the employee to whatever job was lost because of discrimination.
- Pay any salary and benefits the employee lost as a result of being fired, demoted, or forced to quit because of discrimination. This might include lost wages, pension contributions, medical benefits, overtime pay, bonuses, shift differential pay, vacation pay, or participation in a company profit-sharing plan.
- Pay damages to compensate for personal injuries caused by the discrimination, including emotional distress damages

and reimbursement for medical expenses. (These damages, along with punitive damages, are limited to between $50,000 and $300,000, depending on how many employees you have.)

- Change your policies to stop the discrimination and prevent similar incidents in the future.
- Pay the employee's attorneys' fees.

RESOURCE
For more about Title VII. You can find a comprehensive discussion of Title VII and other federal employment laws in *The Essential Guide to Federal Employment Laws,* by Sachi Clements (Nolo).

Every state and many cities and counties also have laws prohibiting discrimination in employment. These prohibitions often echo federal laws in outlawing discrimination based on race, color, gender, age, disability, national origin, and religion.

But some state and local laws go into more detail, sometimes creating additional categories of protected workers that are not covered by federal law. In California, for example, it is illegal to discriminate on the basis of a worker's political activities. In Minnesota, for example, it's illegal to discriminate against people who are collecting public assistance.

Beware the Cat's Paw

Employers can be liable for discrimination even if the person who made the ultimate decision (to fire an employee, for example) doesn't intend to discriminate. In this so-called "cat's paw" situation, one supervisor has a discriminatory motive, but a different supervisor makes the adverse decision. In a case involving discrimination against an employee because of his military service, the Supreme Court found that an employer is liable if a supervisor with a discriminatory motive takes action with the intent of causing negative treatment of an employee, and that supervisor's action is the proximate cause of such negative treatment. In other words, if the supervisor's discriminatory motive taints the decision-making process and ultimately causes the employee to be mistreated, the company is liable. (*Staub v. Proctor Hospital*, 562 U.S. 411 (2011).)

You could find yourself in this position if a higher-level manager relies too heavily on a supervisor's word against an employee, without looking at the situation independently. For example, let's say a supervisor did not want any Latino employees promoted to management positions. To achieve this discriminatory goal, the supervisor gave poor performance reviews, more discipline, and less training and other assistance to Latino employees. When a higher-level manager simply relies on these tainted actions in deciding whom to promote, the company's promotion decisions become discriminatory, even if that wasn't the intent of the ultimate decision maker.

And in Michigan, employers can't discriminate on the basis of height or weight. Also, some state laws cover employers with fewer than 15 employees.

State laws prohibiting discrimination in employment are listed in Appendix B. You can likely find out about city or county anti-discrimination laws on your city or county government's website (find it at https://library.municode.com). You can also research local antidiscrimination laws at the headquarters of your community's government, such as your local city hall or county courthouse.

Harassment

The same statutes that ban discrimination also prohibit harassment based on a protected characteristic. These laws are enforced by the EEOC at the federal level and by fair employment agencies at the state level.

Harassment based on any protected characteristic is illegal. However, sexual harassment is the most well-known type of harassment. And, as the #metoo movement has made clear, sexual harassment is still common in all kinds of workplaces, from fast food restaurants to the sets of Hollywood movies.

Sexual harassment is any unwelcome sexual advance or sex-based conduct on the job that creates an intimidating, hostile, or offensive work environment or that conditions employment benefits on the employee's acceptance of sexual conduct or advances. More simply put, sexual harassment is any offensive conduct related to an employee's gender that a reasonable person of that gender shouldn't have to endure at work.

Sexual harassment can take a wide variety of forms: It can be sexual in nature or it can be nonsexual harassment based on the victim's gender (for example, threatening or bullying the only woman in an otherwise all-male workplace). An employee who has been led to believe that going on a date with the boss is required in order to avoid getting fired has been sexually harassed, as has one whose coworkers regularly tell offensive, sex-related jokes. An employee who is pinched or fondled against their will by a coworker has been sexually harassed, as has one whose colleagues leer at them nonstop. An employee who is constantly belittled and referred to by sexist or demeaning names has been sexually harassed, as has one who is subject to threats of violence or danger because of gender.

Discrimination Based on Sexual Orientation and Gender Identity

For years, the legality of discrimination based on sexual orientation or gender identity depended on the laws of the state and local government where a company did business. Some states and cities prohibited this type of discrimination; others didn't. No federal law protected employees, because courts generally agreed that Title VII didn't extend to sexual orientation. Although Congress tried many times to add sexual orientation to Title VII as a protected characteristic, those efforts failed.

In the last decade or so, some courts and agencies began to reexamine their interpretations of Title VII. Some courts found that Title VII's ban on sex discrimination also prohibited discrimination based on sexual orientation and gender identity. The EEOC also adopted this interpretation. And, in 2020, the Supreme Court agreed. In *Bostock v. Clayton County, Georgia*, 590 U.S. 644, the Court decided in a 6-3 decision that discrimination based on sexual orientation and gender identity are forms of illegal sex discrimination under Title VII. Harassment based on sexual orientation and gender identity are prohibited as well.

An employer who makes job decisions based on these traits is, by definition, penalizing an employee for acting in ways that would be accepted in an employee of a different gender. For example, it's illegal to fire a gay man for marrying or dating another man, because the employer presumably wouldn't fire a woman who married or dated a man. Similarly, firing a transgender woman for dressing in women's clothing is illegal, because the employer wouldn't fire a cisgender woman for doing so. These types of decisions are based on assumptions about how men and women should behave, dress, and carry themselves—in other words, they're based on gender, a protected trait under Title VII.

Although less common, harassment based on other protected characteristics also can create serious problems. For example, an employee who is teased or called names because of national origin or religion could have a harassment claim, as might one who is subject to racist jokes. Any workplace conduct that is unwelcome, offensive, and related to the employee's protected characteristic could constitute harassment if it's severe enough or happens often enough.

An employer has a duty to take reasonable steps to stop harassment. Having a strong written antiharassment policy and a procedure for investigating harassment complaints can serve as a defense in a harassment lawsuit. An employee who fails to take advantage of such policies and doesn't report harassment has a much weaker claim. However, if an employer only pays lip service to preventing harassment—by failing to distribute its policies or failing to investigate complaints, for

Policies With Discriminatory Effects

Many discrimination claims focus on situations in which an employer *intends* to discriminate— that is, an employee can prove that the employer treated the employee differently because of the employee's race, sex, or other protected characteristic. These are called "disparate treatment" claims.

However, there is another type of discrimination claim that doesn't require this intent. In this type of lawsuit, the worker claims that the effect of an employer's workplace rule or job requirement was to screen out large numbers of employees of a particular race, sex, or other protected characteristic. For example, a rule requiring workers to be a certain height might result in excluding a disproportionate number of women. Or, an employer who screens out applicants with arrest records might exclude more Black and Latino employees, who have historically been subjected to more frequent encounters with police. Discrimination claims

that are based on the effect of an employer's actions are known as "disparate impact" claims.

An employer can defend itself against these claims by showing that the particular rule or requirement was job related and necessary to the business. For example, a strength requirement would certainly be allowed if the job required heavy lifting. The fact that more women than men would likely be screened out by the requirement wouldn't make the employer guilty of discrimination.

We don't cover disparate impact claims in detail here, because they rarely come up in the context of firing or disciplining a single employee who's having (or causing) problems at work. Disparate impact claims rarely challenge an individual employment decision, but more often take on a rule or requirement used as a screening or selection tool. Examples include prerequisites for hiring, exams used for promotions, and layoff criteria.

example—the employee has a stronger claim. See Chapter 5 for more details.

RESOURCE

Want more information on harassment? There's lots for free at the EEOC's website at www.eeoc.gov.

Disability Discrimination

The Americans with Disabilities Act, or the ADA (42 U.S.C. §§ 12102 and following), is a federal law that prohibits discrimination against people with physical or mental disabilities. The ADA covers companies with 15 or more employees and applies broadly to private employers, employment agencies, and labor organizations. Although state governments must follow the ADA, state employees cannot sue to enforce their ADA rights.

The ADA bans various practices throughout the employment process, such as asking applicants questions about their medical conditions or requiring preemployment medical examinations. In the firing context, the ADA prohibits an employer from terminating a worker because of a disability or because the worker needs a reasonable accommodation.

What Is a Disability?

The ADA protects "qualified workers with disabilities." A qualified worker is a worker who can perform the essential functions of the job, with or without reasonable accommodation.

A worker who falls into any one of the following three categories has a disability:

- The worker has a physical or mental impairment that substantially limits a major life activity (such as the ability to walk, talk, see, hear, breathe, reason, work, or take care of oneself) or a major bodily function (such as the proper functioning of the immune system, cell growth, brain, or respiratory system). Impairments that are episodic or in remission qualify as disabilities if they substantially limit a major life activity when active. Measures an employee takes or uses to mitigate the effects of a disability (such as prescription medication or prosthetic devices) may not be considered in determining whether the employee's impairment limits major life activities or major bodily functions. The only exception to this rule is for the corrective power of ordinary prescription glasses and contact lenses, which may be considered when determining whether an employee has a disability.

EXAMPLE: Brian has bipolar disorder, a mental condition most commonly associated with wide mood swings, from euphoric highs to depressive lows. Currently, Brian's condition is largely controlled by medication and careful monitoring. However, Brian still has a disability under the ADA because his major life activities would be limited were he not using these mitigating measures.

- The worker has a record or history of such an impairment. In other words, you may not make employment decisions on the basis of your employee's past disability.

  EXAMPLE: Dan had a heart attack and bypass surgery. Since then, he has worked hard to improve his diet, get more exercise, and lower his blood pressure. Although Dan had a few medical restrictions following his surgery, his doctor quickly lifted them and pronounced him fit to work. If Dan's employer fires him, fearing that he might have another heart attack and become unable to work, that employer has discriminated against Dan based on his record of disability.

- The worker is regarded by the employer— even incorrectly—as having such an impairment. You can't treat workers less favorably because you believe them to have disabilities. An employee who brings a lawsuit for being "regarded as" having a disability doesn't claim to have an actual disability (nor is the employee entitled to a reasonable accommodation, covered below). Instead, the employee argues that the employer incorrectly treated the employee as if the employee had a disability and couldn't do the job. These claims tend to come up when an employee has some kind of impairment that doesn't rise to

the level of a legal disability or when an employer acts on the basis of stereotypes about certain impairments rather than on the actual abilities of the employee.

EXAMPLE 1: Diego walks with a slight limp from a childhood accident. Although his gait is slightly impaired and he can't run quickly, Diego is able to walk and stand for long periods of time. He was not promoted to the position of plant foreman because his employer believed he would be unable to walk the plant floor as the job requires. Diego has been discriminated against because he was regarded as disabled, even though his limp is not a disability under the ADA. Although he was capable of doing the job, his employer treated him as if he were not.

EXAMPLE 2: Mihran became depressed when his marriage ended. He sought assistance from a therapist, who counseled him and referred him to a doctor for antidepressant medication. Although Mihran has been down, his depression is relatively mild; he hasn't missed any work or suffered any work-related problems because of it. Mihran's boss fired Mihran upon learning of his condition, believing that a person with a mental illness was more likely to miss work, act irrationally, or even become violent in the workplace. Mihran's employer acted on the basis of stereotypes about mental illness rather than on Mihran's abilities and job performance. Mihran could sue his employer for regarding him as disabled.

Congress amended the ADA in 2008 to strengthen its protections for people with disabilities and to overturn several Supreme Court decisions that limited the scope of the law. The EEOC's final regulations interpreting the amended ADA make crystal clear that the law is to be interpreted in favor of broad coverage for employees. Once you're aware that an employee might have a disability, you must make certain you don't discriminate, for example, by making assumptions about what the employee can and can't do. You should also begin discussing reasonable accommodations with the employee, as described below.

Reasonable Accommodation

Accommodating a disabled worker means providing assistance or making changes in the job or workplace that will enable the worker to do the job. For example, an employer might raise or lower the height of a desktop to accommodate a worker who uses a wheelchair; provide TDD telephone equipment for a worker whose hearing is impaired; or provide a quiet, distraction-free workspace for a worker with attention deficit disorder.

It's your employee's responsibility to inform you of the disability and request a reasonable accommodation; you aren't legally required to guess that an employee might need help to do the job. However, once an employee tells you about a disability, you must engage in what the law calls a "flexible interactive process": essentially, a brainstorming dialogue with your worker to figure out what kinds of accommodations might be effective and practical. You aren't required to provide the precise accommodation the worker requests, but you must work together to come up with a reasonable solution.

Nevertheless, an employer isn't required to provide an accommodation if doing so would cause the business "undue hardship." For this analysis, courts will look at the cost of the accommodation, the size and financial resources of your business, the structure of your business, and the effect the accommodation would have on your business.

> **EXAMPLE 1:** Doris has a spinal cord injury. She suffers from some paralysis and uses a wheelchair. Doris applies for a position as a secretary in a new accounting firm. Because she is physically unable to type, Doris asks her employer to accommodate her disability by giving her typing responsibilities to another employee. Because the company is new and is running on a tight budget, it can't spare any employee hours to do this work. The company proposes, instead, that Doris use voice recognition software when she needs to use her computer, to which Doris agrees.

EXAMPLE 2: Erik has attention deficit disorder. He is easily distracted and unable to concentrate on a project when there's too much background noise or activity. Erik has worked in the financing department of a car dealership for a year. His employer accommodated his disability by allowing him to have his own office, with a door that closes, in the back of the dealership.

Alcohol and Drugs

Alcohol and drug use pose special problems under the ADA. Employees who use (or have used) alcohol or drugs might have a disability under the law. However, an employer can require them to meet the same work standards—including not drinking or using drugs on the job—that apply to all other employees. Here are some guidelines to follow when dealing with these tricky issues:

- **Alcohol.** Alcoholism is a disability covered by the ADA. This means that an employer can't fire or discipline a worker simply for being an alcoholic. However, an employer can fire or discipline an alcoholic worker for failing to meet work-related performance and behavior standards imposed on all employees, even if the worker fails to meet these standards because of drinking.

EXAMPLE 1: Mark has worked as a secretary in Laura's law firm for five years. He has always received glowing performance evaluations. One day, Laura discovers that Mark attends Alcoholics Anonymous meetings every Saturday night. She fires Mark because she doesn't want people with alcohol problems working for her. Her actions violate the ADA because she based her decision solely on Mark's status as an alcoholic.

EXAMPLE 2: Maria runs a small hometown newspaper. John, her city council reporter, periodically misses the city council meetings or shows up late. Maria has noticed that this happens when the meetings are held on Friday mornings. John's poker night is Thursday night, and he tends to drink to excess. Maria has used progressive discipline with John, giving him a verbal reminder and a written reprimand. She has even offered to give John time off to enter an alcohol treatment program. He refused the offer. Maria has told John that the next time he misses a city council meeting, she will terminate him. The termination is allowed under the ADA, because she is firing him for failing to meet the same performance standards that she expects of all of her reporters and not for having an alcohol problem.

- **Illegal drug use.** The ADA doesn't protect employees who currently use illegal drugs or who abuse legal drugs (such as prescriptions). Because using illegal drugs isn't a disability within the meaning of the law, these employees don't have the right to be free from discrimination or to receive a reasonable accommodation based on their drug use. However, the ADA does cover workers who are no longer using drugs and have successfully completed (or are currently participating in) a supervised drug rehabilitation program.

- **Use of legal drugs.** If an employee is taking prescription medication or over-the-counter drugs to treat a disability, you might have a responsibility to accommodate that employee's use of drugs and the side effects that the drugs have on the employee. However, you don't have to accommodate legal drug use if it would cause an undue hardship or the employee cannot perform essential functions of the job.

EXAMPLE: Elaine works as a seamstress at a textile plant. The plant operates on three shifts. Elaine takes medication to treat depression. The medication makes her lethargic for a few hours after she wakes up in the morning. To accommodate the medication's effects on Elaine, the textile plant allows her to work a midday shift, from 11:00 a.m. to 7:00 p.m.

RESOURCE
Want more information on the ADA?
Check out these resources:

- the U.S. Equal Employment Opportunity Commission at www.eeoc.gov
- the U.S. government's Office of Disability Employment Policy at www.dol.gov/agencies/odep, or
- the Job Accommodation Network (JAN) at https://askjan.org.

You can also find a comprehensive discussion of the ADA and other federal employment laws in *The Essential Guide to Federal Employment Laws,* by Sachi Clements (Nolo).

Pregnancy Discrimination

The Pregnancy Discrimination Act or PDA (42 U.S.C. § 2076) amended Title VII to prohibit employers from discriminating against an employee because of her pregnancy, childbirth, or related medical condition. This means you may not fire, demote, or take other negative action against an employee because they are pregnant.

Employers get into legal trouble under the PDA when they make unwarranted assumptions about pregnant employees. For example, some employers assume that pregnant employees won't be able to work, and fire them, force them to take leave, or transfer them to positions with lesser

Avoiding Disability Discrimination Claims

The ADA can be confusing to employers. Courts are constantly redefining its terms and scope, and Congress has amended the law to make it more protective of those with disabilities. As a result, employers are sometimes left unsure of precisely what the law requires. Because of this uncertainty, it's a good idea to consult a lawyer before firing a person with a disability, especially if the reason for termination is related to the disability (such as absenteeism).

Here are a few general guidelines to help you avoid problems:

- **Talk to the affected employees.** Once a worker tells you of a disability and need for an accommodation, ask what changes would help the worker do the job. If the worker proposes an unreasonable change, suggest alternatives that might be effective. Have a discussion periodically to make sure things are going smoothly.
- **Respect employee privacy.** The ADA requires you to keep certain medical information confidential. It's good policy to treat *all* medical information about workers on a "need to know" basis. A supervisor might need to know about the limitations a particular worker has, but coworkers do not. Similarly, you need to know how your worker's disability affects job performance, but not what impact it has had on the worker's personal relationships. Detailed discussions of a disability can lead the disabled worker to feel stigmatized and resentful, a potent recipe for a lawsuit.
- **Make objective evaluations of performance.** Apply the same performance standards to all employees. This will help ensure that you don't let unconscious negative attitudes about disabilities color your employment decisions.
- **Take steps to include disabled workers in all company activities.** Often, employees with physical disabilities are unintentionally left out of company activities—particularly those held off site—because of accessibility problems. When planning company picnics, holiday parties, training sessions, or team-building activities, make sure disabled employees can attend and participate fully.

duties. This is illegal. It is also illegal for an employer to fire a pregnant employee based on the assumption that they won't want to work once they have a child.

> **EXAMPLE:** Hermione works for a shipping company. She used to work in the office, doing administrative work and keeping track of orders. For the last year, she's worked loading packages into the company's trucks, a job with better pay and benefits. Hermione is pregnant. If her employer transfers her back to her office job because he assumes she won't be able to load packages, that could be an act of discrimination if she is still able to do her job. However, if Hermione's doctor restricts her from all lifting during her pregnancy and Hermione requests the transfer, the same job move would be perfectly legal.

The PDA doesn't explicitly require employers to make reasonable accommodations for pregnant employees. Because the goal of the law was to prohibit employers from treating pregnant employees differently from other employees, courts held that the law required accommodations only if such accommodations were provided to other employees. For instance, if an employer provided light-duty work to injured employees, it would also have to provide such work to pregnant employees who needed it. However, an employer that never provided light-duty work to anyone wouldn't have to make an exception for pregnant employees, under the PDA.

A number of states have stepped into the breach, explicitly requiring employers to make reasonable accommodations for an employee's pregnancy-related work restrictions. And in 2022, Congress followed suit, passing the Pregnant Workers Fairness Act (PWFA). The PWFA requires employers to provide reasonable accommodations to pregnant employees' known limitations relating to pregnancy or childbirth, unless doing so poses an undue hardship to the business. Examples of reasonable accommodations include allowing a pregnant employee to sit or use a stool on the job, providing more frequent bathroom and rest breaks, giving leave or time off, allowing flexible scheduling, and allowing pregnant workers to avoid strenuous activity or exposure to substances that are potentially hazardous to their pregnancy. The EEOC offers resources and other information about the PWFA at www.eeoc.gov/wysk/what-you-should-know-about-pregnant-workers-fairness-act.

Age Discrimination

The Age Discrimination in Employment Act, or ADEA (29 U.S.C. §§ 621–634), makes it illegal for employers to discriminate against workers on the basis of age. However, the ADEA protects only those workers aged 40 or older. The ADEA applies to private employers with 20 or more employees, employment agencies, and labor organizations. Although state governments must follow the

ADEA, state employees can't sue to enforce their ADEA rights.

Many states also prohibit age discrimination; some of these laws cover younger workers as well or offer wider protections. See Appendix B for more details on state antidiscrimination laws.

A couple groups of workers are excepted from the ADEA:

- **Police officers and firefighters.** Local governments may establish a retirement age of 55 or older, as long as they provide a valid alternative test that employees can take to prove that they remain physically fit after reaching that age.

- **High-level executives.** The ADEA allows private employers to require retirement if (1) the employee is 65 or older, (2) the employee has worked for at least the previous two years as a high-level executive or policy maker, and (3) the employee is entitled to retirement pay of at least $44,000 per year from the employer. The employee must be eligible to start receiving this pay within 60 days of retirement, and the pay cannot be "forfeitable." If the retirement plan allows the company to stop payments or reduce the amount of pay to an amount below $44,000 per year because of the employee's actions (if the employee sues the company or goes to work for a competitor, for example), the pay is forfeitable and the exception doesn't apply.

RESOURCE

For more about the Age Discrimination in Employment Act. You can find a comprehensive discussion of the ADEA and other federal employment laws in *The Essential Guide to Federal Employment Laws,* by Sachi Clements (Nolo).

Genetic Discrimination

The most recent addition to the civil rights laws is named GINA: the Genetic Information Nondiscrimination Act. (42 U.S.C. §§ 200 and following.) GINA prohibits health insurers from using genetic information to deny insurance coverage or determine premiums. It also prohibits covered employers from making employment decisions based on applicants' or employees' genetic information, and it requires employers to keep employee genetic information confidential. GINA applies to private employers with 15 or more employees, the federal and state governments, employment agencies, and labor organizations.

In addition to prohibiting an employer from making employment decisions based on an employee's or applicant's genetic information, GINA prohibits discrimination based on the genetic information of an employee's or applicant's family member. Genetic information includes the results of genetic tests or the manifestation of a particular disease or disorder in the employee's family. For example, an employer can't refuse to hire an applicant because she carries BRCA1 or BRCA2 (the genes thought responsible for most inherited breast cancers), or fire an employee because he carries the trait for sickle cell anemia. Whether the employer is motivated by stereotypes or stigma associated with the disease or by a desire to reduce health care costs, decisions like these are illegal.

Watch Your Language

Most people are mindful that disparaging comments about race, gender, or religion are strictly forbidden in the workplace. For some reason, however, managers and employers seem to be less inhibited when it comes to age-related remarks. Court decisions about age discrimination are replete with employer comments about old-timers, senior moments, and old dogs who can't learn new tricks. While these statements alone might not be enough to prove discrimination, they will certainly upset older workers (not to mention a jury).

Apparently, even Dick Clark, referred to by some as the "World's Oldest Teenager," wasn't immune. He was sued in 2004 by Ralph Andrews, a 76-year-old producer, who claimed the 74-year-old Clark refused to hire him because of his age. Andrews's complaint stated that Clark wrote him a rejection letter stating that he had recently hired a 27-year-old and a 30-year-old, and that "[p]eople our age are considered dinosaurs!" Clark also promised to consider Andrews if a project came up that required "experienced hands."

Acquiring Genetic Information

With a few exceptions, GINA also prohibits employers from requiring or asking employees to provide genetic information (for example, by requiring genetic testing as a condition of employment). Employers also can't purchase genetic information about employees or their family members.

It isn't illegal for an employer to obtain genetic information on an employee or employee's family member in certain circumstances. Even if one of these exceptions applies, however, the employer still can't make employment decisions based on this information and must keep it confidential:

- The employer obtains or requires such information inadvertently (for example, by overhearing a conversation among coworkers or because the employee volunteers it).
- The employer acquires the information through health or genetic services it offers (as part of a wellness program, for example). The services must meet several conditions for this exception to apply, including that the employer doesn't receive any individually identifiable information about any employees.
- The employer requires a family medical history from the employee in order to comply with the certification requirements of the Family and Medical Leave Act or a similar state leave law.

- The employer purchases documents that are commercially and publicly available and that include family medical history. This exception applies to newspapers, magazines, and books, for example, but not to medical databases or court records.
- The employer conducts DNA analysis for law enforcement purposes as a forensic laboratory or to identify human remains, and requests or requires genetic information from its employees only for analysis of DNA identification markers as a means of detecting sample contamination (that is, to separate employee DNA from the DNA the lab is examining).
- The information acquired is to be used for genetic monitoring of the biological effects of toxic substances in the workplace. The monitoring must meet a number of standards to fall under this exception, including that the employer doesn't receive any individually identifiable results.

Confidentiality of Genetic Information

Employers that have genetic information about employees must keep it on separate forms and in separate files, and treat it as confidential medical records. This means an employer must treat this information as it treats medical information under the ADA: The information must be kept separately from regular personnel files and revealed only in limited circumstances to certain people (for example, to government officials investigating the company's compliance with the law).

Retaliation for Complaints

All of the antidiscrimination laws discussed in this section prohibit employers from retaliating against employees for either filing a complaint of discrimination or for cooperating in an investigation of a discrimination complaint. Many state laws contain a similar ban. These claims are especially dangerous to employers, because juries seem particularly offended by retaliation and routinely deliver the highest damages awards for these claims.

To prove retaliation, employees must show that they were punished for making a complaint in good faith. Any action that could deter a reasonable employee from complaining about discrimination or harassment could constitute retaliation. Employees are also protected from retaliation for participating in an investigation of discrimination or harassment. In other words, an employee need not be the source of the complaint: If an employee acts as a witness or answers an investigator's questions about another employee's complaint, both employees are protected.

As a practical matter, an employee's retaliation claim will fail unless the employee can show that the person who imposed the discipline knew about the complaint. The greater the time interval between the complaint

Employees Win Retaliation Cases in the Supreme Court

For a couple of decades now, the Supreme Court has been viewed as pro-business. In retaliation cases, however, employees have had some big wins. Here are some examples:

- **Any "materially adverse" action can constitute retaliation.** An employee need not be fired for retaliation to occur: Any negative action that might deter a reasonable employee from making a complaint might be retaliation, including shift changes, pay changes, and reassignment to less desirable job duties. (*Burlington Northern & Santa Fe Railway v. White*, 548 U.S. 53 (2006).)

- **Employees who participate in an investigation are protected.** The Court found that employees may not be retaliated against for participating in a company investigation of another employee's complaint; the employee who filed this lawsuit went on to win $1.5 million. (*Crawford v. Metropolitan Government of Nashville and Davidson County, Tennessee*, 555 U.S. 271 (2009).)

- **An employee can sue for retaliation based on his fiancée's legal claims.** In this case, the Court found that a man could sue for retaliation after he was fired because his fiancée filed a sex discrimination lawsuit against their mutual employer. Even though one employee complained of discrimination and the other suffered the negative job consequence, the Court found that this is the sort of reprisal that could dissuade employees from asserting their rights. (*Thompson v. North American Stainless*, 562 U.S. 170 (2011).)

- **Oral complaints can give rise to a retaliation claim.** In this case brought under the Fair Labor Standards Act, an employee claimed that he was fired after making repeated oral complaints that the company time clocks were located in a place that required employees to clock in after donning their protective work gear and to clock out before they took that gear off. As a result, employees weren't paid for time that must be compensated under the law. The Court rejected the employer's argument that such a complaint must be in writing to form the basis of a retaliation claim. As long as the employee's complaint is sufficiently clear and detailed for the employer to understand it as an assertion of statutory rights, the employee is protected from retaliation. (*Kasten v. Saint-Gobain Performance Plastics Corporation*, 563 U.S. 1 (2012).)

and the negative action, the more likely it is that a jury will conclude that the complaint and the discipline were not related.

The best way to avoid a retaliation claim is to not fire or discipline employees who have complained unless the reasons for your decision are well documented, persuasive, and sound. If you're able to show that the reason for your action—be it performance problems, insubordination, or misconduct—predated the employee's complaint, your defense will be stronger. Avoid any reference to the employee's complaint in the disciplinary or termination process and related documents. And, of course, if you refer to the employee derogatorily as a "troublemaker," "squeaky wheel," "complainer," or the like, a jury could decide that you actually punished the employee for complaining.

Unfair Labor Practices

The National Labor Relations Act (NLRA), the federal law that governs the relationship between unions and management, outlaws certain practices as unfair infringements on this carefully balanced playing field. For example, employers may not discriminate or retaliate against employees who support a union, refuse to bargain collectively with a duly elected union, or change workplace rules unilaterally without the union's agreement.

Currently, relatively few private employees are union members; according to the Bureau of Labor Statistics, only 5.9% of private sector employees were union members in 2024. However, the NLRA imposes some rules on nonunion companies as well, intended to protect employees' rights not only to organize a union, but also to talk to each other about and act together to improve their working conditions (these are called "protected concerted activities"). For example, you may not fire or discipline employees simply because they have asked for higher pay, better benefits, or additional safety precautions for employees who work late.

In recent years, the NLRB has begun to take a close look at how this right to engage in protected concerted activities intersects with modern methods of workplace communication, including employee posts on blogs and social media. What do employee posts have to do with labor relations? Plenty, if employees are fired or disciplined for (or prohibited by policy from) communicating with each other about the terms and conditions of employment and joining together to bring their concerns to their employer.

The NLRB has ruled against employers that fire or discipline employees for posting critical comments about the company on social media sites or blogs. (You can find several NLRB reports on these cases at its website, www.nlrb.gov.) For example:

- A collections agency was found to have illegally fired an employee for Facebook posts complaining about her transfer. The employee used expletives and said she was done with being a good employee; her coworkers who were Facebook friends posted comments expressing support, criticizing the employer, and suggesting a class action lawsuit. Because the employees were discussing taking action regarding the terms of their employment, the NLRB concluded that they were engaged in protected concerted activity.

- An employee at a veterinary hospital posted to her Facebook page after being denied a promotion. Several coworkers responded to the post, and engaged in a conversation in which they complained about the person who received the promotion, the company's practices regarding raises and reviews, and so on. The NLRB found it illegal when the employee and one coworker were fired and the other two participants in the conversation disciplined.

- A group of employees took to Facebook to complain about a coworker who they felt had been criticizing their performance. A conversation about the employer's policies toward its clientele ensued, then five of the employees were fired. The NLRB found the firings illegal, because the employees were discussing the terms of their employment and considering how to raise those concerns with their employer.

As part of these enforcement actions, the NLRB often scrutinizes the employer's workplace and social media policies, to determine whether they are likely to discourage employees from exercising their right to engage in protected activity. The level of enforcement tends to fluctuate depending on the administration.

Because of these shifts, there will likely be stops and starts as courts try to figure out how employee rights play out in the digital age. For the time being, however, employers should think twice before disciplining or firing an employee for criticizing company rules, complaining about managers, or raising concerns about pay, hours, and working conditions, whether those issues are raised face to face or on Facebook. This is an area where a consultation with a lawyer will help you stay on top of rapid legal developments. ●

Performance Evaluations

As the saying goes, "An ounce of prevention is worth a pound of cure." In the workplace, the high cost of problem employees—in terms of money, time, and lost productivity—means that the most effective management tactic is to prevent problems in the first place. Performance evaluations are a great way to nip developing problems in the bud. If you adopt a sound performance evaluation process and use it consistently with all employees (not just the ones giving you trouble), you'll prevent a lot of problems.

Of course, no system is foolproof. Sooner or later, you're bound to have difficulties with an employee or two. When this happens, your performance evaluation system will be there as your first line of defense. Not only will it help you identify and deal with most problems early on, but it will also lay the groundwork for discipline and, if necessary, legally defensible termination if the problems just won't go away.

Structured communication between you and your employees is at the heart of a good evaluation system. We do not use the word "structured" lightly. For your evaluation system to be effective—both practically and legally—you must do much more than occasionally check in with employees. You must instead:

- Work with employees to set job-related goals and requirements for their performance.
- Regularly observe and document their performance in relation to those goals and requirements.
- Meet with them periodically to discuss their performance and to redefine their goals, if necessary.
- Conduct a formal annual performance appraisal.

Don't make the mistake of equating a performance evaluation system with feedback. Some employers think that as long as they periodically let employees know how they're doing—a pat on the back here, a shake of the finger there—they've got the evaluation angle covered. Far from it. Although casual feedback is part of an overall evaluation system, you must supplement it with thorough, planned, and well-documented reviews.

Performance appraisal is a process, not a form. If you think that all you need to do to evaluate employees effectively is complete a form at the end of the year, think again. A good appraisal system includes ongoing observation, documentation, and communication.

TIP
Performance feedback and appraisal is especially important for remote and hybrid workforces. Some studies have shown proximity bias against remote employees in many areas, including training and feedback. The closer employees are to their manager(s), the more feedback and guidance they receive. Employees

who work remotely can suffer from this bias, and their job performance might suffer as well. Make sure to touch base frequently with remote workers and provide real-time input on their job performance.

The Benefits of an Evaluation System

An effective evaluation system will help you tap into the potential of every employee. Indeed, a performance evaluation system provides a solid foundation for all aspects of the employment relationship, helping you to:

- examine employees as individuals, and evaluate their strengths and weaknesses
- identify and reward good employees, thereby fostering loyalty and providing motivation for them to continue to work hard
- keep employee morale high through continuous feedback
- stay on top of the needs of your workforce, thus increasing employee retention, productivity, and innovation
- reduce legal risk by ensuring that employees feel that they are treated fairly and are not surprised by management decisions, and
- identify and deal with problem employees, sometimes allowing you to help them become valuable, productive workers, and other times laying the groundwork for discipline and, if necessary, legally defensible termination.

A performance evaluation system can also help you avoid lawsuits (or cut them short). The documentation will support your decisions and help defeat employee claims of illegal treatment. Faced with a personnel file containing written proof of your repeated attempts to correct a seriously wayward employee, a lawyer might think twice before agreeing to represent that employee in a wrongful termination lawsuit.

Consistent evaluation also provides an objective framework for all of your employees, which makes it harder for any employee to claim that you singled them out for discriminatory reasons.

Step 1: Create Performance Objectives

The foundation of any performance evaluation system is a set of performance objectives that identify what you expect of an employee. Performance objectives give employees something to strive for. As the year progresses, employees can refine and adjust their work to make sure they are on track. You might even find that employees exceed your (and their own) expectations.

Different companies call performance objectives different things: responsibilities, deliverables, duties, results, outputs, targets, and so on. Regardless of what you call them, objectives are essentially a way to define what you expect from an employee and to measure the employee's performance.

Beware of Implied Contracts

One unhappy truth of employment law is that instituting a sound and effective performance evaluation system might limit your options. The more consistently you apply the system (especially in conjunction with progressive discipline, discussed in Chapter 4), the more likely a court is to find that you've limited your ability to terminate employees at will. If you always follow a careful system of giving employees feedback, warnings, and opportunities to improve before resorting to termination, a court could find that you've created an implied contract that limits your right to fire at will.

Even so, the benefits of a performance evaluation system far outweigh the risks. Indeed, the rewards you reap in terms of improved performance, productivity, and morale will make you less likely to need your at-will power anyway. After all, you always have the right to fire an employee for cause, and a sound performance evaluation system strengthens, rather than destroys, that right. Furthermore, firing for cause is always a safer bet legally than firing at will.

You can lessen the risks of creating an implied contract by following the guidelines in Chapter 2. Require your employees to sign a hiring letter that states that their employment is at will. Insert at-will clauses into your employee handbook, if you have one. Never make promises to employees about the length of their employment. If you make it clear to your employees that you are an at-will employer—through your actions and through writings signed by employees—a court is quite unlikely to find that you've created an implied contract simply by instituting a performance evaluation system like the one suggested in this book.

This book uses the terms "requirements" and "goals" when referring to an employee's performance objectives to mean the following:

- **Job requirements** reflect how you want all employees who hold a certain job to perform.
- **Developmental goals** reflect the ways in which both you and a specific employee would like to see the employee grow and improve over a set period of time.

This section explains how to identify job requirements and developmental goals. If your company already has an evaluation system in place, you can use the information here to troubleshoot the requirements and goals set for each position and employee.

If you don't have an evaluation system (or if your company simply uses the same generic form for everyone), you'll need to develop goals and requirements before starting to assess employee performance. After all, employees need to know what they are expected to accomplish and how you want them to do their work. It's neither fair nor sensible to hold employees to standards they don't know about.

As explained below, you'll review and revise performance requirements and goals each year, at your annual appraisal meeting. If you're just starting out with an evaluation system, the process of coming up with these performance standards will mark the beginning of the evaluation year. Once you've finalized your expectations, write them down and rank the entries in each category from most to least important. This way, employees will know how to allocate their time and energy. An employee who isn't able to make it through the entire list by the time the next review rolls around should have addressed at least the most important items.

Job Requirements

Requirements describe what you want an employee in a particular job to accomplish and how you want that job to be performed. Every employee who holds a certain position should meet the same set of requirements. In other words, the requirements reflect the features of the job, not the abilities or skills of the particular employee who fills it.

There are two kinds of requirements to consider: result requirements and behavior requirements:

- A "result requirement" is a concrete description of a result that you expect from any employee who holds a particular job. For example, a result requirement for newspaper reporters might be to write three

stories a week; for proofreaders, to miss no more than one error per story; for a salesperson, to make $50,000 in sales each quarter.
- A "behavior requirement" is a description of how you want employees in a particular job to behave while getting the job done. Often, behavior requirements reflect a company's values. For example, if you value stellar customer service, a behavior requirement might be that a salesperson must answer all customer questions cheerfully and respectfully.

Identifying Job Requirements

To identify the requirements of a job, look at how the job fits within your business. What are the job's essential elements? Its purpose? Historically, what have employees in that job been able to accomplish?

TIP
Get your job requirements straight from the job description. If you already have an up-to-date job description for the position, you're way ahead in the evaluation game. The job description should clearly set out job duties and functions, which you can use to draft the job requirements for the evaluation. You'll find more information on job descriptions in Chapter 11.

Employees themselves can also be a valuable resource for pinning down requirements for the jobs they hold. Consider talking to them first. Don't forget to talk to others in your business who interact with and depend upon the person who fills a particular job. For example, when defining a vehicle dispatcher's job, you might learn from the drivers that a key factor in making their jobs go smoothly is the dispatcher's ability to give clear and concise directions. The actual dispatcher might not have thought of that.

Only choose requirements that are job related. This is important for both practical and legal reasons: It doesn't do any good to force the employee to live up to a requirement that doesn't help your business. Furthermore, the law won't look kindly on you if you punish an employee for not living up to a requirement that isn't business related.

Job requirements must be specific. Employers often make the mistake of using vague language when describing requirements. For example, an employer might say its employees should "take initiative" or "be self-starters." But what do these really mean? If you and the employee could potentially disagree on what's expected, it will be difficult to decide whether the employee has fulfilled the requirement.

To guard against vagueness, focus on what you want employees in that job to do, not on who you want employees to be. For example, instead of setting "take initiative" as a job requirement, spell out how you want employees to act or what actions you want them to take. Do you want employees to create their own product ideas? Develop personal sales contacts? Implement their own ways to attract clients? When you focus on

actions instead of traits, you give employees a greater understanding of what you expect, while giving yourself a more concrete standard against which to measure performance.

Here are a few examples:

- **For a call center employee:** "The employee will answer an average of 10 customer service calls per shift. All paperwork for calls received during a shift must be completed and forwarded to the appropriate department by the end of that shift."

- **For a salesperson:** "The employee will generate and develop a customer base. At least half of all new accounts should be accounts developed by the employee. The employee will generate at least $100,000 in gross sales per quarter."

- **For a retail employee:** "The employee will greet customers when they enter the store and ask whether they need assistance. If a customer is looking for a particular item, the employee will walk with the customer to the area or aisle where the item is kept, rather than pointing or giving directions."

Communicating Job Requirements

Tell an employee the job requirements during the hiring process or when the employee starts work. If the requirements change—for example, the business downsizes and needs to redistribute responsibilities—tell the employee about the new requirements as soon as possible.

Developmental Goals

Personal, developmental goals are the second measure by which to evaluate employees. Unlike requirements, you should tailor these goals to employees as individuals, depending on their strengths and weaknesses. Goals will not be the same for all employees in the same job category.

Choosing Goals

Together, you and the employee should come up with goals based on:

- weak spots in the employee's overall performance that the employee should improve upon
- strengths that the employee should nurture and develop, and
- skills that will help improve job performance.

For example, a store manager might do a great job overseeing day-to-day operations but have weak writing skills that make her reports difficult to understand. A developmental goal for that employee would be to take a writing course at a local community college. Or your best salesperson might decide that learning Spanish would help him serve your Spanish-speaking customers better. A developmental goal for that employee would be to complete a conversational Spanish course by the end of the year. (Keep in mind that your company must pay for any courses it requires an employee to take, along with compensating the employee for time spent in class.)

Collaboration is the key to successful goal setting. An employee who helps to create the goals will be more invested in meeting them. Asking an employee to join you in setting personal goals has an added bonus: Many employees know their strengths and weaknesses better than you do. They might understand their jobs in ways you haven't considered. You might be pleasantly surprised to hear their ideas on how they can do their jobs better.

At some point, you should meet with each employee formally to discuss goals. For a new employee, schedule a goal-setting meeting in the first few months of employment. That way, the employee will have goals to work toward during the first year with you. Also at that meeting, apprise the employee of the job requirements (as explained above) and give informal feedback on any work the employee has already done for you. For current employees, you can set and reevaluate goals at the year-end evaluation.

Before your meeting, encourage the employee to prepare by thinking about areas for improvement and growth. Explain that you want to identify goals for which the employee can strive, for the benefit of the company and the employee's own career development.

After you've met and identified goals, find out what, if anything, the employee needs from you to meet them. For example, in order to teach more advanced classes, an instructor might need to attend a continuing education course, which you must pay for. Or if you expect a chef to handle a more complicated menu, you might need to provide more helpers in the kitchen. Agree on a time frame and set deadlines that both of you will meet.

Guidelines for Effective Goal Setting

Here are some guidelines to follow when setting developmental goals with an employee:

- **Don't be excessive.** Some managers think, incorrectly, that more goals are always better. On the contrary, you can actually lower employee performance by heaping too many goals (and requirements, for that matter) onto an employee's back.
- **Choose only goals that relate to the job.** Otherwise, at best, you'll be wasting time, energy, and money on skills or interests that don't really help your company. At worst, you'll be courting legal trouble. To be legally safe in basing an employment decision on an employee's ability or inability to meet a goal, that goal must be job related.
- **Be specific.** Research has shown that specific performance measures lead to better performance than vague statements such as "work harder" or "do your best."
- **Avoid personality issues.** Beware of trying to change an employee's personality through developmental goals. For example, if a shy employee has trouble speaking up in meetings, it's not a good idea to try to address this shyness by requiring the employee to attend more after-hours social functions. Think of other ways the employee might improve, such as by working on more committees or making a monthly presentation to the team.
- **Use active verbs.** This will underscore your expectation that the employee, not some disembodied force, is the one who must perform. For example, don't say "deadlines will be met." Rather, say "John will meet 90% of his deadlines this quarter."
- **Be realistic.** Don't ask so much that you doom the employee to failure or burnout. On the other hand, you don't want to make things too simple. Encourage employees to stretch beyond their current level in order to reach full potential.
- **Avoid stereotypes.** Don't assume, for example, that a female employee won't want to learn how to fix machinery or that an older worker can't master new technology. Base your ideas on what you know about the employee as an individual, not as a member of a particular group.
- **Set measurable goals.** If you can identify a fair way to measure a goal, you'll minimize the risk that you and the employee will disagree over whether it was actually accomplished.

Step 2: Observe and Document Employee Performance

An effective evaluation system requires ongoing observation and documentation. This means that you must be mindful of employee performance throughout the year, not just in the days preceding evaluation meetings. When you notice performance issues—either good or bad—record your observations in writing.

Most of your record keeping can be informal and brief. And the work you do throughout the year will pay off later: When you evaluate an employee formally at year's end, you'll have a detailed record of their performance for the entire review period. Instead of racking your brain or spending time reconstructing events, you can simply review your notes.

Documenting employee performance as it happens also increases the fairness of your year-end summation. Having a year's worth of documentation ensures that your evaluation will be based on an employee's entire performance, not just the most recent events or the ones that happen to stick out in your memory. And if you ever have to justify to a judge or jury any negative actions taken against an employee, you'll be more successful if you can point to a complete paper trail.

Finally, your commitment to a regular documentation program can save you from unfair charges of retaliation. Suppose you begin documenting an employee's performance problems only after that employee complains about discrimination or unsafe working conditions. Even if the employee's dismal performance would justify whatever negative action you might take, it will look like you are illegally retaliating against the employee for making the complaint. By contrast, if you have proof that you noticed and documented performance problems well before the employee filed the complaint, you're in a better position to refute a retaliation claim.

In this section, we describe how you can document employee performance completely throughout the year by using three simple tools:

- **Performance logs.** These are records you keep of what employees have done (or have failed to do) throughout the year.
- **Notes of excellence.** Recognition that you give employees to recognize exceptionally good performance.
- **Notes for improvement.** Documentation that you give employees to alert them that they need to improve.

CAUTION
Don't document after the fact. Employers that fail to document performance problems as they happen might be tempted to "catch up" later, after being sued by a disciplined or terminated employee. It's perfectly okay to write down impressions of how an employee performed, even when some time has passed since the incidents you're describing. But it's dishonest to attempt to pass off these writings as having been made earlier. If a judge learns of your attempts, your "documentation" will be disregarded and your credibility as a witness will plummet.

Maintaining a Performance Log

The best way to document an employee's performance is to keep an ongoing list of incidents involving them. We suggest that you keep a log—in a paper file, a computer file, or a notebook—on each employee whom you supervise. When the employee does something noteworthy— either good or bad—take a moment to log it.

Noteworthy actions are those that concern the way an employee performs the job or behaves in your company. Although the vast majority of entries will relate to the goals and requirements that you and the employee have set, there could be times when the employee does something that's outside the context of those performance objectives. Those incidents can go into the log as well. Include comments, compliments, or complaints that you receive about an employee, but ignore rumors and gossip.

Of course, you won't need to make entries for every day that the employee shows up for work. Only include those incidents that are out of the ordinary or contrary to company rules or procedures. For example, you might note when a worker shows up late, makes an extra effort to meet a deadline, or performs exceptionally well on a project.

Once you begin keeping track of negative incidents, you must be consistent. If there is no entry for a date that the employee worked, and your log is later used as evidence in a lawsuit with the employee, a judge or jury will assume that the employee performed at an acceptable level for that day. If you were to testify to details about an employee's performance that you didn't include in the log, you'd have a tough time explaining why your current rendition of events should be believed over the empty spot in your log.

Your log will also serve as your memory when you sit down to evaluate the employee formally. Because it's a tool for you to use, the log isn't part of the personnel file. You don't need to worry about the quality of your writing or the beauty of the presentation.

Despite the informal nature of the log, however, there might come a time when other people will see it. If the employee sues your company, the log will be an important piece of evidence, which the employee's lawyer will inspect. For this reason, don't put anything in the log that you wouldn't want aired in a courtroom. Here are some guidelines to follow when writing log entries:

- Include concrete details like dates, times, places, names, numbers, and so on.
- Be accurate and don't exaggerate.
- Don't use slurs or other inappropriate or derogatory terms.
- Don't use language that could be construed as discriminatory or illegally biased.

- Avoid personal attacks. Instead, concentrate on behavior, performance, conduct, and productivity.
- Make each entry complete, so that anyone reading it could understand what happened.
- Stick to job-related incidents. Don't include entries about the employee's personal life or aspects of the employee that have nothing to do with the job.

If you decide to give an employee some sort of progressive discipline, note that in your log as well. Don't bother including every detail in the log, however; you'll document the discipline separately.

FORM ON NOLO.COM
You can find a performance log template, a disciplinary notice form, and other forms on this book's online companion page. Appendix A explains how to access these materials.

Documenting Ongoing Feedback

In addition to keeping a running log, periodically give employees real-time feedback concerning performance. When an employee does something of note—either good or bad—don't wait until an appraisal meeting or written performance evaluation to let the employee know about it. An effective performance evaluation system requires ongoing feedback.

Let Employees Know When They Do Well

Whenever you can praise an employee for going above and beyond, you should do so. Positive feedback not only raises employee morale, but also gives employees an incentive to do better and improves your overall relationship with your workforce. People are more likely to accept and act on criticism when it's given in the context of a fair and positive employment relationship.

We suggest commending employees in writing when they do something especially well. These kudos don't have to be elaborate. They are simply small notes or emails that you give to employees (with a copy to their personnel file) to let them know that you notice and appreciate their efforts. You don't have to spend a lot of time writing them, but you should observe the same rules as for writing performance log entries. Reserve more formal, written praise for noteworthy times.

(Remember: Never make promises in these notes, such as "You have a bright future at this company" or "You're going to go far here." If you do, a court might find that you've altered the employee's at-will status. Simply thank the employee for doing well and leave it at that.)

Tracking Performance for Remote Workers

According to the latest statistics from the Bureau of Labor Statistics, more than 21% of private-sector employers have employees who work remotely some or all of the time. And surveys show that this flexibility is highly prized by employees. For example, 52% of the employees surveyed by BambooHR in 2024 stated that they prefer to work remotely.

This represents a sea change in the way we work—and in the way managers track employee performance. When employees work together physically, managers can see many attendance, performance, and conduct issues as they arise in real time. It's easy to observe the empty desk of an employee who is frequently tardy, leaves early, or takes long breaks. You can see an employee looking at Instagram, playing solitaire, or making personal calls during work hours. And, you can witness interpersonal problems, violations of work-place rules, and so on, if employees sit right outside your door.

For many employers, it's much harder to monitor and make these direct observations when employees work remotely. Some employers are turning to monitoring technology to keep tabs on remote workers. For most employers, however, this level of surveillance isn't necessary. Rather than worrying about what employees are doing when you can't see them, it makes sense to instead focus on how they're performing. For example, are employees logging into virtual meetings on time, ready to participate, and dressed appropriately? Are employees maintaining customer and client contacts and relationships? Are employees getting the work done that you pay them to do?

As long as your answers to these questions are "yes," you probably don't need to closely supervise and control employees at a distance. Indeed, one of the benefits of remote work is that employees have freedom to balance their work life with other activities and responsibilities—and often, can be more productive as a result. If a problem crops up (for example, an employee isn't meeting deadlines or a coworker complains about inappropriate behavior in a virtual meeting), of course you will need to look into it. But many employers are finding that their employees are working productively at a distance, without the need for constant monitoring. (However, you will need to closely track wage and hour issues for remote employees, such as hours worked, overtime, breaks, and so on.)

Sample Performance Log

Performance Log

CONFIDENTIAL

Employee Name: Paul Nolo

Employee Title: Copy editor

Date	Incident	Memo or Discipline (see personnel file)
1/2/20xx	Paul arrived 15 minutes late for work—did not call me to tell me that he would be late. His only excuse was that he overslept.	N/A
2/3/20xx	Paul worked hard to ensure that he met the deadline for the Single Mothers series.	Emailed Paul to thank him; copy in personnel file.
3/1/20xx	Paul was 45 minutes late for his shift.	Coaching session. See memo in personnel file.
6/4/20xx	Eleanor Lathom (reporter who worked with Paul on the Single Mothers series) told me that she thought Paul was really easy to work with and helped her improve her writing.	Emailed Paul to let him know; copy in personnel file.

Coach Employees Who Veer Off Track

If an employee's performance begins to slip, there's no reason to wait until the formal review to convey your concerns. You can use coaching, covered in Chapter 4, to intervene when a minor performance problem arises. Coaching is often the first step in a progressive discipline approach, and it is different from more serious disciplinary measures, like verbal or written warnings. A coaching session gives you a chance to course-correct at the first opportunity rather than waiting until an employee's performance creates true problems for the company.

A coaching session is typically a short, informal conversation, which you can use to:

- **Provide tips on how to resolve or avoid a problem.** For example, if an employee missed a minor deadline on the way to a major project due date, you might sit down to review the calendar and plan out how and when the remaining work will get completed on time.
- **Correct a minor problem.** For example, if you asked for a PowerPoint presentation and the employee used a different program that lacks the necessary features, you can simply say, "You can't use that program. I asked you to use PowerPoint because your work will be integrated into a larger presentation, which will be made in PowerPoint."

Document your coaching session in a short memo or email, outlining your conversation and the steps you and the employee have agreed to take going forward. (You can find a sample coaching memo in Chapter 4.)

Step 3: Conduct Interim Meetings to Discuss Progress and Problems

After watching your employee work toward requirements and goals for the first several months of an appraisal period, it's helpful to discuss the employee's progress and make any necessary adjustments. We recommend doing this in a meeting six months after the employee's last formal evaluation, which takes place at the end of the employee's work year. For a new employee, you would schedule this meeting six months after the employee started work. You can hold more than one interim meeting during the employee's work year if you like.

Preparing for the Interim Meeting

Prepare for the meeting by reviewing your documentation (performance log, memos or emails, and disciplinary documents, if any) and organizing your thoughts. Be ready to give specific advice and feedback, not merely vague impressions.

The employee should prepare for the interim meeting, too. Give a few days' notice of the date and explain what you want to discuss (covered below). Ask the employee to think about the past six months on the job: what's been good and what could be changed or improved.

Holding the Meeting

Begin your meeting by giving your overall impressions of the employee's performance over the past six months. Note what the employee has done well and what needs improvement. Without mentioning names, share any compliments or complaints you've received from coworkers, customers, and others.

Next, review the requirements and goals that the employee and you chose for the year. If they still seem realistic to you, discuss whether the employee is on track for meeting them. If not, discuss why not and whether you should modify them.

Be sure to give the employee an opportunity to talk, too. What does the employee think they've accomplished over the past six months? Does the employee need any help or additional resources to perform better? Does the employee need assistance or advice from you? Has the employee encountered any obstacles that make it difficult to perform the job?

Whenever possible, be positive and encouraging to motivate the employee. When there have been problems, however, be honest and clear. And, if the employee has done anything that might lead to disciplinary action, discuss it now.

Your demeanor and attitude will make the difference between a meeting that is productive and one that is not. Always treat the employee with understanding and respect. Resist any temptation to become angry or emotional, and never engage in personal attacks.

After the Meeting

While details of the conversation are still fresh in your mind, write a memo to the employee's personnel file that summarizes what each of you said. Include your views on the employee's performance at this interim point and describe what plans, if any, the two of you agreed to. You don't need to give a copy of this memo to the employee.

Step 4: Conduct the Year-End Evaluation

The performance appraisal process culminates at the end of the appraisal period, usually after one year. At this time, you complete a formal written performance evaluation, the employee writes a self-evaluation, and you and the employee meet to discuss them. During this meeting, you also look ahead to the next year by reviewing job requirements and establishing new goals. All of these events together make up the year-end performance evaluation.

As you now know, a performance appraisal involves much more than this year-end evaluation: It requires ongoing documentation and feedback, which will help make the year-end appraisal process go quickly and smoothly. Nonetheless, the year-end evaluation is the culmination of the entire appraisal process. The employee will pay the most attention to the formal, annual evaluation. So will the judge or jury, if an employee files a lawsuit.

Writing the Evaluation

Writing an effective year-end performance evaluation involves much more than simply completing blanks on a form; it involves gathering information, drawing conclusions, and summarizing your conclusions and supporting evidence in a written document. You must make the evaluation clear and useful to the employee and anyone else who might read it, including your human resources department and your company's lawyers, should it be necessary.

Gathering Information

Although you might think you know in your gut how an employee has performed throughout the year, you can't draw firm conclusions until you've gathered and reviewed documents, reports, and other concrete evidence that reflects the employee's performance.

An easy way to begin is by gathering objective data your company keeps that demonstrates the employee's performance and productivity. Objective data means facts that aren't influenced by opinions. For example, a report showing that a call center answers an average of 100 calls per day is objective. If you wrote a report stating that

the center did a "good job" of answering calls, however, that would be subjective, because it expresses your opinion about the facts. Objective data often comes in the form of numbers, and you can find it in all kinds of reports and documents that companies generate regularly, from budgets to shareholder disclosures. The following are examples of objective data:

- sales numbers
- earnings reports
- call records
- productivity reports
- deadline reports
- output and production records
- budget reports, and
- attendance records.

As useful as objective data is, however, it won't give you the complete picture of the employee's performance for the year. For one thing, there could be factors to consider behind, or in addition to, the objective data. Let's say one job requirement for newspaper editors is to edit at least 7 articles per night, and you have an editor who edits an average of 12 articles per night during the appraisal period. That objective fact indicates that the editor is highly productive. The editor might be able to edit so quickly, however, by being careless and allowing numerous errors to slip through. A manager who didn't look behind the objective deadline report would miss the editor's carelessness and inaccuracy. This subjective, qualitative information might be necessary to give you the whole picture.

Qualitative data is also important because you might not be able to measure every aspect of an employee's performance objectively or firsthand. For example, if you manage a salesperson, you might want to know if customers trust them. Although sales numbers might provide indirect evidence, more compelling would be interviews with customers and a review of any complaints or compliments.

To gather information not reflected in the objective data, look for records of significant incidents that demonstrate the employee's performance, both positive and negative. In your performance log, memos, and emails, you will already have a record of incidents that you can use. Customer and vendor complaints and compliments can also be used, along with any documents of disciplinary action against the employee.

Also, talk to people who work with the employee: clients or customers, coworkers, other managers or supervisors, human resources personnel, vendors, and so on. Solicit specific feedback asking about any particular events or projects that reflect upon the employee's performance.

Review records of your own observations, such as your performance log. If you save emails or voicemails, check to see if you have any that relate to a noteworthy event or an example of the employee's performance.

If feasible, look at a sampling of the employee's work product.

Finally, look at a copy of the employee's performance appraisal from the previous year and the employee's job description.

Drawing Conclusions

After you've gathered the evidence described above, review it as a whole. You must determine whether the employee met the requirements and goals that you set for the year and why the employee succeeded or fell short. The "why" is perhaps the most important part of the process, because it will tell you whether the responsibility for any shortcomings—or successes—should fall on the employee. And, if the employee failed to meet a requirement or goal, it will help you develop strategies for improvement.

If you're feeling overwhelmed, start by looking at the employee's requirements and goals for the appraisal period. For each, look at all the items you have that relate to it. You might even try making lists—or literally separating the papers into stacks on a table or the floor—to help you organize what you've got. Then, for each requirement and goal, ask yourself the following questions:

- Has the employee met this requirement or goal?
- Why or why not?
- How do I know this?
- What is the supporting evidence?
- What was the impact on the department? On the company?
- How can the employee do better?

- How can I do a better job of supporting the employee?
- How can the company do a better job of supporting the employee?

When faced with a performance or productivity problem, look beyond the employee's willingness (or lack thereof) to perform or make an effort. Consider other factors that might have played a role, such as the work environment. Simply telling the employee to work harder or do better will accomplish little if, for example, the employee's supervisor is the true cause of the problem. Similarly, if the employee doesn't have the necessary skills to do the job or is having health or family problems outside of the office, you'll have to take these factors into account when shaping a solution.

If an employee is new to the job, consider the following issues before reaching a conclusion about performance:

- Did you give the employee adequate training?
- Does the employee have the skills necessary for the job?
- Does the employee understand what you expect?
- Have you provided the employee with adequate tools and resources for doing the job?
- Does your company have rules or systems that make it difficult for the employee to do the job?

If the employee has been in the job for a while, think about the following possible causes for the drop in performance:

- Has something changed in the employee's work situation that might explain the trouble? For example, does the employee have a new supervisor, new coworkers, or new customers who are difficult to work with? Or is the employee struggling with new duties or responsibilities?
- Has the employee told you of personal issues that could be affecting performance, such as a new child, a family health problem, or a divorce?
- Has the employee developed a substance abuse problem or a mental health problem, such as depression or anxiety? If so, consult with your human resources department or with your company's attorney. Not only is this a time for tact and understanding, but it's a situation that might fall within the scope of the federal Americans with Disabilities Act and similar state laws.

Summarizing Your Conclusions and Evidence in a Document

After collecting your observations and drawing conclusions about the employee's performance, it's time to write them down, along with the supporting evidence.

The sample performance evaluation form contains a series of sections, one for each requirement or goal. Address the employee's job requirements first, in order of importance, and then turn to the goals in order of priority. (You should have prioritized both when setting them with the employee, as explained above.) For each requirement or goal, the form provides a numbered area for you to do the following:

1. State the requirement or goal.
2. Rate the employee's performance in achieving the requirement or goal.
3. Explain the reasons for your conclusion and provide supporting evidence.
4. Record the employee's comments.

After rating the employee's performance and providing a narrative evaluation for each requirement and goal (Parts I and II of the form), it's time to summarize the employee's performance. Part III provides a space for you to include your impressions of the employee's overall performance during the review period, including strengths, areas for improvement, disciplinary history, and any other relevant facts. To complete the section, you'll need to weigh the relative importance of the requirements and goals: An employee who misses the mark on a relatively minor developmental goal but exceeds expectations in other ways has performed significantly better than an employee who has failed to meet a basic job requirement. An employee might have an attendance problem, but perform excellently when at work. An employee might

---

Common Appraisal Errors

As you review the information and draw conclusions about an employee's performance, be mindful of common pitfalls that can lead to the wrong conclusions and undermine the value of your appraisal. Common problems include:

- **Playing the blame game.** Don't blame employees just because things are going poorly or, conversely, take credit yourself when things are going well. When looking at the "why" behind someone's performance, you might have to acknowledge that you were the source of the problem or, if something good happened, that you weren't behind it. Give credit where credit

is due, and take responsibility when the fault lies with you. Most employees will recognize your honesty and respond accordingly.

- **Focusing on first impressions.** Don't allow your first impressions of an employee to color your opinions. It's unfair and unprofessional and will create problems in your workforce. Good employees who can't seem to do anything right because your first impression of them was bad will quickly learn that there's no use in trying. And bad employees to whom nothing negative sticks because you liked them right away will have no incentive to do well.

Common Appraisal Errors (continued)

- **Liking people like you.** Don't judge employees who are similar to you more favorably and judge employees who are different from you less favorably. This is particularly troubling when you do so—even unconsciously—based on legally protected characteristics, such as race, gender, nationality, disability, or religion. But beyond these traits, be mindful not to judge workers differently based on such things as your shared personality traits, values, skill sets, political opinions, hobbies, outlook, and the like.

- **Being misled by the "halo/horns effect."** Don't allow one aspect of an employee's performance—whether good or bad—to blind you to everything else the employee does. Almost every employee has positive and negative work attributes. It's up to you as the manager to consider all aspects of an employee's performance.

- **Calling everyone "average."** Don't try to play it safe by judging all employees as average. You might think that no one will complain if everyone gets essentially the same review, but it's actually a problem. If an employee performs exceptionally well but gets the same review as one who performs poorly, you've created a disincentive for the good employee to continue performing so well. And you've created an equally powerful disincentive for the bad employee to improve. If your evaluations should become evidence in a lawsuit, having judged everyone the same means your reviews aren't accurate—a big problem for your company in the courtroom.

- **Placing more weight on recent events.** Don't overemphasize an employee's recent performance. It might be fresh in your mind and therefore seem more important than things that happened in the past, but it's unfair and contrary to the goal of the review for you not to assess performance over the entire appraisal period.

- **Stereotyping employees.** Stereotypes based on characteristics protected by law (such as race, gender, nationality, religion, and so on) are illegal. But basing decisions on even legal stereotypes can damage the fairness and accuracy of your evaluation. Don't make assumptions; base your conclusions on objective and qualitative information.

- **Avoiding confrontation.** Sometimes managers will soften their reviews because they're afraid of making employees mad or hurting their feelings. Although you should always use tact and respect, downplaying poor performance only leads to trouble. Not only do you rob your department and your company of the benefits of the performance appraisal process, but you risk sabotaging your ability to terminate an employee should the need arise. Manage with courage and write an honest, straightforward review.

have been struggling in the beginning of the review period, but dramatically turned things around after a verbal warning and coaching session. These "big picture" observations belong in the summary section.

Follow the same guidelines as you did when writing the narrative portions of the evaluation. When you're done, read through the form to ensure that, as a whole, it reflects what you think about the employee's performance. Are all of the statements you made true? Is the appraisal consistent with the feedback you gave the employee throughout the year? If not, then the review might come as a surprise to the employee, which means that you need to improve your ongoing feedback skills throughout the year and that you have a tough year-end appraisal meeting ahead of you.

The example below shows how to complete Part I of the performance evaluation form. You can download a blank copy of the performance evaluation form from this book's online companion page; see Appendix A for details.

Planning the Appraisal Meeting

After writing the initial portions of the evaluation, it's time to prepare to meet with the employee.

Choosing a Time and Place

Given the importance of the year-end performance appraisal meeting, be sure to set aside sufficient time. Schedule at least an hour. It's insulting to an employee to give a

performance appraisal while you're distracted or in a rush. Talk to the employee so that you can pick a day that will work for both of you and be relatively stress free. Choose a time when phone calls and interruptions will be minimal.

Then pick an appropriate place to meet. If you can, avoid your office: It's your space and the base of your power; the employee will feel more comfortable in a neutral environment.

Find a private place where other people can't see or hear you. A conference room is usually ideal, unless it has a lot of glass that allows people to look in. If you can, find a place with a big table so that you can spread out your records and documents and sit next to (rather than across from) the employee; this is a subtle but important affirmation that the evaluation is meant to be a discussion, not a lecture.

Preparing the Employee for the Self-Evaluation

After scheduling the meeting, give the employee an idea of what to expect. Explain that you'll be talking to the employee about the past year's performance and that you'll be using a written evaluation as a framework for that discussion.

Virtually all effective performance evaluation systems—including the one here—ask employees to evaluate themselves as part of the process. Research has shown that this puts them in a better frame of mind for evaluation meetings and makes

Sample Performance Evaluation

Performance Evaluation

Employee Information	
Employee Name: Paul Nolo	Date of Review: 1/11/20xx
Employee Job Title: Copy Editor	Review Period: 1/11/20xx – 1/11/20xx
Manager Information	
Manager's Name: Amy Means	
Manager's Job Title: Copy Desk Chief	
Part I – Job Requirements	
Please rate the employee on each job requirement according to the following scale:	

5	Outstanding	Employee consistently exhibits a high degree of skill and execution and far exceeds the requirements of the job at all times.
4	Exceeds Expectations	Employee exhibits competent skill and execution on a consistent basis and exceeds job requirements in many areas.
3	Meets Expectations	Employee consistently performs job in a competent and effective manner.
2	Improvement Needed	Employee performs job in a competent manner in some areas, but falls below job expectations in other areas.
1	Unsatisfactory	Employee consistently falls below job expectations in multiple areas.

Job Requirement #1	meet all deadlines in a timely fashion.
Rating	1 2 3 ④ 5
Manager's Comments	Paul did very well meeting his deadlines during the appraisal period. As the attached deadline report shows, Paul missed an average of only .048 deadlines per month. Paul did not meet this requirement last year, so we spent a significant amount of time at last year's appraisal meeting figuring out what Paul could do to improve. Throughout this year, I personally observed Paul making a concerted effort to meet this requirement. He received no reminders this year to talk less at work (he received five last year), and he took fewer personal calls. As the attached time report shows, he reduced his average editing time per column inch from two minutes last year to one-and-a-half minutes this year.
Employee's Comments	

them more satisfied with the process. Employees who evaluate themselves tend to be less defensive and to view both the appraiser (you) and the appraisal process as fair.

In doing the self-evaluation, the employee should review much of the same materials that you did: the job description, performance plans, requirements and goals, emails and memos, reports, last year's evaluation, and so on.

Employees can either write a self-evaluation or simply come to the meeting prepared to discuss their own views on their performance. In any event, the employee should prepare to answer the following questions:

- Was each of the previously agreed-to requirements and goals met? Why or why not?
- What things has the employee done over the review period that they are most proud of?
- In what ways was the employee disappointed in their performance?
- Looking to next year, in what ways would the employee like to improve or change?
- Is there anything more that the company, the department, or the supervisor/manager can do to help support the employee's work or improvement in performance?

- Is the employee unclear about any requirements, goals, or expectations in the current job?

Finally, tell the employee that, at the end of the meeting, the two of you will reassess the job requirements and set new performance goals for the coming year, so the employee should come prepared for that discussion as well.

After the meeting, you'll finalize the evaluation. If the employee wrote a self-evaluation, attach it to your evaluation. If the employee didn't write one, then you should incorporate information that the employee gave you at the meeting into your form in the Employee Comments section.

Conducting the Appraisal Meeting

For most employees, the performance appraisal meeting is the most significant and important interaction the employee will have with you all year. Not only will you assess their performance for the entire appraisal period, but you will also give advice, offer coaching on ways to improve, and set new goals for the upcoming year.

This is also an important meeting for you. Hopefully, you will get feedback from the employee to help you support them, improve your own performance, and improve the performance of your department or company. What does the employee think of the job? The workplace? Your company as a whole? Has the employee encountered any obstacles that make it difficult to do the job well? Does the employee see areas in which you could help improve performance and productivity? Are there resources the employee needs that you aren't providing?

Meeting Atmosphere

When you meet with the employee, the feeling in the room should be businesslike, yet friendly. Because this is a collaborative process, you want the employee to feel relaxed, comfortable, and safe. This is an important meeting, though, so you don't want to be so informal that you indicate a lack of respect for the process. The meeting tone should feel like "business casual": not as relaxed as blue jeans, but not as formal as a suit.

To set this sort of tone, be friendly when greeting the employee. Smile and express thanks for coming. Spend the first few minutes on appropriate small talk: Ask about the employee's day or a recent vacation. If you two always talk about a local sports team or each other's children, then engage in a little of that now.

Also, set the room up so that you sit beside each other at a table or in comfortable chairs, rather than across from each other.

When opening the discussion of the employee's performance, be conversational. Be warm, upbeat, and supportive: Focus on "we"—you and the employee—for example,

"I'm excited that we have this opportunity to sit down and talk about your work and goals."

All employees benefit from consistent feedback on their performance, but it can be especially valuable—and necessary—for employees working from home. Because they might not be interacting regularly with supervisors or coworkers, remote employees might not have a strong sense of how they're performing. And, it can be more challenging for you to remember to give this feedback to employees you don't run into at the elevator or see every day outside your office. Make a point of checking in regularly with remote employees to let them know how things are going.

TIP

Meet in person—or at least virtually—with remote employees. If possible, you should physically meet with the employee for the appraisal. This communicates the importance of the meeting and allows you to have spontaneous personal interactions and nonverbal communication that just aren't captured as well at a distance. If distance or safety concerns make this impossible, meet by video conference for the meeting, so you can share screens in real time and see each other face to face. Don't resort to phone or email to evaluate employees. It's too impersonal and inefficient.

Meeting Agenda

Taking time to explain the order of events at the beginning of the meeting will make the whole process go more smoothly. Feel free to conduct the meeting in a way that feels natural and appropriate for your employee and you. Below is a suggested sequence of events and topics.

1. **Start with introductory remarks.** Thank the employee for coming. Explain why performance appraisal is important. Make it clear that you take this seriously and expect the employee to do so as well.

2. **Exchange documents.** if you didn't give each other copies of your evaluations before the meeting, do so now.

3. **Go through each requirement and goal.** The employee should give the self-evaluation first, and then you should give your opinion. If you have judged the employee much more negatively than the employee's self-evaluation, ask the employee for thoughts. Consider them, and then give insight into your own thought process.

   Keep an open mind: Could some of what the employee is saying be true? If, in the end, you stand by your initial conclusions, reassure the employee that you have considered everything they've said, but that you still feel the same way. Explain why.

   Be sure to give the employee enough time to talk. If you don't listen to employees, you undermine the appraisal process, and you don't want to miss this opportunity to learn about your company from someone who works on the front lines.

4. **Reassess the requirements that apply to the employee's job.**

5. **Choose goals for the coming year.**

6. **End the meeting on a positive note.** Thank the employee for the time and effort it took to prepare for and participate in the meeting, and leave the employee with words of encouragement for the coming year.

7. **Ask the employee to sign the evaluation form.** Employees who are unhappy with their evaluations might be reluctant to do so, believing that a signature indicates their agreement with the evaluation. As our performance appraisal form makes clear, however, such signatures acknowledge only that the employee participated in the evaluation process and received a copy of the form. You should sign and date the form as well.

Your Tone and Conduct

The words you use and how you conduct yourself in the meeting are just as, if not more, important than what you say. If your manner is off-putting or naturally leads to a defensive response, then the employee won't hear what you have to say.

Pay attention to what some experts call "relationship management": Be sensitive to the feelings your words will create. You know the employee will have an emotional response to what you say, and you can usually predict what that response will be. Take this into consideration when conducting an evaluation meeting. Too often, employers ignore their employees' emotions. But ignoring them doesn't make them go away; it often makes the situation worse.

Also:

- **Think about the process from the employee's perspective.** Evaluating employees might be a routine matter for you, something you have to do regularly throughout the year, depending on how many employees you manage. For employees, however, it's a once-a-year opportunity to get your full focus and attention on their job and career path. Don't make jokes and don't treat it lightly. Even if the meeting feels like an annoying chore to you, don't let it show.
- **Show respect for the meeting, the process, and, above all, the employee.** This means really listening to what they have to say rather than simply waiting for them to finish talking so that you can launch into your evaluation. It also means showing that you are listening by taking notes, asking about key points, making comments, making eye contact, and nodding your head. When the employee says something important, say it back in your own words.

If the employee has raised any concerns, address them squarely. Even though you're higher up the company ladder, don't act superior. Consider yourself as an equal who wants to work collaboratively to help the employee, the department, and the company succeed.

- **Don't use the meeting as a forum for attack.** The purpose is to help the employee improve, not to belittle or punish the employee for past mistakes. Be empathetic: Use the meeting to help the employee develop strategies for improving performance in the future.
- **When you have to be critical, remember that criticism alone is not helpful.** You must combine it with a conversation about why the poor performance happened in the first place, the impact it had on the department and the company, and what can be done— by the employee, by you, and by the company—to improve.
- **Be prepared for defensiveness.** Nothing in your review should be a surprise to the employee, but if it is, then you must be prepared for the employee to be defensive. Try not to let the defensiveness get to you; don't react to it. Rather, try to listen through it so that you hear what the employee has to say. Not only will you glean valuable information this way, but you will also defuse the situation by hearing the employee out.

- **Don't forget to say something positive when you can.** Identify what you like about the employee's performance and focus on it. Be specific and concrete. Don't make the employee feel cheated by giving compliments only as a setup for criticism (as in "your coworkers really like you but you spend too much time talking to them"). Give a compliment and end it with a period.

Reassessing Job Requirements and Setting Goals

In the final portion of the year-end evaluation meeting, you and the employee should review the requirements for the employee's position and choose new goals for the employee for the coming year.

Reassessing Job Requirements

Regardless of whether the job requirements change, the year-end meeting is a good time to reassess. Together, you and the employee should review the requirements and talk about whether they still make sense.

Establishing New Goals

Near the end of the appraisal meeting, you'll establish new goals for the upcoming year (Part IV of the form). The process of goal setting is important, possibly as important as the goals themselves. Together, you should brainstorm goals that will help the employee and the company. Work together to decide how those goals will be measured. This gives the employee a sense of worth and a sense of how to contribute to the company's success.

Although you might have come to the meeting prepared with ideas for goals, keep an open mind. The employee will also come prepared, and you could end up choosing the employee's goals over your own. After finalizing these goals, include them on the form and give a copy to the employee.

Progressive Discipline

Motivating employees to improve their performance is every employer's goal, and managing through progressive discipline is a great way to achieve it. Progressive discipline is a system that provides a graduated range of responses to employee performance or conduct problems. Disciplinary measures range from mild to severe, depending on the nature and frequency of the issue. Many companies use some type of progressive discipline program, although they might call it positive discipline, performance management, performance improvement, corrective action, or something else. Whatever it's called, a workplace discipline program is "progressive" if it follows the principle that the company's disciplinary response should be appropriate and proportionate to the employee's conduct.

If your company already has a progressive discipline system, you can use the principles and strategies in this chapter to make that system more effective. If you don't yet use progressive discipline, you can adapt the discipline policy at the end of this chapter to suit your workplace (see Appendix A for instructions on how to download a digital copy). This chapter explains the benefits of progressive discipline, covers the basic disciplinary measures available in a typical progressive discipline system, describes how to administer discipline effectively, and provides guidelines that will help you avoid legal problems when disciplining employees.

The Benefits of Progressive Discipline

Using progressive discipline can help get employees back on track and avoid the consequences of continued poor performance or misconduct, or expensive replacement costs.

The essence of progressive discipline is not to threaten or punish, but to collaborate and be fair. As you administer discipline, you communicate with employees, listen to their views, and invite them to participate in finding a resolution to the problem. When employees are included in creating an improvement strategy, they become invested, increasing the likelihood that they will actually follow through and improve. And, by treating employees fairly and with respect, progressive discipline fosters feelings of employee loyalty and morale.

Done right, progressive discipline can:

- allow managers to intervene and correct employee behavior at the first sign of trouble
- enhance communication between managers and employees
- promote greater employee performance and productivity
- improve employee morale and retention through highlighting the rewards for good performance and consequences for poor performance
- avoid the expenses of having to find replacement employees
- ensure consistency and fairness, and

- lay the groundwork for fair, legally defensible employment termination of employees who can't or won't improve.

Unless you intervene, an employee might not know that certain behavior or actions are considered unacceptable. Your company will suffer the direct consequences: reduced productivity; quality control problems; dollars, opportunities, or customers lost; or worse.

There could also be indirect consequences, such as low employee morale, lack of confidence in your management skills, and high turnover.

The Steps of Progressive Discipline

Effective progressive discipline systems offer the best of both worlds: They give managers the structure they need to treat employees consistently, with the flexibility to take unique situations and problems into account. In most progressive disciplinary systems, managers deal with first-time problems by administering a verbal coaching or warning, then escalate to more serious measures if the problem continues or if the employee develops other problems. For more serious issues, the manager can start the process at a higher disciplinary level, including termination for very significant offenses.

The disciplinary measures typically available in most companies' policies (although they might go by different names) include:

- coaching
- verbal warning
- written warning, and
- termination.

Coaching

In today's workplace, most managers know that creating successful employees isn't always about directing and controlling; it's often about coaching: encouraging and developing. In this context, coaching is a positive engagement with employees to help them maximize their performance and build their skills and competencies.

As such, coaching isn't simply—or even primarily—a disciplinary measure, but instead a management approach that emphasizes communication, collaboration, goal setting, mentoring, and assistance to help employees realize their full potential.

In this chapter, however, we use the term "coaching" in a more limited sense, to refer to the first step of a progressive discipline system. Although you might be coaching employees in the broader sense all the time, you are coaching under our definition only when using your collaborative and communication skills to correct a disciplinary problem. While it requires the same set of skills, coaching in the disciplinary system ensures specified goals are reached, and it gives you options to escalate the discipline if they aren't.

What Is Coaching?

A coaching session is simply an informal, one-on-one meeting with an employee to discuss a performance or conduct problem. The tone of a coaching session should be relaxed and comfortable; your goal is to collaborate with the employee to come up with some workable solutions to a relatively minor problem. In the session, let the employee know what the problem is and how it's affected the company, ask the employee for ideas about how to turn things around, and come up with a strategy for improvement together. When the coaching session is over, you should document your discussion in a brief memo, like our sample below.

When Is Coaching Appropriate?

Coaching can be used at the first sign of relatively minor trouble. The purpose of coaching is to work through and correct an action or behavior before it becomes a larger problem.

Of course, the disciplinary response you choose will depend on your company's policy and practices. Typically, however, coaching is appropriate for first-time problems involving:

- poor performance
- poor attendance or tardiness, or
- very minor misconduct (for example, if the employee unintentionally violated a rule).

If the employee has already been coached for the same problem or the employee's behavior has caused significant harm to the company or violated the law, you should probably skip the coaching and escalate to a more serious disciplinary measure.

Verbal Warning

If a problem continues despite your coaching efforts, a formal verbal warning is often the next step.

FORM ON NOLO.COM

A disciplinary notice form is available online to use for verbal warnings. You can download the template, and other forms mentioned throughout this book, on this book's online companion page. For details on how to access these materials, see Appendix A.

What Is a Verbal Warning?

Typically, a manager delivers a verbal warning in a formal meeting, where the employee is told that the behavior or action is unacceptable. The term "warning" is used to communicate that there is a real problem, one that must be resolved if the employee is to get back on track. Verbal warnings differ from coaching because they're more formal. The employee is notified that this is a disciplinary procedure, and the incident is documented in the employee's personnel file.

When Is a Verbal Warning Appropriate?

A verbal warning is probably appropriate if:
- The employee hasn't responded to your efforts to coach them through a performance problem or a relatively minor conduct problem.
- The employee has violated a company rule, but it doesn't appear to have been deliberate or malicious, and hasn't caused significant harm to the company.
- The employee's behavior or poor performance is causing some problems for the company, but the employee seems to be unaware of the issue and is genuinely interested in improvement.

Written Warning

A written warning is typically reserved for fairly serious problems. It can have serious consequences, affecting an employee's opportunities for advancement and eligibility for merit raises, bonuses, and consideration for special projects. Because of these

---

Sample Coaching Memo

To: File

From: Michael Norris

Date: August 31, 20xx

Re: Dan Warburg

Met with Dan today, August 31, 20xx, to discuss the product release. I told Dan that I'd heard Dylan was working on a database project and that Sasha was updating the department's internal communications protocols, rather than working on the new product. I told Dan I was concerned that his group might not hit the milestones and release schedule.

Dan informed me that he had sent the team an email outlining the due dates, but hadn't followed up and met with each team member to assign interim deadlines and establish priorities. We agreed that Dan would write up a plan by tomorrow afternoon, detailing how his team would complete the remaining work. I'll review that plan, then Dan will meet with each team member and explain the priorities and due dates. If any problems come up, Dan will discuss them with me immediately.

---

potential consequences, the written warning gives the employee an extra incentive to make a change for the better. If the employee can't or won't improve, it also lays the groundwork for a fair and legally defensible termination.

What Is a Written Warning?

A written warning is both a conversation and a document. It used to be standard practice for a written warning to simply appear on a worker's desk or locker, unaccompanied by any discussion. In today's workplace, however, the term "written warning" normally refers both to the actual written document and to the conversation that accompanies it.

Giving a written warning doesn't simply mean handing over a piece of paper; it also means explaining the warning to the employee and talking about what will happen next.

When Is a Written Warning Appropriate?

Because a written warning is a serious disciplinary measure, it isn't the right response to minor problems or many first-time offenses. Here are some situations when you might consider a written warning:

- The employee hasn't improved a performance, attendance, or misconduct problem, even after you've provided coaching and given a verbal warning. In this situation, a written warning is appropriate as the next step in the discipline process.
- The employee has taken an extended unexcused absence, failed to turn up at a mandatory event, or otherwise engaged in a serious or flagrant violation of the company's rules. Typically, a first-time attendance problem would be handled through coaching. If that first absence is prolonged or causes extreme

hardship, however, stronger discipline might be appropriate.
- The employee has committed misconduct that is serious but doesn't warrant termination. Examples typically include horseplay, violations of safety rules, problems dealing with customers or clients, or mistreatment of coworkers.

Termination

Nothing has worked. All attempts to correct an employee's performance or behavior have failed. The employee's unacceptable actions continue, despite numerous warnings. Or, the employee has done something so egregious that immediate termination is appropriate (for example, stealing from the company or threatening violence).

Termination of employment isn't really a disciplinary measure: It represents the failure of the disciplinary process. Despite your best efforts to help the employee improve, you know that there's nothing more you can do. Chapter 7 explains how to decide when it's time to fire an employee, including offenses for which firing is often appropriate.

How Progressive Discipline Works

The steps in your progressive discipline system are the tools at your disposal for dealing with misconduct or poor performance. How you use those tools determines how effective your disciplinary efforts will be. How do you decide what type of discipline is appropriate

Sample Verbal Warning

Employee Disciplinary Notice

Employee's Name: Luis Guerrero	
Manager's Name: Pedro Salazar	**Date of incident:** July 11, 20xx
Type of Warning: ☑Verbal Warning ☐ Written Warning	

Incident Description	On July 11, Ken Schwarz complained to me that the tables at your station often are still dirty and/or have dirty dishes on them when he seats customers. Since receiving that complaint, I have checked the entire restaurant a few times each day and have noticed that only your tables are left unbussed for more than a minute or two. When you do not bus your tables promptly, our customers have to wait longer to be seated or have to sit at tables that have not been cleaned properly. This reflects badly on all of us. I met with you earlier today to discuss this problem. You told me that you were working as quickly as you can and that you believe you have improved since our last discussion.
Prior Incidents	We met on June 12, 20xx, to discuss this issue. At that time, I told you that I had received complaints from customers that your tables were not properly cleaned, and that I had noticed that you were not bussing your tables as quickly as the other staff. We agreed that you would clear and wipe down each table within a few minutes after customers leave. We also agreed that you were spending too much time hanging out with the dishwashers in the kitchen and that your speed would improve if you waited at your station in the dining room with the other bussers. During the last week, I have observed that you are still spending time in the kitchen, rather than with the other bussers in the dining room. I also noticed that you do not bus tables immediately after customers leave. During the dinner rush last Friday, for example, one of your tables was not bussed for eight minutes after the customers left.

Sample Verbal Warning (continued)

Improvement Plan	We have agreed that I will spend 15-20 minutes with you each day for the next two weeks, observing your work and giving you feedback on how to improve. At the end of that time, I expect you to bus each table in your section within two minutes after the customer leaves.
	To do your job properly, you must be at your station. Therefore, we have also agreed that you will remain at your station in the dining room at all times, unless you are on break.
Employee's Comments	

Manager's Signature: Pedro Salazar   Date: July 18, 20xx

Employee Acknowledgment

I acknowledge that I have received and understand this document.

Employee's Signature: Luis Guerrero   Date: July 18, 20xx

Write Your Warning After the Meeting

At some companies, managers are told to draft their written warning before they meet with the employee, then hand it over during the meeting. There are several problems with this approach, however:

- You can't be sure that the facts warrant a written warning until you meet with the employee. If you were wrong in your assessment of the situation, you'll have to get your piece of paper back from the employee and start all over again.
- You won't be able to include the employee's response in your documentation. Sometimes, the employee says something during your meeting that should be memorialized, such as admitting to wrongdoing or providing an explanation for poor performance.
- Once you hand over the written warning, the employee will start reading and stop listening to you. The employee might also be upset that you decided how to handle the situation without even asking for input and possibly another side to the story.

For all of these reasons, we recommend writing your written warning after you meet with the employee, as you would with any other disciplinary documentation.

in any given situation? And how do you deliver that disciplinary message in a way that produces actual improvement?

When confronting a situation that might call for discipline, follow these steps:

1. **Gather information.** Before you act, make sure you know what happened.
2. **Assess the severity.** Consider how the problem is affecting the employee, the team, and the company.
3. **Decide how to respond.** Choose the appropriate disciplinary measure, based on the severity and frequency of the problem and how your company has addressed similar issues in the past.
4. **Prepare to talk to the employee.** Plan your disciplinary meeting, including what you will say and how you will say it.
5. **Meet with the employee.** Talk about what has happened and collaborate to create an improvement plan.
6. **Document.** Make a written record of the discipline imposed and the improvement plan.
7. **Follow up.** Check back in to make sure the employee is improving as agreed.

Gather Information

Before you take action, you have to understand what's really going on. Some situations are relatively clear-cut; perhaps an employee has shown up late to work, missed a deadline, or failed to follow required safety

Sample Written Warning

Employee Disciplinary Notice

Employee's Name: Dave Costello	
Manager's Name: Claude Washington	Date of incident: February 11, 20xx
Type of Warning: ☐ Verbal Warning ☑ Written Warning	

Incident Description	On February 11, 20xx, I overheard part of a conversation you had with Crystal Cavalier in her cubicle. I heard you questioning her about her boyfriend, then saying something like "Are you sure you don't want to go out with me instead?" I also observed that Crystal did not respond. Instead, she turned away from you and focused on her computer screen. I called Crystal into my office and asked her what happened. She said you were asking her questions about her relationship with her boyfriend, even after she told you she didn't want to discuss it. She confirmed that you said, "Are you sure you don't want to go out with me instead?" even though she previously turned down your request for a date. She told me that she felt very uncomfortable about your interest in her and that she felt you were not getting the message that she does not want to have a romantic relationship with you. When I talked to you later that same day, you confirmed that you had said these things to Crystal.
Prior Incidents	No prior reported incidents of similar behavior.
Improvement Plan	Dave, your conduct violates company policies on appropriate workplace behavior. Specifically, your conduct violates our policy on Professional Behavior (p. 23 of the Employee Handbook) and Harassment (p. 12). Your comments and requests for a date made Crystal very uncomfortable. She has stated that clearly to you, but you have persisted. You are not to talk to Crystal about her personal life or ask her out on dates. In addition, because you seem unclear about what constitutes appropriate workplace behavior, I have scheduled you to attend a sexual harassment training workshop on February 19. Following this training, we will meet again to make sure that you understand the types of comments and behavior that are inappropriate in the workplace.

Sample Written Warning (continued)

Employee's Comments	
Manager's Signature: *Claude Washington*	Date: February 11, 20xx
Employee Acknowledgment	
I acknowledge that I have received and understand this document.	
Employee's Signature: *Dave Costello*	Date: February 12, 20xx

procedures. You might not know all of the reasons for the employee's actions, but you do know that something's amiss and that the employee is responsible. In this scenario, you can move on to assessing the severity of the problem.

Other situations are trickier to untangle, especially if more than one employee is involved. If, for example, your team isn't meeting its performance goals, you might not know exactly who or what caused the problem. Or, if one employee accuses another of misconduct (like harassment or threats of violence), you might need to gather more information before deciding what to do. If you can't figure out who's responsible for a problem, you might need to investigate before considering discipline. See Chapter 5 for tips on conducting an investigation.

Assess the Severity

Finding out how the problem is affecting the team or business is necessary because:

- The disciplinary measure you impose should depend, in large part, on how serious the problem is. If the employee's behavior is having or could have a direct and significant impact on the company's ability to deliver its products or serve its customers, a higher level of discipline could be in order.
- It will be easier to leave your emotions at the door and make objective, fair disciplinary decisions if you focus on the effect of the employee's behavior, not on your own anger or disappointment. It's easy to let negative feelings enter into your decisions, especially

if the employee's actions have undermined your authority or caused you to miss your own performance goals.

- Having a few examples of the impact ready when you meet with the employee—communicates the importance of the issue, and it gives the employee the proper context to understand the problem. It demonstrates that the employee is a crucial member of the team, whose performance plays an important role in the company's success. And it will help both of you brainstorm solutions that address the employee's concerns as well as the needs of the company.

EXAMPLE: You sit your accounts payable clerk down and say, "Your lack of attention to detail is causing us to have to double-check your work and is making our customers doubt the integrity of their invoices. This is costing the company money and time, and we need to figure out a way to fix it." His first response is to ask for more information: What lack of detail? Who has had to go over the work in which accounts? Which customers are upset?

Because you took the time to consider the impact of the clerk's problem, you are armed with a few examples, such as, "The Jones Company found errors in their invoices twice. This means that our sales rep, Tom, had to spend time assuring them that we will correct the invoice and won't charge them for products they didn't order. This embarrasses our company, hurts our reputation, and threatens

our future business. Because Tom's time with them is limited, this means we're using it to correct a problem instead of giving Tom the opportunity to sell more product. Long-term, persistent errors like this make it look as though our company doesn't take its billing or its invoicing seriously, signaling that clients shouldn't take our invoices seriously either."

Once the clerk understands that his performance actually endangered the company's relationship with a customer, wasted a coworker's time, and squandered a chance for the company to make more money, he can see how important it is for him to do the job right. It's also more likely that he will understand why you feel the need to intervene. Now, you can begin to collaboratively find a solution.

Decide How to Respond

The whole point of progressive discipline is to facilitate responses that are proportionate to the situation at hand. In other words, the disciplinary measure you choose should reflect how serious the problem is. If, for example, your employee has been late to the office one time, a written warning is too harsh. A simple coaching session—even a brief chat at the employee's desk—will probably do the trick.

When trying to figure out how serious a particular problem is, consider:

- **The effect of the behavior.** Understanding how an employee's problem affects other employees, customers, and business opportunities is fundamental to deciding how to respond.

- **The frequency of the behavior.** One missed deadline is less worrisome than an ongoing pattern of late assignment submissions. A repeat problem means that the employee doesn't understand your expectations, doesn't know how to meet them, doesn't have the resources to meet them, or simply has entrenched behaviors—like procrastination, in the case of the employee who keeps missing deadlines—that must be improved.

- **Disciplinary history.** If you've already met with the employee about the issue and come up with a reasonable action plan that hasn't been executed, tougher discipline will be necessary.

- **The legality of the behavior.** If the employee has done something illegal, such as threatened another employee, misrepresented the company's financials to shareholders, or used a company computer to download pirated software, a very serious response is in order. In these situations, how the company responds could determine its liability to a third party.

EXAMPLE: Steve asks Claudia out several times, but she turns him down. When Steve asks her to be his date at a company party, Claudia says, "Look, I've tried to be polite about this, but I just don't want to go out with you. Please stop asking me; I'm not going to change my mind." Steve then begins leaving romantic notes on the windshield of Claudia's car in the company parking lot as well as on her desk. Claudia tells him to stop and reports his behavior to John, the human resources manager.

John gives Steve a verbal warning, and tells him to stop bothering Claudia. Steve stops leaving notes for Claudia, but begins going out of his way to see her. He times his arrival and departure from the office to coincide with hers, he hangs out in the hallway outside of her office and stares at her, and he "just happens" to cross her path during her twice-weekly lunchtime walks on a nearby bike path. Claudia again complains to John, who gives Steve another verbal warning.

What's wrong with this picture? Steve is stalking Claudia and receiving nothing more than a slap on the wrist. The company hasn't let Steve know that his actions are inappropriate and won't be tolerated. Claudia will be able to argue that the company should be legally responsible for any harm she suffers as a result of Steve's actions, including her emotional distress.

Prepare to Talk to the Employee

Even if you will just be engaging in simple coaching, prepare your approach. Planning will give you some important breathing space so you won't respond emotionally. It will also help you get all your ducks in a row prior to taking action so you can explain the problem and its effects to the employee.

TIP

Where should you "meet" with remote employees? It's best to meet in person for disciplinary discussions: This allows you and the employee to communicate more effectively, share documents, and feel more like a collaborative team. If you're disciplining a remote employee who comes into the office sometimes, schedule the meeting for an at-work day if possible. However, for fully remote employees, a video conference might be your best or only option (and better than trying to handle the conversation by phone or email). Make sure you set a professional tone for the virtual meeting by setting aside enough time, preparing your documentation and what you plan to say, and making sure you have no distractions.

The keys to good preparation are:

- **Gather the specific facts you need.** Be prepared to offer concrete examples of the issue needing correction and to explain how this behavior falls short of your expectations. Also be prepared to explain clearly what the employee needs to improve and why. You might find it helpful to bring a copy of particular company policies, the employee's job description, performance appraisals, or other documents where these expectations are expressly stated.
- **Solicit feedback from others, if necessary.** Some companies require managers to get permission—from their manager or the human resources department, for example—before imposing a verbal or written warning. However, even if your company doesn't require this, feedback from others can give you ideas on what to say, how to say it, and what solutions might work. You can also find out how similar situations have been handled in the past to make sure you're being consistent. This is a critical factor in making sure that your disciplinary decisions don't appear discriminatory.
- **Think about what you'll say.** No matter what type of discipline you're using, you'll have to sit down and talk with the employee. Script your first few sentences: What are the most important points you want to make? Because the meeting should be a collaborative exchange between you and the employee, you shouldn't write out everything you plan to say; just consider how you'll open the conversation and make a list of key issues to cover.
- **Prepare for possible responses.** Will this employee take responsibility and immediately move to solving the problem? Or will you be met with resistance? If you're uncomfortable about emotional confrontations, plan how you will respond if the employee reacts with anger or tears.

Meet With the Employee

The face-to-face meeting is where your preparation will pay off in an honest, respectful session that paves the way for improvement. A typical meeting will progress through the following steps:

1. **State the issue.** At the outset, tell the employee exactly what you're there to discuss. This sets the stage for an honest conversation and avoids making the employee feel sandbagged. Follow up with a sentence or two explaining the impact on others or the company.

   EXAMPLE: "Kay, I asked you to meet with me today to talk about your weekly reports. Twice in the past six weeks, your reports haven't been completed by Friday morning at 10:30, when they are due. Your report wasn't turned in until Friday at 1:00 p.m. six weeks ago, and last Friday your report wasn't handed in until after 3:00 p.m. Mark uses everyone's weekly reports to put together his figures for the central office. If he doesn't get them in time, his figures are late, which makes our team look bad. Last week, it also meant we didn't get our purchase order in on time, which has caused delays for customers this week."

2. **Review previous discussions, if any.** If you and the employee have already talked about this issue—whether in a disciplinary meeting or a casual conversation—briefly summarize those discussions. This will serve as a reminder that the employee knew about the problem and agreed to improve. It helps justify your continued attention to the problem and focus the employee on what needs to change.

   EXAMPLE: "Six weeks ago, when your report was late for the first time, we met. As you'll recall, I reminded you that one of your job duties as a customer representative is to complete your weekly report on time. You agreed that you would get your report in by 10:30 a.m. on Fridays from then on."

3. **Get the employee's buy-in.** Before you move on, make sure the employee agrees about what happened. You need to be sure you fully understand what's going on before you try to begin solving a problem you might not have. And, if the employee reacts defensively or with anger, you'll want to make sure that you can at least agree on what happened, even if you disagree about why.

   EXAMPLE: Kay responds to the statement above by saying, "It couldn't have been after 3:00 p.m. Anyway, I was too busy training Sarah to get to it."

   Rather than arguing, simply restate the facts and ask the employee to agree to them. "The time stamp on your email to Mark says 3:14 p.m. As you know, weekly reports are due at 10:30 a.m. Before we start talking about why the report was late, I want to make sure you agree that the report was late."

4. **Hear the employee out.** Once you and the employee agree on the facts, the employee will probably want to offer reasons (or excuses) for the problematic behavior. Listen carefully to what the employee says; you might learn things you didn't know, including how your employees get along or understand their work assignments. Show that you're listening by repeating back what you hear.

> **EXAMPLE:** Kay says, "I didn't realize it was that late; I'm sorry. I spent the morning training Sarah on the new customer management software, and she had a lot of questions that I couldn't answer easily. I was on the phone with IT for a long time, and I even missed lunch on Friday. I got to the report as soon as I could." You respond, "So your report was late because you were busy training Sarah and talking to the IT department?"

5. **Start working together on solutions.** During this process, help the employee come up with ways to solve the problem and offer any resources or help you can.

> **EXAMPLE:** You move the conversation to problem solving by saying, "Kay, I understand why your report was late. But those reports need to be in Friday morning by 10:30 a.m. so that Mark can meet his deadline to get our figures to the central office and make sure we have the resources we need. What can you do to make sure you get your reports in on time from now on?"

6. **Decide on a plan.** Sometimes you and the employee will come up with several ideas; other times—particularly when there's misconduct—the only solution is for the employee to stop the problem behavior. Either way, once you determine the best course of action, restate it so you both are clear on what will happen next.

> **EXAMPLE:** Kay says, "Since I've started training new reps, I've found it hard to get to all of my own work. Last week and six weeks ago, my weekly reports were late. Other weeks, I've gotten the weekly reports in on time but I've had to stay late to finish all of my paperwork and return calls. I think I might need some help prioritizing all the work I have to do now." Good thing you had this meeting! Kay has told you about an important problem that needs to be solved. Although her reports were late, it happened because she wasn't clear about work priorities—and perhaps, because you've put too much work on her plate. You respond, "I'm sorry, Kay, I didn't realize that your new training responsibilities were taking up so much time. I don't want you to have to put in extra hours just to get your work done. How many hours per week would you say it takes to train a new rep?" Kay responds, and you have a conversation about shifting some of her work to accommodate her training responsibilities. Once you've reached a decision, you state it clearly, "I'm going

to take you off the phones for four hours a week, two hours on Tuesday morning and two hours on Thursday morning. You can use this time to train new reps. I'm also going to reduce your sales goals proportionately. And you are going to prioritize getting those weekly reports to Mark on time."

7. **Decide what will happen next.** If you're managing a performance problem, state the changes you want to see and by when. Also plan to check in with the employee in the interim, to make sure things are moving forward as planned.

> **EXAMPLE:** "Let's check back with each other in three weeks, to make sure these changes are giving you enough time to get your work done. If the solution we've come up with is working, I'll rewrite your job description and performance goals to reflect that you have taken on these training responsibilities and that your sales goals have been reduced as a result."

Document

It's vitally important to document disciplinary matters. Of course, you'll want written proof that the employee was aware of the problem and was given a fair chance to improve, should the issue ever end up in court. But there are many other reasons to put your disciplinary decisions and actions in writing:

- It helps you make sure that you and the employee agree on what happened, what is expected, how the employee will improve, and by when.
- It creates a record for you or the employee's future managers to use if discipline becomes necessary again.
- It can help you identify patterns on your team. For example, if several of your employees have trouble meeting deadlines, you might want to examine your own scheduling practices. Are you giving people enough time? Does your team know why these deadlines are important? Does the team have enough resources to get the job done? Do you need to create a calendaring system, send out email reminders, or come up with another way to keep everyone on track?

Follow Up

Now that you've completed the difficult meeting and have an action plan for fixing the problem, you might be tempted to sit back and congratulate yourself on a job well done. But remember, the ultimate goal of workplace discipline is to improve the employee's performance. The only way to do this is to adhere strictly to your agreements, stay on top of the employee's performance going forward, check in often on the status of the action plan, and work closely with your employee to ensure a positive outcome. Progressive discipline is a process, not a single meeting or document. To get the most out of the process, you need to stay involved until the problem is truly resolved.

Guidelines for Avoiding Legal Trouble

One big reason why discipline can be stressful is that mishandling a disciplinary situation can lead to a lawsuit. Unfortunately, avoiding discipline altogether can also lead to legal trouble and allow workplace problems to grow unchecked.

The disciplinary process we describe in this chapter will help you stay on the right side of the law. To use progressive discipline effectively, you must: have legitimate, objective reasons for your actions; be fair and consistent in applying disciplinary measures; consider the employee's situation carefully; communicate your expectations clearly; and thoroughly document your discussions and decisions. What's more, employees who are treated fairly and respectfully through progressive discipline are less likely to consider legal action.

This section provides some guidelines that will help you make legally sound disciplinary decisions.

Don't Compromise At-Will Employment

As explained in Chapter 2, most employees work at will unless they have contracts that limit the company's right to fire. But not all contracts are in writing, or even explicitly stated out loud: Some contracts are implied from your words and actions, or even from the language of a poorly drafted discipline policy.

There are two ways discipline can undermine the at-will relationship: through company policies and through the actions of those who impose discipline. If a company's discipline policy appears to require particular disciplinary responses to particular actions, an employee might point to that as proof of an implied contract, guaranteeing the employee every step in the disciplinary process before being fired. Similarly, if the policy reserves termination only for a specified list of offenses, that might give an employee the right not to be fired unless they've committed one of those acts. You can avoid these problems by adopting a policy that doesn't tie your hands. Our sample policy, at the end of this chapter, leaves your disciplinary options open for just this reason.

Even if your company's policy doesn't create any legal problems, managers can create legal trouble by giving employees the impression that they will be disciplined or fired only for certain reasons. Typically, this issue comes up when managers are discussing the consequences of continued poor performance or misconduct, or the rewards of improvement. If managers go beyond setting measurable goals and standards for improvement and tack on a threat or a promise of what will happen in the future, they could endanger the at-will relationship.

> **EXAMPLE:** Constance is a highly skilled writer and editor for a website on technology issues. Tom, who owns the company, would like to promote her to manager of the editorial department, but he is concerned about her communication skills. Although her writing is clear and concise, she is not a model of clarity

in face-to-face conversation. In fact, Tom is having a coaching session with Constance to discuss the problem. After Constance was asked to lead a team of employees in developing a series of weekly columns for the site, two people complained that she didn't provide enough guidance and wasn't clear about the project's timeline and deliverables.

If Tom says, during his coaching session, "Constance, I'd like to promote you to manage the editorial department, but first you're going to have to improve your one-on-one communications skills," he has tied his hands. What if Constance improves somewhat, but not enough? What if Tom finds a perfect outside candidate to manage the department? Even though his statement was well intended, it could backfire. The better approach is simply to discuss the communication problem, without mentioning what might or might not happen in the future.

Be Consistent

Done properly, progressive discipline offers a lot of flexibility: You and the employee work together to come up with ways to solve whatever problem the employee is having. This allows you to craft a plan that accounts for the employee's unique situation and perspective, as well as the needs of the company.

But with this flexibility comes the responsibility to be consistent. You must adhere to the basic disciplinary steps and your company's discipline policy every time, and you must always impose the same disciplinary measures for similar problems.

Achieving Consistent Treatment of Remote Employees

How can you treat remote employees consistently, when everyone's home life and work-from-home setup are different? The key is to set clear expectations, then enforce them with an even hand. For example, if you allow flexibility for female employees to pick up their kids from school or daycare, or to care for a sick child, you must allow the same flexibility to male employees. It's fine to allow employees who work from home some leeway in setting their schedules, but you must apply the same rules to everyone.

It can be even tougher to be consistent in a hybrid workforce, where some employees work from home and others come in to the workplace. After all, you can't really make an "apples to apples" comparison when some employees are sitting outside of your office and others check in with you virtually a few times a week. But again, clarity about performance expectations and conduct rules will go a long way toward promoting fairness.

The biggest legal danger of inconsistency, as explained in Chapter 2, is discrimination claims. Employees who are treated differently quickly start to wonder why. And if employees have any reason to believe that your inconsistent treatment is based on a protected characteristic, such as gender or religion, you could be facing major legal trouble.

As a practical matter, being inconsistent will undo all of the benefits of progressive discipline. Employees won't feel respected or treated fairly, and they won't understand the consequences of poor performance or behavior. Instead, they'll believe that rewards flow from being on your good side, not from doing what the company needs them to do.

Be Objective

To discipline effectively, you must be objective. Stay above the fray, figure out what happened and why, and then decide on the appropriate disciplinary measure based on the facts, not based on your feelings or frustrations, or what you privately think of the employees involved.

Making objective, business-based decisions about discipline has two important legal benefits. First, it helps avoid discrimination claims. Employees won't be able to successfully argue that you had illegitimate motives if you can point to sound, objective reasons for imposing discipline. Second, you'll be able to turn the focus away from your feelings and toward the actual effect of the employee's actions on the company. This will help you choose a proportionate disciplinary response and explain it to the employee.

Don't Retaliate

If you discipline an employee because that employee has recently exercised a legal right, you could be slapped with a retaliation lawsuit. As explained in Chapter 2, it's illegal to act against an employee for: complaining of unsafe working conditions; complaining of, or filing a charge of, discrimination or harassment; blowing the whistle on potentially illegal or unethical conduct; filing a workers' compensation claim; or taking legally protected time off (such as FMLA leave).

Even when you have perfectly legitimate reasons for disciplining an employee, the timing of the discipline can create problems. If you discipline shortly after an employee has exercised a legal right, your discipline could appear to be retaliatory. Of course, nothing prevents you from disciplining an employee for violating workplace rules or poor performance. But you must make sure that you'll be able to prove that your action was entirely independent of the employee's protected activity. Before you discipline or terminate employment in this situation, you should talk to a lawyer to make sure that you're on safe legal ground.

Consider Reasonable Accommodations

If an employee's performance or conduct problems are the result of a disability, you have special obligations. You must consult with the employee to figure out whether a reasonable accommodation would help them do the job successfully. However, you aren't required to lower your standards or avoid disciplining disabled employees who can't meet the company's expectations.

Sometimes the first sign that an employee's disability might require an accommodation—or even that an employee has a disability at all—is a performance or attendance problem. An employee's disability might make it difficult to perform certain job duties or follow certain work rules. If an employee points to a disability as the reason for a performance problem, this is your cue to begin a conversation about reasonable accommodations.

> **EXAMPLE:** Colin works in the call center of a large software company. Colin is absent from his desk four or five times a day, in addition to his regularly scheduled lunch hour. These absences last anywhere from a few minutes to almost half an hour. Sean, Colin's manager, has already coached him on this issue, but the absences continue. When Sean decides to give Colin a verbal warning, Colin reveals that he has diabetes. He needs breaks several times a day to eat and drink, and he also has to test his blood sugar levels and adjust his insulin. If his blood sugar gets too low, he might also have to rest briefly before returning to work.
>
> Because Colin has disclosed that he has a disability, Sean must speak to him about reasonable accommodations. In this situation, the call center operates 12 hours a day, and there are other employees who can answer the phones in Colin's absence. Therefore, Sean and Colin agree that Colin can take half an hour for lunch and put the additional half hour toward breaks during the day. If he needs more time, he can make it up at the end of his shift. They also agree to meet once a week to make sure the plan is working. Although Colin violated a work rule by taking unauthorized breaks, Sean decides not to give him a verbal warning after all.

As long as you've met your obligation to provide a reasonable accommodation (if one is available), it's perfectly acceptable to discipline an employee with a disability for failing to meet performance or conduct standards. In some cases, a performance problem might indicate that an employee with a disability can't perform the job's essential functions. As explained in Chapter 2, only employees who can do these functions, with or without accommodation, are protected by the Americans with Disabilities Act (ADA).

Be Careful When Disciplining for Absences

Attendance is a basic requirement of most jobs: If an employee doesn't show up regularly, the work won't get done. This is why many companies have adopted attendance policies, often providing that employees who exceed a certain number of absences will be subject to discipline.

You must be very careful to avoid disciplining employees for taking leave to which they are legally entitled, however. If, for example, you discipline an employee for taking FMLA leave, you could be sued for violating the employee's right to leave. Federal law also gives employees the right to take time off to serve in the military or, in some circumstances, for a disability covered by the ADA. Some states also give employees the right to time off for sick leave, jury duty, to vote, for a child's school conferences, to attend to needs resulting from domestic violence, to donate bone marrow, or for a workplace injury for which the employee is receiving workers' compensation. (To find out about your state's laws, contact your state labor department.) You may not impose discipline for legally protected absences, nor may you consider such absences in determining whether an employee has taken too much time off.

You must also take special care not to make any exceptions from your attendance policies. Unless an employee's absence is excused or legally protected, you should apply your rules consistently across the board. Employees pay close attention to issues involving time off, and they'll notice any exceptions you make. Not only can this lead to discrimination claims, but it can also demoralize and anger employees who are disciplined for behavior that others get away with.

Deal With Dangerous Situations Right Away

If an employee is endangering coworkers or company property, you must step in immediately. There are, of course, many practical reasons for doing so, from maintaining morale to keeping workers safe. But there's also a very important legal reason to act: Any harm a dangerous worker causes after the company becomes aware of the problem could be legally attributable to the company. (Chapter 7 explains this in more detail.)

Keep It Confidential

It's never a good idea to discuss specific instances of employee discipline with anyone who doesn't have a need to know. First and foremost, it shows disrespect for any employees you've had to discipline, who certainly don't want their failures broadcast throughout the workplace. It could also breach the trust you've established through collaboration. Once you start talking about an employee's performance problems or misconduct, you can be sure that other employees will too, which can lead to gossip, bad feelings, and wasted time.

An employee who believes that you've spread false, damaging information about them might have more than hurt feelings: The employee might also have a valid legal claim for defamation. When you discipline, you're communicating that the employee has done something wrong or failed to meet company expectations in some way. If you're wrong about the employee's performance or conduct, or if you make the discipline public in a way that falsely maligns the employee, you might be vulnerable to a defamation claim. (For more on defamation, see Chapter 8.)

Another danger of talking unnecessarily about discipline is that it compromises employee privacy. Often, personal problems spill into the workplace to create performance problems. So when you meet with an employee to talk about performance or conduct issues, you shouldn't be surprised if you end up hearing more about their private life than about the job.

But this doesn't give you carte blanche to repeat that information to others in the company. This is not only disrespectful and very hurtful to the employee who confided in you, but also could lead to legal claims of invasion of privacy. Even though you (hopefully) didn't pry this information out of the employee, you could face a lawsuit if you reveal it to others who have no legitimate need to know about it.

The best practice is to reveal information an employee tells you in confidence only when you must. For example, if you have a coaching session with an employee whose performance is slipping, and she tells you that she's having trouble concentrating at work because a coworker is sexually harassing her, you can't keep that information confidential. You have a duty to the company and the employee to escalate the complaint appropriately and make sure it's investigated. If, however, the employee tells you that her performance is suffering because her husband is having an affair, that would be something to keep to yourself.

Sample Progressive Discipline Policy

In this section, we provide a sample progressive discipline policy that you can distribute to employees or include in your employee handbook. Of course, you might have to tailor it to meet the needs of your business and employees. Appendix A explains how to download a customizable version.

If you choose to draft your own policy (or you already have a policy you'd like to troubleshoot), keep these tips in mind:

- If you list types of conduct that might result in discipline, state that the list is not exhaustive and that the examples included are merely illustrations. This will give you the latitude you need to respond appropriately to problems as they come up. It will also help you defeat a claim that the policy creates an implied contract.
- Avoid tables that match disciplinary actions with types of misconduct.
- Don't use any terms that could be interpreted as a guarantee of continued employment, such as "permanent employee," "guarantee," "due process," and "grounds" or "cause" for termination.
- Make it clear that you can deviate from the policy if you feel it's appropriate to do so.
- Reserve your right to terminate employment at will.

Sample Discipline Policy

Progressive Discipline Policy

Any employee conduct that violates company rules or that, in the opinion of the company, interferes with or adversely affects our business is sufficient grounds for disciplinary action.

Disciplinary action can range from coaching to immediate discharge. Our general policy is to take disciplinary steps in the following order:

- coaching
- verbal warning(s)
- written warning(s), and
- termination.

However, this is not a guarantee of any particular treatment in a given circumstance. We reserve the right to alter the order described above, skip disciplinary steps, eliminate disciplinary steps, or create new or additional disciplinary steps.

In choosing the appropriate disciplinary measure, we may consider any number of factors, including:

- the seriousness of the conduct
- any history of misconduct or performance problems
- your employment record
- the length of your employment with the company
- the strength of the evidence against you
- your ability and willingness to correct the conduct
- your attitude about the conduct
- disciplinary actions taken in the past for similar conduct by other employees
- how your conduct affects the company, its customers, and your coworkers, and
- any other circumstances related to the nature of the conduct, your employment with this company, and the effect of your conduct on the company.

We will give these considerations whatever weight we deem appropriate.

Sample Discipline Policy (continued)

Depending on the circumstances, we may give some considerations more weight than others, or no weight at all.

Some conduct might result in immediate termination of your employment. For example, you might be subject to immediate termination for:

- theft of company property
- excessive tardiness or absenteeism
- arguing or fighting with customers or coworkers
- brandishing a weapon at work
- threatening the physical safety of customers or coworkers
- physically or verbally assaulting someone at work
- any illegal conduct at work
- use or possession of alcohol or illegal drugs at work
- working under the influence of alcohol or illegal drugs
- failing to carry out reasonable job assignments
- insubordination
- making false statements on a job application
- violating company rules and regulations, and
- discrimination or harassment.

Of course, it is impossible to compile an exhaustive list of the types of conduct that will result in immediate termination. The above examples are merely illustrations.

This policy does not change the fact that your employment with the company is at will. Being an "at-will" employee means that you or the company can terminate the employment relationship at any time, for any reason, and with or without advance notice.

Complaints and Investigations

Employers can learn of problems at work in many ways. Customers, vendors, or other third parties might complain of an employee's conduct, or a manager or supervisor might observe the behavior personally. Sometimes, you'll discover evidence of misconduct—such as theft or vandalism—and have no idea who did it. But perhaps the most common way employers find out about misconduct is through employee complaints.

When faced with the possibility of an incident of workplace wrongdoing, even one that you've witnessed firsthand, your first step must be to figure out what really happened.

A complete, impartial, and timely investigation is one of the most important tools an employer has for dealing with problem employees. An investigation will help you manage misconduct and assure workers that their complaints and concerns are taken seriously. The very existence of an investigation procedure will emphasize the importance of following workplace rules and might even provide a valuable defense to a harassment, discrimination, or wrongful termination lawsuit.

To get these benefits, however, an employer must investigate every incident and complaint of serious misconduct quickly and thoroughly. This chapter will explain:

- when an investigation is necessary
- how to create a complaint policy and procedure that will encourage employees to come forward with concerns

- how to plan the investigation
- techniques for interviewing and gathering evidence
- how to investigate without invading workers' privacy, and
- how to reach a decision and take action, if necessary.

CAUTION

If your workers are unionized, they might be entitled to special rights and procedures during the investigation. All of your workers have certain rights, such as the right to a workplace free from harassment and discrimination. However, unions often negotiate additional rights for their members. If your workplace is unionized, check the collective bargaining agreement to find out if there are special procedures you must follow in your investigation.

RESOURCE

Get detailed information on investigating common workplace problems. *The Essential Guide to Workplace Investigations*, by Lisa Guerin (Nolo), offers step-by-step instructions for investigating any type of employee complaint or dispute, with separate chapters devoted to discrimination, harassment, theft, violence, and alcohol and drug use.

When Investigation Is Necessary

Not every infraction of workplace rules demands a full-scale investigation. For example, no investigation is necessary at all if everyone agrees on what happened. Or, if the person accused of misconduct fesses up, you can move on to figuring out an appropriate way to resolve the problem.

Minor Problems

For a relatively minor problem, consider a scaled-down investigation. For example, if an employee is accused of misconduct that wouldn't merit a written warning or other serious disciplinary measure, such as being tardy a single time or playing a radio too loudly, you can probably dispense with the detective work. Simply speak to the person who complained and to the accused employee, warn the employee that the behavior needs to stop, and document your conversations.

When deciding whether an investigation is warranted, think about how similar incidents or complaints have been handled in the past. If you usually investigate similar problems, consider doing so now. If legal trouble later develops, you want to be able to show that you were fair and consistent with employees and that you treated their complaints with equal concern.

Incidents That Require More Attention

Often, there will be some dispute over the basic facts of an allegation of significant wrongdoing. The employee accused of wrongdoing could deny having said or done anything wrong, argue that the complaining employee misunderstood the situation, or even claim

that the complaining employee is lying. Witnesses—if there are any—might lend support to the complaining employee, might back up the accused employee, or might tell a different story altogether. Documents relating to the incident might be inconclusive or nonexistent. In these situations, an investigation is necessary to get to the bottom of things.

Allegations of Harassment

While every complaint of serious workplace misconduct should be investigated, complaints of harassment merit special attention. Having an investigation policy that you promptly implement when learning of a complaint can help you avoid liability in some circumstances.

If one of your managers or supervisors harasses an employee and the harassment results in negative, job-related consequences for the employee—such as getting fired, demoted, or reassigned—your company will always be legally responsible for your managers' or supervisors' harassment. This is true even if the employee never complained and you had no idea what was going on.

You will also be responsible for harassment by a supervisor or manager that you know about—even when it doesn't result in a job-related action against the employee (for example, if you see or hear a manager telling sexual jokes or repeatedly asking an employee out on dates).

However, if a manager or supervisor subjected employees to this second type of harassment (harassment that doesn't result in a negative job action against the worker) and you didn't know about it, you might be able to avoid liability if all of the following are true:

- You had a policy prohibiting harassment that includes a procedure for filing complaints.
- You regularly conducted prompt, complete, and impartial investigations of harassment complaints.
- The harassed worker delayed in making a complaint or failed to complain at all.

The reasoning behind this defense is pretty simple: If an employer has an investigation policy that it follows faithfully, an employee should use it to give the employer a chance to fix the problem. If the employee fails to make a complaint, you will have no notice of the problem and, therefore, no way to know that you should investigate or take action.

In order to ensure that you can call on this defense if ever needed, you must make it clear to your employees that it's your policy to investigate their complaints fully and fairly—and actually follow through when faced with a complaint. This way, employees can't argue that they failed to report harassment because they didn't think you would do anything about it. Remember that once you learn of a manager's or supervisor's harassment of this second type—through

a complaint or in any other way—you are responsible for any harassment that continues after you find out.

This gives you an incentive to investigate and take effective action quickly.

EXAMPLE 1: Sheila's boss, Roger, has asked her out several times. She has turned him down each time, explaining that she has no romantic interest in him and would prefer to keep their relationship professional. Roger refuses to approve Sheila's scheduled raise because she will not go out with him. Roger's employer will be legally responsible for Roger's harassment, even if Sheila never complains about it, because she has been subjected to a negative job action.

EXAMPLE 2: Katherine works on the production line in an auto manufacturing plant. Her coworkers and supervisor, mostly men, constantly tell sexual jokes and refer to women in crude terms. The top executives in the company visit the plant. Although the men are on their best behavior during the official tour, several executives remain in the building after the tour to review paperwork, and they overhear the men's crude remarks. The company will be liable for any harassment Katherine suffers following the visit. Although she hasn't made a complaint, the company now knows about the problem and has a duty to act.

EXAMPLE 3: Same as the second example, above, except the executives never visit the plant. If Katherine wants to hold the company responsible for her harassment, she will have to make a complaint to put the company on notice of the problem. If Katherine fails to make a complaint, she can hold the company responsible only if she can show that (1) the company had no policy against harassment, or (2) the company didn't take complaints seriously, failed to investigate, or failed to act on reported problems. For example, if Katherine can show that several women from her plant had complained in the last year and nothing was done about the problem, the employer will be liable despite her failure to complain.

These rules apply to harassment by managers or supervisors. If coworkers harass an employee, the company will be liable only if it knew or should have known about the harassment and failed to take appropriate action to stop it. The employee will have to prove this in court. If a supervisor commits harassment, the company bears the burden of proving that it shouldn't be liable because the employee failed to utilize the company's complaint procedures. This distinction is very important in court. At your company, however, the upshot is the same: You should investigate all complaints or situations involving harassment immediately, no matter how you learn of them and no matter what position the accused employee holds. Not only will this give you the best chance of prevailing in court, but it will also help you maintain a productive and respectful workplace.

> **CAUTION**
> **You can learn more about your liability for your managers' or supervisors' acts from the EEOC (the Equal Employment Opportunity Commission).** Read its guidelines, entitled *Enforcement Guidance on Harassment in the Workplace* (April 29, 2024), available from the EEOC's website at www.eeoc.gov/laws/guidance/enforcement-guidance-harassment-workplace.

> **CAUTION**
> **State law might differ.** Although many states have adopted the rules explained in this section (which come from federal law), there might be a few states that buck the trend. States that have stronger antiharassment laws might take a different approach. An employment lawyer can help you figure out if your company needs to take additional protective steps.

Complaint Policies and Procedures

If your company has an employee handbook, a policies manual, or any form of written guidelines for employees, it should have a written complaint and investigation policy.

Some employers feel intimidated at the thought of writing their own personnel policies. But a complaint policy needn't be filled with legalisms or technical language; in fact, the best policies aren't. The primary goal of having a policy is to encourage your employees to come forward with complaints. A short statement, written in simple, direct language, is the best way to accomplish this.

What Your Complaint Policy Should Include

Your policy should describe the conduct about which employees can complain, how to make a complaint, and what will happen once a complaint is filed.

Prohibited Conduct

A complaint policy should spell out, in simple terms, what conduct will be investigated. If you already have a progressive discipline policy, sexual harassment policy, or other written guidelines describing unacceptable workplace behavior, you can use those policies for guidance.

List the types of misconduct employees should report (for example, harassment, discriminatory conduct or comments, violent behavior or threats of violence, safety violations, and theft or misuse of company property). Include a catch-all category at the end of your list, allowing employees to raise concerns about any type of behavior that makes them feel uncomfortable, upset, or unsafe. Even if these other complaints don't rise to the level of serious workplace issues, your employees will feel that you are interested in their well-being, and you will be able to nip developing problems in the bud.

How to Make Complaints

Next, explain how employees can make a formal complaint if they are victims of, or witnesses to, any of these prohibited behaviors. Encourage employees to come forward by making the process as clear and easy to follow as possible.

Many employers ask workers to complain to their direct supervisors or managers. If you choose this option, make sure that employees can also complain to someone outside of their chain of command, such as a human resources manager, another supervisor, or even the head of the company. If an employee is being harassed or mistreated by their supervisor, this allows the worker to bypass that person and complain to someone else. Also, workers might simply feel more comfortable talking to someone who won't be responsible for evaluating their performance and making decisions on promotions, raises, and assignments.

Make sure that the people whom you designate to take complaints are accessible to employees. For example, if your human resources department is located in a distant office or your local human resources manager works a part-time schedule, choose alternate people to take complaints who are local and available.

Investigation

While you need not describe your investigative procedures in detail, your policy should assure your employees that serious complaints will be investigated quickly, completely, and fairly.

Retaliation

It's illegal to punish or otherwise take any negative action against an employee who comes forward with a good-faith complaint of harassment, discrimination, illegal conduct, or health and safety violations. A complaint is made in good faith if the employee honestly and reasonably believes the complaint to be true.

The most obvious forms of retaliation are termination, discipline, demotion, pay cuts, or threats of any of these actions. More subtle forms of retaliation can include changing the shift hours or work area of the accuser, changing the accuser's job responsibilities or reporting relationships, and isolating the accuser by leaving them out of meetings and other office functions. Employers can get in trouble here. Although it often makes sense to change the work environment so that the accuser doesn't have to report to or work with the accused, those changes can't be detrimental to the accuser.

Your complaint policy should assure employees that no action will be taken against them for complaining in good faith or participating in an investigation. Promise to take all necessary steps to prevent and discourage retaliation. Assure employees that you will act quickly to prevent any further harassment or mistreatment while the investigation is pending.

Managers' Responsibilities

Your managers and supervisors can help you ferret out workplace misconduct. Your policy should state that managers and supervisors are responsible for reporting violations of company rules and for taking complaints from employees.

Confidentiality

Your policy should make clear that you will keep the complaint confidential *to the extent possible.* You cannot reasonably promise not to tell anyone about the complaint, because you might have to tell the alleged wrongdoer about the complaining employee's statements and perhaps interview witnesses about the incident. However, you should disclose information about a complaint strictly on a need-to-know basis.

Corrective Action

Your policy should state that you will conduct a prompt and thorough investigation after receiving a complaint. Make it clear that you will take immediate disciplinary action if you decide that the accused employee violated company policy.

Sample Complaint Policy

Below you'll find a sample complaint policy that you can add to your employee handbook, distribute to your employees, or post in your employee lounge or break room.

You can find a downloadable version of the Company Complaint Policy at this book's online companion page; see Appendix A for details on how to download it.

This sample policy assumes that you have other written personnel policies spelling out standards of workplace behavior, including policies regarding workplace discrimination and harassment. If you have no such written policies, you will have to explicitly describe the types of conduct that are prohibited. The policy also assumes that you have a human resources department. For smaller employers, you can delete these references and replace them with the names of your designated complaint takers.

Remember that this policy is only a sample. You might have to adapt it to meet the needs of your employees and work-place, to conform to your other written policies or to comply with state law. (For more information on workplace policies—including a list of topics you might want to cover in an employee handbook—see Chapter 11.)

Preparing to Investigate

Once you receive a complaint or otherwise learn of potential misconduct, it's time to plan your investigation. After you figure out who will investigate, the investigator will decide whom to interview and what documents to review. And you might have to take some immediate action before the investigation is complete to prevent further misconduct.

Choose the Investigator

Who investigates a complaint will depend on the size of your company, the identities of the complaining employee and accused employee, and the severity of the charges. Regardless of workplace size or type of complaint, however, your investigator must possess two essential attributes: experience and impartiality.

Experience

An experienced investigator who knows what to look for, how to find it, and how to evaluate that information will likely do a better job for you than someone who hasn't tackled a job like this before. Your investigator should have some experience in investigating complaints, or at least some education and training on the subject. For larger companies, someone from the human resources department is usually the best bet. Human resources personnel can get training and educational materials on investigation techniques through professional associations. (See also *The Essential Guide to Workplace Investigations,* by Lisa Guerin (Nolo).) Smaller companies without a human resources staff can use other managerial employees to conduct the investigation, as long as they have experience in personnel matters.

There's another reason to choose someone with experience: If you're sued by the employee who complained or the employee who was disciplined, the investigation will become crucial evidence. You will rely on it to show that you reacted reasonably to the complaint, while the employee will argue that your investigation, or the conclusion reached, was faulty. If the employee can show that your investigator had no experience or training in conducting investigations, a jury is more likely to second-guess the investigator's decisions and disregard the investigator's findings.

This doesn't mean that even the smallest company must have an experienced investigator on staff, however. You can supplement your designated investigator's lack of practical

Sample Company Complaint Policy

Company Complaint Policy

Our Company is committed to providing a safe and productive work environment, free of threats to the health, safety, and well-being of our workers. These threats include, but are not limited to, harassment, discrimination, violations of health and safety rules, and violence.

Any employee who witnesses or is subject to inappropriate conduct in the workplace may complain to _____ or to any Company officer. Any supervisor, manager, or Company officer who receives a complaint about, hears of, or witnesses any inappropriate conduct is required to immediately notify _____ . Inappropriate conduct includes any conduct prohibited by our policies about harassment, discrimination, discipline, workplace violence, health and safety, wages and hours, and drug and alcohol use. In addition, we encourage employees to come forward with any workplace complaint, even if the subject of the complaint is not explicitly covered by our written policies.

We encourage you to come forward with complaints immediately, so we can take whatever action is needed to handle the problem. Once a complaint has been made, _____ will determine how to handle it. For serious complaints, we will immediately conduct a complete and impartial investigation.

We expect all employees to cooperate fully in Company investigations by, for example, answering questions completely and honestly and giving the investigator all documents and other material that might be relevant. All complaints will be handled as confidentially as possible. When the investigation is complete, the company will take corrective action, if appropriate.

We will not engage in or allow retaliation against any employee who makes a good-faith complaint or participates in an investigation. If you believe that you are being subjected to any kind of negative treatment because you made, or were questioned about, a complaint, report the conduct immediately to

_____

_____ .

experience by providing educational materials and sending the investigator to seminars and trainings on investigative techniques. When faced with serious complaints, consider bringing in an outside investigator.

Impartiality

The person who investigates must be perceived within the workplace—and particularly by the employees involved in the complaint—as fair and objective.

Someone who supervises, or is supervised by, either the complaining employee or the accused employee shouldn't perform the investigation. Similarly, you shouldn't choose an investigator who has known difficulties with any of the main players. Once you have come up with a potential investigator, you might want to ask whether the complaining employee believes that person can be fair and impartial. If not—and if those concerns seem reasonable—choose someone else.

Of course, a small business might not have a wide range of potential investigators to choose from. In that case, just make sure that whoever does the job doesn't have an ax to grind with either the complaining or the accused employee.

Outside Investigators

In some situations, it makes sense to ask for professional help to investigate a complaint of workplace wrongdoing. Many law firms and private consulting agencies investigate workplace complaints for a fee.

When to Call a Lawyer

If you have in-house counsel, you always have a lawyer available to help you with your investigation planning and strategy. (But see "Attorney-Client Privilege," below, to learn why your in-house counsel shouldn't be the investigator.) If you don't have an attorney on the payroll, however, you might need some outside legal help in some investigation situations.

Consider bringing in a lawyer during your investigation if any of the following are true:

- Any employee involved (whether the employee who made the complaint or the employee accused of wrongdoing) has hired a lawyer.
- The employee has filed a charge or complaint with an administrative agency (such as the Equal Employment Opportunity Commission).
- The employee has filed a lawsuit.
- The underlying problem involves serious allegations of harassment, discrimination, stalking, threats, violence, and so on.
- A number of employees have complained about the same problem.

It's much better to get legal advice at the outset than to realize later that you made some mistakes a lawyer could have helped you avoid. A lawyer can help you plan the investigation, document your findings, and minimize your company's legal exposure.

CHAPTER 5 | COMPLAINTS AND INVESTIGATIONS | 139

Consider an outside investigator if:

- You receive more than one complaint about the same problem (for example, several women complain that a particular manager has harassed them).
- The accused is a high-ranking official in the business (such as the president or CEO).
- The complaining employee has publicized the complaint in the workplace or in the media.
- The complaining employee has hired a lawyer, filed a lawsuit, or filed charges with a government agency, such as the Equal Employment Opportunity Commission, the Occupational Safety and Health Administration, the Department of Labor's Wage and Hour Division, or a similar state agency.
- The accusations are extreme (allegations of rape, assault, or significant theft, for example).
- For any reason, no one is available to investigate the complaint fairly and objectively.

You can get referrals for professional investigators through management newsletters, trade associations, and other business contacts. For complaints of discrimination and harassment, your state's fair employment practices agency might be able to provide referrals. These agencies are listed at www.nolo.com/FEPA.

If you take action against an employee based on an outside investigator's report, you might have to give the employee a summary of that report. This obligation is imposed by the Fair and Accurate Credit Transaction Act (FACTA), an amendment to the Fair Credit Reporting Act. (15 U.S.C. §§ 1681 and following.) For more information on FACTA and the Fair Credit Reporting Act, visit the website of the Federal Trade Commission, at www.ftc.gov.

> CAUTION
> **Even if you hire an outside investigator, you are responsible for any actions you take based on the investigator's findings.** Hiring an outside investigator doesn't insulate you from liability for the investigation or the decisions you make based on that investigation. For this reason, work closely with the outside investigator to make sure that they receive all relevant information, conduct a thorough and fair investigation, and document the findings. And although a professional investigator can certainly give you advice about what action to take when the investigation is through, you should always make the final decision.

Specialized Investigators

Sometimes the nature of the complaint should affect your choice of investigators. For example, some women might feel more comfortable discussing a sexual harassment complaint with a female investigator. Some larger companies try to make an investigator of each gender available for just this reason. Or, if the investigation involves technical issues (figuring out whether an employee sabotaged a computer program or violated safety rules in a production line, for example), you should try to choose an investigator—or make someone available to assist the investigator—who has the relevant background needed to understand the details.

Starting the Investigation

For the balance of this discussion, we'll assume that you are the one doing the investigating, rather than other staff or an outside investigator. Start by reviewing relevant policies, gathering background information and possible evidence, and planning whom to interview.

Review Policies

You'll need to determine which company policies and guidelines might apply to the situation. Even if you're familiar with your company rules and procedures, it's a good idea to review these policies before proceeding.

Review and Gather Background Information and Evidence

The next steps are to review background information and gather evidence. You should:

- Read the complaint and gather and read any relevant paperwork (such as personnel files, attendance records, emails, performance reviews, or documentation of previous misconduct).
- Collect and review any physical evidence (such as a weapon, illegal drugs, graphic images, or relevant work materials).

Once collected, these documents and items should be placed in a locked file cabinet or another safe place.

Attorney-Client Privilege

Whenever you talk privately to a lawyer for the purpose of obtaining legal advice, that conversation is protected by the attorney-client privilege. This means that no one can force you or the lawyer to reveal what either of you said. The purpose of the privilege is to encourage full and frank discussion from both sides.

However, you can lose this privilege if you don't honor it. For example, if you tell another person what you said to your lawyer, your conversation is no longer privileged. Similarly, if your company defends against a harassment lawsuit by relying on the results of your investigation, the person who conducted the investigation will need to testify. If your lawyer conducted the investigation, the lawyer could be forced to reveal the contents of conversations with company representatives, which would otherwise have been protected by the attorney-client privilege.

This is why some companies with in-house counsel choose not to use their own lawyers as the investigators. If your in-house counsel becomes a witness in a later legal proceeding about the investigation, your company could lose its attorney-client privilege as to conversations with the lawyer about the investigation. Because of this, companies often reserve their in-house counsel for privileged conversations, and leave the investigation to a nonlawyer employee, an outside lawyer, or an outside investigator.

Plan the Interviews

In some cases, only the complaining employee and the accused employee should be interviewed (for example, if the complaint is about an incident that no one else witnessed, heard, or was told about later). In other situations, there could be many potential witnesses. For example, if the incident underlying the complaint occurred during a staff meeting or company social event, there could be dozens of potential witnesses. In such cases, the investigator should ask both the complaining and the accused employee which workers were most likely to have seen or heard the disputed event.

Regardless of the number of people whom you ultimately interview, you should interview the complaining employee first, followed generally by the accused employee, and then witnesses. You can vary this order to accommodate employees' schedules in the interests of moving as quickly as possible.

It's helpful to have some idea of what questions you will ask each person interviewed. You don't need to script every interview question in advance, but you should take a few notes on topics to cover in each interview.

Take Immediate Action If Necessary

Sometimes an employer learns of possible misconduct so egregious that immediate steps must be taken, even before the investigation is complete. For example, if an employee complains that a supervisor has committed a sexual assault, an employee threatened to bring a gun to work, or a worker appears to be giving company trade secrets to a competitor, you don't have the luxury of waiting until your investigation is complete. Some action must be taken at once to protect your employees and prevent further harm.

If the misconduct is between two employees (sexual harassment, insubordination, or fighting, for example), an employer might choose to separate the employees until the investigation is finished. By assigning one or both to different shifts, or switching managers or job responsibilities temporarily, an employer can alleviate the immediate problem and investigate more thoroughly. But be careful not to take any action against the complaining employee that could be construed as retaliation. For example, if one employee must move to a less desirable position temporarily, it's best to move the accused employee.

If one employee is accused of (or has been reported for) extreme misconduct, consider suspending that employee, with pay, while you investigate the situation. When you suspend the employee, explain the complaint or behavior at issue and ask to hear the accused employee's side of the story. Provide assurance that you will investigate the incident and reach a decision as quickly as possible.

Get Started Right Away

Ideally, you should begin investigating within a day or two of receiving the complaint, and complete the investigation within a week or two, depending on how complicated the allegations are. Of course, there will be times when outside circumstances and conflicting schedules make immediate investigation tough. These brief, unavoidable delays can't be helped. However, if you drag your feet unnecessarily, you'll send the message that you don't take the complaint seriously. And if the misconduct continues in the meantime, a court might find you responsible for failing to investigate or resolve the problem right away.

Conducting Interviews

Most investigations consist primarily of interviews with the employees involved, including the employee who complained, the employee accused of wrongdoing, and any witnesses to the incident. At the end of the investigation employers might have to rely solely on statements from the main players and witnesses to get to the truth, and these statements might contradict each other.

If the main participants in the incident flatly deny each other's claims, you'll have to sort out who is telling the truth. How can you decide whose story is more credible in such situations? The first step is to conduct interviews designed to elicit as much information as possible. The more facts an interviewer can draw out of each witness, the easier it will be to figure out what happened and why.

TIP

Schedule interviews as close together as possible. Once you start conducting interviews, employees are bound to start talking to each other. As noted under "Keep It Confidential," below, you might not be able to prohibit employees from discussing the investigation. But you can minimize these conversations by interviewing witnesses on a tight schedule. The less time between your interviews, the fewer opportunities employees have to talk to each other and influence each other's statements.

Tips on Conducting Effective Interviews

Your goal is to elicit as much information as possible from your witnesses. Use the tips below to maximize the utility of the time you spend interviewing the person who complained, the person accused, and witnesses to the wrongdoing.

Keep an Open Mind

Some employers tend to make light of complaints of wrongdoing—they don't want to believe that misconduct is taking place right under their noses. Other employers are at the other end of the spectrum—they automatically assume that an employee wouldn't complain without good cause. Neither approach is sound. If you start your investigation believing you already know what happened, you'll inevitably miss some important details. By contrast, if you keep an open mind until your investigation is complete, you'll conduct more thorough interviews and receive more candid answers to your questions.

> EXAMPLES:
>
> **Don't ask:** Why did you pressure Maria to falsify her time card?
> **Ask:** Did you and Maria discuss her time card? What did each of you say?
>
> **Don't ask:** What were you thinking, bringing a knife to work?
> **Ask:** Did you bring a knife to work last Thursday? Why?

Ask Open-Ended Questions

The best way to encourage your witness to talk is to pose open-ended questions that ask what the witness heard, said, or did, and why. If you ask questions that suggest the answer or that call only for a yes or no answer ("leading" questions), you will be doing all the talking.

> EXAMPLES:
>
> **Don't ask:** Did you arrive at three o'clock?
> **Ask:** What time did you arrive?
>
> **Don't ask:** Did you hear John tell Ping that she would not be paid for her overtime work unless she agreed to have lunch with him?
> **Ask:** Did you hear John and Ping talking last week? Tell me what you heard.

Keep Your Opinions to Yourself

As your investigation progresses, you will inevitably start to develop some opinions about what really happened. Don't share these opinions with your witnesses. If your statements or the tone of your questions suggest that you have already reached a decision, witnesses will be less likely to speak freely with you. Some might be afraid of contradicting your version of events. Others might feel there is no point in explaining what really happened if you have already made up your mind. In the worst-case scenario, a witness might believe you are conducting an unfair or biased investigation and challenge the outcome in court. Avoid these problems by keeping your conclusions to yourself until the investigation is complete.

> EXAMPLES:
>
> **Don't ask:** I have already heard from several people that Sameh was absent from last week's mandatory meeting. Is that what you remember?
> **Ask:** Who attended last week's mandatory meeting?
>
> **Don't ask:** Can you confirm that Michael punched Darrell on the loading dock?
> **Ask:** Did you see an incident between Michael and Darrell on the loading dock? Tell me what happened.

Focus on What the Witness Knows

Many people have a difficult time distinguishing fact from opinion when describing what they have seen or heard. For example, a witness who tells you why another person did something is really giving you a subjective opinion of why that person acted that way. By keeping your witnesses focused on the facts, you can prevent speculation and rumor from affecting your decisions.

EXAMPLES:

If you're told: Lawrence has been out to get Graciela since the day he started working here. But I'm not surprised; he doesn't like reporting to a woman.

You might ask: What have you seen or heard that leads you to believe Lawrence is out to get Graciela?

If you're told: Everyone knew that Evelyn was going to lose her temper and get violent. It was just a matter of time.

You might ask: What do you mean by get violent? What did you see or hear Evelyn do? Why did you believe Evelyn was going to lose her temper? What did she say or do to make you think she was on edge? When you say "everyone knew," do you mean that you discussed this with others? Who did you talk to about it, and what did they say?

Find Out About Other Witnesses or Evidence

In order to conduct a complete investigation, you should ask the employees you interview whether they know of other witnesses or physical evidence relating to the incident. If the witness is the accused or complaining employee, ask if anyone else saw or heard the incidents in question and whether the witness told anyone about it when it happened. Find out if either took any notes about the problem or if any workplace documents— emails, memoranda, or evaluations, for example—relate to the incident.

EXAMPLES:

If you're told: Robert and I had a loud argument by the elevators. He told me I wouldn't get my raise unless I agreed to withdraw my complaint that he had harassed me. Afterwards I was so upset that I ran back to my office in tears.

You might ask: Was anyone else near the elevator when the argument took place? Did anyone hear what Robert said to you? Did you see anyone on your way back to your office? Did you talk to anyone about what happened?

If you're told: Julie sent me an email apologizing for giving me a bad review. She said her manager made her change my performance appraisal after I filed a workers' compensation claim.

You might ask: Do you have a copy of Julie's email to you? Did she copy anyone on the email? Did you see the performance appraisal before it was changed? Do you have a copy?

Ask About Contradictions

Sometimes one witness contradicts what another has said. The accused and complaining employees are perhaps most likely to contradict each other, but even uninvolved witnesses might give conflicting stories. The best way to get to the bottom of these disputes is to ask about them directly. Once you get down to specifics, you might find that everyone agrees on what happened, but not on whether it was appropriate.

If the witnesses continue to contradict each other even after you point out the conflicts in their stories—if the accused flatly denies the complaining employee's statements, for example—ask each witness why the other might disagree.

> **EXAMPLES:**
>
> **If you're told:** I never sexually harassed anyone. I treat the women who work for me with respect.
>
> **You might ask:** Tanya says that you touched her waist and hips several times while she was distributing paperwork to clients and says that you made a joke about her spending the night at her boyfriend's house. Did this happen? Could Tanya have misinterpreted something you said? Do you think Tanya might have made up these allegations? Why?
>
> **If you're told:** Darnell told us at last week's morning meeting that anyone who complained about safety problems in the warehouse would get in trouble. He basically threatened to fire anyone who reported an accident.
>
> **You might ask:** Two other people in your work group said that Darnell told all of you he had reported two safety violations to his manager. They said he encouraged you to bring any safety concerns to him, and he would bring them to the company's attention. Did this happen? Did you have a different conversation with Darnell? Why do you think these people remembered the meeting differently?

Keep It Confidential

Complaints can polarize a workplace. If workers side with either the complaining employee or the accused employee, the rumor mill will start working overtime. What's worse, if too many details about the complaint get out, you could be accused of damaging the reputation of the alleged victim or alleged wrongdoer and get slapped with a defamation lawsuit.

Avoid these problems by practicing confidentiality in your investigation. Set a good example by being discreet. Hold interviews in a private place where you won't be overheard (or off site, if the workplace doesn't allow for privacy). Don't discuss the investigation at staff meetings or in the lunchroom, and avoid gossip.

Tell each witness only those facts necessary to conduct a thorough interview. The accused employee deserves to hear details of the allegations, but peripheral witnesses don't.

> **EXAMPLES:**
>
> **Don't ask:** Sylvia says that Roger asked her out several times and tried to bring her back to his room after the holiday party. She also says that Roger made a lot of X-rated jokes in front of clients and that you might have heard some of these jokes during the meeting with Pets-R-Us. Did you hear any of these jokes?

Interviewing Remote Employees

You will need to consider some additional issues if any employees you need to interview are working remotely.

- **Where to hold the interview.** If possible, you should interview employees in person. When in the same room with the employee, you can more easily establish rapport, review documents, and gauge demeanor and body language. If you can't conduct the interview in person, however, a video conferencing platform (like Zoom) is the best alternative. At least you'll be able to see the employee, establish a professional tone, and review documents by screen share. Don't conduct interviews by phone unless you have no other options.

- **Planning for a remote interview.** Before the interview, familiarize yourself with the platform you'll be using. Prepare the documents you'll be sharing on your screen. Make sure you have a professional setting on your end, including your attire, visible surroundings, and backdrop. And, remember that you might need to schedule extra time for remote interviews. You might need to take breaks to counter the inevitable fatigue of video conferencing; because video conferencing can also come with technical and practical glitches, it could take you a bit longer to get through your questions.

- **Preserve confidentiality.** Use the options available through the video platform, such as a waiting room feature and password protection, to keep your interview private. Let the employee know ahead of time that the interview will be confidential, so they can prepare to be in a private space where family members, roommates, or patrons of their local coffee shop won't overhear the conversation. And, make sure you have a private space for your end of the interview.

- **Start the interview right.** When you're ready to begin, remind the employee that this is a private conversation, and ask whether the employee is alone. Let the employee know that they can ask for a break if they are getting fatigued or need to use the restroom. If you plan to record the interview, make sure you get the employee's consent up front. Most video conferencing platforms have consent features built in.

Ask: Did you attend the pitch meeting with Pets-R-Us? Who else was there? Did Roger make any jokes during this meeting? Tell me what he said.

Don't ask: Fernando has complained that Martin gave him a bad performance evaluation, and he thinks it's because Martin dislikes Latinos. Fernando believes that he has made more successful cold calls than anyone else on his shift. He thought you might be able to confirm this, since you compile the monthly productivity reports. Is this true?

Ask: Do you compile monthly productivity reports? Do these reports contain the cold call success rate for each salesperson? Do you recall who had the highest success rate for the afternoon shift? May I see a copy of these reports for the last year?

It's one thing to control what you say during an investigation, but it's much harder to control what employees say. Maintaining confidentiality in an investigation can be a tricky legal issue as well. In the past, both the EEOC and the National Labor Relations Board (NLRB) found that forbidding employees who participate in an investigation from discussing the matter with anyone could violate laws prohibiting retaliation and unfair labor practices. Although both agencies recognized that a particular investigation might require employee silence (for example, if the employer reasonably fears that evidence could be destroyed), these decisions had to be made on a case-by-case basis. Blanket

"gag rules" that apply to everyone involved in every investigation didn't usually make the cut, particularly if employees felt that they couldn't raise concerns or talk to their coworkers about workplace problems.

Because of these conflicts and shifting interpretations, you should get legal advice if you want to impose an employee confidentiality requirement in a particular investigation.

Don't Retaliate

It's against the law to punish someone for making a complaint of harassment, discrimination, illegal conduct, or unsafe working conditions. As explained above, your commitment to compliance should be clearly reflected in your complaint policy, and this is the time to honor it. Assure every person you interview that you're eager to hear their side of the story and that they won't face retaliation for coming forward.

> **EXAMPLES:**
> **If you're told:** I'm having some problems working with Maurice, but I don't want to cause trouble.
> **You might ask:** I'm glad you brought this issue to my attention. Coming forward with a problem does not cause trouble. We would really be in trouble if you kept this information to yourself and your team's work suffered as a result. No one in the company will retaliate against you or take any action against you for coming forward. Now, what has been happening with Maurice?

If you're told: I've seen some pretty heated conversations between Maria and Simone, but it's really none of my business. I don't want Simone to think that I'm not a team player.

You might ask: I need to find out what's been going on between Maria and Simone, and anything you can tell me about those conversations will help me get to the bottom of this. If there are problems in your work group, everyone's work suffers and everyone feels uncomfortable. No one will be allowed to retaliate against you or treat you poorly because you spoke to me. Both Maria and Simone have been told that these issues would be investigated. I've warned both of them not to retaliate, and I'll make sure that they don't. What have your heard Maria and Simone say to each other?

Respect Your Workers' Privacy

Keep your questions focused on work-related issues, not on your workers' private lives. Although the law differs from state to state, employers are generally on shaky legal ground if they ask about—or make employment decisions based on—a worker's conduct off the job. Instead, limit your questions to the worker's performance or conduct on the job. Even if a worker's problems on the job are related to personal concerns, you're free to discipline or counsel the worker as you see fit as long as you stick to job-related criteria.

Sometimes a worker will volunteer personal information during an interview. For example, one might tell you about a private problem that's affecting their work demeanor and performance. Feel free to offer a sympathetic ear (as long as the worker feels comfortable confiding in you) and try to come up with helpful workplace solutions. However, you shouldn't ask probing questions about an employee's life outside the workplace, even if the employee raises the issue. The deeper you delve into personal issues, the greater your risk of invading privacy.

EXAMPLE: Although Jack has always been a considerate and competent employee, he has been acting erratically at work for a couple of months. He has seemed tired and short-tempered, and his attention to detail has really suffered. Last week, Janice complained that Jack had neglected to follow safety procedures while loading packages and that his carelessness caused her a minor injury. When Janice spoke to Jack about it, he cursed at her and stormed away. The drastic change in behavior leads his employer to believe that something in Jack's private life might be affecting his work.

Don't ask: Is everything okay between you and your boyfriend?

Ask: Your coworkers and I have all noticed that you just haven't seemed yourself lately. You've been short-tempered and careless, and your performance has really suffered. Why has this happened?

After the employer asks why Jack is having work problems, Jack says that he is having a rough time in his personal life right now and would prefer not to talk about it.

Don't ask: But if your personal life is affecting your work, I need to know what is going on. Did you and your boyfriend break up? Are you having health problems?

Ask: I understand that you want to keep your personal life private, and I respect that. If there is anything that I can do to help, please let me know. But we do need to talk about your work performance. Let's talk about how you can get back on track here.

Ask to Be Contacted With New or Additional Information

Close every interview by thanking the witness and asking them to contact you if anything else comes to mind. You'll be surprised by how frequently a witness will return with follow-up information. For example, a witness might see or hear pertinent new information or remember a significant detail later. And some witnesses might hold back important information during the interview, trying to decide whether to come clean. If you offer every witness an opportunity to continue the conversation, you're more likely to get the full story. And should your investigation be challenged in court, you'll be able to prove that you made every effort to gather all the facts.

EXAMPLE:

Don't say: Have you told me everything you remember about these incidents? Because you won't be able to change your statement once I start talking to other witnesses.

Say: Please remember that my door is always open if you remember anything later or there is something you need to add to your statement. Also, if you learn of any new information that relates to the complaint, please bring it to my attention right away.

Write It All Down

Take notes during every interview. Before you begin, note the date, time, and place; the name of the witness; and whether anyone else was present. Write down all important facts that the witness relates or denies. If the witness offers opinions, be sure to identify them as such. Before the interview is over, go back through your notes with the witness to make sure you got it right. These notes will help you remember what each witness said later when you are making your decision.

Although it might sound like overkill, consider asking each witness to sign and date a written statement of what was said during the interview. A signed statement will help you in court if the investigation is challenged as biased or incomplete and will discourage people from changing their stories on the witness stand.

It's Never Too Late

What should you do if a worker comes to you with new information only after you've reached a decision or even acted based on it? The answer depends on whether the new information, if accurate, would change your conclusions. If not, you can simply make a note of the new information and stick with your earlier decision.

If the new information might change your mind, you will have to look into it. If, after investigating, you're satisfied that the information is accurate, you should make any necessary adjustments to your conclusions and actions. For example, if you receive new information showing that the misconduct was worse than it seemed, you might have to impose more severe discipline. If the additional details show that another employee was actually responsible for the problem, you might have to rescind your discipline of one employee and impose discipline on the other.

One thing you can't do: Ignore the new evidence. Although it might be tempting to simply stick with your original conclusions and disregard the new information as "too late," this will get you into trouble. If the new information shows that you disciplined a worker unjustly or failed to discipline a worker who engaged in serious wrongdoing, you are responsible for correcting the situation.

As you take notes and document your investigation, remember that every document you create could become courtroom evidence. If your company is sued over the incident underlying the investigation (for example, a harassment complaint) or the action it takes based on the investigation (for example, firing the employee accused of harassment), your investigation will play an important role in the case: It's your company's way of showing that it met its legal obligations. And, the employee who feels mistreated will want to use your notes and other documents to show that your investigation was somehow inadequate or ineffective. All of this means that your investigation documents will likely be pored over in court. Keep all this in mind as you take notes on witness interviews. Your notes should be accurate, complete, and above reproach.

EXAMPLE:

Don't write: I spoke to Joan today. She said that Richard has been acting strange lately, but she hasn't really seen any fights between Sam and Richard. She thinks Richard might act out violently sometime soon.

Write: I interviewed Joan Suzuki today, June 14, 20xx, regarding Sam Levine's complaint (see complaint form in file). We met in my office at 3 p.m. I asked Joan whether she had seen any incidents between Richard Hart and Sam in the last two weeks. Joan said that she thought Richard had been acting very strange lately. When I asked her to explain, she said that Richard seemed distracted and angry and that he had been complaining to others in the work group about his ex-wife's petition for an increase in child support. Richard told her that Sam had denied his request for a raise and that Sam was responsible for all of his problems. Joan also said that Richard had made several jokes during shift meetings about "going postal" and that he told Sam "you will be the first to go." This is the only incident she has seen between Sam and Richard. Joan said that she was frightened by Richard's change in behavior.

Joan confirmed that Jose, Jocelyn, and Cherise heard Richard's jokes at the meetings. I thanked her for her information, and encouraged her to come forward with any additional information immediately. I assured her that Richard has been suspended pending the outcome of the investigation, and that the company would act swiftly to deal with the situation as soon as the investigation was complete.

Interviewing the Complaining Employee

Often, you'll become aware of a problem employee by way of a complaining coworker. Your interview with the coworker might be straightforward and lowkey, or be laden with emotion and tension, or something in between. Here are the steps to get you through whatever happens.

Questioning the Complaining Employee

Start your investigation by getting the details from the complaining employee. Remember to use the tips explained above. Here are some sample questions to consider:

- What happened? If the complaint involves several incidents or a pattern of misconduct over a period of time, start with the most recent problem and work backward.
- Who was involved? What did that person say or do?
- What was your response or reaction, if any?
- When and where did the incident(s) take place?
- Did anyone witness the incident(s)?
- Did you tell anyone about the incident(s)?
- Do you know of anyone who might have information about the incident(s)?
- Have you been affected by the incident(s)? How?
- Do you know of any similar incidents involving other people?
- Do you know of any evidence— documents or otherwise—relating to your complaint?

Difficult Interviews

Employees often find it extremely difficult to come forward with a complaint, especially one about discrimination or harassment. Many employees complain only as a last resort, after trying informally to stop the misconduct. An employee who complains could be wrestling with difficult feelings of embarrassment, anger, sadness, and fear.

When an employee finally does decide to complain, these emotions might spill out during the interview. The worker might cry, become angry, or even have a change of heart halfway through the process. Your best response is to listen and be understanding.

Acknowledge to the employee that you recognize that this is difficult and emotional and that you want to get to the bottom of things. If the complaining worker tries to "take back" the complaint, say that you'll have to investigate anyway and would like the worker's cooperation. If the employee is afraid of the accused employee, think about what immediate steps you can take to calm these fears, such as separating the workers. However, don't try so hard to sympathize that you lose your objectivity in the investigation. Remember, your job is to find out all the facts before making a decision.

> **EXAMPLE:**
>
> **If you're told:** If Thomas finds out I complained about him asking me out, he'll never promote me to the team leader position. I've worked so hard for that promotion; maybe it isn't worth filing a complaint.
>
> **Don't say:** I can't believe Thomas was so disrespectful to you! By the time I'm through with him, he won't be in a position to be deciding on any promotions. He'll be lucky to have a job!
>
> **Don't say:** If you aren't willing to make a formal complaint, there is nothing I can do to help you. You will just have to decide whether this is important enough to warrant a full-fledged investigation.
>
> **Say:** I understand that you are worried about your promotion. But I won't allow anyone, including Thomas, to retaliate against you for coming forward. And once I know about potential harassment, as I do now, I have a legal responsibility to investigate and figure out what to do. I am going to look into what happened, talk to Thomas and any witnesses, then decide what the company will do.

If requested, you might let the complaining employee bring a friend to the interview. You aren't legally required to allow this, and there are pros and cons to having another person present. If the employee is highly emotional, having a support person might make things more comfortable and help the employee tell the story more completely. And if your investigation is challenged later, the support person will be one more witness to your conscientious efforts. However, having a third party present might make it more difficult for you to establish a rapport with the complaining witness. And it will add one more person to the list of those who know about the complaint and investigation, which makes confidentiality more difficult.

Concluding the Interview

Once you've finished your questions, conclude the interview by giving the employee some idea about what to expect. Tell the employee that you plan to interview the accused worker and any other witnesses, review any additional evidence, and complete the investigation as soon as possible. Emphasize that you will keep things confidential to the extent possible but might have to reveal some information to conduct a thorough investigation.

Thank the employee for bringing the complaint to your attention. Offer assurance that the worker will not be retaliated against for coming forward, and ask to be told of any retaliatory conduct, whether by the accused employee or anyone else. Finally, because complaining employees often don't remember all details during the initial interview, stress that your door is always open if additional facts come to light.

Interviewing the Accused Employee

Your goal when interviewing accused employees is to get their side of the story. The best way to do this is to be forthright, by explaining that a complaint was made (or potential misconduct was noted by management), describing the conduct in question, and asking the employee to respond.

Questioning the Accused Employee

It can be very difficult to interview someone accused of wrongdoing. The accused worker could be angry, frightened, and upset about the accusations and will certainly see you as the enemy. After all, a worker who actually committed the misconduct in question will be worried about keeping their job. A worker who didn't will be upset about being accused. Either way, these can be very uncomfortable situations, for the employee and the investigator alike.

Give the accused employee every opportunity to offer their side of the story.

Here are some sample questions to consider:

- What is your response to the complaint or allegations?
- What happened (if the accused employee doesn't completely deny the allegations)? When and where did this happen?
- Why might the complaining employee lie (if the accused employee says the allegations are false)? Could the complaining employee have misunderstood your actions or statements? Have you and the complaining employee had problems working together?
- Did anyone witness the incident(s)?
- Did you tell anyone about the incident(s)?
- Do you know of anyone who might have information about the incident(s)?
- Do you know of any evidence—documents or otherwise—relating to these allegations?

Concluding the Interview

Close the interview by telling the accused employee what will happen next. Explain that you will interview witnesses and review other evidence before reaching a final conclusion. Give assurances that you will keep the investigation confidential to the extent possible. Stress that retaliation against the complaining employee is strictly prohibited. Finally, ask the employee to bring any new or additional information to your attention at once.

Interviewing Witnesses

There are many kinds of witnesses. Some have seen or heard, firsthand, the misconduct at issue, while others have heard only rumors. Some will be privy to an entire dispute, while others will have only a bit of information to share. And some might have an ax to grind (or favor to curry) with either the complaining or the accused employee.

Your goal in interviewing witnesses is to find out what they know without unnecessarily revealing information. While the accused employee has the right to know what allegations have been made, third-party witnesses have no such right. And you have good reasons to maintain confidentiality. If the allegations turn out to be false, the accused employee can sue you for defamation if you publicized them recklessly. Even if no lawsuit is in the offing, you can cut down on gossip and rumor in the workplace by keeping a tight lid on the investigation.

When deciding what to ask a witness, think about who suggested the witness and why. Did the complaining employee tell you that the witness saw the misconduct? Did the accused employee claim to have confided in the witness after an incident? Sticking to the facts the witness is supposed to know will help you keep things confidential.

Here are some questions to consider for third-party witnesses:

- What did you see or hear?
- When and where did this take place?
- Did you tell anyone about the incident(s)?
- Did the complaining employee tell you anything about the incident(s)?
- Did the accused employee tell you anything about the incident(s)?
- Have you personally witnessed any other incidents between the complaining employee and the accused employee?
- Have you heard these issues discussed in the workplace? When, where, and by whom?
- Have you ever had any problems working with the complaining employee? The accused employee?

When your questions have been answered, thank the witness for participating.

Written and Physical Evidence

In many cases, there will be no evidence of wrongdoing other than witness statements, especially when the alleged misconduct consists of verbal or physical harassment, threats, or violence.

Sometimes, however, documents play a role in the investigation. For example, if an employee complains of discrimination by a supervisor, you might review the employee's personnel file to see how the supervisor has documented their exchanges. Similarly, if an employee claims that her coworkers sexually harassed her by sending her obscene messages and images over the office email system, you can review those materials directly.

Documents might also help you pin down crucial details. For example, if an employee claims to have been out of the office on a day when the workplace misconduct allegedly happened, you can check attendance records to find out the truth. Or, if an employee accuses a supervisor of giving a poor performance review in apparent retaliation for a recent complaint of harassment, you can find out when the employee made the complaint, when the performance review was drafted, and whether the review was changed at any time.

Finally, consider whether any physical evidence other than documents might be relevant. If the company confiscated a weapon or illegal drugs that the employee is accused of bringing to work, for example, those should be part of the investigation. If the company's trade secrets have been stolen, you might need to examine your computer system and access codes. However, don't be so zealous in your evidence gathering that you invade worker privacy, as discussed below.

Employees' Rights to Privacy

As you decide how to conduct your interview, be mindful of your employees' privacy rights. Depending on your state's laws and your own policies, you might be on shaky ground if you rummage through your workers' lockers or desk drawers. More stringent rules apply to intrusive searches, like drug tests and lie detector tests.

The Right to Privacy in the Workplace

The law protects a worker's right to privacy, but this right is limited. After all, the workplace is less private than the bedroom or the doctor's office. The workplace belongs to your company, and you are entitled to take some steps to make sure workers are performing their jobs safely and appropriately. However, if you intrude unnecessarily into employees' private concerns or property, you can get into legal trouble.

How can you tell whether you've crossed this line? Unfortunately, there are few hard-and-fast rules. The best you can do is to look at the question the way a judge would if faced with the facts in your workplace incident. A judge will evaluate the strength of two needs—the worker's reasonable expectations of privacy and your justification for performing the search—and determine which need is stronger. Your search will be considered legitimate and legal if your justifications outweigh the worker's reasonable expectations of privacy.

Employees' Reasonable Expectations of Privacy

The key to understanding whether employees have a reasonable expectation of privacy is to focus on the word reasonable. From a legal standpoint, a reasonable expectation is one that the average person would have in the same or similar circumstances. In other words, just because a person expects to have privacy in a certain situation doesn't mean that the law will defer to that expectation; it must be one that most reasonable people would share.

When trying to figure out whether your workers have a reasonable expectation of privacy in a given situation, you need to consider your policies and common sense.

Your policies. Your workers don't have a legitimate expectation of privacy if you have warned them that their communications or workspaces aren't private. Many companies limit their workers' privacy expectations by adopting policies that explicitly allow searches of work areas, email monitoring, and so on. If you have a policy stating, for example, that lockers are subject to search or that all company emails may be read, your workers won't be able to argue that they nonetheless expected that their lockers or email would be private. If you have this type of policy, you are free to conduct a search as long as you have a valid, work-related justification.

Common sense. Another way to measure a person's expectation of privacy is to simply subject it to the test of common sense. Think about whether the average worker would consider a particular space private. For example, if your employees routinely share desks, they probably have no reasonable expectation that their desks will remain private. However, if your workers keep personal items in their desks and take care to lock their desk drawers, they might reasonably expect more privacy. If your workers wear uniforms that are laundered on the premises, they probably have no expectation of privacy if they leave something incriminating in a pocket. However, many workers would feel violated if you searched the pockets of the clothes they were wearing.

Common sense also tells us that workers' expectations of privacy in their private belongings or their bodies are very strong. If you're considering a more intrusive search of a worker's own property—of purses and backpacks, for example—you must have a very compelling justification. And physical searches of an employee's body are always a bad idea. Talk to a lawyer before wading into these dangerous legal waters.

> ⓘ **CAUTION**
> **If your policies don't warn your employees that you might search and monitor the workplace, consider talking to a lawyer before you conduct a search.** The law in this area tends to change rapidly, as new technologies make it ever easier to monitor workers. Every year,

CHAPTER 5 | COMPLAINTS AND INVESTIGATIONS | 157

state legislatures and Congress consider proposed laws to protect workers' privacy rights. If you misjudge the situation, the searched worker can sue you for invasion of privacy.

Your Need to Investigate

A judge will balance your employees' reasonable expectations of privacy against your company's need to intrude. Only if your need is legitimate and overriding will your search pass legal muster. For example, if an employee complains about receiving harassing emails, you have a strong justification to find out who sent them. If you have been told that an employee's desk contains a weapon, you have compelling reasons for a search. And if you have had persistent theft problems during one shift, a locker search limited to employees on that shift will probably withstand legal scrutiny.

In considering your justifications, a judge might also consider how you conduct the search. If your methods are particularly intrusive, you could get into trouble, even if you have a legitimate purpose in conducting the search. For example, let's say you are searching a locker to investigate the theft of a fairly large item. Although you have a strong justification to search, you have no reason to read the worker's diary, rifle through the worker's wallet, or examine prescription drug bottles, even though all of these items might be in the locker that you are entitled to search.

Lie Detector Tests

If a worker denies accusations of wrong doing, you might be tempted to use a lie detector test (or polygraph) to get to the truth. However, these tests have been virtually outlawed by the federal Employee Polygraph Protection Act (29 U.S.C. § 2001), which generally prohibits private employers from requiring their workers to submit to lie detector tests or from disciplining workers who refuse to take such a test. This law makes an exception for workers who are accused of theft or embezzlement that causes the company to lose money. Even in these circumstances, however, strict rules govern how the test can be conducted. To find out more about the act, out the U.S. Department of Labor's website on the Act, at www.dol.gov/agencies/whd/polygraph.

RESOURCE
For more about the Employee Polygraph Protection Act. You can find a comprehensive discussion of the EPPA and other federal employment laws in *The Essential Guide to Federal Employment Laws,* by Sachi Clements (Nolo).

Drug Tests

Drug testing is a legal issue employers should approach with caution. Drug tests are highly intrusive, yet they can also be invaluable tools for preventing drug-related accidents and safety problems. Although you aren't legally prohibited from performing drug tests, you must have a strong, legitimate reason for doing so.

Because drug testing is intrusive, a worker who convinces a jury that the testing was illegal could cost you a lot of money and ruin your reputation as a fair employer. Before you perform any drug test or adopt a drug test policy, we strongly advise getting legal advice. In the event that you proceed, do so with legal assistance, and consider the following guidelines.

Whom to Test

A drug test is most likely to withstand legal scrutiny if you have a particular reason to suspect an employee of illegal drug use or if the employee's job involves a high risk of injury. Avoid a policy of testing every employee for drugs or randomly testing employees. Unless all of your workers perform dangerous jobs, random tests cast too wide a net. If you test all of your workers across the board, you are, by definition, not acting on a reasonable suspicion about a particular worker.

When to Test

Your drug testing will be on the safest legal ground if your primary motive is to ensure the safety of workers, customers, and members of the general public. You should limit testing to:

- employees whose jobs carry a high risk of injury to themselves or others (such as a forklift operator or pilot) or involve

security (such as a security guard who carries a gun)

- workers who have been involved in accidents, such as a delivery driver who inexplicably ran a red light and hit a pedestrian, and
- workers whom a manager or supervisor reasonably suspects of illegally using drugs (for example, because a manager notices signs of impairment like slurred speech or glassy eyes, sees the worker using an illegal drug, finds illegal drugs in the worker's possession, or observes a pattern of abnormal or bizarre behavior by the employee).

How to Test

Even with the strongest reasons for testing, you can still get into legal trouble over the way that you test. To be safe, make sure that you do all of the following:

- Use a test lab that is certified by the U.S. Department of Health and Human Services or accredited by the College of American Pathologists.
- Consult with a lawyer in developing your testing policy and procedures.
- Use a testing format that respects the privacy and dignity of each employee, to the extent possible. If your chosen drug test requires a urine sample, allow workers to give the sample privately or provide a monitor of the same sex, for example.

- Have a written policy in place about drug use in the workplace (including a discussion of the disciplinary steps you will take and under what circumstances) and your testing procedures (including when the test will be given, how it will be administered, and what substances—and at what levels—it will detect).
- Require employees to read your drug and alcohol policy and testing policy and sign an acknowledgment that they have done so.
- Document why you felt the test was necessary and how it was performed, each time you administer a drug test.
- Keep the test results confidential.
- Be consistent in how you deal with workers who test positive.

You can't force a worker to take a drug test. However, you can fire an employee who refuses to take a drug test, as long as you had sound reasons for testing.

CAUTION

Get help from a lawyer. Many states have their own drug testing rules that address when, how, and whom you may test. You might be required to have a written policy, provide employees with advance notice, or follow other requirements. Before you adopt a drug testing program, you should talk to an experienced local employment lawyer, who can make sure your policy doesn't violate any applicable laws.

Making the Decision

Now comes the hardest part: Once you've interviewed all the witnesses and gathered all the relevant evidence, you have to decide what really happened. If the complaining employee and the accused employee have offered conflicting stories—as they often do—you'll have to figure out who is telling the truth. After making your assessments, you must decide what action to take (if any) and document your decisions.

Interview the Main Players Again

Before making your decision, consider setting up another interview with the accused employee. Have you heard new allegations or information since you last interviewed the accused worker? If witnesses have added significant details or documents supporting the complaining employee have surfaced, it's probably a good idea to get the accused employee's response. Courts are more likely to find an investigation was fair and thorough—and its outcome reliable—if the accused employee is given the opportunity to respond to all the evidence before the employer makes a final decision.

Also consider conducting another interview with the complaining employee, if the accused employee or witnesses have denied the allegations or offered reasons why the complaining employee might not be telling the truth.

Evaluate the Evidence

If there is no dispute about what actually happened, you can skip this step. However, if there are important disagreements between witnesses—and particularly if the accused worker denies the facts of the complaint—you will have to figure out where the truth lies.

To begin, review the evidence you have gathered and your notes from interviews. Are there any facts to which everyone agrees? What are the major points of contention? As to each of these disputes, what did the witnesses say? Are there any documents supporting one version or the other?

Now you have to assess the credibility of each version of the facts. Although figuring out who's telling the truth can be difficult, your common sense will help you sort things out. As you're sifting through the evidence, consider:

- **Plausibility.** Whose story makes the most sense? Does one person's version of events defy logic or common sense?
- **Source of information.** Did the witness see or hear the event directly? Did the witness report firsthand knowledge or rely on statements from other employees or rumors?
- **Corroboration and conflicting testimony.** Are there witnesses or documents that support one side of the story? Does the evidence contradict someone's statements? Do the witnesses support

the person who suggested you interview them?
- **Contradictions.** Did any of the witnesses contradict themselves during your interview?
- **Demeanor.** How did the witnesses act during the interview? Did they appear to be telling the truth or lying? Did the accused employee overreact to the complaint or have no reaction at all? Did the complaining employee seem genuinely upset?
- **Omissions.** Did anyone leave out important information during the interview? Is there a sensible explanation for the omission?
- **Prior incidents.** Does the accused employee have a documented history of this type of misconduct?
- **Motive.** Does either the complaining worker or the accused worker have a motive to lie about or exaggerate the incident? Is there any history between these employees that affects their credibility?

Once you've considered these factors, you'll often find that one version of the events is really implausible, or at least that it makes a lot less sense than the other. In investigations, as in science, the adage holds true: The most obvious explanation is usually correct. However, if the web remains hopelessly tangled, you might have to end the investigation by admitting that you can't figure out what really happened. If there's evidence on both sides and it could've happened either way, this is your best option. We explain how to do this below (under "Inconclusive Results").

EXAMPLE 1: Stuart complained that Darcy had threatened to fire him for reporting to jury duty. Stuart said that Darcy made this threat in the lunch room on April 28, 20xx. Darcy seemed very surprised by this allegation; she agreed that she spoke to Stuart in the lunchroom about his jury summons but that she said only that she hoped Stuart didn't get picked to sit on a jury because jury duty can be so boring. Darcy suggested that the investigator speak to several witnesses, all of whom confirmed her side of events. Darcy also said that Stuart had seemed upset since his last performance review, when Darcy noted that Stuart hadn't met several of his performance goals for the year. When the investigator interviewed Stuart a second time to get his reaction to this, Stuart admitted that the witnesses were there but insisted that they must have heard Darcy incorrectly. He also admitted his bad feelings about the performance review.

In this case, the investigator can conclude that there was no wrongdoing. All of the witnesses support Darcy's version of events. Stuart can't explain this discrepancy.

Darcy has also offered a reason for Stuart's complaint, which Stuart hasn't denied.

EXAMPLE 2: Same as above, but one witness (a friend of Darcy's) confirms Darcy's version of the conversation and one witness (a coworker with whom Stuart often has lunch) confirms Stuart's version. Although Stuart admits his bad feelings about the performance review, he points out that he went to Darcy's manager shortly after his evaluation to talk about the review. The manager confirmed Darcy's opinion of Stuart's performance and explained how Stuart could improve. Stuart says that he felt more comfortable about the evaluation after this conversation, although Darcy was upset that Stuart went over her head and complained. Darcy denies being upset about this.

Without more evidence, the investigator can't reach a conclusion. There is a witness on each side. Both Stuart and Darcy claim that the other has a motive to lie, and both claim to be telling the truth. Darcy's manager can confirm his conversation with Stuart but doesn't know if Darcy was upset about the conversation or if Stuart remained upset about the evaluation. In short, this one could go either way.

Decide What to Do

Once you've evaluated the evidence, you must decide whether company policies were violated or misconduct occurred. This decision will dictate what actions you should take and what you should tell the employees involved.

Role of the Complaining Employee

Even if you take immediate and effective action against the wrongdoer, the complaining employee might be upset. Perhaps the complaining employee believes a harsher punishment should have been imposed, feels that their job performance or reputation have suffered because of the complaint, or doesn't believe the wrongdoer will shape up.

You are under no obligation to impose the punishment your complaining employee favors; your obligation is to be fair and reasonable to the accused employee and the rest of your workforce. However, you should listen carefully to the complaining employee's concerns. Perhaps the employee who claims that the wrongdoer will never change is worried about retaliation or further misconduct. If so, you can assure the complaining employee that you will deal swiftly with any such behavior. An employee who claims to have suffered unfairly because of the misconduct might have a point, for example, if they were unfairly denied a promotion, raise, or leave. Consider conferring such benefits retroactively.

Although complaining employees might well have their own axes to grind, they can also help you figure out whether you've chosen an effective remedy. If it isn't actually going to work, better to hear about it now when you can fix the problem than later from a jury.

No Misconduct

There are several situations in which you might find that no misconduct occurred. If something happened between the complaining and accused employee but it wasn't illegal or prohibited by your company policies, you might find that there was no misconduct. In these situations, you should consider whether the accused employee's behavior (or the complaining worker's conduct) warrants counseling or warning.

In rare cases, you might conclude that the complaint was false. If the complaining employee acted in good faith (for example, they misunderstood an incident or were confused about the accused employee's actions), no further action will likely be necessary. If the complaining employee lied intentionally, however, discipline against the complaining worker is in order. Consider the employee's motives, how serious the allegations were, and the disruptions to your workplace to determine an appropriate response.

Inconclusive Results

If the results of your investigation are inconclusive, you should tell both the complaining and the accused employee why you reached this conclusion. You might also remind the accused worker about the rule allegedly violated, to make sure everyone understands your expectations. If your investigation uncovered confusion about a particular policy (such as what constitutes sexual harassment or what is required under a safety rule), consider providing workplace training for all of your employees.

Misconduct

If you find that the accused employee has engaged in serious misconduct, you must take immediate corrective action. Use your progressive discipline policy as a guide. When you make your decision, consider the strength of the evidence. Remember, you might have to defend whatever action you take in court. Do you have strong, firsthand, and corroborated evidence of wrongdoing? If you are going to take harsh disciplinary measures, consider whether the evidence you gathered will support your decision.

After deciding how to discipline the wrongdoer, take care of it immediately. Meet with the employee to inform them of the results of the investigation and the discipline you will impose.

You must also meet with the complaining employee. Explain what you discovered in your investigation and that the accused employee has been disciplined, and describe any future steps you'll take to prevent further problems. Invite the employee to come to you with any future concerns about the situation.

TIP

If you decide that misconduct occurred, consider whether your workplace needs some training. If your investigation turned up significant confusion about company rules or appropriate workplace behavior, prevent further problems by training your employees on what you and the law require.

Document Your Decision

If you've followed the advice in this book, you've already documented every step of your investigation. At this point, you should have a written complaint (or notes from meeting with the complaining employee), notes from your other interviews (or written statements from the witnesses), and copies of any relevant documents or policies. You should also make a note of any proposed witness whom you were unable to interview and the reasons why.

Some investigators, particularly consultants who specialize in conducting investigations, prepare investigation reports. Although the contents vary, most contain a summary of the complaint, a list of witnesses contacted, a summary of each witness's statement, a list of documents or policies consulted, the investigator's conclusions and recommendations, and the reasons for those conclusions.

Attention to Detail

Figuring out how much detail to include in an investigation report or other documentation of an investigation can be tricky. If your investigation doesn't end the matter and you are later sued by the complaining employee or by the accused employee, you will almost certainly have to hand over this document to your opponent.

Your documentation doesn't have to memorialize every thought that crossed your mind during the investigation, nor should it. If you include a lot of extraneous detail, a jury might have trouble following your decision-making process. But make sure to write down all of the major decisions you made and why. For example, if you didn't believe a witness's statement, make a note of that and the reasons for your skepticism. Similarly, if you concluded that no misconduct occurred, write down all of the reasons for your decision. If you write extensive notes but later claim to have left out an important detail, the jury might decide that you're trying to build a case after the fact.

You don't have to prepare an exhaustive report. However, you should preserve your notes from the investigation and write down your conclusions.

If the results of your investigation were inconclusive, document the reasons why you were unable to sort things out. Note the conflicting evidence carefully. This documentation will be invaluable if similar allegations are later made against the accused employee—you'll have a record of previous problems to support any discipline you might impose.

Your documents should include a notation of any disciplinary steps taken. If your meeting with either the wrongdoer or the complaining employee was eventful, you might want to include notes from that meeting as well.

Once you've written down your conclusions, place them—along with all other documents relating to the investigation—in a special file devoted to the investigation. Don't place any documents relating to the investigation in any employee's personnel file. Although you might need to include some information in an employee's records (for example, the discipline imposed or the fact that an employee made a complaint that you found to be false), you should keep your notes and report in a separate investigation file. Keep the file with your other confidential employment records (such as employee medical records). This will help you avoid claims that you spread private or damaging information about your workers.

Sample Written Investigation Report

FROM: Myrtle Means

TO: File

RE: Investigation of Cynthia Smith Complaint

DATE: September 3, 20xx

I completed my investigation of Cynthia Smith's complaint against Jackie Starr on August 27, 20xx. Cynthia complained that Jackie had harassed her about her disability. Cynthia said that Jackie had made jokes about her wheelchair and had complained about having to make the restroom wheelchair accessible. (See notes from my interview with Cynthia on August 19, 20xx.)

I spoke to Jackie on August 20, 20xx. Notes from this interview are in the file. Jackie denied treating Cynthia any differently from her other direct reports. However, Jackie admitted that she had joked about Cynthia's wheelchair when her team was planning the company picnic; Jackie said she made these jokes because she felt bad that Cynthia would not be able to participate in some of the activities. She said Cynthia laughed, and she was surprised to hear that Cynthia was upset. Jackie also said that she complained about having to wait in line to use the women's restroom, because a stall had to be removed to make the room accessible to Cynthia.

Three witnesses heard Jackie's comments about the picnic: Tom Jones, Kathleen McDermott, and Diego Cameron. Tom and Diego both felt uncomfortable about Jackie singling out Cynthia; Kathleen didn't think Cynthia minded the jokes. All three confirmed that Jackie made jokes about Cynthia participating in the three-legged race and the volleyball game. (See my notes from these interviews.)

Martina Kowalsky heard Jackie complain about the restroom. Martina said that Jackie complained that 20 women were inconvenienced just so Cynthia would be more comfortable. (See my notes from my interview with Martina.)

I concluded that Jackie had acted inappropriately toward Cynthia. All of the witnesses confirmed the details of Cynthia's complaint. Jackie also confirmed the facts of the allegations, although she denied that she mistreated Cynthia.

Sample Written Investigation Report, continued

I gave Jackie a written warning on August 28, 20xx. I explained to her that she had violated company policy, had treated her employee disrespectfully, and had used poor judgment. I warned her that her behavior had to improve immediately. I arranged for her to attend a diversity management seminar next month.

I informed Cynthia of the results of my investigation on August 28, 20xx. I also told her that I had given Jackie a written warning and required her to attend training on diversity in the workplace. I asked Cynthia if she felt comfortable continuing to report to Jackie. Cynthia said that she did. She said that Jackie treated her fairly in work assignments and evaluations. Cynthia said that she hoped the training would help Jackie understand workers with disabilities. I told Cynthia that the company was very sorry for what happened to her and that she should feel free to come to me with any concerns about her working relationship with Jackie in the future. I also told Cynthia that the company planned to move the company picnic to a location with paved walkways and ramps and to hold events and games in which every worker could participate.

Dispute Resolution Programs

As we've stressed throughout this book, the best way to deal with any type of employee problem is to nip it in the bud. But first, you need to spot that bud. And the best way to do that is to encourage employees to come forward with their problems or complaints and to provide an effective means of resolution.

The formal complaint and investigation procedure described in Chapter 5 is intended primarily to handle potential illegalities, such as theft, harassment, or violence. What about problems that don't rise to this level but nonetheless have a negative effect on employee morale? For more important problems, what should you do if the employee isn't happy with the outcome of the investigation?

Many companies have responded to such challenges by adopting alternative dispute resolution (ADR) programs. These take many different forms: They can be voluntary or mandatory, they might be run by management or include a peer review component, they might be free or cost a fee, and so on. They run the gamut from simple open-door policies that encourage employees to bring their concerns to management to mandatory arbitration programs that require employees to give up their right to sue the company in exchange for using a private trial-like procedure.

What ADR programs have in common is that they're intended to be an alternative to litigation (hence their name). By offering employees other ways to have their grievances heard and addressed, companies hope to resolve these problems internally, without costly lawsuits. And some companies take things a step further by making participation in the program mandatory: A worker who wants to bring a claim against the company must use the company's procedures, not the court system.

TIP

Lower your insurance premiums with an effective ADR program. Many employers purchase employment practices liability insurance (EPLI) to limit the risk associated with employment lawsuits. When insurance companies decide whether to offer a company this coverage, and at what rates, they will typically consider any steps the company has taken to minimize the possibility of facing lawsuits, such as having an at-will employment policy, a written sexual harassment policy, and effective internal ADR procedures. If you have EPLI, talk to your carrier to find out whether adopting a particular type of ADR policy will save you some money.

This chapter explains the variety of ADR mechanisms that companies use, describes benefits and drawbacks of each, and provides tips on how to create and implement an ADR program at your company.

(!) CAUTION

Union employers: Check the collective bargaining agreement. If your work-place is unionized, internal grievance procedures are probably already required by the collective bargaining agreement. These detailed contracts between unions and employers typically include procedures that union members must use to raise complaints about pay, performance, discipline, and other personnel matters. If your workplace already has union grievance procedures in place, the union might well view any ADR program as an effort to replace those procedures or avoid your duty to bargain, which could lead to big trouble.

Types of Alternative Dispute Resolution

There are many types of ADR in the workplace. Some companies choose just one type; others adopt a multistage set of procedures. This section explains some common options and describes the primary benefits and disadvantages of using each.

Open-Door Policies

The least formal type of ADR programs are open-door policies: written policies inviting employees to bring their concerns and ideas to their immediate supervisors or to others within the company. Some open-door policies require workers to contact people directly up the company ladder. If the employee doesn't wish to go to an immediate supervisor, or if the supervisor's response doesn't satisfy the employee, the employee is then asked to take the problem to the next level of management. Other policies allow workers to bring issues to any manager in the company or to the human resources department.

Open-door policies tend to improve communication between employees and management, encourage employees to come forward with concerns early on, and signify to employees that you value their input. It's also very easy to implement an open-door policy. You won't need any outside experts, so these policies are free. Although your managers will need to know how to deal with employee concerns—and which concerns (such as allegations of harassment) to bring to the attention of higher management—these are things you'll want your managers to know anyway.

The only downside is that open-door policies can take up a lot of time. Your managers will have to listen attentively to employee concerns, no matter how seemingly unimportant. Yet the benefits gained by an open-door policy far outweigh the costs. And no matter how small a concern might seem, if an employee bothers to raise it, it's affecting at least that employee negatively, so time spent listening isn't necessarily wasted.

Designated Ombudsperson

Some companies designate an ombudsperson, whose primary job is to be available to workers raising complaints or concerns. When an employee comes forward with a problem, the ombudsperson tries to help the employee resolve it through informal means like counseling, talking to any other employees or managers who are involved, or presenting possible options for finding resolution.

Typically, the ombudsperson operates outside of a company's formal management structure. The purpose of this is to assure employees that the ombudsperson is neutral and independent. For the same reason, most ombudsperson programs offer employees the option of coming forward confidentially. At some point, however, especially with complaints of serious wrongdoing like harassment or other illegal behavior, this confidentiality might have to give way to the company's obligation to stop the misconduct.

> **EXAMPLE:** Hal owns a large software company in the Silicon Valley. His company has several hundred employees, 15 departments, and 40 managers or officers. The employees perform a variety of jobs. One of the company's several ADR offerings is having an ombudsperson available to talk to employees who don't feel comfortable raising concerns with their supervisors or the company's human resources department. Among the problems employees can bring to the ombudsperson are disputes with supervisors, concerns about working conditions, performance evaluation issues, and problems relating to coworkers. The ombudsperson will help the employee try to come up with creative ways to resolve the problem. If the employee gives permission, the ombudsperson will intervene and try to resolve the dispute in a way that's satisfactory to all parties.

Ombudsperson programs are quite common in large institutional settings, like colleges and hospitals. In these multilevel organizations, individuals can easily feel lost in the shuffle, and having a place to take their concerns can help diminish this feeling. Large companies can get this same benefit from designating an ombudsperson.

In smaller companies, however, it can be difficult to establish an ombudsperson program. For one thing, employees are less likely to believe that the ombudsperson is truly neutral in this setting. And problems are more likely to be known in a small company, so the confidential, behind-the-scenes nature of going to the ombudsperson could be lost. Smaller companies are also less likely to have the budget to devote a position entirely to the informal resolution of employee problems (and, hopefully, less likely to have enough problems to justify such a position).

Peer Review Programs

In a peer review program, employee complaints that can't be resolved informally are heard by a group—typically composed of some employees and some managers—that decides how the issue should be handled.

EXAMPLE: During Rachel's performance evaluation, her supervisor, Charles, told her that she wouldn't be receiving a merit raise. Charles said that Rachel's productivity as a salesperson was solid, but that her numbers weren't as high as some others on her team. Rachel agreed but said that her performance still warranted a raise because she had taken on additional responsibilities for her group, including training new salespeople and helping set up the team's software system for tracking leads, which took time away from her sales. Charles acknowledged Rachel's contributions but refused to change his mind about the raise.

When Rachel was unable to resolve the issue with Charles, she made a formal request to have the dispute heard by her company's peer review panel. A week later, four employees and three managers from outside Rachel's department met in a conference room. Rachel and Charles both had an opportunity to tell their sides of the story, and both brought documents, including Rachel's written performance appraisals, job description, and time sheets, as well as productivity numbers for the team. The panel asked both some questions, then met privately to reach a decision.

The panel decided that, even though Rachel's extra job duties weren't mentioned in her job description or performance evaluation, it seemed clear that Charles had asked her to handle them. The panel also found that Rachel's numbers weren't much lower than those of the other employees in her group, and that her customers seemed very satisfied with her work. As a result, the panel decided that Rachel deserved a merit raise. The panel also decided that Charles should update the job descriptions and performance targets of all of his reports to reflect their current job duties.

Often, companies limit the scope of issues the peer review panel can hear in order to reserve management's right to make and change policy. For example, a company might provide that the panel can deal only with alleged violations of company policy but can't handle complaints that a company policy should be changed or a new rule should be instituted. Even in these companies, however, the panel can make recommendations to management based on what it hears from employees.

As you can see from the example above, one benefit of a peer review program is flexibility. Because the panel is composed of company employees, it can come up with solutions tailored to the unique features of the workplace. It can also make recommendations that deal with the underlying reasons for a dispute: The panel recommended updating job descriptions and performance targets, so Charles and the employees he supervises could all be on the same page about expectations.

Another advantage of this type of system is credibility. Because employees have a seat at the table, they're more likely to see a peer review panel as fair and interested in their concerns. And this credibility will, in turn, encourage employees to come forward with issues, so the company has a chance to deal with them early on. To take advantage of this benefit, however, the company must let the panel do its work independently. If employees see the peer review program as a smokescreen and don't believe that employee panel members have a real say in outcomes, the program won't be effective.

Among the disadvantages of a peer review program are lost time and productivity. The company will have to train those who will sit on the panel, allow them to take time away from their other duties to hear and resolve complaints, and allow those involved in the dispute to spend some time preparing for and attending the hearing. And, of course, the company will have to abide by the panel's decisions, which can make for a tough transition if your company is used to a top-down management style.

Step Grievance Procedures

Modeled on union grievance procedures, a step program is a set of increasingly more formal options for handling complaints. It often includes some of the other ADR processes described here, each offered as a way to take the complaint further if the prior step doesn't resolve the issue to the employee's satisfaction.

A typical step program might start by asking employees to discuss the issue with their supervisors or another manager. If that isn't successful, the employee might next have the option of filing a formal written complaint, to be heard by a designated upper-level manager, a peer review panel, or some other decision-making person or body. If the employee isn't satisfied with the decision on the complaint, an appeal might be available, often to the company president or to an executive in charge of employee relations. Some companies include mediation or arbitration (described below) as a final step in the process.

EXAMPLE: Al's Appliances is a chain of warehouse stores that sells electronics, appliances, and other gadgets. The company has about 100 employees who work at its three stores. When two employees filed charges of discrimination with their state's fair employment practices agency, Al's management learned that a store manager was using derogatory language toward nonwhite employees, and that workers didn't know how—and were afraid—to raise this issue with management. Al's president decided that the company had to figure out a way to give workers a chance to raise issues and concerns internally, both to avoid future legal claims and to improve employee morale.

The company adopted a three-step grievance procedure. The first step was the company's open-door policy, which encourages employees to bring concerns to their immediate supervisor or the human resources department. If the issue isn't resolved at that level, the employee can file a formal complaint to be heard by a peer review panel: a group of four employees and three managers (the company chose an odd number of peers to avoid tie votes). An employee who doesn't like the peer review panel's decision can take the issue to arbitration, with fees to be paid by the company.

Because a step grievance procedure is essentially a combination of several types of ADR programs, you'll have to carefully consider each component to make sure it will work at your company. These procedures can have plenty of benefits, with employee satisfaction topping the list. Because a step procedure mimics a legal claim—with the equivalent of the right to appeal—employees are more likely to feel that they've had a fair chance to get their complaints heard. Also, a step program helps avoid personality disputes, because the employee will have an opportunity to voice concerns to various decision makers. And this type of program offers employees plenty of options: A worker who simply wants to raise a concern with a supervisor can do that, while an employee who wants to file a formal complaint has that opportunity as well.

The drawbacks of a step grievance procedure include lost time and resources. These programs typically offer employees a series of appeals. If more than a few employees wish to have their claims heard and reheard, the process will quickly become unwieldy, especially in smaller companies.

Mediation

Mediation is a process in which two people or groups involved in a dispute come together to try to find a fair and workable solution. They do so with the help of a mediator: a neutral third person trained in conflict resolution. Unlike a judge or an arbitrator, a mediator doesn't make decisions about the dispute. Instead, the mediator's job is to help the participants evaluate their goals and options to find their own solution or compromise.

Mediation can be very helpful in the employment context because of its ability to repair relationships—often, the employees will need to continue to work together. By allowing each person to give their side of the story, mediation can help improve employees' communication and understanding of one another. And because any solution that comes out of mediation must be mutual, mediation encourages problem solving, working together, and making some level of investment in a shared future.

Workplace mediation can take many forms. A company can hire or make available an outside mediator to resolve disputes, or it can train company employees or managers to act as mediators. Mediation might be available only for interpersonal disputes—for example, difficulties between coworkers or a disagreement over a performance appraisal—or it might be offered to resolve larger legal disputes between employees and the company (for example, if an employee claims to have been discriminated against).

Because it requires buy-in from all participants and offers flexibility in choosing solutions, mediation is often very popular with employees, who see it as an opportunity to participate in resolving their concerns.

However, the fact that mediation is noncoercive—that is, that no outside person makes a decision and that no resolution will be reached unless all parties agree to it—means that mediation has the potential to be a waste of time. Some employers complain that mediation is too open-ended because of the possibility that no conclusion will be reached. Also, mediation can be expensive, whether you hire outside mediators or train your own employees.

Arbitration

Of all the varieties of ADR programs used by employers, arbitration has gotten the most attention from courts and the public. Many companies routinely require all new hires to sign an arbitration agreement. These agreements often require employees to give up their right to sue over any workplace issue and instead bring any legal claims to arbitration—a trial-like procedure in which disputes are heard by an arbitrator who acts as a judge. After hearing evidence and arguments, the arbitrator issues a decision. If the arbitration is "binding," both parties are stuck with the arbitrator's ruling and can appeal to a regular court only in very limited circumstances (for example, if the arbitrator was biased). In nonbinding arbitration, both

sides are free to accept or reject the arbitrator's decision.

Mandatory arbitration programs, under which an employee must participate in arbitration before or instead of suing, once generated a lot of controversy and a lot of litigation. In a mandatory, binding arbitration program, employees are required to give up their right to sue their employers in court over disputes arising from the employment relationship. Because employees are giving up an important legal right, the process that takes its place must meet certain minimum standards of fairness. In the early days of mandatory arbitration, some employers instituted programs that were too favorable to themselves. Employees challenged these programs in court, where judges expressed disapproval of requirements that tipped the scales too heavily in the employer's favor.

> CAUTION
> **Enforcement agencies likely aren't bound by your arbitration agreement.** Some enforcement agencies, such as the EEOC, are empowered to bring cases against employers on their own behalf. If, for example, an employee complains to the EEOC about discrimination, the EEOC may decide to sue the employer itself. In this situation, the agency won't be required to arbitrate, even if your employee has signed an arbitration agreement. This same reasoning has been applied to lawsuits brought by the U.S. Labor Department.

Courts have, for example, struck down required mandatory arbitration programs that:

- require the employee to pay for all or most of the cost of arbitration
- limit the participants' rights to engage in "discovery"—the process of exchanging documents, questioning witnesses, and otherwise gathering evidence before the arbitration
- require employees to arbitrate all claims against the company but allow the company to decide whether to arbitrate or go to court, and
- limit the monetary damages employees can receive to amounts far less than what an employee could be awarded in court.

Now that many of these disputes have been hammered out, courts routinely uphold employer efforts to enforce mandatory arbitration agreements that meet basic fairness requirements. (See "What Makes an Arbitration Program Fair?" below.) However, mandatory arbitration programs remain unpopular with employees, who often see them as an effort to take away workplace rights and avoid responsibility for wrongdoing.

No Arbitration of Sexual Harassment and Sexual Assault

Although legal claims for sexual harassment have been recognized by courts since the 1970s, the #MeToo movement has laid bare a dirty secret: Despite legal protections, workplace trainings, and company policies prohibiting harassment, sexual harassment continues to be a pervasive and destructive problem for working women, with very serious consequences.

#MeToo activists argue that harassment has persisted, in part, because of secrecy. They have targeted two strategies employers have used to keep harassment claims out of the spotlight: confidentiality provisions in settlement agreements and mandatory arbitration agreements, which require harassment claims to be raised in private proceedings rather than in open court.

In response to these concerns, Congress passed the Ending Forced Arbitration Act in 2022. This law prohibits employers from enforcing pre-dispute arbitration agreements in cases involving sexual harassment or sexual assault.

The courts are still sorting out how the Ending Forced Arbitration Act will apply in practice. However, for employers who require employees to sign mandatory arbitration agreements, the upshot is clear: Those agreements will likely not be enforceable if an employee is raising issues of sexual harassment or sexual assault.

Mandatory Versus Binding Arbitration

It's easy to confuse "mandatory" arbitration with "binding" arbitration; after all, they sound pretty similar. But the legal meanings of these two terms are different from what you might expect.

Mandatory arbitration means that the employee is required to arbitrate disputes, either as a first step before filing a lawsuit or as a substitute for filing a lawsuit.

Binding arbitration means that the decision is final and that both parties must abide by it. Although they might have a limited right to appeal for extreme arbitrator bias or misconduct, the arbitrator's decision is ordinarily the last word.

Mandatory arbitration can be binding or nonbinding. If the arbitration is intended as a substitute for litigation, it will typically be binding. However, some companies require employees to submit disputes to nonbinding arbitration before filing a lawsuit. An employee who is pleased with the arbitrator's decision can accept it, and that's the end of the problem. An employee who is unhappy can file a lawsuit.

Similarly, binding arbitration can be mandatory or voluntary. Some companies give employees the option of submitting disputes to binding arbitration. If the employee agrees, the arbitrator's decision will be final.

Options that are more employee friendly include voluntary arbitration, in which employees can choose whether or not to arbitrate their claims, and nonbinding arbitration, in which either the employee or the company can reject the arbitrator's decision and sue. Because these options preserve the employee's right to sue, they also face far fewer legal challenges.

However, voluntary and nonbinding arbitration have drawbacks, as well. First and foremost, they don't offer the prime advantage of mandatory arbitration: limiting employee lawsuits. If an employee can sue after arbitrating, your company will potentially pay twice to decide the same claim. If an employee can sue instead of arbitrating,

your arbitration program will have saved you nothing. As courts have increasingly upheld mandatory arbitration requirements, these kinder and gentler alternatives have become less popular.

TIP

Consider reserving arbitration for legal claims. Because arbitration is an involved procedure that requires significant time and money, many companies make it available only for legal claims: that is, claims that employees could raise in court. This helps employers avoid shelling out substantial fees and spending valuable time planning a defense to claims like "I should have received a '7' rather than a '6' for 'Teamwork' on my performance evaluation."

Which Procedures Are Right for Your Company?

Now that you know something about the various types of ADR programs, you can start thinking about whether to adopt one at your company.

To achieve your goal of encouraging employees to voice their concerns, you will need to come up with a program that fits your company's style, resources, and needs.

What Is Your Company's Style and Culture?

Some companies are laid-back, informal places, while others have a more traditional, buttoned-down hierarchy. Where your company falls on this spectrum should inform your ADR program. A formal dispute resolution mechanism, such as arbitration or grievance hearings, might work well for a very structured company but fail miserably in a company where workers are used to sitting down with managers to talk things out.

Also consider your workers' attitudes toward the company. Does your company encourage and listen to employee input? Do employees feel like valued parts of the company team? If so, you should probably look at dispute resolution methods that involve teamwork, such as open-door

What Makes an Arbitration Program Fair?

The American Arbitration Association (AAA) is one of the nation's largest providers of arbitration and mediation services. Many contracts—including many in which the parties agree to arbitrate employment disputes—specifically state that the parties agree to use an arbitrator provided by the AAA or to use the AAA's arbitration rules.

For employment disputes, the AAA has adopted national rules for employment arbitration. Under these rules, employers that name the AAA in their arbitration contracts must submit the program to the AAA at least 30 days before putting it into effect, so the AAA can make sure the program meets its standards. Among other things, the AAA rules provide all of the following:

- All participants must have the right to counsel or some other representative in the arbitration.
- The parties are entitled to discovery necessary for a full and fair exploration of the issues in dispute.
- The arbitrator may make any award that would have been available in court.
- The employer must generally pay all costs of the arbitration, other than a fee capped at no more than $1,000 to be paid by the employee.

To view the AAA rules, go to the organization's website at www.adr.org and search for "Employment Arbitration Rules & Mediation Procedures."

Mediation and Arbitration Hybrids

Hybrid variations on the basic processes of mediation and arbitration combine elements of both in an effort to bring more finality to mediation or limit the power of the arbitrator. Here are some common variations:

- **Mediation with a recommendation.** If mediation ends without an agreement, the parties can ask the mediator for a written recommendation. The parties can accept the recommendation, reject it, or use it as a way to restart their negotiations.

- **Mediator's proposal.** If the parties agree, the mediator can propose a settlement (often simply a dollar figure), then show it to each party separately. The parties then tell the mediator privately whether they accept or reject the proposal. If both parties accept, the mediator lets the parties know and the dispute is settled as the proposal indicates. Otherwise, the mediator simply says the proposal failed, without saying who accepted or rejected.

- **Med/arb.** If mediation is unsuccessful, the mediator (or a new neutral party) then acts as an arbitrator and makes a binding decision. This hybrid provides assurance that, one way or the other, the dispute will be resolved.

- **High/low arbitration.** To reduce the risk of an unacceptable binding arbitration award, the parties agree in advance to parameters of high and low dollar amounts that limit the arbitrator's authority in deciding a damage award. For example, they might agree that the arbitrator can award no less than $5,000 and no more than $20,000 to the winning party.

- **Baseball arbitration.** After presenting evidence and arguments, each party gives the arbitrator a figure for which they would be willing to settle the case. The arbitrator must choose one party's number.

- **Night baseball arbitration.** As in baseball arbitration, each party sets a settlement value on the case and exchanges it with the other party. However, these figures aren't revealed to the arbitrator; it's called "night baseball" because the arbitrator is in the dark. The arbitrator makes a decision, then the parties must accept whichever of their figures is closer to the arbitrator's award.

programs, peer review, or mediation. An arbitration program or required grievance procedure could lead employees to feel that their rights are being diminished, which could cause resentment and morale problems.

On the other hand, if your company is more hierarchical and workers are comfortable with a top-down management style, a formal complaint and decision-making procedure might be a better fit. An arbitration program or internal appeal procedure could be less disruptive than a process that requires employees to take on new roles as decision makers in resolving disputes.

What Resources Can You Devote to the ADR Program?

Some ADR procedures require very little money and training. For example, an open-door policy takes advantage of your existing structure and the skills of your managers. A step grievance procedure might also require minimal resources, if your managers are up to the task. Other types of programs, such as peer review and mediation that uses employees as mediators, will require some initial training for the employees who will be making and facilitating decisions.

At the other end of the spectrum, programs that rely on outside personnel, such as mediators or arbitrators, will be far more expensive. And if you decide to use arbitration, you will need to consult a lawyer to make sure your program will stand up to legal scrutiny.

What Are Your Goals?

Although all ADR methods are designed to resolve disputes and allow for the airing of grievances, other goals might dictate that you choose one type of program over another.

For example, if you're eager to improve communication and encourage employee participation in making company decisions, open-door policies, peer review programs, and mediation are all good options. If you're more interested in avoiding lawsuits, you might want to choose methods that give employees their "day in court," such as step grievance procedures or arbitration. (And if your top priority is to stay out of court, talk to a lawyer about mandatory arbitration.)

How Large Is Your Company?

The fewer employees you have, the less sense it makes to adopt formal procedures, such as arbitration or a step grievance program. If your company is small, you're less likely to have the human resources to offer peer review, levels of appeal, and decision makers outside of the employee's chain of command.

So what can you do at a small company?

Adopt an open-door policy, for starters. If possible, give employees the option of taking their concerns up the ladder; if your company ladder more closely resembles a step stool, you could simply say that employees who aren't satisfied with their supervisors' responses can take their concerns straight to the president or owner.

Do You Have Established Policies and Procedures?

As you have no doubt concluded, we believe that consistent application of fair, established company policies is essential for preventing and dealing with employee problems. It also gives you more options when designing an ADR program. Procedures that call for final judgments—such as an appeal process or arbitration—are better suited to companies that have clear written procedures in place. Otherwise, decision makers won't have much to go on when trying to figure out how the problem should be resolved.

> **EXAMPLE:** Ron's Repairs started as a 2-person mechanic shop but now employs 40 people in 3 locations. The company grew fast, and Ron hasn't made the time to create an employee handbook or write down company policies. As a result, the manager of each shop does things a little bit differently.
>
> Ron reads an article about ADR and decides it sounds like a good idea. He adopts a step grievance procedure, by which employees bring issues to their own store manager, then to a peer review panel, then finally to Ron for a final resolution. In the very first grievance filed, a mechanic complained that he was being asked to work too much overtime. Many employers have policies that lay out the rules for who gets priority to work overtime or avoid overtime. Ron's doesn't have any overtime policies, however, so each store follows the rules set by its manager.
>
> The complaining employee's manager quickly dismisses the employee's concerns, because the manager faithfully followed his own system for assigning overtime. The peer review panel can't reach a decision: Because each shop has a different procedure, no one can figure out what the company's policy is, and the panel doesn't have the authority to create policies. When the dispute finally reaches Ron's desk, all he can say for sure is that he should have come up with an overtime policy a long time ago.

If you don't yet have written policies, please heed our advice to create them as soon as possible. (See Chapter 11 for tips that will help you get started.) In the meantime, you'll probably be better off using less formal ADR methods—such as an open-door policy or ombudsperson—that don't require anyone to try to figure out what your policies are (or should be).

CAUTION

If using ADR, talk to a lawyer. You can do a lot of the initial work yourself, but definitely consult a lawyer before instituting your policy. ADR programs create plenty of legal risks. For example, many courts have held that a mandatory ADR program can create an implied contract that employees won't be fired for misconduct unless they've had a chance to "grieve" the issue through the company's program, an outcome you want to avoid. On the other hand, if you work too hard to avoid creating a contract, you will have trouble arguing that employees must use the program: If the company doesn't have to, then why should they? A lawyer can also help you think through options and come up with a program that will minimize your legal risks. And you should absolutely talk to a lawyer before adopting any kind of arbitration program.

Tips for Creating an Effective ADR Program

Once you've considered all the angles and decided what type of ADR program will work for you, it's time to sit down with a lawyer and come up with a detailed written program.

No matter what type of ADR program you adopt, experts agree that all effective workplace programs have some things in common. Here are 10 tips that will help you make your program a success.

1. Get With the Program

Once you decide to adopt an ADR process, don't sabotage your efforts by denying it the resources necessary to succeed. Establishing an effective program will require the company to commit time and money. You might need to: train managers, peer reviewers, and internal mediators; create an ombudsperson position or designate someone to assist employees who wish to bring complaints; ask company bigwigs to set aside some valuable time to make decisions on employee grievances; and pay a lawyer to review your program and policies.

This investment will pay off in the long run, as you realize the benefits an effective ADR program offers. But you won't reap any advantages unless you commit the necessary resources to your ADR program up front.

2. Train Managers

Your managers might not share your enthusiasm for an ADR program. To some managers, giving employees a way to raise concerns and complaints will sound like more work, more challenges to their authority, and more oversight from senior company executives. And they're not entirely wrong; they just aren't seeing the whole picture. You'll want to supplement this view by letting managers know that effective ADR will also make their employees happier, save the company money, and help identify policies that aren't working—goals that all managers should share.

3. Generate Employee Support

Of course, there's no point in adopting an ADR program unless employees are going to use it. And employees won't use it unless they feel that the program is fair and effective.

Having a peer review component will go a long way toward building credibility for the program. Following the tips in this section will also help you create procedures that employees can support.

In addition, you might want to create some way for employees to give feedback on the program. In soliciting employee feedback, it's always a good idea to give employees the option of making their comments anonymously, through an unsigned written evaluation form, anonymous suggestion box, or online survey.

4. Prohibit Retaliation

As explained in Chapters 2 and 5, an employer engages in retaliation when it disciplines, fires, or takes any negative action against a worker for coming forward with a good-faith complaint. Retaliation is illegal in many circumstances, which should be reason enough to avoid it. But if you need another incentive, consider that employees won't bring concerns to your attention if you punish them for doing so. The goal of your program is to find out about problems by encouraging employees to come forward, not to scare employees into silence.

5. Offer Some Confidentiality

The best ADR programs give employees a variety of options for raising complaints. After all, your employees have different personalities and styles, so it shouldn't be surprising that one employee might be comfortable filing a formal complaint while another might want to seek help behind the scenes.

You can't—and shouldn't—promise complete confidentiality for all complaints. As explained in Chapter 5, if an employee tells you or any manager about certain kinds of problems (such as harassment), the company is legally responsible for taking action. And you won't be able to investigate and deal with the problem effectively if you have to protect the complaining employee's identity throughout the process.

However, you should tell employees in any written materials about your ADR program that you will try to keep their complaints as confidential as possible, if that is their wish. This will encourage hesitant employees to come forward while preserving the leeway you might need if serious problems surface.

6. Make Employee Assistance Available

Experts say that the most successful ADR programs offer some kind of help to employees who want to raise concerns. This assistance can include having someone (perhaps from the human resources department, for example) available to explain the ADR process, allowing the employee to bring a coworker or friend to internal hearings, or paying part of the cost of an employee's legal consultation.

Why would a company pay a lawyer—even in part—to oppose the company? For one thing, doing so can increase employee support of the ADR program (which can save the company more money in the long run). If employees know that they can get independent legal advice, they're more likely to feel that the process is fair. And employers who've been around the legal block know that sometimes an employee's lawyer can be their best friend: If the employee is emotionally invested in a dispute but doesn't stand much chance of success in court, a good lawyer can convince the employee to drop the issue and move on.

7. Communicate the Program's Goals and Procedures

Employees also won't use the ADR program unless they know about it. And they won't know about it unless you tell them—positively and repeatedly—how the program works and why you adopted it. Explain that you want to know about employee problems so you can resolve them quickly. Tell employees about their options and how to begin the process. Some experts also advise employers to periodically report back to employees on how the program is doing: how many complaints have been filed, how many were resolved, whether employees were generally satisfied with the procedure, and so on.

TIP

Employees probably don't see avoiding lawsuits as a worthy goal. Although staying out of court is a major motivation for companies to adopt an ADR program, it's not one you should necessarily advertise to your workers. The more you talk about helping the company avoid lawsuits, the more workers are likely to suspect that you are more interested in limiting their rights than in hearing and resolving their concerns. Instead, emphasize how the program will benefit workers by giving them an inexpensive (or free) forum where their concerns can be heard—and resolved—quickly.

8. Take Action to Address Valid Complaints

Your ADR program won't have much credibility with employees—and you won't get the full benefit of adopting it—unless you deal with legitimate employee concerns. For example, if several employees complain that a manager is playing favorites and causing resentment, you should look into it. Of course, it's possible that the employees have misjudged the situation, but it's certainly also possible that you have a problem manager on your hands.

Similarly, if a particular policy or procedure seems to be fueling a lot of grievances, you should consider whether the policy could use some tweaking or should be tossed out altogether. For example, if you adopt productivity quotas that employees aren't meeting, you should think about whether you've set them too high.

Your first sign of trouble could be a raft of complaints in your internal ADR system from employees who disagree with poor performance ratings they received after the quotas were adopted.

Once those problems surface through internal complaints, take advantage of your opportunity to intervene and make corrections early.

Doing so will quickly gain employee respect for your ADR program and encourage employees to raise concerns.

9. Give Employees a Forum

Successful ADR programs let employees tell their sides of the story. Many employee lawsuits are fueled by the feeling that no one is listening and no one cares; employees who have no meaningful forum for their complaints within the company are more likely to seek their day in court to share those concerns with a judge and jury. When you give employees a meaningful opportunity to be heard, you take away a major motivation for litigation and you gain valuable insight into what's wrong and what's right in your organization.

10. Don't Be Greedy

Employers get into trouble—with their employees and with the courts—when they come up with rules and procedures that stack the deck too heavily in their favor. This comes up most often in mandatory arbitration, where businesses have had their ADR programs invalidated by courts because the programs limited employee damages or forced employees to pay prohibitively expensive fees. But even less formal types of ADR can seem unfair to employees if avenues for complaint are limited, if concerns aren't taken seriously, or if procedures the company establishes seem to favor the company (such as instituting short deadlines for making complaints, prohibiting employees from questioning witnesses or looking at relevant company documents, or empowering decision makers who are seen as biased).

Making the Decision to Fire

No matter how good your employee relations, your workplace policies, and your intentions, you'll eventually face one of the toughest decisions employers have to make: whether to fire an employee.

This chapter will take some of the guesswork and anxiety out of that decision. First, we discuss the types of misconduct, performance issues, and other problems that should prompt you to think about letting a worker go. Then we explain, step by step, what to consider when making the decision. These guidelines will help you figure out if you have a valid, legal reason to fire, when to consider salvaging the employment relationship, and whether you've done all you can to protect yourself from a wrongful termination lawsuit.

Is It Time to Consider Firing?

Most employers start thinking about terminating an employee in one of two situations. In the first, a worker commits a single act of serious misconduct that's dangerous or potentially harmful to the business. Employers usually learn about these problems immediately, through reports from coworkers or customers, or from firsthand experience with the employee. These problems must be handled quickly and carefully.

In the second common scenario, an employee's performance or conduct problems have persisted, despite the employer's efforts to counsel and correct. Although these problems aren't immediately threatening to the company, they will eventually erode the morale and discipline of other workers and the productivity of the business. Once a worker demonstrates an inability or unwillingness to improve, it's wise to consider termination.

Dangerous, Illegal, or Deceptive Conduct

If an employee commits any of the following types of misconduct, even a single time, you should immediately investigate and consider firing:

- **Violence.** This includes fighting with coworkers; pushing and shoving; throwing books, furniture, or office items; vandalizing company property; or any other physical acts against people or property.
- **Threats of Violence.** Statements about plans to harm, "get," or kill anyone (including self-harm) or bring a weapon to work merit immediate attention.
- **Stalking.** This comes up most often in cases of sexual harassment or workplace romance gone awry but can also arise out of pure hostility. An employee might stalk a supervisor or manager in order to intimidate that person, for example.
- **Possession of an unauthorized weapon.** Your workplace policies should make it clear that weapons aren't allowed in the workplace unless authorized and necessary to perform work duties.

- **Theft or other criminal behavior directed toward the company.** These acts include embezzling, defrauding the company, or illegally using the company's intellectual property.
- **Dishonesty about important business issues.** The occasional fudge about progress on a project or reasons for time off is probably not a termination-worthy offense, but an employee who lies about whether orders have been filled or customers have been served, for example, must be dealt with.
- **Use of illegal drugs or alcohol at work.** Using drugs or alcohol at work (other than drinking in moderation at company events where alcohol is served), or showing up at work impaired, is cause for concern.
- **Harassing or discriminatory conduct.** Accusations of serious harassment—including touching another employee sexually or insisting on sexual favors—must be dealt with immediately. Investigation is also warranted if an employee has been accused of discriminatory conduct.
- **Endangering health and safety in the workplace.** An employee who fails to follow important safety rules, uses machinery in a dangerous way, or exposes coworkers to injury—whether intentionally or through inattention or lack of care—could be a huge liability for you.

- **Assisting a competing business.** Revealing your trade secrets to a competitor or using your intellectual property to work for or start a competing company is extremely serious misconduct.

Dealing With Dangerous Employees

Taking any negative employment action against a worker who threatens or commits violence can be scary. However, it might help to know that experts believe employment policies that encourage open communication, mutual respect, and an opportunity to air grievances—like the policies we describe in earlier chapters—go a long way toward diminishing the potential for violence.

If you're faced with suspending a worker for violence, threats, or carrying a weapon, make sure to communicate the reason for your decision calmly and respectfully, giving the employee an opportunity to respond. Provide reassurance that you want to hear the worker's side of the story, that you'll investigate the situation quickly, and that you won't make any final decisions until you've talked to everyone involved. Don't lose your temper or speak with sarcasm or humor.

If you believe that the employee could become violent, have security personnel stand by to assist you. Hold your suspension meeting at the end of the last day of the work week, when fewer workers will be on site. Also consider getting advice from a workplace violence consultant.

Lawsuits for Failure to Fire

In some states, you can actually be sued for not firing a worker (or in legal parlance, for "negligent retention"). If you knew—or should have known—that your employee posed a risk of danger to other employees or the public, and that employee harms others while working for you, you can be sued for failing to fire that worker.

For example, if you discover that one of your employees threatened to harm a coworker and you fail to take the threat seriously, the coworker might be able to sue you if the threat is carried out. Similarly, if you suspect that your delivery worker is driving under the influence but you fail to take steps to investigate or put a stop to the situation, you could be liable to a pedestrian whom the worker hits while driving drunk.

To avoid these problems, investigate quickly and carefully. Don't think that a "what I don't know won't hurt me" approach can shield you from legal liability. Judges have ruled that even employers that don't know of an employee's dangerous conduct may be held responsible if a reasonable employer would have known. Once you have investigated, immediately discipline or terminate the worker, as appropriate.

As soon as you learn about these types of misconduct, suspend the worker immediately (with pay) and investigate the incident. Get the employee out of the workplace, but don't immediately fire the worker. Instead, take the time to figure out what really happened.

Persistent Issues

Some workers are just unable or unwilling to improve, no matter how many times they're counseled, warned, or disciplined. At some point, you'll have to decide whether they've reached the last rung of your progressive discipline policy's ladder. If an employee fails to improve after a couple of written warnings, you'll have good cause for termination. Persistent problems that might warrant termination include:

- **Poor performance.** Workers who can't measure up to your reasonable expectations drain resources and cause morale problems among the employees who pick up the slack.
- **Violations of minor safety and health rules.** An employee who violates a major rule usually falls in the "one time only" category, described above. However, an employee who repeatedly fails to follow minor health and safety requirements— like a ban on smoking or a requirement to use equipment in a particular way— is either extremely careless or unwilling to follow the rules. Either way, it's a problem you must address.
- **Insubordination.** A worker who always bucks authority, who refuses to take orders, or who questions your every request will quickly compromise your leadership and ability to get things done.

Don't Be Afraid to Fire Poor Performers

For many employers, firing a worker is cause for anxiety and perhaps even a little guilt. It's a big decision, and one that can have far-reaching effects on the life of the fired worker and your company. But don't let these concerns stop you from firing a truly incompetent worker. Retaining a problem employee decreases workplace morale, reduces your company's productivity, encourages other workers to behave badly, and causes you no end of frustration. Even with the risk of litigation that comes with any firing, your business will ultimately be better off.

When you consider whether to fire someone for persistent misconduct, look at the history of prior warnings or coaching sessions. For example, a worker who has been late several times in the last few months presents a larger problem than one who has been late several times in the last few years. If the misconduct is spread over a long period of time, consider giving the worker another chance, even if you've reached the end of your progressive discipline policy. Juries tend to be a bit skeptical about employers that rely on stale infractions as a reason to fire.

- **Sleeping on the job.** Probably most of your workers have the occasional low-energy day after a late night. But an employee who regularly uses the workday to catch up on sleep is affecting productivity.

- **Abuse of leave (taking unauthorized leave or using leave for improper purposes).** Employees who take unfair advantage of your leave policies (by, for example, using sick leave to extend a vacation) not only hurt your company's productivity but also set poor precedent for other employees.

- **Excessive absences or tardiness.** An employee who's rarely working can't get a lot done. At some point, a worker's repeated absences or lateness will affect both your bottom line and the morale of your workers who show up faithfully, on time.

Making the Decision to Fire: An Employer's Checklist

Although workplace difficulties can be broadly grouped into types, every worker's situation is unique. This can make it tough for employers to be sure that their management decisions are consistent and fair.

It can also be difficult for employers to sort out their own feelings about a worker who might have to be fired. After all, we spend many of our waking hours at work, developing relationships that are not only professional, but social and personal, as well. Your intuition about people, your sense of whether they'll be able to improve and turn things around, and your knowledge of how their personal situations might be affecting their workplace conduct can all help you make smart management decisions. But employers have to be careful not to let personal feelings dictate their firing decisions. Any appearance of favoritism can lead to bad feelings, anger, and lawsuits.

Minimize these problems by following the same basic decision-making process every time you face a potential firing. Follow the 10 steps explained below to ensure that you've considered every angle before firing that problem employee.

You can find a checklist with these steps at the end of this chapter, as well as on this book's companion page (see Appendix A for details).

Step 1: Investigate the Conduct or Incident

If you've already investigated the incident or if the accused worker admits committing the misconduct in question, move on to Step 2. If there's some question as to what has happened, however, your first step is to investigate, no matter how serious the offense—even when you catch the employee apparently "in the act." There's always the possibility, no matter how slim, that things aren't what they appear to be. And the worker might have an explanation or reason for the misconduct that isn't immediately apparent.

For serious offenses, impose a paid suspension to remove the worker from the workplace while you investigate. Follow the guidelines in Chapter 5 to get to the bottom of things.

Take Away the Element of Surprise

When you consider whether to fire a worker, picture yourself breaking the news to the employee. What reaction do you imagine the worker will have? If your answer includes the word "surprised," proceed with caution: Chances are that you haven't done everything you should to protect yourself from a lawsuit.

A worker won't be surprised by the possibility of termination if you publicize your workplace policies widely; give fair, accurate, and regular performance evaluations; and follow your progressive discipline policy consistently. A worker who's genuinely surprised by a firing discussion is one who wasn't aware of company policy, didn't understand that their behavior was falling short of expectations, or didn't think the company would enforce its own rules. In almost every case, workers should know there's a problem well before receiving a pink slip.

Step 2: Check the Worker's Personnel File

Never proceed without reading the personnel file, even if you think you know its contents. What you find—and what you *don't* find—can have important legal repercussions.

Persistent Problems

Hopefully, if you are dealing with persistent problems in performance, attendance, or attitude, these issues will be documented in the file. If you have proper documentation of the worker's problems, move ahead to Step 3.

If you don't find sufficient documentation on file, you should seriously consider giving the employee another chance. This time, make sure to follow your discipline policy to the letter and document each step.

> **EXAMPLE:** Ramon's employer is considering firing him for poor performance. When she reviews Ramon's personnel file, she finds that he received a written warning from his new supervisor three months ago for failing to meet his sales quota. The employer knows that Ramon has had performance problems for more than a year. However, Ramon's previous manager failed to keep track of these problems, choosing instead to speak informally to Ramon without documenting the conversations. Because of the lack of documentation, it's a wiser decision at this point to discipline Ramon instead of firing him. If he fails to improve after the company has properly implemented its discipline policy—with documentation—the employer will be in a safer legal position to fire him.

Does the File Contain Evidence of Good Performance?

When you review your employee's personnel file, pretend you're a lawyer representing your employee. Are there documents you could use to show that the worker shouldn't have been fired? If your answer is yes, think twice before firing, or the next time you see those documents might be in a courtroom, as exhibits in your former employee's wrongful termination lawsuit.

Favorites of the employee's lawyer include glowing performance appraisals, merit raises, commendations, and promotions, particularly if they appear to contradict your reasons for firing. Of course, even the worst employee might have some good qualities, which you've duly recorded in evaluations. But if you're firing a worker for poor performance despite positive reviews and merit increases, you're asking for trouble.

This advice goes for almost any persistent offense. An employee who gets fired for insubordination shouldn't be able to point to a performance review praising their teamwork, people skills, and willingness to go the extra mile. When reviewing the file, make sure that what you see is consistent with your reason for firing. If it isn't, your employee should probably be given more time to improve. Or you should consult with an attorney.

A Single Offense

If your worker has committed a serious or egregious offense, there might be no previous signs of trouble in the personnel file. That's nothing to worry about: The severity of the offense gives you good cause to fire, even if the employee was previously a shining star. Sometimes, however, the employee will have a history of misconduct. You might have decided to give the worker another chance, or perhaps the previous incident warranted only minor discipline. In these cases, the file should document all prior incidents, your discussions with the worker about them, and the discipline imposed.

> **EXAMPLE:** Carrie shows up at work with a handgun in her purse. When her supervisor talks to her about it, Carrie claims that she did not know she was prohibited from bringing her gun into the workplace. Although she knows of the company's "no weapons" policy, she says that she believed the policy didn't apply if the weapon was properly licensed. Carrie's explanation, though thin, might have been enough to give her another chance; however, in her personnel file is a previous written warning from her supervisor at a different branch of the company. That supervisor documented that Carrie had brought her gun to work there as well, used the same explanation, and was told that the policy applied to licensed weapons, including her gun. Carrie is out of excuses and out of a job.

Evidence of an Employment Contract

As you read through the file, be on the lookout for evidence of an employment contract limiting your right to fire at will. As explained in Chapter 2, employees with these contracts can still be fired for cause— that is, a good business reason—but the existence of the contract makes it especially important that you document reasons for the termination.

Also, because you can create a contractual relationship with an employee even if the two of you haven't signed a document clearly labeled as an employment contract, check to see whether you made any oral agreements with your employee that are memorialized in the file. (Also think back on your conversations with the employee, as discussed in Step 4 below.) If there are promises of continued employment, or if your performance evaluations and disciplinary documents contain language contradicting the at-will relationship, you might have created an implied contract, especially if the employee hasn't signed an at-will statement.

An employment contract doesn't make a worker termination proof, but it could limit your options. Remember that the language of the contract governs when you can fire an employee. For most contracts, this means you need only have a good business reason to end the employment relationship. However, if you agreed to different restrictions (for example, that the worker could only be fired for committing a criminal act or for defrauding the company), you must decide whether termination is justified under the contract's terms.

EXAMPLE: Leif is considering firing his company's CFO, Oz, for poor performance. Oz has a written employment contract, guaranteeing him the position for two years unless the company is sold or he commits a criminal act or misconduct that causes "severe financial harm" to the company. The company hasn't been sold, and Oz hasn't committed a crime. However, he is performing poorly as CFO: His filings are always late, his sloppy practices have resulted in a bank audit, and the board of directors has complained about his sparse financial reports. Although these are serious problems that would give Leif good cause to fire Oz in general, they haven't resulted in severe financial harm and therefore do not fall within the contract's provisions. If Leif fires Oz before the two-year contract period ends, he could lose a lawsuit for breach of contract, despite Oz's undisputedly poor performance.

Step 3: Examine Your Written Policies

Next, gather together your employee handbook, personnel manual, and any other written policies that have been in effect during the worker's tenure. Review them to make sure the worker had sufficient notice that particular conduct could result in getting fired. One or more of the following can put an employee on notice:

- **Clearly written policies.** Your written policies, in a handbook or other material, might address the issues that you're dealing with now.
- **Other written communications.** You might have given adequate notice in some other way—through performance evaluations or written warnings—that the worker's conduct or performance was falling short of the mark.
- **Obvious misconduct.** Some behavior, like threatening violence or selling trade secrets to a competitor, is so outrageous that explicit notice is unnecessary. You can be sure that the worker knows this type of conduct is completely unacceptable.

Check to make sure you have followed your progressive discipline policy. If you're dealing with a one-time serious offense, does your policy give you the right to fire immediately? Or, does your policy reserve your right to fire for any reason? If you're facing an employee with persistent problems, have you done everything promised in your discipline policy? Have you gone through each progressive step and documented your efforts?

As you did when reviewing the personnel file, read through your policies to see whether you've placed any limitations on your right to fire workers. If there are written statements that could be construed as creating an implied contract, make sure the worker's misconduct gives you good cause to fire (it probably will).

EXAMPLE: Marisa has had persistent performance and attitude problems since she came to work for Lorenzo, all of which Lorenzo has faithfully documented. After her last written warning, Marisa was told that she would be fired for her next offense. Lorenzo came upon Marisa using the office copier to run off invitations to a friend's wedding shower. Lorenzo decided this was the last straw, until Marisa explained that she didn't know employees were prohibited from using the copier to make personal copies. Marisa pointed out that Lorenzo and several managers had all used the copier for personal copies in the last few weeks. Because no written policy prohibited personal use of the copier, and because the issue was, understandably, unclear to Marisa, Lorenzo decided not to fire her over this.

Step 4: Review Statements Made to the Employee

What you say to a worker can be just as important as your written communications and policies. Take a moment to think back on conversations or statements that aren't memorialized in the employee's personnel file or the personnel handbook.

Oral Statements That Contradict Written Statements or Policies

Consider whether you have said anything to the worker that is contrary to your written policies and the documents in the personnel file. For example, have you led the worker to believe they would not be fired despite poor

performance or other problems? Think about whether you've made any comments that might lead the worker to believe there was no risk of being fired for the conduct at issue.

If you remember conversations or statements that contradict written evidence, you can be sure that your employee will, too. If you made general statements that might be construed as creating an implied contract not to fire without good cause (such as, "You won't be fired as long as you do a good job"), then you can still fire the worker, as long as you have a legitimate business reason for doing so. However, if you made more specific promises to the employee, talk to a lawyer before proceeding.

Oral Statements That Cast You in a Bad Light

Because firing an employee always carries with it the possibility of a lawsuit, you must think not only about whether you can show a judge or jury a documented, believable picture of your problem employee, but also about what kind of picture the employee's lawyer will paint of you.

When you reflect on your conversations, consider first whether you've said anything that could be construed as discriminatory or harassing. Have you made any comments about the worker's race, national origin, gender, age, religion, or disability? Have you made any general remarks on these subjects that could be considered derogatory? Have other workers complained about your comments? If there's enough evidence to pin one of these transgressions on you, you could find yourself answering harassment or discrimination charges.

> **EXAMPLE:** Reginald, who is 70 years old, has worked for Tim, who is 35, for the last 10 years. They have become friends outside of work and often engage in friendly joking and teasing in the workplace. Reginald often calls Tim "pipsqueak" or "the kid," while Tim calls Reginald "old-timer" or "gramps." Neither minds these jokes. However, when Tim fires Giselle, who is 68 years old, for documented performance problems, Giselle files a lawsuit complaining that Tim discriminated against her because of her age—using his pet names for Reginald as one piece of evidence. Although those statements wouldn't be enough by themselves to win the case for Giselle, they won't help Tim in front of a jury.

Consider also whether your worker might have legitimate cause to feel sexually harassed. If you, other managers, or coworkers have asked the worker out, made comments about the worker's sex life, or commented excessively on the worker's appearance, you could be headed for big trouble. An employer with *any* concerns about discrimination or harassment should put the firing decision on hold and speak to a lawyer.

Step 5: Examine Your Treatment of Other Workers

A fired employee's most effective argument to a jury is that you've acted unfairly by treating the employee differently than others in the same position. Even an employee who has performed poorly or committed misconduct can make this argument. The employee won't claim to have been perfect—instead, they'll argue that you've come down harder on them than on others who have committed the same transgression.

To counter this argument, make sure that you've been consistent in your handling of similar offenses or misconduct by other workers. Have you always fired for this type of behavior? Or have you given other employees another chance?

If you've treated other employees differently, there might be a good reason for the difference. Perhaps one worker's conduct was worse, lasted longer, or caused the company more trouble. Make sure that your choice to fire this worker, while allowing others to remain, will make sense to a jury as a valid business decision.

> **EXAMPLE:** Vanessa is considering firing Jodi for repeated tardiness. Jodi has been warned and coached half a dozen times but has continued to arrive for work 15 to 20 minutes late at least once a week. Jodi is a shift supervisor for a delivery company. The drivers can't leave the company's warehouse until Jodi hands out their route assignments, so the company's entire fleet of trucks sits idle when Jodi is late. Vanessa has retained Morris, although he has also been late many times. However, Morris hasn't been late as often as Jodi. Also, because Morris works as a janitor, his tardiness doesn't affect anyone else. Because Jodi's lateness posed much larger problems for the company, Vanessa will have no trouble justifying her decision.

If you've been inconsistent with your employees and there's no valid reason for the difference, the employee could accuse you of unfair treatment. In the worst-case scenario, the fired worker could file a claim for illegal discrimination. Carefully review the demographics of the workers who have committed similar offenses. If the fired worker can show that you fired only nonwhite workers, for example, or that you were more lenient toward women or quick to get rid of employees with disabilities, you're at risk for a lawsuit. Talk to a lawyer before making a decision. Your inconsistencies might mask a deeper problem in fairly applying your policies to your entire workforce—one that you should deal with immediately to avoid legal trouble.

Step 6: Consider the Possibility of a Lawsuit

Now it's time to think about whether the context of the circumstances or other factors, such as the employee's personality, make it more likely that a particular worker will sue, and win.

If your situation fits into one of the following scenarios, it certainly doesn't mean that you can't fire the employee. It just means that you should make extra sure that your reasons are well documented and business related before you take action. And, in more questionable cases, it means you should consider consulting with an attorney.

The Context of the Termination

Your decision to terminate an employee doesn't arise in a vacuum. Surrounding events and circumstances—even if completely unrelated—can be used by an employee's lawyer in a way that makes you look biased, unfair, or just plain mean. Here are some issues to watch out for:

- **Timing.** If the worker recently complained of illegal activity in the workplace, such as discrimination or harassment, firing that worker could lead to a retaliation claim. Similarly, a worker who is fired shortly after exercising a legal right or complaining of improper or illegal activity (such as having to work unpaid overtime or work in hazardous conditions) might bring a claim that the firing was retaliatory or violated public policy. If the worker recently criticized, or discussed trying to change, the working conditions or job terms (like compensation) with other employees, you might face an unfair labor practices claim. And a worker who gets fired shortly after telling you that they are pregnant, have a disability that requires accommodation, or hold certain religious beliefs could decide that the firing and the disclosure are linked. If this argument is plausible, the employee might find a lawyer willing to handle the case.

- **Workplace demographics.** If firing this employee will significantly change the demographics of your workforce, it might look like a discriminatory firing to a judge or jury. Are you firing the only worker with a disability or the only vocal born-again Christian on your payroll? If so, consider whether the employee has any grounds to file a discrimination lawsuit.

- **Other terminations.** Consider any other employees you have fired. Do you see a pattern that could be used against you? Have you fired only women? Have you fired workers who have raised complaints about health and safety issues? Have you fired several workers on the verge of collecting their pensions? The fired employee might be able to use these similarities to prove that your motives are suspect. This kind of evidence is especially powerful in discrimination lawsuits.

EXAMPLE: Curtis is considering firing Magda for poor performance. Magda has failed to meet her sales targets for the past two quarters and doesn't appear to be showing much improvement. Magda filed a sexual harassment complaint one month ago, complaining that her supervisor had repeatedly asked her out and made her uncomfortable. After investigating the complaint, Curtis concluded that Magda's supervisor had acted inappropriately and issued him a written warning. If Curtis fires Magda now, she might conclude that she got fired because of her sexual harassment complaint, and the short period of time between the firing and the complaint will only help her claim. Also, it's possible that Magda's work has been suffering because of her concerns about the supervisor's behavior. In this case, Curtis should probably give Magda time to improve, as well as offer her any assistance she might need to get back on track.

CAUTION
Don't forget wage and hour issues. As explained in Chapter 2, even an employee who is fired for good cause might have legal claims against your company for wage and hour violations. If you have concerns about whether you've properly paid the employee over the course of the employment relationship, talk to a lawyer before you make the decision to fire.

The Employee's Personality

Consider whether the worker seems likely to file a lawsuit. Of course, this isn't something you can predict with certainty. Nevertheless, considering the following factors will help you decide whether to offer a severance package or some other incentive in exchange for the worker's agreement not to sue, and whether to consult with a lawyer before the actual termination:

- **Threats to sue.** A worker who has said or hinted that a lawsuit could be in the offing, who has already hired a lawyer, who has filed lawsuits against other employers, or who has assisted someone else (a spouse or coworker, for example) in bringing a lawsuit should be considered a risk.
- **Financial problems.** An employee who will have trouble finding another job or who is the sole financial support for a family might have a stronger incentive to file a lawsuit.
- **Psychological issues.** A worker who has already displayed a self-perception as a victim or tends to blame others for problems might resort to a lawsuit to correct this perceived injustice. Similarly, an employee who has a rigid belief in right and wrong might be more likely to sue based on a perception that these rules have been violated.
- **Fairness.** We've said it before, but it bears repeating: A worker who feels like a victim of unfair treatment is more likely to file a lawsuit. Consider whether the employee will think you have acted reasonably and fairly.

See Chapter 9 for more information on severance pay and releases (agreements not to sue).

Step 7: Consider the Alternatives

You've likely already thought about whether some disciplinary measure short of termination might be effective. However, now is a good time to quickly revisit the issue. Do you think it's likely that the employee will be able and willing to improve? If so, a lesser punishment could work well for both of you. However, make sure that you aren't playing favorites or bending your rules without a good reason. If you've consistently fired other workers for the same behavior, you'll have to consider whether making an exception in this case will be perceived as unfair.

You might want to consider an alternative to termination if the worker's problems are due to difficulties outside of work, increased responsibilities that the employee can't handle, or trouble working with a particular supervisor (or if you've made some managerial missteps in your dealings with the worker).

Step 8: Get a Second Opinion

If possible, have a second person from within your company review the decision to terminate. The purpose of this review is to make sure that your decision is legitimate, reasonable, and well supported. The reviewer should consider how the termination would look to someone outside the company. The reviewer should also make sure that the decision is based on objective, work-related concerns and hasn't been influenced by favoritism, discrimination, or other subjective factors.

Ideally, the person who does this review won't have a stake in the outcome. A supervisor from a different department or a manager at another store location might be a good choice. The less contact the reviewer has had with the people involved, the more likely the opinion will be objective. Make sure the reviewer knows that you want an honest opinion and not simply a rubber stamp approval of your decision. The reviewer should look at the worker's personnel file, the written policies, and any report or notes from an investigation. The reviewer needn't go through the entire process outlined here, but should consider all documents relating to the firing, as well as how other employees have been treated.

Take the reviewer's comments seriously. If the reviewer finds that your decision could be challenged, find out why. Use the reviewer's comments to figure out how you can either salvage the employment relationship or properly document and support your decision.

> **EXAMPLE:** Maurice plans to fire Geri and has asked Antoinette to review his decision. Geri works as a cashier in a supermarket Maurice manages; Antoinette manages a different supermarket in the same chain. Antoinette notices that Maurice has fired two other cashiers in the past year; when she reviews their files, she sees that each of them received two written warnings for major cash shortages (over $50) from their register drawers before being fired for a third shortfall. Geri's drawer has been short only once and for a much lesser amount. When Antoinette asks Maurice about this apparent inconsistency, Maurice says that Geri seems distracted at work since having her baby, and he is convinced that she will have further cash shortages if he keeps her on.
>
> Antoinette tells Maurice to put the firing plans on hold. Although he might have legitimate concerns about Geri's attentiveness, his comments sound perilously close to admitting that he's treating Geri differently—more harshly than the other cashiers whose drawers were short—because she is a new mother. He seems to be making an assumption based on the fact that she's a mother rather than on her performance. Better for Maurice to talk to Geri about her attentiveness and see whether her performance improves.

Step 9: Consult a Lawyer, If Necessary

When you're faced with a close call of any kind—or are unsure that your decision will hold up in court—consider talking to a lawyer before taking action. Except in very complex cases, an experienced employment lawyer should be able to review the facts and give you some legal advice in a few hours. Chapter 12 provides more information on finding and working with employment lawyers.

You would be wise to run your decision by a lawyer in the following situations:

- The employee recently filed a complaint of discrimination or harassment.
- The employee recently exercised a legal right, filed a complaint, or complained to you of illegal or unethical activity.
- The employee recently revealed that they are in a "protected class." If you want to fire a worker who just told you she is pregnant or has a disability, for example, you should have your decision vetted by a lawyer.
- Firing the employee would change your workplace demographics. Before you fire the only woman in the accounting department or the last Latino engineer, for example, talk to a lawyer.
- The worker is due to vest benefits shortly. If a firing will prevent the employee from vesting stock options, retirement money, or other benefits, you might be hit with a claim that you fired in bad faith.
- The employee has an employment contract (whether written, oral, or implied) limiting your right to terminate, and you are concerned that you don't have good cause to fire.
- The employee denies the acts underlying the termination. If an employee has been accused of misconduct and denies the allegations, or if an employee disputes performance or attendance problems, consider asking a lawyer to double-check your decision.

FORM ON NOLO.COM
Use our termination risk assessment form. Our checklist will help you determine the risk level of a termination and whether you should consult with a lawyer before taking action. See Appendix A for details on how to access this form.

Step 10: Document the Reasons for Firing

Once you've considered all the angles, the only thing left to do is document your decision in an internal memorandum to the worker's file.

Your written documentation should be short and to the point. Completely and accurately describe the reason(s) why you decided to fire the worker. If the worker committed a one-time serious offense, write down what happened and why it's cause for termination. If possible, specify the policy the worker violated. If the worker engaged in persistent misconduct over a period of time, specify not only the misconduct but also your efforts to remedy the problem. Write down the dates of disciplinary meetings and warnings.

EXAMPLE 1: On June 13, 20xx, Brian Thomas brought a gun to the office, in violation of the company's workplace violence policy. Brian showed the gun to several coworkers, who felt threatened by his actions. Brian was immediately suspended with pay. When we investigated the incident, Brian stated that he intended to use the gun to intimidate his supervisor. Brian was terminated on June 19, 20xx.

EXAMPLE 2: During a performance evaluation on March 24, 20xx, I informed Katie St. John that her monthly reports had been consistently late. Katie apologized and told me she would work on timeliness. In June 20xx, I gave Katie a verbal warning on this issue. I explained that her lateness was affecting the entire department and could even delay our tax and corporate filings. In September 20xx, I gave Katie a written warning because she continued to file her reports late. On December 15, 20xx, after Katie could provide no reasonable explanation for her continued late filings, I terminated her employment.

As long as you have a lot of documentation about the worker's problem already, this memo can be fairly short and to the point, as long as it is also accurate and complete.

Checklist of Considerations Before Firing an Employee

Don't proceed with a decision to terminate a problem employee until you've covered the steps listed below.

☐ Perform an investigation, if necessary.

☐ Check that the employee's personnel file contains:
- documentation of persistent problems or prior incidents
- no evidence contradicting reasons for firing, and
- no employment contract (or evidence of good cause to fire, if there is a contract).

☐ Examine written policies to check that:
- Worker had notice that the conduct might result in firing.
- Company has followed its progressive discipline policy.
- No employment contract exists (or there is good cause to fire, if there is a contract).

☐ Review statements to the worker to ensure that none were:
- discriminatory or harassing, or
- contrary to company policy.

☐ Compare treatment of other workers to ensure that:
- Similar offenses were handled consistently.
- There is no appearance of discrimination.

☐ Consider the possibility of lawsuits based on:
- timing problems or appearance of retaliation
- altered workplace demographics, or
- a pattern in recent firings.

☐ Consider alternatives to firing.

☐ Get a second opinion within the company.

☐ Consult with a lawyer, if necessary.

☐ Document the reasons for firing in an internal memo.

Planning for the Aftermath

Once you've made the decision to terminate an employee, you're probably anxious to get it over with. You can't, however, proceed with the actual firing before considering what will happen after the termination. If this seems a bit like putting the cart before the horse, it is; but it's a necessary process. Now's the time to decide how to handle certain aspects of the termination, such as what you'll tell coworkers and reference seekers, whether you'll offer the employee continued health insurance, and whether you'll challenge the fired employee's application for unemployment benefits.

As discussed further in Chapter 10, part of your termination meeting with the employee will consist of explaining how you'll handle these very issues. The only way you can give an effective and complete explanation is if you have thought things through beforehand.

Legal Constraints on What You Say

Throughout this book, we've advised you to choose your words carefully when speaking with an employee whom you're reviewing, coaching, or disciplining, and when speaking with others about the employee's work.

After you've fired a worker, it's doubly important to speak cautiously, whether to the rest of your company, to prospective employers, or to the world at large. If you don't watch what you say, you can get into legal trouble. Before you can decide how to handle such post-termination issues as what to tell coworkers and reference seekers, you must understand the laws on defamation and blacklisting.

Defamation Laws

Terminated employees who think that you've wrongly maligned them to others can sue you for defamation. This means that they can sue you for what you tell prospective employers who seek a reference or for what you tell their former coworkers about the termination.

Before you decide to zip your lips rather than talk about the termination, understand that if you tell the truth, defamation generally won't be an issue for you. To win a defamation case, the former employee will have to prove both of the following:

- You said things about them that weren't true.
- The false statements damaged the former employee in some way (for example, by convincing a prospective employer not to hire them).

Defamation is called "slander" if your words are spoken and "libel" if your words are written down.

Although employers tend to fear these types of cases, the reality is that they're very difficult for former employees to win. In all states, you will prevail if you can prove that the statements you made were true.

Most states have laws protecting employers from defamation lawsuits for certain statements they make to prospective employers seeking a reference. These laws differ in the details; see the "State Laws on Information From Former Employers" chart in Appendix B to find out your state's rules. Broadly speaking, however, you'll be on safe legal ground as long as you confine yourself to work-related topics and speak in good faith and without malice. Essentially, this means you must have a reasonable belief that you are speaking the truth, and you must not be acting intentionally to harm the employee's job prospects.

Of course, there's the truth, and then there's what you can prove. Unfortunately, the latter is what really matters in the world of the law. To be safe, don't exaggerate when talking about the termination, and don't air your opinions and impressions about why the worker failed.

Only give information that you can prove, such as information that you documented through your progressive discipline and performance evaluation systems.

Blacklisting Laws

To safeguard a worker's ability to hunt for a job, some states have passed "blacklisting" laws that allow former employees to take legal action—criminal, civil, or both—against those who try to sabotage their efforts to secure new employment.

Truthful, well-meaning comments to prospective employers or to your workforce won't normally get you into trouble. The former employee must prove that you actively attempted to prevent them from getting a job, which means proving that you did something more than simply answer questions from prospective employers or coworkers. Indeed, many blacklisting laws specifically protect employers that make their statements only in response to someone seeking a reference. These laws state that only unsolicited comments can be the stuff of blacklisting.

The typical blacklisting case occurs when an employer makes unsolicited calls or sends unsolicited communications to companies where a terminated employee is likely to seek employment, with the intent to prevent the employee from getting work.

The majority of these laws were passed during the early, tumultuous days of the labor movement, when pro-union organizers were routinely fired and powerful employers banded together to try to neutralize employees' power by making it impossible for them to secure new jobs. Although we trust that you don't fit the picture of such an employer, blacklisting laws can still be used against you if you stray too near their prohibitions. This means that you shouldn't make well-meaning phone calls to competitors to warn them off of an employee whom you just terminated, for example.

What to Tell Coworkers

If you think the termination is going to be traumatic for you, imagine how your other employees will feel when they learn that a coworker—perhaps a friend—has been forced out of their midst. Not only will the rest of your employees want to know why you decided to take action, they might also start to fear for their own jobs. Rumors might circulate. Morale could drop.

The terminated employee will be nervous as well. After all, a termination is a humiliating event, and the employee will no doubt want to know exactly how public the humiliation will be. Think about this issue now, so that you can let the terminated employee know exactly what you will tell coworkers.

What course of action should you take? Given the difficulty of the situation, you might be tempted to simply avoid the issue altogether and say nothing to your workforce about the termination. Although this instinct is understandable, it will probably only heighten workplace anxieties. Other employees aren't going to simply ignore the termination, no matter how difficult the terminated employee was. Termination is the secret fear of every employee, and it's unsettling at best when it happens to a coworker.

To acknowledge the event and to encourage the rest of your employees to move past it, consider calling a meeting to announce the fact of the termination.

Tell your workforce the employee has been terminated and the effective date of the action. Don't give reasons. Don't express anger or relief. Be professional and neutral. Tell your workforce that you can't go into details because you must respect the fired employee's privacy.

When telling your workforce about the termination, you might be tempted to explain and justify your actions, both to reassure other employees that they won't be getting the ax and to cast yourself as a fair and friendly employer. In most cases, however, you should resist this temptation. If you say too much in your own defense, you will necessarily be saying negative things about the terminated employee. It can only make your remaining employees uncomfortable to hear you trashing their coworker, even if the trashing is deserved.

In addition, the terminated employee will likely find out what you say to other employees. After all, most employees have a workplace friend or two. You can bet that those friends will report back on your comments. If you allow yourself to talk at length about the termination, you risk saying things that aren't absolutely provable and risk a defamation lawsuit in the process. Even if you do stick to provable facts, you risk humiliating the terminated employee giving details. As we explain more fully in Chapter 10, humiliation often leads an employee to a lawyer's doorstep.

Of course, this doesn't mean that you can never discuss your reasons with anyone. If you have a compelling business need to tell an employee your reasons for the termination, then do so one on one in a private and confidential setting. Instruct the employee that nothing you say can be revealed to anyone else in the organization. And if you do make such a disclosure, remain mindful of the defamation and blacklisting laws described above.

What to Tell Reference Seekers

The fired employee might ask if you'll provide a reference. After all, the employee will have to find another job, and could be concerned about responding to questions from prospective employers. Decide before the termination meeting how you're going to handle this.

Unfortunately, the issue of giving references for terminated employees is a complicated one. You'll find yourself feeling tugged in a number of directions, some of them diametrically opposed, such as:

- "I want to tell the truth about the former worker, even though it's negative, but I worry that doing so will prevent the worker from finding another job."
- "I want to warn prospective employers against hiring this person, but I don't want to risk a defamation or blacklisting lawsuit."

- "I want to appease an angry worker by helping with the job search, but I don't want to risk a lawsuit from the new employer, who might claim that it hired a dangerous employee because I wasn't completely forthcoming."

Decide How Much Information to Give

Given the pitfalls described above, you might be inclined to give as little information as possible when prospective employers call. In fact, many employers have gone this route, choosing to simply verify the employee's position and dates of employment and leave it at that. This is a reasonable and perfectly legal option.

There are, however, reasons to be more forthcoming with prospective employers. Many employers ask for and check an applicant's references. You could severely hamper an employee's job search by refusing to give information, especially if that employee has some decent qualities that might make them a better fit elsewhere.

In addition, think about the plight of other employers. Like you, they rely on references to help them determine if someone will be a good fit for a job. If you refuse to give reference information, you could potentially leave them vulnerable to hiring someone whom you know isn't qualified or, worse yet, is dangerous.

Don't immediately decide to adopt the bare-bones approach. Although no law requires you to provide more than the basic "name, rank, and serial number," this response sends an unspoken message: You're choosing silence because you have nothing good to say. In fact, you might have something bad that you don't want to share. If your reticence results in your former employee's not getting work, they might be inspired to sue you over anything possibly related to the employment or termination. To avoid that unfortunate turn of events, it might be wiser to respond more fully, as explained below.

Follow Safe Reference Procedures

You can respond to reference requests without risking a lawsuit from the terminated employee if you stick to provable documented facts, remain mindful of the defamation and blacklisting laws described above, and follow the safe reference procedures described in this section.

TIP

Pick a reference policy and stick with it. Apply the policy to all your employees, not just the ones you fire. Otherwise, you leave yourself vulnerable to claims of discrimination or unfair treatment.

Make One Person Responsible for References

If it's feasible, designate someone at your business as being responsible for handling references for former employees. That person should be familiar with the legal pitfalls involved and the guidelines provided in this section.

Ideally, pick someone trained in human resource issues. For a small business, however, that might not be an option. In that case, the person should be in management and should be discreet.

Keep a Record

As you'll see below, we recommend that you require all reference requests to be made in writing. We also recommend that all of your responses be in writing. Keep a copy of every request you receive and every response you send out. You should also keep notes of any phone calls you receive, even if your response is simply to ask that the request be made in writing.

Keep copies of all correspondence with the employee about references, including any letters informing the employee about reference requests and any releases that the employee signs. In addition, keep notes of all conversations you have with the employee and anyone else about this issue.

If you're never sued, these files will simply take up space until you decide to destroy them (keep them for at least four years, however). If you're sued, they will come in very handy for these reasons:

- You can prove what you said and to whom.
- With your file cabinet full of similar requests and responses, you can argue that your normal business practice is to

respond in writing to reference requests. This makes it harder for an employee to claim that you made oral statements that were defamatory.

Tell the Terminated Employee What You'll Say

The most common reason employees consult lawyers about references is that the reference contained unexpected information. To avoid surprising the employee, you should tell the employee what you plan to say to prospective employers. A good time to do this is either at the termination meeting or at the exit interview. Make sure the employee understands exactly what you'll reveal when called for a reference. Don't use vague words such as "positive" or "negative." Be precise and concrete.

Ordinarily, former employers will tell prospective employers dates of employment, job title(s), and responsibilities. They also give factual information—both positive and negative—about the terminated employee's performance and productivity.

In addition to telling the employee what information you'll give in a reference, explain your reference policy. Explain that you'll notify the employee each time someone requests a reference and will give out information only to prospective employers who send you a release signed by the employee.

Only Respond to Written Requests

Precision is important when giving references. That's why you'll want to demand that all requests be made in writing. That way, you can determine exactly what information is being requested and by whom.

Insist on a Release

A release is a document that the employee signs, giving you and others permission to provide information to a prospective employer. The prospective employer, not you, has the responsibility for getting the terminated employee to sign a release. If you get a written request for a reference that doesn't contain a release, reply that you won't respond until you receive a release signed by the employee.

Respond in Writing Only

To keep out of legal hot water, you'll need to carefully craft your reference using the guidelines in this section. For that reason, you should respond only in writing to reference requests. Otherwise, you might find that you slip up in a casual conversation and say things that you shouldn't have. And once you say something, you can't take it back.

In addition, putting your response into writing means that a former employee can't later claim that you said things about them that you didn't say (or in a manner or tone of voice that you didn't use).

Give the Former Employee Notice of the Request

Even if you have a signed release, let the employee know (by letter or email) when you receive a reference request, and from whom.

Review the Former Employee's Personnel File

If you follow the guidelines in this book, you'll discuss references with the employee at either the termination meeting or the exit interview. You'll also include notes of that discussion in the employee's personnel file.

When you receive a reference request, don't rely on your memory of the employee's tenure with you or of the conversation regarding references. Instead, review the employee's personnel file prior to sending out a reference letter. Make sure that everything in the letter is grounded in factual and verifiable information contained in the employee's file.

Also, if you want to include something in the letter that you didn't talk to the employee about, inform them. You don't want anything in the letter to come as a surprise to the employee.

If You Speak, Speak Fully

As we explained above, the law doesn't require you to give a reference for a former employee. If you choose to go beyond the minimalist approach, however, you must include any information you have indicating that the employee might harm someone (for example, that the employee committed or threatened violence or put others in danger).

If you give a lot of information in a reference but don't include this information, and the employee turns around and injures someone at the new job, you could be liable for damages.

It's important to understand that this rule doesn't affect you if you choose not to say anything about the employee other than the bare minimum (for example, verifying positions held and dates of employment).

This rule applies only when you choose to say something substantive in response to a reference request.

Not every state follows this rule, although there appears to be a growing trend to hold employers liable for giving a misleading positive reference for an employee who is truly dangerous. Here are a few examples from real cases:

- A California middle school hired a vice principal who had glowing letters of recommendation, including one that recommended him for an assistant principal position "without reservation." In fact, the vice principal had been accused of sexual misconduct with students at the previous school. When a student at the new school accused him of similar behavior, the California Supreme Court allowed her to sue the previous school district for damages, finding that it had a duty not to misrepresent the facts when describing the employee's character and qualifications.

- A psychiatric hospital hired a mental health technician after receiving a very positive letter of reference from his previous employer, the county detention center. The county failed to mention that the employee had been accused of—and disciplined for—sexually harassing female inmates and had, in fact, resigned before a disciplinary hearing on some of the charges. When a female patient at the psychiatric hospital claimed that the employee had sexually assaulted her, the New Mexico Court of Appeals found that she could sue the county for providing a misleadingly positive reference.

- An anesthesiologist was fired for abusing Demerol on the job; his termination letter stated that he had been fired for cause for reporting to work in an impaired condition and putting patients at risk. Nonetheless, he received positive reference letters from two of the doctors in the partnership that had fired him, stating that he would be an asset to any anesthesia service, was an excellent clinician, and was recommended highly. No mention was made of his drug abuse. In his new position, the anesthesiologist failed to resuscitate a patient who was in for routine surgery; the family of the patient—who ended up in a permanent vegetative state—sued the new employer. The new employer, in turn, sued the former employers for misrepresentation. The 5th Circuit Court of Appeals found that the former employers had no stand-alone duty to disclose the employee's drug abuse. However, once they provided a reference, they had a duty not to affirmatively misrepresent the facts. Because their referral letters were false

and misleading, they could be partially liable for the patient's injuries.

Stick to the Facts

In your reference letter, give only information that is true and that you can verify in some way.

Don't pass on gossip or conjecture. Don't pass on your opinions or theories. Avoid stating what you believe might be true; only say what you know is true and can back up with documentation.

> **EXAMPLE 1:** Stephanie owns a café in a trendy part of town. She has one of the busiest cafés in town, and wait staff must work at a swift pace to keep up with the customers. Stephanie recently fired Jan because numerous customers complained that Jan, although friendly, was too slow and kept mixing up their orders. Although Stephanie gave Jan a number of chances, Jan never improved. A few days after firing Jan, Stephanie received a call from another café looking for a reference for Jan. Stephanie asked that the café owner make the request in writing. When she received the request and a release signed by Jan, she sat down to write the reference. The request specifically asked Stephanie to address how Jan related to customers.
>
> **Wrong:** "Jan had poor relations with our customers. Her mind was always somewhere else, and she never paid much attention to her work. She didn't try very hard and didn't care if she made a lot of mistakes. She was lazy and a bit of an airhead. I don't think that she is very smart. She isn't cut out for the café world. I wouldn't hire her again."

Right: "Numerous customers commented that they liked Jan's personality. To my knowledge, she never yelled at a customer or was rude to a customer. However, I received an average of five customer complaints per week about Jan. About half of these complaints were from customers who felt that Jan was too slow in filling their orders. The other half of the complaints were from customers who indicated that Jan had mixed up their orders and given them the wrong drink."

EXAMPLE 2: Lewis is the senior partner in a law firm. He recently fired Mark after receiving complaints from two female secretaries and one female attorney that Mark made lewd and sexually suggestive comments and gestures in their presence. Another law firm has now asked for a reference for Mark. In the reference letter, Lewis indicates that Mark's legal work is excellent and that he has never received a complaint from any client about Mark. He also notes Mark's win/loss record in the courtroom. Because he has decided to give some information about Mark, he must also address the sexual harassment issue.

Wrong: "I think Mark is some sort of sexual deviant. He has a demeaning attitude toward women and thinks they are nothing more than sexual objects for his amusement. He doesn't have any respect for them at all, and he shouldn't be left alone with any female employee. He made lewd gestures and disgusting comments to female members of my firm. When I asked him about this, he didn't even have the decency to look embarrassed."

Right: "I received complaints from two female secretaries and one female attorney that Mark had made lewd and sexually suggestive comments and gestures in their presence. I received a total of five complaints during a one-month period. As part of my investigation into the complaints, I asked Mark for his side of the story. He verified what the secretaries and the attorney said."

> **CAUTION**
> **Know the rules about salary information.** Some states and local governments forbid prospective employers from asking about an applicant's salary history. These laws recognize that using salary history to decide what to pay someone might perpetuate historical pay discrimination. Some states allow prospective employers to ask about salary history at a certain point in the job process, or if the employee volunteers the information; others don't. Make sure you know the rules that apply to you before supplying any information on salary for former employees.

Include Both Positive and Negative Information

It's a rare employee who lacks even one redeeming feature. When giving a reference, don't forget to include any positive facts about the employee. Remember, an employee who was a bad fit at your business might nevertheless fit in somewhere else.

Saying something positive, however, doesn't mean you have to perfectly balance the reference by saying one positive thing for every negative thing. After all, if you fired the employee, there's probably a lot more negative than positive to say. That's fine; just be sure you include the relevant facts.

Don't Answer Every Question

Some references will specifically ask questions that require you to break the rules we've set out in this section. You don't have to answer all of the questions you're asked, especially those that seek your opinion or conclusions. Stick with the verifiable and relevant facts.

Avoid the Possibility of Blacklisting

As explained above, blacklisting is an employer's deliberate effort to prevent a former employee from finding a job. You are always within the law when you respond truthfully to reference requests from prospective employers. The mere fact that a former employee has to work hard to find a new job usually isn't sufficient evidence to suggest blacklisting.

But you could stray dangerously close to legal trouble if you talk about your former employee in contexts other than a formal request for a reference, such as social gatherings where colleagues might be present. While you might have no intention of preventing employment, your loose lips could be all that a lawyer needs to begin a lawsuit.

To avoid problems, be especially careful not to talk about former employees at informal gatherings, when your guard might

be down. If a colleague tells you at a cocktail party that she's looking forward to interviewing a former employee of yours—and that person was a particular thorn in your side—it might be best simply to nod and smile and shift the conversation to another topic. Never call prospective employers and volunteer information when you haven't been asked for it.

Continuing Health Insurance

Given the ever-increasing cost of medical care, health insurance has become a coveted employee benefit. Whether your plan will continue to provide coverage will be one of the first questions a newly terminated employee will likely ask.

Many employers offer to foot the bill to continue insurance coverage—at least for a time—as part of the severance package. Often, this benefit helps give former workers peace of mind and makes them feel more kindly toward a former employer.

Warm sentiments aside, federal and state laws that might require you to make continued coverage available for former employees, though you won't necessarily have to pay for it.

Federal Law

A federal workplace law, the Consolidated Omnibus Budget Reconciliation Act, or COBRA (29 U.S.C. § 1162), applies to your business if you have 20 or more employees and if you offer a group health care plan.

Among other things, it requires you to offer former employees the option of continuing their health care coverage for 18 months if you fire them for any reason other than gross misconduct. The employee's spouse and dependents are also eligible to continue coverage under COBRA.

The employee must pay for continuing coverage under COBRA, including both your share and the employee's share of premiums. You can charge the employee up to 102% of the premium cost, using the extra 2% to cover your administrative expenses.

COBRA applies to HMO and PPO plans as well as more traditional group insurance plans. COBRA also covers all other types of medical benefits, including dental and vision care and plans by which you reimburse employees for medical expenses.

RESOURCE

Get more information about COBRA. You can find a comprehensive discussion of COBRA and other federal employment laws in *The Essential Guide to Federal Employment Laws,* by Sachi Clements (Nolo).

State Laws

Laws in most states grant former employees the right to continue with their group health insurance after their employment ends. You need to know about these state protections, because you have to comply with both state and federal law. In many instances, simply complying with COBRA will not get you off the hook. State protections are generally more detailed and more generous to workers than COBRA. In addition, even small businesses, which escape the purview of COBRA, might have to comply with state laws. For basic information about your state's law, see the "State Health Insurance Continuation Laws" chart in Appendix B.

RESOURCE

Find out more about your state's law. While the basic coverage of the state health insurance laws is usually easy to understand, your role in complying with them and the state's practice in enforcing them can get rather complicated. For more specific information, contact your state's insurance department.

Unemployment Compensation

An employee you terminate will likely ask for information about unemployment compensation. This is understandable, as life—and bills—won't stop just because the employee lost a job. As with the other issues discussed in this chapter, you must be prepared to answer these questions. Anticipate that you'll be asked whether whether the termination will make the employee ineligible for benefits and whether you will contest the employee's claim for benefits.

Will the Employee Be Eligible?

Employees can claim unemployment benefits if they weren't at fault in being terminated—for example, if it was because of financial cutbacks or because they simply weren't a good fit for the job for which they were hired. They can also receive benefits if their actions that led to termination were relatively minor, unintentional, or isolated.

An employee who was fired for "misconduct" won't be able to receive unemployment benefits. Although you might think that any action that leads to termination should constitute misconduct, not all state unemployment laws look at it that way.

Some actions that result in termination simply aren't serious enough to be viewed as misconduct and justify denying benefits to the terminated worker.

How serious does an action have to be to rise to the level of misconduct? Although states define misconduct differently, an employee will normally be viewed as having engaged in misconduct after willfully doing something that substantially injured the employer's business interests.

Thus, revealing trade secrets or sexually harassing coworkers is misconduct, while mere inefficiency or an unpleasant personality might not be. Other common types of actions that constitute misconduct under most states' laws include extreme insubordination, chronic tardiness, numerous unexcused absences, intoxication on the job, and dishonesty.

Actions that typically don't constitute misconduct include: poor performance because of lack of skills, good-faith errors in judgment, off-work conduct that doesn't impact the employer's interests, and poor relations with coworkers.

Remember that the issue of what constitutes misconduct is a matter of interpretation and degree. Annoying a coworker might not be misconduct, but intentionally angering an entire department even after repeated warnings might be.

Should You Contest the Claim for Benefits?

Your state's unemployment office will ultimately decide whether the terminated employee can receive unemployment benefits. You, however, do have the option of contesting the employee's application, which gives you a great deal of power as far as the employee is concerned. In California, for example, the unemployment board presumes that a terminated employee didn't engage in misconduct unless the employer contests the claim. The effect of this presumption is that all terminated employees normally receive unemployment benefits unless the former employer intervenes.

When Not to Contest the Claim

There's no reason—and no grounds—for you to contest an unemployment claim when the employee is fired for sloppy work, carelessness, or poor judgment. Similarly, if the worker simply failed to meet your performance expectations or wasn't able to learn new skills, you probably have no basis for challenging the claim.

Even in cases where an employee engages in misconduct, you might want to waive your right to contest unemployment as part of a severance package that you give to the employee. (See Chapter 9 for more about severance packages and unemployment insurance.)

When to Contest a Claim

You should contest a claim only when you truly believe that the employee engaged in misconduct.

And even then, you should contest a claim only when you have a good reason for doing it. Employers will typically fight for one of three reasons:

- They're concerned that their unemployment insurance rates might increase. After all, the employer pays for unemployment insurance. The amount paid is often based in part on the number of claims made against the employer by former employees.
- They're concerned that the employee plans to file a wrongful termination action. The unemployment application process can be a valuable time for discovering the employee's side of the story, and it can also provide an excellent opportunity for gathering evidence, both from the employee and from witnesses.
- The employee's claim alleges an illegal basis for the termination. For example, if you fired an employee for poor performance but the employee's stated reason for termination says, "I was fired for reporting sexual harassment by my manager," you can't let that stand uncontested. If you face this type of situation, you should speak to a lawyer before the unemployment hearing.

If you're leaning toward fighting an unemployment compensation claim, proceed with caution. Such battles not only cost time and money, but also ensure that the fired employee will become an enemy. You might even inspire an employee to file a wrongful termination action who otherwise might not have. If the fired worker has friends who remain on the job, they, too, might doubt and distrust your tactics.

Before deciding, do some research about what constitutes misconduct in your state. Also ask what effect a successful claim will have on your insurance rates. If it's relatively small, you might be wise to back off.

If you still want to fight the claim, however, consider paying for a consultation with a lawyer. In addition to advising you about the claim, the lawyer can counsel you on whether it's wise to tell this particular employee during the termination meeting or exit interview that you plan to contest any claim.

Written Explanations of the Termination

When you conduct the termination meeting, try to give the employee a brief but truthful explanation for the termination. Sometimes an employee will ask that you put the reasons in writing. If this makes you nervous, it should. Unfortunately, about half the states have laws requiring employers to do as the employee asks. Although you don't have to provide this document when you fire the employee, it's a good idea to begin preparing it now.

The Anatomy of an Unemployment Compensation Claim

Although the details of unemployment compensation vary in each state, some general principles apply in most cases. An unemployment claim typically proceeds through the steps described below.

The employee files a claim. The process starts when the former employee files a claim with the state unemployment program. You'll receive written notice of the claim and can file a written objection, usually within 7 to 10 days.

The agency determines eligibility. The state agency makes an initial determination of whether the former employee is eligible for unemployment benefits. Usually there's no hearing at this stage.

The referee conducts a hearing. You or the former employee can appeal the initial eligibility decision and have a hearing before a referee (a hearing officer who is on the staff of the state agency). Normally conducted by phone or in a private room at the unemployment office, this hearing is the most important step in the process. You and the former employee will each get to have your say. In addition, you're entitled to have a lawyer there and to present witnesses and any relevant written records, such as employee evaluations or disciplinary warnings.

Administrative appeal. Either you or the employee can appeal the referee's decision to an administrative agency, such as a board of review. This appeal usually is based solely on the testimony and documents recorded at the referee's hearing, although in some states the review board can receive additional evidence. While the review board is free to draw its own conclusions from the evidence and overrule the referee, more often than not, it goes along with the referee's ruling.

Judicial appeal. Either side can appeal to the state court system, but this is rare. Typically, a court will overturn the agency's decision only when the decision is contrary to law or isn't supported by substantial evidence.

Laws that require employers to give former employees letters describing their work histories are known as "service letter" laws.

These laws vary widely from state to state. In Minnesota, for example, an employer must provide a written statement of the reasons for an employee's dismissal within 10 days after the employee requests it in writing. (Minn. Stat. § 181.933.) Kansas also has a service letter law, but it doesn't require employers to provide a reason for the firing; they need only state length of employment, job classification, and wage rate. (Kan. Stat. § 44-808(3).)

A former employee who asks you to provide a service letter is usually asking for the truth, meaning the whole truth about the firing. Chances are, the terminated employee won't like the contents of this letter. Fortunately, a number of states specifically prevent employers from being sued for defamation because of what they write in a service letter, as long as the employer's statement is "truthful" or "in good faith." Keep in mind, however, there's usually nothing to be gained from being painfully blunt. Even though the law protects you in telling the truth, a modicum of politeness is always the best approach.

The "State Laws on Information From Former Employers" chart in Appendix B gives a brief summary of the laws in your state.

Severance and Releases

f you've decided to fire a problem employee, you're probably not eager to offer a severance package, particularly if the employee has caused you nothing but trouble. However, there are several reasons why you might need or want to pay severance:

- **To fulfill a legal obligation.** If, by word or by deed, you've led employees to believe that they would receive severance, you must follow through.

- **To help the worker out.** You might want to give a severance package to an employee whom you've had to fire, especially if the employee tried (but failed) to improve.

- **To avoid lawsuits.** A severance package can help a fired worker find a new job, ease the transition, and demonstrate that you care about the worker's well-being. A worker who receives these benefits will have an easier time moving on and letting go of any bad feelings toward your company and will be less inclined to sue. If you're concerned about lawsuits, you might want to ask the employee to sign a release (an agreement not to sue you).

- **To get something you want in exchange.** You can offer a severance package (or an enhanced package, if you're already legally obligated to pay severance) in exchange for the employee's agreement not to sue you. Or, you can offer severance contingent on the employee's signing a noncompete, nondisclosure, or nonsolicitation agreement.

TIP
Severance packages and releases are related, yet distinct, concepts. A **severance package** refers to the combination of items—often including money, insurance continuation, outplacement services, or other benefits—that you might give to a departing worker. A **release** is a legal agreement between you and the worker, in which the worker agrees not to sue you in exchange for some benefit you provide: often, a severance package. You can give a severance package without a release, or you can condition your severance package on the worker's signing the release. Both options are explained below.

Are You Obligated to Pay Severance?

Although many employers assume they must offer a severance package to fired workers, no statute requires it. However, you might still be legally obligated to pay severance if you led employees to believe they would be paid. In short, you can obligate yourself to pay severance.

CAUTION
If your workplace is unionized, you might be required to pay severance or other benefits to fired workers. Check the terms of your collective bargaining agreement.

When Severance Is Required

You will have to pay severance if you've made an enforceable promise to do so, either in a contract with the fired worker or in your written policies. You might also have to pay severance if you've regularly done so in the past.

Written Contracts

If you and the employee have a written employment contract in which you promise to pay severance, you must honor it. Some employment contracts promise severance if the worker is fired before the end of the contract term, meets certain performance goals, or stays at the company for a certain period of time. The contract might also include restrictions on severance, most notably that it won't be paid if you fire the worker for willful misconduct. Whatever the language of the contract, you must honor its terms.

Oral Promises

An oral promise to pay severance is as binding as any written contract or written policy—you're legally bound to follow through.

Although it can be tough for an employee to prove that an oral promise was made, there is always the possibility that a judge or jury might find in the employee's favor and order you to pay up.

Written Policies

If you have a written policy stating that you will pay severance, you must follow that policy. Such a policy might be included in your employee handbook or documented in another communication from management, such as an email or memo to all employees. A policy of paying one week's salary for every year of service was once common (although it's less so now). Like employment contracts, written policies often carry their own conditions or limitations. For example, your handbook might specify that severance will be given only to employees who have been with the company for a minimum number of years.

Employment Practices

Your conduct as an employer can be every bit as important as your written words. If you have an unwritten company practice of paying severance to employees in certain positions or to workers fired for certain reasons, you might subject your company to a legal challenge if you make an exception for a particular employee.

> **EXAMPLE 1:** Manolo owns a clothing store. He fires Josh, a salesperson, for persistent absences. Manolo has fired four other employees: Two were laid off during tough financial times and two were fired for performance problems. He paid severance to all. Because Manolo has always paid severance to fired employees, he might be obligated to pay Josh.

> **EXAMPLE 2:** Same as above, but Manolo paid severance only to the two employees he had to lay off. Manolo has a good argument that his practice is not to pay severance to every fired employee, but only to those fired for economic reasons that aren't related to their performance or productivity. Because Josh was fired for cause, he isn't entitled to severance.

Special Rules for Mass Layoffs

Some states require an employer to pay a small severance amount to workers who are laid off in a plant closing or mass layoff (when more than a certain number of employees—usually 50 to 100 workers—are laid off at the same time). Because these laws don't apply when you fire an individual employee, we don't cover them here.

CAUTION

This book covers only severance payments to problem employees who are fired. It doesn't explain the full gamut of possible severance policies you might adopt to cover your whole workforce.

Assessing Your Current Severance Practices

Having read the above section, you should be able to figure out whether you have, even unwittingly, instituted a severance policy at your company. (Readers who are satisfied that they haven't can skip ahead to "Should You Pay Severance?" below.) If the conclusion is yes, consider what you have promised. Does your policy or practice obligate you to pay severance to the problem employee whom you plan to fire?

The answer depends on the scope of your policy. Most employers adopt one of four basic severance arrangements, sometimes with slight variations.

Severance for All Employees

Some employers adopt a policy or practice of paying a set severance amount to all fired employees. This amount might be fixed or might depend on the employee's salary and tenure at the company. A common formula is one or two weeks of severance pay, at the employee's current salary, for each year of service.

If your policy is a blanket approach like this, you don't have much leeway now, even if the employee whom you're terminating is one who you feel doesn't deserve the benefit. If you decide to depart from your established practice, do so at your own risk. Your ex-employee could argue that your policy is like a contract, which binds you to its terms. Employers that get into legal fights over severance benefits often discover that their legal bills quickly outstrip the amount of pay involved.

Severance for Some Employees

If your company has a policy that limits severance to only certain employees, and the employee you intend to terminate fits within the exception to your policy, you don't have to pay severance to that worker.

Deciding whether an employee fits within your stated exceptions—particularly a "serious misconduct" exception—can be tricky. Even if your policy is clear and the reasons for termination well documented, you might have a hard time deciding whether the employee's problem qualifies as serious misconduct. Some cases will be easy:

An employee who threatens violence, steals, or engages in egregious harassment won't be entitled to severance. For those employees whose acts or intent are not so clearly bad, the safest approach is to err on the side of paying severance.

Severance at the Discretion of the Employer

Some companies reserve the right to make decisions about whether to pay severance (and how much to give) on a case-by-case basis. Unlike the approaches explained above, this approach starts with the assumption that no employees will receive benefits unless the employer decides otherwise. The factors the employer might consider often aren't announced. These written policies might include language like "severance will be paid at the sole discretion of the employer" or "the company will decide whether to pay severance on a case-by-case basis."

Although this type of policy gives you the most leeway, it also exposes you to possible legal trouble from employees claiming that the policy was applied in a discriminatory fashion. Even if you have sound, decent reasons for your decisions, your employees won't know what factors you considered, and they might suspect that you had improper motives when picking and choosing among your workers.

Legal Requirements for Severance Policies

Under a federal law known as ERISA (the Employee Retirement Income Security Act of 1974), employers are required to follow strict requirements in administering severance plans. If you have a regular policy or practice of paying severance to fired employees under all circumstances, even if the policy is unwritten, chances are good that this law applies to you. ERISA doesn't apply to payments that are individually negotiated with a fired worker, such as payments made in exchange for the employee's agreement not to sue (called "releases," these agreements are covered below).

ERISA is a notoriously confusing and technical law. Its purpose is clear enough: to ensure that employers provide workers with information about their retirement and severance plans and treat them fairly when administering the plans. ERISA requires an employer to use a plan administrator, provide workers with a written summary of the plan, file a copy of the plan with the U.S. Department of Labor, establish a written procedure for employees to file and appeal claims under the plan, and follow a host of other rules. If you believe your plan might be covered under ERISA, consult a lawyer to make sure you are in compliance with the law.

EXAMPLE: Ash has fired six workers in the last two years. Her severance policy allows her to pay severance at her sole discretion. Ash has paid severance to only two of the workers fired, both of them women. She decided to pay these workers severance because both had worked for the company since its inception 10 years before. Ash felt bad about firing them and wanted to reward their loyalty.

Ash didn't pay severance to the other four workers, because all were fired within a couple of years of starting with the company. However, these four other workers were all men. Even though Ash's decisions weren't based on the sex of the fired worker, one of these fired men might believe differently and might even find a lawyer willing to take the case.

No Severance Policy

You might have run your company without ever giving a thought to severance benefits.

Perhaps you're just starting out, or you've been fortunate enough not to have had to terminate many employees. Or, you might have subconsciously decided that no one will receive benefits, but haven't made that decision a known policy. Can you decide to give severance now?

Yes, you can. There's no legal requirement that you announce a policy before giving severance. However, an employer that suddenly decides to bestow benefits puts itself legally "at risk" in the same way as the employer who gives benefits according to its sole discretion. Because you haven't shared your criteria for giving severance, you make it possible for someone to believe illegal motives could be at work.

Should You Pay Severance?

If your policies, written or oral, obligate you to pay severance to all or some fired employees, or if you have made a practice of doing so in the past, you should pay fired problem workers according to your usual formula. However, if your policy allows you to give severance at your discretion—or if you have no policy at all—you have two choices to make: whether to offer severance and whether to condition your offer on the worker signing a release.

Reasons to Offer Severance

The problem employee whom you intend to let go might be completely responsible for their predicament, particularly if it's the result of willful misconduct, calculated and serious dishonesty, or premeditated violence. If you were unlucky enough to have hired a truly bad egg, you probably feel that you've already paid enough, and you certainly don't want to reward egregiously bad behavior. In such cases, you won't find yourself losing sleep over the employee's departure or wishing there was something you could do to soften the blow. But as counterintuitive as it might seem, this undeserving employee could still be a candidate for a severance offer, for reasons explained below.

On the other hand, you might be terminating a problem worker for whom you feel some sympathy, even though the worker's behavior or performance proved to be ultimately unacceptable. For instance, the worker who couldn't learn new skills required for the job, the employee whose divorce affected productivity, and even the worker whose drinking or temper got out of control might still have to go, but you'd like to do something for them. In these situations, offering severance might feel like the humane thing to do.

Providing some funds to live on until the worker finds another job can also provide a little insurance against future lawsuits. A severance package could help defuse the anger a worker feels about being fired. And a happier former employee is a less-litigious former employee.

Particularly if some responsibility for the employee's problems rests with you or other members of your company, it might make good business sense to pay severance now rather than legal fees and jury awards later. Remember, however, that paying severance alone is no guarantee that you will avoid a lawsuit: You can do that only with a release, discussed below.

Risks of Offering Severance

Sadly, even if you have good reasons for handing out severance benefits, whether you're trying to do the right thing or trying to avoid a lawsuit, there's a risk involved. Consider not what the fired worker might do, but what remaining employees—some of whom you might have to fire later—will expect.

For example, suppose you're firing a single mother and you know that she'll have a tough time financially until she's reemployed. If the reasons that led to her firing weren't extreme, she could be a candidate for severance. But what happens if the next person you terminate is a single father? If you don't extend the same severance to him, he could charge you with sex discrimination. Even if his sex had nothing to do with your decision not to offer a severance—perhaps his income level was higher or he had another job lined up, for example—it might seem unfair to him.

And if you decide to buy off employees who threaten to sue or act as if they might, you could be encouraging others to make the same threats. Most employees won't be surprised when they're fired, and some might begin to think about what they can get out of you before the ax falls. Knowing that a threat to sue has been met with "hush money" in the past, the next employee might make hollow threats just to see what you'll cough up.

Should You Ask for a Release?

If you're lucky, the employee you've decided to fire will pose little threat to you in terms of future lawsuits. Perhaps the employee has acknowledged their failings or has simply accepted the inevitable and wants to move on.

A Release by Any Other Name

Lawyers have come up with a lot of different terms for a release. It might be called a "release of claims," a "waiver of rights," a "covenant not to sue," a "separation agreement," or a "nonsuit agreement." All of these terms refer to the same thing, however: a contract in which the employee agrees to give up the right to sue you in exchange for something of value.

Unfortunately, there are other employees who will walk out the door and head straight to a lawyer's office. Workers with persistent problems might have seen the writing on the wall and talked to a lawyer even before the firing. Sometimes you'll be tipped off by references to lawyers or even by the employee's use of legal terminology that you can assume was picked up during conversations with counsel. Other times, the employee's level of anger and general disposition will lead you to reasonably conclude that there's trouble ahead. And if your own conduct has been less than stellar—if you've been harsher with this employee than others, for example—the chances of legal trouble increase.

This is the time to consider whether to ask the problem employee to sign a release: that is, a contract in which you give the worker something of value (usually the same things you might consider in a voluntary severance package, like compensation, continued

insurance coverage, and/or other benefits) in exchange for the worker's agreement not to sue. The employee "releases" or gives up potential legal claims against you. A release buys you protection against the unpredictable (but assuredly high) costs of defending a lawsuit in the future.

Getting a Release When You Have a Severance Policy

If your policies or practices have led the employee to expect a severance package if they're fired, you might need to give more than the expected package if you want to extract a promise not to sue. After all, you're asking for something extra from the employee, so you have to give something extra in exchange to make the agreement legally enforceable. In short, you need to sweeten the deal.

You can add to your usual severance package by throwing in money, paying for COBRA coverage, or providing any of the benefits explained in "What Should You Offer?" below. The important thing is to make sure that you're giving the employee something extra that wouldn't ordinarily be available under your severance policies, in exchange for signing the release and giving up the right to sue you.

Getting a Release When You Don't Have a Severance Policy

If your policies and practices don't require you to offer severance, you could still choose to do so, as explained above. If you want the employee to sign a release, you can simply condition receiving the severance on the employee's promise not to sue. Without a release, a voluntary severance package is a gift from you to the employee. However, if the employee is asked to sign a release in exchange for the severance, that gift becomes a contract.

Pros and Cons of Asking for a Release

Releases can be invaluable to employers. A release buys you peace of mind: A worker who signs away these rights cannot bring a lawsuit. If the employee tries to sue you, a court will throw out the claim as long as the release is valid. (See "Preparing a Release," below, for tips on what makes a release enforceable.) For the price of an enhanced severance payment now, you can buy protection against the possibility of lawsuits in the future. For this reason, some companies routinely request a release from every fired worker.

However, there are drawbacks to asking for a release. You will have to weigh what you might gain from a release against what it might cost you.

When a Release Makes Sense

When deciding whether to ask for a release, your first consideration should be the strength of the worker's potential legal claims. Have you documented the

employee's problems? Have you fulfilled your legal obligations? Have you followed your own policies? Aside from whether you've implemented the employment policies outlined in this book, consider whether there are skeletons in your closet that might also surface in a lawsuit—unless you squelch them with a release.

Next, consider the context of the employee's firing. Might the employee suspect—or allege—mistreatment, regardless of your true motivation? For example, did the employee recently make a complaint of discrimination, harassment, or illegal activity? Is the employee the only member of a particular demographic group in your workplace or a particular work group (for example, the only woman or Asian American)? Even if you had a legitimate reason to fire the worker, consider offering an enhanced severance package in return for the employee's agreement to release such claims.

Finally, think about the worker's attitude about litigation. Has the employee threatened to sue you, hired a lawyer, or talked generally about taking you to the cleaners? Has the worker been involved in other lawsuits, even ones brought by a friend or family member? If you have any indication that the worker is thinking about suing, and the worker was mistreated or there's an appearance of mistreatment, a release is probably a good idea.

Risks of Asking for a Release

Consider the potential drawbacks to asking for a release: Offering a release might convince some workers that they have legitimate legal claims against you; why else would you offer to pay them to give up those claims? Other employees might feel so resentful at being asked to give up their rights that they start to consider legal action they might never have entertained otherwise. A worker asked to release claims often decides to talk to a lawyer before signing away the right to sue, which could result in a protracted round of negotiations and, ultimately, a higher severance payment. And, if you ask for a release from an employee who wasn't contemplating a lawsuit in the first place, you'll end up paying severance money you otherwise could have saved.

What Should You Offer?

Whether you decide to offer severance voluntarily or only as a condition of signing a release, your goal is to offer enough to ease the worker's transition, forestall a lawsuit, and successfully obtain a signed release, without giving away the store. Here are ideas to consider.

How Broad Can a Release Be?

The scope of a release—the types of claims that the worker agrees to give up—can be quite broad. As explained below, employers routinely ask workers to give up any and all claims arising from the employment relationship, not just claims of wrongful termination. And these broad clauses are just as routinely enforced by courts.

There are a few exceptions to this expansive rule, however. Some states' laws put certain types of claims off limits, including claims for unemployment compensation, workers' compensation, or other benefits provided, at least in part, by state funds. Even if a worker agrees to release these claims, courts in these states will allow the worker to seek benefits anyway.

A release of wage and hour claims under the Fair Labor Standards Act may not be enforced unless the release is approved by a court or supervised by the Department of Labor. Although workers can waive the right to sue in court for discrimination and harassment, they may not waive the right to file administrative charges with government agencies that investigate these claims (nor may they waive the government's right to pursue these claims on its own). And some states impose special rules if an employer wants the employee to release "unknown claims" (claims based on facts that the employee doesn't know at the time the release is signed). These claims are discussed in "Preparing a Release," below.

Money

Realistically, cash is what most fired workers want. How much is enough? That will depend on how you answer the following.

How much can you afford to pay? Consult the bottom line before making any decisions. If you're paying a worker out of a sense of generosity, the amount should be well within the bounds of what you can afford. If your goal is to forestall a lawsuit or convince a worker to sign a release, you might be willing to pay a bit more, knowing that the alternative—litigation—will be more expensive.

How strong are the employee's potential claims against you? When deciding whether to ask for a release, assess your potential legal exposure. If you have well-founded concerns about serious legal trouble, you'll want to offer more. This is a tough balancing act. On the one hand, you should be willing to pay an employee with a potential blockbuster discrimination claim much more to go away than you would pay an employee who has been treated fairly from start to finish. On the other hand, offering a lot of money out of the gate could raise the employee's suspicions (and narrow your wiggle room if you end up in a protracted negotiation). If facing the possibility of a significant legal claim against your company from this employee, you should definitely talk to a lawyer about crafting your severance and release.

How long will it be until the employee finds another job? Take a look at the job market for this particular worker. If it will be tough to find a comparable job, you might want to pay as much as possible to provide support during the weeks of searching. On the other hand, an employee who can walk across the street and land a similar position might not need a generous severance package.

Can you cash out the employee's unused vacation time? You might also consider cashing out a worker's unused vacation time, if your policies and state law don't already require you to pay the worker for this time. Many states require employers to pay a terminated worker for all accrued vacation days that have not been used. If your state is one of them, this vacation pay is money to which your employee is already entitled, apart from any severance arrangement. Contact your state labor department for details. (Visit www.dol. gov/agencies/whd/state/contacts for contact information.)

Insurance Benefits

Some employers offer to pay the full cost of continued insurance coverage for a period of time after an employee is fired. Although COBRA and similar state laws require most employers to offer fired employees the opportunity to continue their health insurance, they don't usually require employers to foot the bill.

You might also consider continuing to pay for other insurance benefits, such as life or disability insurance.

Uncontested Unemployment Compensation

Fired employees can claim unemployment benefits if they were terminated for reasons other than deliberate or repeated misconduct. As you probably know, the former employer pays a portion of these benefits through payroll taxes. For this reason, after a worker applies for benefits, the employer has an opportunity to fight the worker's claim.

If you're terminating an employee for unintentionally poor performance, you have no grounds to dispute their application for unemployment benefits. In this situation, your agreement not to contest any unemployment application as part of a severance package will be meaningless. But if you're firing someone for reasons that arguably fall within the scope of misconduct, your promise not to contest the application has real value. By agreeing not to fight the claim, you make it more likely that the employee will be found not to have engaged in serious misconduct and will receive benefits.

Outplacement Services

An outplacement program helps an employee find a new job. It might offer counseling on career goals and job skills; tips on résumé writing; help in finding job leads; use of computers, printers, scanners, and other office technology for the job search; practice interview sessions; and assistance in negotiating with potential employers. Some programs also offer therapeutic counseling to help the employee deal with losing a job and move on.

The cost of outplacement services depends on the kinds of services included. Many firms will give a discount if you are offering outplacement to a number of workers or if you enter multiple contracts for services within the space of a year or so. Because competition among outplacement service providers is fairly stiff, you will likely have leeway in negotiating the price you pay and the services you receive.

For some employers, the cost is worth it: Former employees whose time and minds are taken up by a new job are far less likely to sue for wrongful termination or to file claims for unemployment.

Other Benefits

You might consider offering other benefits, such as allowing the fired worker to keep advances or money paid for moving expenses, letting an employee keep company equipment (like a laptop, mobile phone, or car), or releasing an employee from contractual obligations, like a covenant not to compete (explained below).

<table>
</table>

Should You Let a Fired Worker Use Your Office Resources?

If you own a small business, you'll probably balk at the cost of hiring a consulting firm to provide outplacement services to your employees. Some employers avoid these costs by allowing the fired employee to use company resources to search for another job. For example, you might offer to let a former employee use office equipment, such as the copy machine, scanner, computer, laser printer, and telephone.

There are pros and cons to opening your doors to a fired employee. Of course, if you have any reason to fear that the fired employee poses a threat of sabotage, violence, or theft, don't let that employee back into the workplace, period.

However, if you believe that a worker could benefit from using your office resources, and you feel that it's appropriate given the circumstances, you can offer valuable help—within limits. For example, you might allow the worker to use your equipment only for a set amount of time (one or two months, say). Or you could arrange to have the worker come in only at certain times and on certain days.

Designing a Severance Package

Now that you have some idea of the range of possible benefits, you will need to make up a benefits package for your situation. A good way to figure out exactly what combination of benefits will be the most helpful while costing you the least is to talk to the employee. Certain items—like continued health insurance coverage or outplacement assistance—might be particularly important to a fired worker. If possible, have an honest discussion to find out what your worker would like.

A fired worker might approach you with a wish list of benefits. Be prepared to negotiate, and create a ready list of items you might be willing to offer in a counterproposal. As always, don't forget your motivation for offering severance: Are you leading with your heart or with your head? If you're mollifying an employee whom you suspect might sue, be ready to offer a bit more, knowing that it will be money well spent if it helps avoid litigation.

! CAUTION
Proceed cautiously if there's a lawyer in the picture. If an employee who asks for severance has consulted an attorney, you will probably want to tie your benefits to a release, which will remove the possibility that you will be sued over the termination. Also contact your own attorney for advice.

Preparing a Release

Because a release is a legal contract, you must follow certain rules to make it valid. You might also want to take additional steps to make sure that a court will enforce the agreement, should the worker later have a change of heart and try to sue you anyway.

> ! CAUTION
> **Some states have specific require-ments about the form and content of releases.** You might have to use particular words and phrases, type the agreement in a specified font size, or provide certain information about the worker's rights. If you don't follow these rules to the letter, a court could later decide that the release is invalid and let the worker sue you anyway. Because of these technical requirements, you should have a lawyer draft the release for you, or at the very least review it before you give it to the employee.

Release Basics

Your release must meet a few basic legal requirements. If it's lacking in any one respect, your former employee might be able to disregard it and sue you. A valid release, on the other hand, will be upheld by a judge, who will use it to dismiss any lawsuits that the employee might file con-cerning the termination or other aspects of your employment relationship.

Giving Something Valuable

Every legal contract involves the exchange of value. For example, in exchange for your money, which is valuable, Nolo will send you a book, which is also valuable. In legal terms, the valuable things—like money, goods, services, or benefits—that each party to the contract promises to give the other is called "consideration."

Because a release is a legal contract, you must give the employee something of value—benefits, money, or services—in exchange for their agreement to give up legal claims against you (claims that are valuable because the employee could otherwise sue you and perhaps win money). As explained above, if you have a severance policy, you must offer additional benefits that aren't already in the package.

Any of the items you might offer as severance could qualify as consideration, as long as the employee isn't already entitled to them. Once you've decided what you want to offer, specify each item in the release and state that you are giving it in exchange for the worker's release of claims.

> **EXAMPLE 1:** "As consideration for his release of all claims relating to his employment, Lloyd Astin agrees to accept a lump sum cash payment of $20,000 and continued payment of his health and disability insurance premiums for three months. Mr. Astin will

also be allowed to keep the computer he has used while employed at Company, after all Company-related materials are removed from the computer by a technical support person of the Company's choosing."

EXAMPLE 2: "In exchange for his agreement to release all claims relating to his employment, the Company agrees to reimburse Greg Borden for costs he incurs for outplacement services up to a maximum of $3,000."

Release of Claims

In exchange for your consideration, the worker should agree to give up the right to sue you for all employment-related claims. Legally, a release can cover almost any claim the worker might have against you that relates in any way to the employment. You don't have to limit the release to claims relating only to the worker's termination, for example. However, a release can only cover claims arising up to the date the release is signed. If you and the worker have problems later—for example, if the worker claims that you've blacklisted or defamed them by giving a false and harmful reference—those disputes won't be included, which means that the worker can still sue you over them.

The key to a solid release—one that will give the most protection against legal trouble—is to be all-inclusive. Don't limit it to only those claims you are most concerned about. For example, if you fire someone with whom you had an employment agreement,

don't ask the worker to give up only the right to sue you for breach of contract—a worker can bring myriad claims for wrongful termination. For example, a worker who had an employment contract might believe the firing was for discriminatory reasons or in violation of public policy. If you limit your release to only contract-related claims, you leave yourself open to lawsuits based on other legal theories.

At the same time, however, the release must be specific enough to inform the worker of the rights being given up. Some courts even require employers to list the specific antidiscrimination laws—like Title VII, the ADA, or the ADEA (see Chapter 2 for more about these laws)—that provide the rights the worker is waiving. In fact, if you want the employee to waive ADEA claims, you will have to follow a set of special rules or risk a court finding that your waiver is invalid; see "Special Rules for Older Workers," below, for more information. If the employee can later argue successfully that they didn't know what the release covered, your contract will not provide you with much protection. A typical release states that the worker is giving up any right to sue you for claims arising out of their employment or the termination of that employment and then lists the specific types of claims that might include. The release should also explain what a release entails: that is, that the worker is giving up the right to sue you.

EXAMPLE: "In exchange for the consideration provided in Paragraph A, Sean Dennis, on behalf of himself and his heirs, executors, successors, and assigns, agrees to unconditionally release the company and its past and present officers, directors, employees, agents, parent and subsidiary companies, affiliates, successors, and assigns, from liability for any and all claims or liabilities arising out of his employment or the termination of his employment. This release expressly includes, but is not limited to: claims of discrimination under federal or state law (including Title VII, the ADA, the ADEA, and California's Fair Employment and Housing Act); claims for breach of contract and breach of the covenant of good faith and fair dealing; claims of wrongful termination in violation of public policy; tort claims (including claims of fraud, intentional and negligent infliction of emotional distress, and intentional interference with contractual relations); claims under the Occupational Health and Safety Act and similar California laws; claims under the Family and Medical Leave Act and California's Family Rights Act; and any and all other claims related to his employment.

"By signing this release, Mr. Dennis understands that he is giving up his right to sue the company for any of the claims that he has released."

Written and Signed

A release should be in writing, signed, and dated both by the worker and by someone authorized to sign on the company's behalf (typically, an officer or executive). You and the worker should each sign and date two copies, so you will each have a document with original signatures for your files.

Special Rules for Unknown Claims

Even if you use very inclusive language in your release—like that in the example above—it might not cover every claim an employee could bring. Some courts have held that releases generally don't prevent employees from suing over issues that they didn't know about when they signed the release. A worker who later learns of facts that would support a legal claim—for example, that the employer illegally withheld money from a paycheck or exposed the worker to toxic chemicals—might still be able to sue over those claims.

To forestall future lawsuits based on unknown claims, an employer might have to include specific language in the release. The employer must state that the release includes claims that aren't known to the worker at the time the release is signed. Some states require the employer to use particular words in this portion of the release and/or require particular typeface and font size. The lawyer who drafts or reviews your release can make sure it meets any state requirements.

Knowing and Voluntary Waiver

A release is valid only if the worker enters into it freely, knowing that signing it means giving up the right to sue. The release won't be enforceable if the employee is coerced or threatened into signing or if the agreement isn't voluntary for any other reason. Also, if the language of the release is too vague, the employee might later claim not to have understood its effect.

Avoid any hint of coercion in asking an employee to sign a release. Don't threaten or talk tough in order to convince the employee to sign. And don't withhold any benefits to which the worker is entitled— such as a final paycheck or payment for accrued vacation time—until the worker signs. These tactics will only create ill will, and you won't gain anything for your actions if the release gets thrown out of court.

To ensure that your release will be enforced, include language stating that the employee is entering into it knowingly and voluntarily. You can further protect yourself from claims of coercion by giving the worker ample time to consider the release and suggesting that the worker consult a lawyer.

EXAMPLE 1: "This release has been negotiated between Ms. Hernandez and the company. Ms. Hernandez has agreed to this release knowingly and voluntarily. Her signature on this release acknowledges that she has not been coerced in any way and that she has been advised to consult with a lawyer about the legal rights she is giving up and the terms of this release."

EXAMPLE 2: "I have had the opportunity to read and carefully consider this release. I have also been advised to consult with a lawyer about the release. I am signing this agreement voluntarily" (followed by the employee's name and signature).

Special Rules for Older Workers

If firing a worker who is 40 years of age or older, a federal law—the Older Workers' Benefits Protection Act, or OWBPA—requires you to include additional terms in a release. Among other things, you must:

- specifically refer to the Age Discrimination in Employment Act (ADEA) in the release
- advise the worker, in writing, to consult with a lawyer before signing
- give the worker at least 21 days to consider the release before signing, and
- allow the worker to revoke the agreement (in other words, to back out of the deal) for 7 days after signing. (Don't provide the employee with the severance check until this revocation period has expired. It's easier to hold on to your money in the first place than to try to get it back.)

For more information on the OWBPA, check out the Equal Employment Opportunity Commission's (EEOC) website, at www.eeoc.gov.

Tips on Making Your Release Stronger

In addition to including the foregoing release requirements, consider these tips to make your release more likely to be enforced.

Use Clear Language

Your release should be as clear as possible, using language the employee can understand. If it uses a lot of legalisms and technical terms, workers who aren't familiar with that language might legitimately argue that they didn't understand what they signed. And if the employee challenges your release in a lawsuit, the court will be required to interpret any ambiguities in the worker's favor. Gear the release toward the employee: If you've dealing with a well-educated and savvy businessperson, you don't need to worry as much about sticking to basic terms.

Make Sure the Employee Knows the Rights Being Released

A court will be more likely to enforce a release if the employee knew what rights it covered. If the worker threatened to sue or talked to an attorney before signing the release, a judge will likely presume that the worker was aware of these rights. The best way to prove the employee's knowledge is to include a list of rights in the release, as illustrated in the example above.

Encourage the Worker to Talk to a Lawyer

When discussing the release, suggest that the worker consult a lawyer to review it and decide whether to sign. If the worker decides to talk to a lawyer first, add language to the release stating that the worker consulted with a lawyer before signing the release. If the worker doesn't take your suggestion, put in a sentence stating that you advised the worker to consult a lawyer about the release before signing and that they had an opportunity to do so.

Negotiate the Release

A court is more likely to find that a release was made voluntarily if you negotiate its terms—particularly the consideration offered—with the employee. You don't have to negotiate every term, but you should have a serious discussion about what the worker would like in the release. There could be any number of possible compromises that offer the worker a better deal without necessarily costing you more money. For example, a worker who can get insurance through a spouse might ask you to fund outplacement services instead of paying the full cost of continued health insurance. Or a worker might ask to receive half the severance payment immediately and half in the following year, to save on taxes.

Give the Worker Time to Decide

It's reasonable for an employee to take a few weeks to decide whether to give up the right to sue you. The shorter the time you allow for reflection, the more likely it is that a court will find that the worker was coerced. For example, if you hand a worker a release agreement and insist on a signature by the end of the day, you might be in trouble. State in the release how much time you gave the worker to decide.

If the employee asks for more time to consider the release, you should strongly consider granting the request. A worker who wants a lawyer's opinion before signing the release will have to find an attorney, make an appointment, and attend the actual consultation before making a decision. Your best course of action is to give the employee as much time as needed—within reason—to make an informed decision now, rather than face the possibility of a lawsuit later.

Consider a Revocation Period

You might want to give the employee an opportunity to change their mind—to revoke the release—for a few days after signing. There are pros and cons to allowing revocation.

The biggest drawbacks are that the agreement isn't final when the employee signs and that the employee might back out. The main benefit is that the worker will have a very hard time proving coercion if you provided time to undo the agreement.

If you're dealing with a particularly slippery character or a worker who just doesn't seem able to decide, offering a revocation period might make sense. Just remember not to release the severance check until the revocation period is over.

Additional Release Terms

You can include other terms in the release as well. For example, some employers include a statement denying any wrongdoing. These provisions typically state that the employer doesn't admit any liability for the claims being released.

You might also wish to include information on the employee's rights and obligations in the release. For example, you might indicate the date on which the employee was fired, a list of any benefits or payments to which the employee is entitled, and a statement of the employee's obligations, such as returning company property, paying back loans from the company, and maintaining the confidentiality of the company's trade secrets.

Until the last few years, employers routinely included confidentiality clauses in their settlement agreements. A confidentiality clause prohibits the employee from revealing the settlement terms, the underlying issues, or sometimes even the fact that an agreement was made. The purpose of these provisions is to protect the employer's reputation and to prevent other employees from finding out about the arrangement and arguing for similar terms if and when they get fired.

Confidentiality provisions came under a lot of scrutiny during the #MeToo movement. Activists pointed out that sexual harassment and discrimination had continued under the radar, in part, because companies and perpetrators were allowed to hide their misdeeds behind a wall of confidentiality. As a result of this public reckoning, a number of states (including California) passed laws prohibiting confidentiality provisions that would prevent employees from discussing harassment, discrimination, or retaliation. In 2022, the federal government followed suit in the Speak Out Act, which prohibits employers from enforcing general confidentiality provisions against employees who are talking about sexual harassment or sexual assault.

The National Labor Relations Board recently weighed in, finding that a general confidentiality provision in a severance agree- ment might be illegal if it prohibited employees from talking to each other about the terms and conditions of their employment.

Similar objections and legal claims have been made against nondisparagement agreements: clauses some employers have long included in settlement agreements that prohibit the employee from criticizing the employer or harming its reputation. As a result of these recent legal changes, any employer that wants to include a confidentiality or nondisparagement provision in its release or severance agreement will need legal advice.

Agreements to Protect Your Business

When a worker leaves a company, voluntarily or otherwise, there's a risk that the worker will take confidential information to a competitor. You might also worry that such a worker will hire away your remaining employees. You can protect your business by asking the worker to sign a nondisclosure or nonsolicitation agreement.

Each of these agreements is a contract between you and the worker. This means that, like a release, you must give the worker something of value in exchange for a promise not to disclose or solicit. To exact this promise, you might choose to pay voluntary severance or pay additional severance over and above the package to which the employee is already entitled.

Noncompete Agreements

By entering into a noncompete agreement, an employee agrees not to compete directly with your company by working for a competitor in the same capacity or by starting a competing business, at least for a certain period of time after leaving your company. Once common in many states, noncompete agreements have come under heavy criticism recently. Employee advocates argue that they suppress workers' wages and mobility, by preventing them from accepting work that pays more or offers other benefits. Some business advocates also oppose non-compete agreements, arguing that they prevent employers from casting a wide net to hire the best available talent.

Employees Who Change Their Minds

If a worker tries to sue you after signing a release, traditional legal principles require the worker to first return whatever you paid in exchange for the release. This requirement, referred to as the "tender back" rule, prevents workers from having their cake and eating it, too. After all, a worker who is arguing that the release is invalid—which the worker has to do in order to bring a lawsuit—shouldn't be able to keep amounts received under the contract.

Most courts require the worker to return the consideration upon learning that the release is invalid; otherwise, the worker has "ratified" the agreement by acting as if it was valid. However, workers who file lawsuits based on the Age Discrimination in Employment Act (the ADEA) aren't required to tender back: Older workers may keep their release money *and* file ADEA claims. The employer might be entitled to an offset or reimbursement of the money paid for the release, but only if the worker wins the lawsuit. (Courts thought it would discourage employees from filing lawsuits if they had to pay back their employers if they lost.) The employer may recover up to the full amount of the severance, or the full amount of the worker's award, whichever is less. For example, if you paid the employee $5,000 in severance, but the employee is awarded $2,000 by a jury, you can recover only $2,000.

A handful of states don't enforce noncompete agreements at all, including California, Minnesota, North Dakota, and Oklahoma. Many more states will enforce noncompete agreements only for highly paid employees. In 2024, the Federal Trade Commission (FTC) announced a rule banning noncompete agreements. The rule was challenged in court, and a federal district court issued an order stopping the FTC from enforcing the rule. Initially, the FTC appealed the ruling, but in 2025 with the change of administrations, the FTC stayed (paused) all appeals. It appears unlikely that the FTC will try to enforce any ban on noncompetes at any point in the near future, but employers should keep abreast of any new developments in the federal law.

Nondisclosure Agreements

At some point, you might have to fire a worker who has access to your company's most confidential information. To prevent the worker from profiting off your trade secrets, you can ask them to sign a nondisclosure agreement. This type of contract restricts the employee's ability to use or disclose to others the confidential information learned while working for you.

Courts are most likely to enforce a nondisclosure agreement if the fired employee had access to the company's trade secrets. A trade secret is information that gives your company a competitive advantage because it's not generally known, you have taken steps to keep private, and others can't readily figure out. Examples include chemical formulas, customer lists, recipes, software programs, and manufacturing processes. If you can demonstrate in court that the employee had access to your company's most sensitive confidential material, the court will be more likely to restrict the employee's use of that information.

Nonsolicitation Agreements

If you're concerned about a fired worker luring away your employees or customers, consider a nonsolicitation agreement. These agreements prohibit the worker from recruiting your staff or soliciting your clients for their new employer or business.

A court is more likely to enforce a limited nonsolicitation agreement: one that prohibits the fired employee from soliciting only a specific list of customers or only the customers with whom that employee had a professional relationship while working for you. If you try to keep the employee away from every one of your customers, a court might decide that you're asking for too much. A court will also look more favorably upon a nonsolicitation agreement that is limited in duration.

For example, an agreement not to solicit customers for one year after leaving the company will fare better than an open-ended agreement.

Keep in mind that a nonsolicitation agreement limits only the former employee's actions. If your customers or other employees decide, on their own, to join or patronize the fired employee's new business, they are free to do so, and you can't require your former employee to turn them away at the door. ●

How to Fire

Telling an employee face to face that you've decided to terminate their employment is, no doubt, one of the saddest and most difficult tasks you will encounter as an employer.

Unfortunately, there's little we can tell you to make you feel better about firing, and we would be doing you a disservice if we made your comfort the focus of this chapter. This is because how you fire an employee—what you say, where you say it, how you say it, and so on—could determine whether the employee decides to sue you for wrongful termination. In addition, you need to keep in mind the practical risks involved in terminating an employee—risks such as theft and sabotage and violence—when deciding how to proceed. Your feelings, then, must take a backseat to these legal and practical considerations.

TIP

The advice in this chapter is just that: advice. As always, you might need to tailor this information to meet the needs of your particular situation. You know your workplace and your employees best. Often, this means you might do things differently from the way we suggest (within legal limits). In the end, common sense should be your guide. If you treat the employee with care and respect, you should do just fine.

The first step is the actual termination, and the second step is an optional exit interview that takes place several days after the termination meeting. This process allows you to break the news quickly to the employee while leaving most of the details of the termination—for example, explaining when the employee's health insurance will end—to a later date, when emotions have cooled. In addition, the exit interview provides a less emotionally charged forum where the employee can vent feelings about your company in general and about the termination in particular.

TIP

Use the same termination process for all employees. This will minimize the chances that an employee will believe you were discriminatory in the way that you handled the termination. If you ever do vary from your standard procedures, you should have a good reason for doing so, such as fearing violence or criminal conduct from the employee.

The Termination Meeting

Your behavior during the 15 minutes or so that it takes to break the bad news might heavily influence whether the employee will sue you, poison coworkers' opinions of you, target your business for theft or sabotage, or leave calmly and without incident.

What Goes Around Comes Around

A study by the Cornell University Graduate School of Business and Public Administration concluded that the primary reason people decide to sue their former employers is the way they were treated during the termination, not the desire for money. The study concluded that, all else being equal, employees who receive unfair and insensitive treatment are more likely to sue than employees who receive fair, honest, and dignified treatment. The study advised that fair and sensitive treatment includes the following:

- giving an employee honest and straight-forward reasons for the termination
- giving an employee advance notice of the termination
- treating the employee with dignity and respect
- reducing the financial burden of the termination (through things such as a severance package and continued benefits)
- allowing the employee to voice opinions about the termination
- offering counseling to ease the psycho-logical shock of termination, and
- offering outplacement services.

Therefore, it pays to carefully plan the termination meeting ahead of time. Don't act on instinct or assume that the right words will come to you during the meeting. Nail down every detail beforehand, including who is going to conduct it and what that person will say to the employee.

Who Should Break the Bad News?

The person who tells the employee that they're being fired should be someone in management or human resources with whom the employee has a positive, or at least neutral, relationship. You shouldn't give this assignment to someone who has an antagonistic relationship with the employee or who is emotionally involved in the decision to terminate.

For these reasons, the employee's supervisor is often the wrong choice for the job. Often, that individual is the one who had to deal with the employee's problems and misconduct on a daily basis, and is emotionally invested in the termination decision. The supervisor's supervisor or someone from human resources might be a better choice.

TIP
The person who breaks the news should not be a stranger to the employee. Choose someone the employee knows and recognizes as an authority figure. For example, a manager from another store wouldn't be a good choice. Nor would a midlevel manager from corporate headquarters whom the employee has never heard of or met.

A Termination Letter: Should You or Shouldn't You?

Many experts advise employers to give the newly terminated employee a letter detailing the reasons for the termination and the status of the employee's benefits. The theory is that the definite and final nature of the letter will dissuade employees from bringing lawsuits, while, at the same time, document the termination.

Termination letters can be beneficial, but also dangerous. Indeed, they can look like "Exhibit 1" to a trial lawyer. They're the first thing an attorney for the terminated employee will ask to see, and likely the first thing the lawyer will introduce at trial, if there's a way to hang you on your own words.

As a result, we advise against using termination letters. You can get the same benefits through conducting a direct and professional termination meeting and through documenting the termination in internal company memos.

Make sure you choose someone who's discreet; don't pick a gossip. If you can, use a person who has some training or background in employee relations. If you have to pick someone who doesn't have this training, take the time to counsel the person beforehand on how to conduct the meeting and what to say (and what not to say).

For the balance of this chapter, we assume that you, the reader, will be conducting this meeting. Obviously, if someone else conducts the termination meeting, make sure that person understands the information provided here. Even though you might not be at the meeting, you could be the one to pay the price if the meeting or the interview doesn't go well.

Who Should Attend the Meeting?

The two essential participants are you and the problem employee. Depending on circumstances and choices, however, you could end up with a larger group.

Representing the Employer

The conventional wisdom is that two people should attend the meeting on behalf of the employer: the person who will break the news and a witness. If the employee files a lawsuit, the wisdom goes, the witness will be there to verify what happened in the meeting.

Recent studies suggest, however, that having more than one employer-side person at the meeting humiliates the employee by making the termination feel more public than private. This humiliation increases the likelihood that an employee will feel upset and angry by the process.

Given this conflict, as always, our advice is to let common sense—and common courtesy—be your guide. If you have an employee who you feel is fairly trustworthy and not likely to sue, we suggest sending only one person to the meeting. If you don't send a witness, make sure that whoever conducts the interview takes detailed notes of everything that both parties say and do.

On the other hand, if you have an employee who has already made noise about contacting a lawyer, you don't have a lot to lose by sending in a witness, and you might even have something to gain.

If you do have a witness attend, it should be a neutral person in management or human resources. The witness shouldn't be the employee's coworker. The less prior connection the witness has to the employee and to anyone involved in the decision to terminate the employee, the better. A manager from another department, another plant, or another store is ideal.

> **CAUTION**
> **Three's a crowd.** The debate over witnesses notwithstanding, it's never wise to have more than two employer representatives at a termination meeting. More than two begins to feel more like an ambush than a conversation.

The Role of the Employer Witness

If you decide to bring an employer-side witness to the meeting, that person's job will be to record what happens. If you and the employee ever disagree over what was said at the meeting, the witness will be there to give an independent recollection.

The witness shouldn't talk at the meeting, except in cases where the witness is a human resources representative who explains the employee's benefits. (Explaining benefits is covered below.) Immediately after the meeting, the witness should write a detailed memo recounting what happened.

When Should the Meeting Take Place?

There are as many theories about which day to fire employees as there are days in the week. One theory holds that early in the week is best. Firing first thing Monday morning allows the fired worker to get on with life and connect up quickly with outplacement services that might help in searching for a new job. It eliminates the weekend downtime the former worker will have in which to mull over the decision and plot revenge. But it also requires the worker to gear up to start the week and commute to work, only to be fired.

Under another theory, it's best to deliver the news last thing on Friday. This approach allows workers to gather their personal possessions at the end of the week, when coworkers are most likely to be gone (or to come in the next day to finish the task in private). Echoing this advice, one recent study indicates that an employee's hostility is greater when terminated earlier in the week. Presumably, an employee is more likely to feel humiliated if sitting at home during the workweek rather than on a weekend.

Intuition must be your guide. You know the employee and your workplace best. Whichever day you choose, we recommend scheduling the meeting for sometime in the morning, which will give the employee a chance to gather their belongings, tie up loose ends, and say goodbyes, all at the employee's own pace.

> **TIP**
> **Pay for the last day.** If you aren't offering a severance package, consider paying the employee in full for the day (or—if you can afford it—the remainder of the week) in which you break the news. This goodwill gesture will reduce the chances that the employee will sue. Explain to the employee that you'll pay this amount even though you don't expect any more work. Paying for the full day is also the safest legal route. In some states, employers are required to pay what's called "show-up pay" or "reporting time pay" to compensate employees who show up to work but are sent home early. In some states, these laws apply even if the employee is sent home early due to termination.

If you fear violence or sabotage from the employee, the best time to break the news is at the end of the last day of the workweek. You will want to get this employee out the door as soon as possible. And the fewer people around when that happens, the better.

Where Should the Meeting Take Place?

Unless you fear violence, sabotage, or theft, your choice of where to hold the meeting will depend primarily on where you can make the employee feel most comfortable. Choose a private place that ensures confidentiality. A noisy cubicle, for example, is not the right spot.

If the employee has a private office, that's the ideal place to hold the termination meeting for several reasons:

- The employee's office is "home turf" and likely their most comfortable environment.
- You want to be able to control the duration of the meeting and end it quickly when you're done. If you're in the employee's office, you can simply walk out when you feel the meeting is over, closing the door behind you.
- Breaking the news in the employee's office spares the employee the embarrassment and discomfort of having to walk through the building and face coworkers immediately after being terminated.

If the employee doesn't have a private office, a conference room or another private area is your next-best choice. If possible, the place should be one where you can leave the employee alone to regain composure after the meeting.

Usually, your office is the least desirable place to hold the meeting, for two reasons:

- Your office is your base of power and authority. Terminating the employee in such a place only increases the employee's sense of powerlessness and humiliation.
- When you are in your office, you can't easily control when the meeting ends. If the employee doesn't gracefully exit on your cue, you'll have to tell them to leave or ask someone to escort them out. Either scenario makes the situation more difficult for both of you.

TIP

Don't escort the employee out the door unless you have to. If you don't fear violence, theft, or sabotage from the employee (and you won't with the vast majority of employees), it's usually best to avoid the strongarm tactic of having the fired employee escorted through the building with a guard or even a supervisor. Not only is it unnecessary, but it's likely to embarrass the fired worker. Many an employee has complained to a lawyer—and to a jury—"After working hard for them all those years, they treated me like a common criminal." In addition, the tactic is likely to unsettle coworkers.

If you fear violence from the employee, choose an area that is as isolated as possible from other employees. It should be private and close to a building exit so that you can escort the employee out of the building as quickly as possible. You might also arrange to have a mental health professional or security personnel stationed near your meeting place. In all but the most extreme cases, however, it's probably unnecessary—and even counterproductive—to have these outsiders at the meeting. Indeed, their presence might further anger or disrupt a potentially volatile employee.

What to Say and How to Say It

No matter how carefully you plan the other aspects of the termination meeting, the words you say and how you say them will determine whether the employee leaves on a positive or a negative note.

In choosing your words, always keep your goal at the front of your mind: You want to terminate the employee, but not hurt or anger them unnecessarily. Be firm, yet kind.

TIP

Avoid any attempt at humor. This isn't a funny event, for you or the employee. Unless you're a true comic genius, your attempts will fall flat, at best, or be insulting at worst.

Prior to the meeting, you should have reviewed the employee's personnel file and learned the details of the misconduct or poor performance that led to the discharge. You should also know what your company has done to help the employee improve and to provide second chances. It's also a good idea to familiarize yourself with the employee's entire history with your company. Although you won't discuss all of these things during the meeting, they'll be helpful to know in case the employee refers to them or wants to ask questions.

Announce the Termination Decision

Start the meeting by informing the employee that they are being terminated and as of what date. Don't ask about the employee's day or family: Such pleasantries will only ring hollow and make the employee feel foolish after learning the real reason behind the meeting.

When breaking the news, be direct and focused. A large part of your job is to convey a sense of serious purpose so that the employee realizes that this is the final word on the situation, not a decision that can be negotiated. For this reason, don't use ambiguous language. For example, avoid phrases such as "This isn't a good fit," "Things just aren't working out," or "We've decided to let you go." Be clear and straightforward. Actually using the words "terminated" or "termination" is often the best approach. For example, you might say, "The company has decided to terminate your employment, effective at the end of the day."

Give Your Reasons

The next step is to explain concisely why you are terminating the employee. This step requires a difficult balance between being direct and clear and being kind and sympathetic. You must do both without straying too far to either side. Don't be so direct that you seem coldhearted, but don't be so sympathetic that you appear to be apologizing or backtracking from the decision. The best tone to strike is objective and professional.

Some employers fall into the trap of thinking they have to justify their decisions during this step. This isn't a wise move. Simply state the reasons and leave it at that. To do any more is to risk hurting the employee's feelings unnecessarily or fostering an argument. In addition, you'll gain nothing by making excuses or by offering defensive or longwinded justifications. For instance,

you might say, "as we've discussed previously, your weekly reports have been late or incomplete too often." You don't need to go into detail about all of the chances the employee was given, the problems their performance caused, or how hard it has been on you.

Resist minimizing the problem that resulted in the termination. Employers sometimes try to spare the employee's feelings this way. If the employee sues for wrongful termination, however, these soothing, disingenuous words will come back to haunt you when attempting to tell the jury about the severity of the misconduct that resulted in the termination.

It's also usually a mistake to try to paint a positive gloss on the job loss by saying things such as:

- "Good jobs are easy to come by these days; it should take you no time at all to find a new one."
- "Now you'll be able to pursue a career that fits better with your interests."
- "This will free you up to spend more time with your kids."

This also isn't the time or the place to communicate what a lout the employee has been. You simply want to end the relationship as quickly and as cleanly as possible. Dwelling on the past problems will only make the employee feel worse.

Don't Debate or Undermine the Decision

You can allow the employee time to vent—to express confusion or anger or disagreement—without being drawn into an argument or debate over the merits of the decision. Tell the employee, "I understand that you feel that way, but the decision is final." If the employee starts to argue with you or mount defenses or objections, end the meeting.

TIP

If you're planning an exit interview, mention this to an employee who wants to argue. Explain that the exit interview is the place to air grievances and opinions about the termination and the entire employment relationship.

It's fine to be sympathetic, but don't offer false hope. If the employee starts to plead for the job, don't flee from the situation by promising to "think it over one more time." You won't be doing yourself or the employee any favors by prolonging the inevitable.

If you're the person delivering the bad news but you don't support the decision, resist the temptation to tell the employee that you are really an ally in a wolfskin coat. Firing a worker isn't the time to seek personal exoneration or to attempt to foster an "us-against-them" mindset by saying, for example: "Off the record, I don't think this is a good decision: I have always enjoyed working with you." Like it or not, you are a messenger with bad news. Deliver it without hesitation and without a hint that you aren't fully behind it. To do otherwise could encourage the employee to file a lawsuit and use your comments to convince a jury that this was a wrongful termination.

RELATED TOPIC

What if the employee mentions a disability? Sometimes, the termination meeting is the first time an employee will bring up a disability. For example, the employee might tell you that a physical or mental condition is to blame for performance problems. Hopefully, if the employee is being fired for performance or productivity problems, you've had evaluations and disciplinary discussions, in which the employee had multiple opportunities to bring up this issue and request a reasonable accommodation. In general, you have no duty to accommodate a disability that isn't obvious unless the employee has requested an accommodation. However, if there's any question as to whether the company has fulfilled its obligations to provide reasonable accommodation, you should consult with a lawyer before terminating.

Explain the Final Paycheck

If you can, have the employee's final paycheck with you at the termination meeting. (In some states, you're required to do so.) When giving it to the employee, state whether it includes accrued vacation and any extra days (for example, if you've paid the employee through the end of the week even though you expect the employee to stop work immediately). If you have a policy of paying departing employees for their accrued sick leave, you should explain that as well.

If it's not possible to bring the employee's final paycheck to the meeting, be prepared

What Not to Say

In this book, we assume that you're only firing the employee because that employee has been a problem, either through continual misconduct (including poor performance) or because of one very severe incident. In such situations, you have what lawyers call "cause" to fire. In this circumstance, you can truthfully tell the employee the reasons for the termination, with little fear of brushing up against wrongful termination laws.

Still, employers occasionally say and do things that make it look like they're violating the law, even when they aren't. Knowing what not to say can be as important as knowing what to say.

Don't Say You're Cutting Back

It's fine to tell a worker that the firing is part of a plan to shed workers, but only when it's absolutely true. Even though it might appear to be more humane to say that a position has been eliminated rather than point to the worker's poor performance, it's a mistake.

If you later get caught in this type of fib by a former employee who claims the real reason for the firing was discriminatory or otherwise illegal, you won't be able to prove your bogus claim. This will look bad to a jury. You could easily find yourself on the losing end of an employee's charge that the firing was based on discrimination or some other illegal motive.

Don't Allude to Changing the Company Image

When firing a worker, don't refer to your desire to change the composition or culture of the workplace. Similarly, avoid either talking of your plans to recast the workforce or implying that the employee somehow does not fit your intended new image. Any of these pronouncements could leave the impression that the employee is truly being fired for any number of illegal discriminatory reasons, such as being the wrong race, gender, or age.

Don't Mention Personal Characteristics

The best way to steer clear of discrimination laws in the termination interview is to never say anything that touches on a person's race, gender, national origin, age, religion, or any other characteristic that might be protected in your state. Obviously, this means no slurs or insults. But more subtly, it means no comments about the employee's protected characteristics, no matter what your intent in making them. When you bring these traits into the termination meeting, the employee will likely think the two could be tied together. For example, let's say you tell an employee, "we were so happy to hire you as the first woman to head a construction team, but your performance just never met our expectations." The employee might believe that she was held to different standards or treated differently based on gender.

What Not to Say (continued)

Don't Mention Physical Limitations

It's also a mistake to mention an employee's injury or physical condition. This can be particularly damaging if the employee has a disability that falls under the protection of the Americans with Disabilities Act.

Mentioning someone's physical condition also holds potential danger if the worker has been injured on the job and has filed a workers' compensation claim. An employee who has filed such a claim is protected under laws that prohibit retaliation. While you can fire an employee for excessive absences or for violating clear-cut safety rules, you can't do so because the employee has filed a workers' compensation claim, even if it causes your insurance costs to skyrocket.

Don't Imply That the Worker Is a Troublemaker

Never say that you are firing someone for "not being a team player" or the like; this is usually code for being a troublemaker. This is especially important if the person truly is someone with a penchant for filing workplace complaints. The employee might believe that the firing was in retaliation for complaining.

---

to tell the employee its amount, everything it will include, and the exact date on which the employee will receive it. Many states have laws specifying when employers must issue final paychecks. Some states require employers to provide it immediately, while others give employers a week or until the end of the pay period. State law also determines whether the employee's final paycheck must include accrued, unused vacation time. The chart at the end of this chapter provides a state-by-state rundown of laws governing final paychecks.

Explain the Severance Package, If There Is One

If you plan to offer the employee a severance package, explain it now rather than at the exit interview. The employee might be worried about surviving financially while looking for a new job; describing the generous severance package now will ease that strain.

If the severance package comes with a catch—such as the employee's signing a release, which waives the right to sue—take care not to pressure the employee into making a decision about severance at the termination meeting. Simply lay out the terms of the severance and give the employee a specific amount of time to make a decision.

Review Any Noncompete and Confidentiality Documents

If the employee signed any noncompete or confidentiality agreements when hired, you'll need to review those with the employee.

An exit interview (if you plan to have one) is the best time to review those documents. After all, a noncompete document means that the employee won't be able to seek employment from your competitors. This isn't the sort of news you want to deliver right on the heels of the termination if you can avoid it. Better to wait and give the employee time to calm down and digest the termination. And, before you talk to the employee about a noncompete agreement, make sure it's still legally enforceable; as explained in Chapter 9, these agreements have been in a state of legal limbo of late.

Explain the Status of Benefits

Having broken the bad news, you must help the employee deal with the practicalities of losing the job by explaining what will happen to any employment benefits.

The length of this discussion will depend on whether you plan to hold an exit interview. If so, you can gloss over this information a bit during the termination meeting. Don't ignore it entirely, however. The employee won't feel comfortable waiting a few days for answers to questions about important issues such as when health insurance coverage will end. If a human resources representative is acting as your witness for this meeting, that person can take over and explain the benefits.

Explain Your Position on References

Many employees will want to know whether you'll provide a reference for prospective employers. In Chapter 8, we explained the issues to think about when deciding whether to give information beyond the dates, job responsibilities, and salary of your former employee. Be prepared to explain your position at the termination meeting.

Discuss what you plan to tell prospective employers: Make sure the employee understands exactly what you will reveal when called for a reference. Don't use vague words such as "positive" or "negative." Employers that choose to give a detailed reference should tell the employee what the prospective boss will hear. Be precise and concrete. This way, an employee who doesn't like what you plan to say can make an informed decision when considering whether to list you as a reference.

In addition to discussing the substance of your reference, explain your reference policy. Say that you will notify the employee each time someone requests a reference and will only give out information to prospective employers that send you a release containing the employee's signature.

Tie Up Loose Ends

After learning of the termination, the employee will most likely feel confused and disoriented. Be prepared to lead the employee through this confusion and answer questions such as:

- "Do I work the rest of the day or leave immediately?"

- "Do other people know this is happening?"
- "When can I collect my belongings?"
- "Can I go home now and come back tomorrow to deal with this?"
- "What do I tell my clients?"
- "I have appointments scheduled for the rest of the week. What do I do about those?"
- "Can I still access my email account?"

We don't presume to be able to give answers that will be appropriate for every situation. However, here are some suggestions that have proved workable in many cases.

Develop a plan for work in progress. Prior to the meeting, find out what the employee is working on and have a plan for passing that work to a coworker or a supervisor. Explain whether you want the employee to complete the work in progress at the moment. It's best not to leave this decision up to the employee. Doing so is unfair and unkind, and it's not in the best interest of your business.

Develop a plan for advising coworkers. Before the meeting, you should have thought about what you'll tell the rest of the company about the termination. Discuss your intentions with the employee and ask for any thoughts. You shouldn't, however, allow the employee to convince you to say anything to the rest of the company that is untrue. Nor should you stray from the advice in Chapter 8 just to please the employee.

Decide about outplacement help. If you're going to provide the employee with any outplacement services, explain them during the termination meeting.

Set up the exit interview. If you're going to conduct an exit interview, explain what this will entail. Schedule the interview for a date and time that's convenient for the employee.

End the Meeting on a Congenial Note

End the meeting on the most positive note possible. Shake the employee's hand and offer your best wishes. If you can say something positive about the employee's tenure at your company, do it. But don't say anything that's untrue or that appears to contradict the termination decision.

Give the Employee a Contact

To facilitate the employee's transition out of your company, provide the name of someone within the company who can answer any questions. Ideally, this would be someone from human resources, but anyone in management who has a positive relationship with the employee will do. This person's job will be to hold the employee's hand through the termination and beyond. The employee may come to this person with questions about any number of things, including:

- handing off remaining work to coworkers
- turning in company materials, such as keys, computers, and cell phones

Termination Meeting Checklist

Before the Meeting:

☐ Notify key people.

☐ Choose someone to conduct the termination meeting (and decide when and where it will take place). Make sure this person is familiar with the employee's performance, personnel file, and benefits.

☐ Notify anyone in management who needs to know about the termination decision.

☐ If you have a payroll or accounting department or service, tell them to drop the employee from payroll.

☐ Choose someone to be the employee's contact after the termination meeting.

☐ Prepare payment.

☐ Check your state's law on timing of final paychecks and whether accrued vacation must be included.

☐ Cut a final paycheck for the employee with all earned wages, including commissions.

☐ Issue any outstanding expense reimbursements.

☐ Decide whether you will offer a severance package to the employee.

☐ Prepare a plan for a smooth transition.

☐ Create an action plan for handing off the employee's current projects to coworkers and supervisors.

☐ Decide what you will tell the employee's coworkers about the termination.

☐ If you think the employee might be violent, arrange for security personnel and an escort out.

☐ Decide how you will handle calls from prospective employers seeking a reference for the employee.

☐ Decide whether you will have an exit interview with the employee.

During the Meeting:

☐ Open with a direct statement about the termination.

☐ Present the employee with the final paycheck, if state law requires it be provided at the time of termination.

☐ Review the employee's benefits and provide any notices required by the state regarding health insurance, unemployment, and other benefits.

☐ Go over the severance package with the employee and present a waiver and release, if applicable.

☐ Remind the employee of any confidentiality obligations.

☐ Collect computer passwords, company credit cards, keys and swipe cards, laptops, phones, confidential documents, and other company property.

☐ Verify the employee's mailing address for purposes of sending the final paycheck or W-2.

After the Meeting:

☐ Make arrangements to have the employee's passwords and computer privileges turned off. (If you're concerned about the employee's stealing company information, you might want to arrange for this to be done during the termination meeting.)

Termination Meeting Checklist, continued	
☐ Remove the employee's name from the various lists you use at your company, including office letterhead, company directories, and email listservs. ☐ Remove the employee's name from your company's website and any online accounts. ☐ Have the employee's emails forwarded to the appropriate person within the company. ☐ Change the employee's outgoing voicemail.	☐ If you assign parking spaces, remove the employee's name from the list and reassign the space. ☐ Cancel the employee's corporate credit card. ☐ Cancel the employee's remote access to work computers. ☐ Identify someone to handle any mail that arrives for the employee after the termination.

- understanding the termination's impact on benefits
- understanding any noncompete, non-solicitation, and nondisclosure contracts the employee signed, and
- understanding the severance package, if there is one.

FORM ON NOLO.COM
A termination meeting checklist is available online. You can download a template of the termination meeting checklist on this book's companion page. For details on how to access this form, see Appendix A.

Document the Meeting

As soon as the termination meeting is over, write down what was said and by whom. You don't have to include every detail, but do note the important facts. Put your documentation in the employee's personnel file.

Collect Company Property and Cancel Passwords

When and how to collect company property and block the employee's access to the building and computer system is a matter of judgment and tact. If you trust the employee and don't fear violence or destructiveness, there's no reason to treat the employee like a criminal, especially at a time when they're apt to be feeling pretty low. Be casual and patient, allowing time to digest the termination before you swoop in for the company credit card and cell phone.

If you do fear violence, theft, or sabotage—or if the employee held a highly sensitive position in your company (such as managing your computer system)—act quickly to block the employee's access to the computer system, confidential files and documents, trade secrets, and the building itself. If you can arrange it, the best time to have access blocked is during the termination meeting.

Terminating Remote Workers

If firing an employee is tough, firing an employee remotely is even harder. It can be especially tricky to convey the right tone—compassionate but firm—on a video conference, let alone to physically collect the company's property or hand over important documents. If you must fire someone remotely, keep these additional considerations in mind:

- **Prepare for the logistical challenges.** Of course, you can't guarantee that you won't face connectivity problems or frozen screens. But think through how you will handle basic physical challenges, such as getting important documents to the employee, getting signatures when necessary, and retrieving the company's property. Some managers follow up the termination video conference with an email that covers practical matters. If necessary, you can also overnight important documents and items to the employee. If you require the employee to return company equipment, arrange for a prepaid self-addressed shipping box to be sent to the employee.
- **Offer kindness and respect.** Because you won't be in the same room, the employee will have a harder time reading your nonverbal gestures, tone of voice, and body language. As we've said, you'll want to be firm yet kind in delivering the news. Think about how to convey this message in two dimensions. You'll also want to

convey respect for the solemnity of the occasion by treating it professionally: Dress appropriately, make sure the visible space behind you is neutral, and eliminate any distractions.

- **Make sure the employee knows that the meeting is important.** Of course, you don't want to ask when would be a good time to schedule a termination meeting. However, you should ask the employee to set aside time for an important meeting, without distractions. And, if you see children or other people in the employee's space when the meeting starts, let the employee know that you need undivided attention and privacy. This will avoid embarrassing the employee in front of family—not to mention having the employee's spouse, roommate, or mother react or join the discussion.
- **Handle the final paycheck.** You won't be able to physically hand over the employee's final paycheck at the meeting, so make sure you get that money to the employee by the deadline set by the state where the employee works. If this is the same day as the termination (as in California, for example), you'll need to make sure the check is delivered—after the meeting ends, of course. You might be able to handle this by direct deposit, if the employee has already authorized this for paychecks. No matter what method you use, however, the money must arrive by the deadline.

Terminating Remote Workers (continued)

- **Decide how you will retrieve property.** Remote employees often have company-owned equipment, such as computers, printers, routers, headsets, and other items. They might also have company documents, from an employee handbook and manuals to sales brochures, client documents, and more. Figure out how you will get these items back, if that's the plan. Should the employee drop them off, will a company representative pick them up, or should the employee ship them? Similarly, an employee who has previously worked at the workplace might have left belongings there.

Company Property

Make sure you collect all company property and turn off all passwords before the employee walks out the door for the last time. Among the things you might need to gather are:

- the company car and keys
- keys or access cards to the building
- corporate credit card(s) (call the credit card company to cancel the account)
- computer password(s)
- confidential files
- client lists
- manuals
- tools or equipment
- laptop computer, and
- cell phone.

Keep It Confidential

As with every other aspect of the employment relationship, keep the termination meeting as confidential as possible. Only tell people about it on a need-to-know basis.

The Exit Interview

Imagine the exit interview as the calm after the storm. The firing was tough—both deciding to do it and breaking the news to the employee—but now everyone has had time to let their emotions cool and get used to the fact that the employment relationship is over. All that remains is to pick up the pieces and move on.

Picking up the pieces is what the exit interview is all about. It gives both employer and employee a chance to reflect on the employment relationship—both the good and the bad of it—and to finish any remaining business. If handled with care and tact, the exit interview can also be a healing process, for both you and the employee.

Not all employees will be interested in attending an exit interview. They might feel too angry, ashamed, or hurt—or might simply be too busy looking for a new job—to return for a final conversation. If you've left any important matters (like benefits, severance, and especially a final paycheck) until the exit interview, this will help convince them to attend. Even in this situation, however, you should use your best judgment as to how long to keep the employee. It's certainly best to try to engage in some conversation and learn what you can about what went wrong. However, at some point, you'll be adding insult to injury if you drag out the discussion with an employee who isn't eager to answer questions.

When and Where Should the Interview Take Place?

Schedule the exit interview for two to three days after the termination meeting, at a time that's convenient for the employee. This way, enough time has passed for the employee to deal with the termination and to start looking toward the future. However, not so much time has passed that memories have faded or that concerns—such as the employee's need for health insurance or questions about trade secrets—are becoming urgent.

Plan to meet off site, if possible. A local park or café might be a good choice of venue. Most terminated employees will be loath to return to the workplace; they won't want to face coworkers and managers. If you must meet at the workplace, schedule the meeting for after work hours and meet in a private place, such as a conference room.

Preparing for the Interview

The exit interview will be more fruitful if you tell the former employee in advance what you'll be covering. When scheduling the meeting, also suggest that the employee give you a list of questions in advance, so that you can prepare.

In addition to answering the employee's questions and explaining the issues listed below, such as health care continuation and benefits, you might want to think about what you can learn from this employee about your company. Some terminated employees feel they have nothing to lose when asked about problems or issues at the company, especially if these issues had nothing to do with the termination. They might give you frank information on supervisors or managers that current employees are reluctant to divulge. The exit interview is a rare chance to get a worker's-eye view on what goes on in your business.

Who Should Conduct the Exit Interview?

Someone who is neutral and unconnected to the termination decision should conduct the exit interview. Usually, the employee's immediate supervisor isn't the best choice. The ideal person would be someone from human resources or an office manager.

If you operate a small business, you probably don't have much choice in who conducts the interview. Just make sure that the interviewer takes care to keep the tone neutral and friendly, especially if there's been any animosity between that person and the employee.

Immediately after the interview, document what was said. As always, keep the details of your conversation confidential and share details only with people who must know.

What Should You Cover During the Interview?

The exit interview is the place to finalize all details of the termination and allow the employee to vent feelings about the company and the termination. We suggest covering the details first, leaving time for the more emotional part at the end. With luck, this will be the last official contact that you or anyone from your company has with the employee.

Benefits

At the termination meeting, you gave the employee a brief explanation of the status of postemployment benefits. Now is the time to go into more depth. Include any information necessary to continue benefits after employment to take advantage of any vested interests such as stock options and retirement contributions.

Among the benefits you should explain are:

- health insurance, including dental and vision
- life insurance
- unemployment benefits
- retirement benefits, and
- stock options.

Confidentiality Agreements

If the employee has signed a confidentiality agreement, provide a copy and review it together. Discuss the employee's past work and give examples of things the employee handled that are confidential. Be careful to explain, however, that these are merely examples and that there could be other information that falls within the confidentiality agreement.

Without appearing threatening or condescending, explain what types of conduct will violate the agreement and what the repercussions of violating it will be.

If the employee still possesses any confidential documents or items, retrieve them at the meeting. If the employee failed or neglected to bring them, set a specific date for the return.

Noncompete Agreements

If the employee has signed an enforceable agreement not to compete with you after leaving your employ, give them a copy of the agreement, review it together, and make sure the employee understands it. Provide example names of companies and businesses that the employee can't work for (but explain clearly that these are just examples and not an exhaustive list). Explain what will happen if the employee violates the agreement, but make sure not to sound threatening.

Outplacement Services

If you plan to offer the employee any assistance in finding another job, explain this at the exit interview.

Company Property

Retrieve any company property the employee still has.

Severance Agreement

If offering the employee a severance package in exchange for a release, now is the time to finalize the agreement. Explain the agreement and, if the employee is signing a release as part of the agreement, review the release together as well.

Before finalizing the severance agreement by signing it, make sure that the employee has turned over to you all confidential documents and all pieces of company property. The severance package is your final bit of leverage. Don't use it until you've gotten everything you want back from the employee.

Final Paycheck

If you didn't provide the final paycheck at the termination meeting, do so at the exit interview, even if the law of your state allows more time. (See the chart "State Laws That Control Final Paychecks" in Appendix B for a list of state laws regulating final paychecks.)

In addition, reimburse the employee any money owed for work expenses.

References

Discuss how you'll handle any request you receive for a reference. You might have already covered this point at the termination meeting, but it's a good idea to review it again in this calmer context.

Listen to the Employee

When we discussed the termination interview above, we cautioned you not to allow the employee to argue or engage in a time-consuming diatribe about the termination. Keep it short; keep it focused.

In contrast, the exit interview is the ideal time to allow the employee to vent and share their thoughts about you and the termination. The employee's emotions have likely leveled out, and time has passed in which to organize thoughts and feelings. Of course, listen with a critical ear and beware of people with axes to grind or grudges to satisfy. And under no circumstances should you allow the employee to go overboard and start abusing you or yelling at you. If the employee can't act professionally, end the interview.

This is also your opportunity to learn things that could make your company better. You might have prepared a list of questions to ask about the worker's experience with your company and supervisors. For suggestions, see "Learn More About Your Company," below.

Learn More About Your Company

Here is a list of issues you could raise with the former employee at the exit interview. It will be a rare exit interview, however, where you would feel it appropriate to ask all or even most of them. Consider asking:

- Describe why you decided to work for this company.
- In what ways did the company meet your expectations?
- In what ways did the company fail to meet your expectations?
- Describe what you liked most about working for this company.
- Describe what you liked least about working for this company.
- Do you think that you were treated fairly by the company? Why? Why not?
- What did you think about your job?
- Do you believe that you were paid fairly?
- How did you feel about the amount of work expected of you? Did you ever feel too much pressure?

- Did you ever want additional training? Did you ask for it? Did you receive it? What did you think about it?
- How would you rate your own job performance?
- Did you get along with your supervisor? How would you rate your supervisor's job performance?
- Did you feel free to talk to your supervisor or manager about problems in your job? Did you feel like your input was appreciated and respected?
- Did your supervisor give you sufficient feedback about your work? Did your supervisor describe areas where you could improve? Did your supervisor recognize your efforts and achievements?
- Did you get along with your coworkers?
- Do you think the company's policies are sensible? If not, please explain.
- What would you do to improve your department?
- What would you change about this company if you were in charge?

Looking Forward

ongratulations! You've solved your employee problem of the moment, either by using evaluations, discipline, and other management techniques to turn a struggling worker around, or by making a careful decision to fire a problem employee and following through. To make sure you don't run into similar problems in the future, you'll have to figure out what went wrong and how you can avoid making the same mistake twice.

Take a few minutes now to think back on your dealings with the problem employee. Were there warning signs, such as offhand remarks or actions that didn't add up to much at the time, but developed resonance as the employment relationship soured? Were you less than enthusiastic when you hired the worker? Were there problems that you could have dealt with earlier? Were your hands tied by your policies (or lack of them)? Were you stymied by a supervisor's failure to manage the worker effectively or document the worker's problems?

Most honest employers would have to answer "yes" to at least one of these questions. In fact, no matter what kind of business, management structure, company culture, or individual employees you have, your preventable employee problems can probably be traced back to one or more of the following three basic sources:

- poor hiring
- flawed (or nonexistent) workplace policies, or
- failing to follow commonsense procedures.

The strategies we've given you in this book can help you deal with employee problems as they crop up—and help you prevent employee problems in the first place.

But to really protect yourself from future problem employees, you'll want to think about revamping any hiring and personnel practices that led to this recent employee problem.

Unfortunately, there's no way to guarantee that you'll never face another difficult employee issue. But by following the tips and strategies covered in this chapter, you can inoculate your workplace against future trouble and give yourself every advantage when dealing with the problem employees that slip through your defenses.

Improve Your Hiring Process

The best way to deal with problem employees is to avoid hiring them in the first place. After all, if you managed to hire only the right people, you'd have a workplace virtually free of employee trouble. What a dream that would be.

Does such a utopian workplace exist?

Probably not. But you can move toward that goal by hiring the right people. We believe that the first step in hiring excellent employees is creating a great workplace. Once you've established that foundation, you can likely improve your hiring process. For many managers and employers, hiring employees is a rushed and poorly thought-out affair. Is it any wonder that problem employees get hired every day, often at the expense of better qualified and more suitable candidates?

In this section, we take a look at some common trouble spots in the hiring process. This isn't a primer on how to hire. Rather, it's a discussion of dos and don'ts intended to help you avoid mistakes that can result in hiring problem employees.

Understand the Position

Before spending the time and money to post a position, sift through applicants, interview, and hire, make sure you understand what the job truly entails. This is an absolutely crucial step because everyone suffers when you hire someone who lacks the proper skills or qualifications. Eventually, the new hire will be miserable if unable to meet your expectations; coworkers will have to take on the burden of doing the new hire's work; the supervisor will have to take time out to train or discipline; and you might eventually have to endure a termination and all the unpleasantness and legal risk that accompanies it.

Consult Previous Performance Evaluations

This process of analyzing a position is similar to that of identifying job standards for a performance evaluation system. In fact, if you're filling a vacant position (instead of creating a new one), a good place to start is to look at the job requirements that you identified in the former employee's performance evaluations. If the requirements are still relevant, use them. But if your recent experience with a former employee has revealed that the standards could be clearer, more precise, or easier to measure, take this opportunity to tweak them.

Talk to Individuals Who Previously Held the Position

You're likely to learn valuable practical information about the position by talking to people who used to hold it. What skills did they feel were most important for doing the job? What were their day-to-day tasks? How did the job fit within the overall business of the company? What qualifications do they think a person needs to perform the job well? What skills would have helped them perform better?

If you conducted exit interviews with former employees who once held the open position, take a look at the notes from those interviews. Perhaps they left because they felt ill-equipped to handle the position, or perhaps they felt overqualified.

Think Back on What Went Wrong Last Time

When filling a position vacated by an employee whom you fired, ask yourself if there's anything the experience taught you about the position. For example, did fuzzy reporting lines contribute to the previous employee's inability to keep the job? Was too much (or too little) expected of one person, or did you assume a level of training or experience that your fired employee was not explicitly expected to have at the time of hiring? It's a rare employer who, deep down, can say, when thinking about a terminated employee, "I did everything right." If improving the job description might have helped, take this opportunity to fix it.

Talk to Colleagues and Customers

You're likely to learn valuable information by talking to the people at your company who interact and work with the person holding the open position. For example, the person who will supervise the new hire might be able to tell you how the job has evolved since you last considered it. Or the folks who will report to the new person might have thoughts on how that employee could better supervise them. If appropriate, consult customers or clients who might have insights on aspects of the job that you are unaware of.

Write a Job Description

Once you've analyzed the position, writing a job description should be a cinch. Not only will it help you choose a person who is a good fit, but it will also help candidates decide whether they are qualified and whether they want the job in the first place. Your job description should include:

- **A job summary:** An overview of the position, with a brief description of its most important functions. Because this will be the first thing applicants read, it's a great place to weed out those who won't be able to meet your expectations.

- **A list of job functions:** Provide a more detailed list of duties to elaborate on the job summary.
- **A requirements section:** A list of the education, certifications, licenses, and experience necessary to do the job.
- **Other important information about the position:** Name any factors you think might be relevant, such as location (is the job remote, hybrid, or in-person?), working hours, travel requirements, reporting relationships, and so on.
- **Salary or pay:** Some states require certain employers to list an expected pay range or salary for the position. Even if not required by law, providing a reasonable pay range can help weed out applicants for whom your pay scale just won't work.

Decide Whether the Position Needs to Be Filled

Having figured out what this job entails, you're now in a position to decide whether you really need to fill it. There are all sorts of reasons why a job might not be necessary, even if it seems indispensable at first blush. Ask yourself:

- Have your business needs changed such that you don't need this position anymore?
- Will changing business needs make this job obsolete in the near future?
- Can you transfer the duties and responsibilities of this position to other people?
- Can you collapse two positions into one?

- Can you purchase new technology that eliminates the need for the position?
- Would it be more economical to use independent contractors for the work?

> 💡 **TIP**
>
> **There are pros and cons to using independent contractors.** On the plus side, you can save money by avoiding costly payroll taxes and benefits. In addition, you can hire someone for a short, specific project without incurring the costs and long-term responsibilities of an employee. On the con side, you lose continuity and control when you have nonemployees coming in and out of your organization. Also, you risk misclassifying the worker, which could result in a government audit, fines, and unpaid wage claims.

Screen Out Poor Candidates

Careful screening will filter out many potential problem employees. You also spare yourself the time and disruption of interviewing people who aren't suited for the job.

Cover Letters and Résumés

Reviewing a candidate's cover letter and resume is an ideal way to separate the problematic candidates from the attractive ones, if you read these documents with a critical eye.

Start by reading the cover letter for more than just content. Look at the candidate's style, spelling, and grammar. Even if you're not hiring a proofreader or an editor, you'll want to see a letter that is done right. Sloppiness at this stage could well presage a sloppy attitude toward work.

Next, look for evidence that this letter was tailored to your company. An applicant who has taken the time and trouble to learn about your company and pitch the cover letter accordingly is one who understands the importance of evaluating a situation individually. This quality is valuable in every employee.

You'll want to use a similar critical eye when evaluating résumés. Look for the following red flags:

- gaps in information (for example, years that are unaccounted for)
- poor appearance and layout
- poor grammar, misspellings, and typographical errors
- vague phrases that give no substantive information (such as "helped," "familiar with," and "have knowledge of")
- possible evasions, such as "attended" a school rather than "graduated from;" and
- incomplete information (for example, listing many former positions, but not providing the dates of employment).

A good résumé will include concrete details about job duties and responsibilities. It should have specific language and details that give a vivid picture of what the candidate did—and, more important, actually accomplished—at each job.

Evaluating Work Histories

Look for candidates with careers that look like logical steps up a ladder. You don't want someone who has been jumping around—or worse, down—in ways that seem puzzling. Look for candidates who have accomplished things in their careers and not just performed various jobs adequately.

Don't be too rigid, however. People who take time off to travel, raise children, or explore different career options can be stellar employees. Is a particular nontraditional job history evidence of a rational yet unusual series of decisions that spell stability for this position, or does it indicate someone who won't stick very long at any job? If the applicant's qualifications look good otherwise, it makes sense to keep them in the pool and find out more.

Don't let stereotypes and biases enter into your thinking. Don't assume someone will make an ideal employee just because they graduated from an Ivy League school, for example. And, similarly, avoid rejecting someone out of hand just who was educated at a state college.

Applications

Cover letters and résumés can be quite valuable, but since they vary so much from candidate to candidate, they can make it difficult for you to compare people using the same criteria. In addition, they might not provide the information that you really want, or they might include irrelevant information that will distract you or cloud your judgment. A way to solve these problems is to have all viable candidates complete the same job application, which forces them to give you just the information you need.

If you're going to take the extra step of sending out applications, don't cut corners by using a generic application from a book or online. The whole point of the application is to get information that's tailored to the job you're trying to fill. Few generic applications will do that for you. They can be helpful in one regard, though: Look at them to get ideas for creating your own application, along with the following tips.

Draft your application while looking at your job analysis. Ask questions designed to elicit information about the skills and qualifications that the position requires. For example, if you're hiring a legal secretary, you might ask:

- How many words per minute can you type?
- Please list the word processing and software programs in which you are proficient.
- Imagine you must file a pleading in an unfamiliar jurisdiction. How would you find out about that court's filing requirements?

Use closed questions. A closed question requests specific information on key issues. Ideally, it calls for a short answer that will quickly tell you whether this candidate is worth pursuing. For example:

- When are you available to begin work?
- When and where did you attend college?
- Did you graduate? With what major and degree?

Avoid questions that would require the applicant to write at length about the topic. Anything that requires more than a sentence or two is probably best reserved for an interview.

Ask "yes" or "no" questions about absolute job criteria so you can quickly cull candidates who don't meet minimum requirements. For example, if hiring for a position that requires driving, ask "Do you have a valid state driver's license?" Or, if hiring for a position that requires travel, ask "Are you willing to travel overnight for work several times a month?"

Don't ask any questions that violate the law. Of course, you wouldn't intentionally do so, but remember that even seemingly innocuous queries can violate the law. For example, a question about the applicant's date of birth could land you in legal hot water if that candidate isn't hired and complains to an attorney or state employment department about age discrimination. (For more on this issue, see "Interview Questions," below.)

Does Your State Ban the Box?

A number of states and local governments have passed laws that prohibit employers from asking applicants about criminal history on an employment application, including requiring applicants to check a box if they have a criminal record. Called "ban-the-box laws," these statutes are intended to give a fair shot to applicants with a criminal record, by encouraging employers to consider their strengths and qualifications rather than automatically rejecting them.

These laws don't necessarily prohibit employers from ever asking about an applicant's criminal record; some just move that conversation to a later point in the hiring process—such as after holding an interview or making a conditional offer of employment. However, a number of states also limit the types of criminal history an employer can ask about or consider at any point in the hiring process. For example, state law might prohibit employers from considering arrest records that didn't lead to conviction or criminal records that have been expunged or sealed. And, even if your state doesn't have any of these laws, a blanket policy of excluding all applicants with a criminal record—without regard to the offense, the job, and other factors—could result in discrimination. (See "Conduct a Background Check," below, for more information.)

CAUTION
State and local laws might prohibit you from asking about salary history. In the past, employers routinely asked applicants—and their former employers, when checking references—what they earned. Employers would often use this information to set the applicant's salary offer for the new position. In recent years, however, many states and local governments have banned such inquiries, which are thought to perpetuate pay discrimination. The bans take different forms: Some bar all inquiries about pay throughout the hiring process, some allow employers to ask once an offer has been made or to ask about salary expectations rather than history, and so on. The safest course of action, to avoid not only violating laws like these but also discrimination claims, is to set salary based on job requirements and applicant qualifications and performance, rather than on what a previous employer was willing to pay.

Assembling Your Application

Take some care in assembling your job application. Don't forget that it represents your company, just as a résumé and cover letter represent an applicant. Make it neat, clean, and professional. Include a cover letter thanking applicants for their interest, congratulating them on making the first cut, and asking them to return the application to you by a particular date. Enclose a release to be signed by the applicant, which gives you permission to talk to references and former employers and to conduct a background check. (For more on this topic, see "Conduct a Background Check," below.)

Evaluate the Returned Applications

You'll find that it's easier to review the completed applications than it was to read through cover letters and résumés. You'll be able to quickly discard applicants whose answers to your "deal-breaker" questions put them out of the running. As for the rest, adopt a set of guidelines that you can apply to each question, and evaluate every application consistently. But don't be too rigid: You don't want to ignore overall impressions, which can be as important as the answer to any one question.

Conduct an Initial Interview on the Phone

Having sifted through the returned applications, your pile of possible candidates for the job should now be manageable. But don't issue invitations for an interview just yet.

Doing an initial interview by phone or video conference can help screen out candidates that the paper screening process doesn't catch, leaving you fairly sure that the people you select for in-depth interviews are top-notch candidates.

The employer isn't the only one who can benefit from a phone interview. Just as you're constantly evaluating candidates, applicants, too, want to evaluate you and your organization. The phone interview could result in some "self-screening" if the applicant decides that the job isn't a good fit. Email the candidate to schedule a phone interview. When you call, have the candidate's résumé, cover letter, and application in front of you. Know what you are going to ask before you call. Prepare some open-ended questions about the applicant's experience, skills, and qualifications. Ask about anything in the applicant's paperwork that you find puzzling or that you'd simply like more information on. Be prepared to answer the applicant's questions about your hiring process, the position, and your company.

Interview Effectively

Once you've screened out unacceptable applicants, it's time for face-to-face interviews. Most employers say that this is the most significant part of the hiring process, the event that determines whether they will hire or reject a hopeful applicant. Yet few take the time to choose the best environment for the interview, prepare questions in advance, create an interview schedule, or plan what to say to the candidate.

If you've ever prepared to interview a candidate by reading the résumé and cover letter five minutes before the interview begins—or, worse yet, while the candidate is waiting at your receptionist's desk—you've turned your hiring process into a game of chance and increased your risk of making a poor hire.

There are a number of popular theories about the best way to interview job candidates. Some are quite complex and require a certain amount of manipulation and deviousness on the part of the interviewer.

Others ask you to orchestrate the interview like a chess match, planning all of your moves beforehand. The one thing all of these theories have in common is that they require you to prepare and think in advance. Even if you do only that, you'll have gone a long way toward improving your hiring process.

Prepare Your Interview Questions

You won't get all of the information you need from a candidate simply by asking whatever occurs to you in the moment. An interview is not a conversation. You need specific information from the candidate, which you'll get only if you ask for it.

Start preparing your questions with the qualifications and skills you want at the top of your mind. For each quality, list questions that you think will elicit information about the candidate's proficiency. Use both closed and open questions, but avoid leading questions:

- **Closed questions invite short factual answers:** "How many people do you supervise?" "Which states are in your sales territory?" "Have you ever written something for publication?"
- **Open questions, by contrast, invite the candidate to speak at length:** "Tell me about a work experience you've had that demonstrates your leadership abilities." "What drew you to the plastics industry?" "Tell me about the accomplishment at your previous job that you are most proud of."

- **Leading questions suggest the answer:** "You have written for child audiences before, haven't you?" "You have a lot of leadership experience, right?" "You must enjoy sales a lot."

Some information—such as number of years of experience, level of education achieved, and licenses held—is fairly easy to elicit through simple closed questioning.

Other information is more difficult to obtain. Does the candidate have problem-solving skills? Is the candidate a motivated worker? Can the candidate work as part of a team? If you ask these questions directly, of course, you're going to get the obvious answers. Can you problem solve? Yes! Do you work well as part of a team? Of course! Not very helpful.

Asking ordinary, open-ended questions might not get you much further. For example, asking, "Describe for me your ability to problem solve" is almost too vague a question to answer.

The ideal way to deal with these difficult areas is to ask open-ended questions that are rooted in real-world examples. This way, the question is specific enough for the candidate to answer and for you to learn the information you need. As a bonus, these answers are often of the sort that can be verified when you talk to the candidate's references. For example, to learn about a candidate's problem-solving skills, you might ask, "Describe a workplace problem that you've faced in the past year and how you resolved it."

Questions that are tied to specific problems or issues are known as behavioral questions. Some common examples of behavioral questions include the following:

- **To elicit information about management ability, ask:** "Tell me about a time when you have had to coach an underperforming employee."
- **To elicit information about sales ability, ask:** "Describe an important sale from your last job. How did you accomplish it? Why are you particularly proud of it?"
- **To elicit information about adaptability, ask:** "Tell me about a time when your current employer changed your job duties. What happened? How did you handle it?"

In most instances, behavioral questions will elicit the most valuable information. When responding, candidates should be able to give specific examples of having performed the tasks or used the skills you are looking for in the current position. In other words, it's not good enough for candidates to say they're capable of doing something; you want to hear about a specific example.

Avoid Illegal Questions

The spontaneous and unpredictable nature of any interview makes it rife with traps even for employers with the best of intentions. Well-meaning comments could be construed by an applicant as prejudicial or could be used later by an unhappy applicant as the basis of a discrimination lawsuit. For example, a casual discussion about a female applicant's home life could lead you to ask if the applicant plans to have children soon. If you don't hire her, she might claim you discriminated based on her gender.

Don't let fear of breaking the law render you speechless. If you follow two simple rules, you'll avoid trouble during the interview process.

Rule One: Don't ask about any characteristic that the law prohibits you from considering in making your decision. For example, don't ask applicants about their race or religion, because you aren't allowed to consider these factors in making your decision. But don't panic if an applicant raises a delicate subject—such as a disability or national origin—without any prompting from you. You can't raise such subjects, but the applicant can. If the applicant does broach the subject, however, tread lightly. Unless the applicant raises an issue that directly relates to the job (for example, the need for a reasonable accommodation—see "Applicants With Disabilities," below), politely steer the conversation in another direction.

Rule Two: Respect the applicant's privacy. Although federal law doesn't require you to do so, many state laws and rules of etiquette require you to respect the applicant's privacy. For example, asking applicants in California about their sexual fantasies (yes, that is an example from real life) violates their state-protected right to privacy.

So, what can you ask? If you've followed the advice in this chapter, you should have analyzed the job and determined the tasks the applicant will have to perform and the skills and experience the position requires. These lists will help you confine the interview to what you really need to know: whether the applicant can do the job. You can ask applicants if they'll be able to perform each essential task, and you can also ask if they have the requisite skills and experience to do so. Remember, the law absolutely allows you to ask questions that directly relate to the job you are trying to fill. In "Interview Questions," below, you can find examples of acceptable and unacceptable questions.

In a rare and narrow exception to anti-discrimination law, you can discriminate against people on the basis of gender, religion, national origin, or age (but not race) if the very nature of the job requires you to do so. And because you can discriminate in this situation, you can ask about the protected trait.

This exception—called the "bona fide occupational qualification" (BFOQ) exception—arises from the fact that some jobs actually require people who have certain characteristics that the law usually protects, such as people of a certain national origin or religion. For example, if you are a movie director searching for someone to play the role of Hamlet's mother, you can discriminate against men in filling the part.

Or if you are an official in the Catholic Church, you can discriminate against non-Catholics when hiring priests.

In order to use this exception, you must prove that no member of the group that you want to discriminate against can perform the job. This is a tough thing to prove. For example, the airlines can't discriminate against older applicants when hiring flight attendants simply because they think that passengers prefer young faces. If you look at the actual job duties—maintaining

order in the plane's cabin, serving meals and beverages—a 45-year-old is just as able to perform the job of flight attendant as a 25-year-old.

Orchestrate the Event

Too often, companies lose out on top-notch hires because they've made the hiring process uncomfortable and confusing. Just as you are evaluating whether you want to hire the candidate, the candidate is evaluating whether to come work for you. The answer

Interview Questions		
Topic	**Acceptable Question(s)**	**Unacceptable Question(s)**
Marital status	If you are married, does your spouse work for this company?	Are you married?
Gender	None	All questions that touch on this topic
Age	Are you 18 years of age or older?	How old are you? What is your birth date?
Religion	None	All questions that touch on this topic
Race or national origin	None	All questions that touch on this topic
Citizenship	Are you legally authorized to work in the United States on a full-time basis?	What country are you from? Are you a citizen of the United States? Are your parents citizens of the United States?
Disability	Please review the attached list of job requirements and duties. Are you able to perform all of them?	Do you have any physical or mental problems that would prevent you from performing this job? Do you have any medical problems that this company should be aware of? Have you ever requested an accommodation from an employer under the Americans with Disabilities Act?

will be "no" if you present the process—and, by extension, your company—as inconsiderate and disorganized.

Choose a comfortable setting for the interview. A conference room is a good choice, but an office with you sitting behind a desk is not. Be prepared to meet the candidate promptly. Notify the receptionist or whoever greets visitors at the door so that the candidate can feel welcome right from the start. You don't want candidates showing up only to find that no one knows who they are, why they are there, or where to find you.

Know in advance which people from your department are going to interview the candidate. They should prepare by reading through the candidate's cover letter and résumé, the application, and your notes from the initial phone interview. You should also meet with them beforehand to discuss what information you want to elicit from the candidate and what information you

Applicants With Disabilities

Of all the antidiscrimination laws, the Americans with Disabilities Act, or ADA (42 U.S.C. §§ 12101–12213), is often the hardest for employers to understand and comply with, especially when it comes to hiring. Employers want to find out if the person they hire can actually perform the job but might not be sure how to explore this issue without running afoul of the law.

If you remember one simple rule, you'll be in good shape: You can ask people about their abilities, but not their disabilities. For instance, you can ask applicants how they plan to perform each function of the job, but you can't ask whether they have any disabilities that will prevent performing each function of the job.

One way to stay within the rules is to attach a job description with specific information about the job duties to the job application. Or describe these things to the applicant during the job interview. Then ask how the applicant plans to perform the job. This way, applicants can tell you about their qualifications and strengths. It also gives applicants the opportunity to let you know if they need a reasonable accommodation. A reasonable accommodation is either something you do or equipment you provide to the applicant that makes it possible to do the job despite the disability.

Some other rules to keep in mind:

- If you have no reason to believe that the applicant has a disability, you can't ask whether the applicant will need an accommodation from you to perform the job.
- If you know the applicant has a disability (for example, the disability is obvious or the applicant has told you about it), you can ask whether the applicant will need an accommodation from you to perform the job.

want to convey. Pick someone to run the interview. That person is in charge of essentially befriending the candidate during the process. Your leader will greet the candidate at the door, usher the candidate to the interview location, make sure the conversation flows during the interview, keep the interview on schedule, and make sure that all relevant information gets covered.

> **TIP**
> **Choose the right social butterfly for the job.** Although we assume in this chapter that the person running the interview is also the person in charge of the hiring process (the "you" we are addressing), it doesn't have to be that way. Interviewing candidates takes a certain amount of social skill. It's not up to the candidate to move the conversation along and make everyone feel comfortable; it's up to the interviewers. If you're painfully shy or have trouble talking to people you don't know, you might not be the best person to run the interview, even if you're the most senior person in the room and will ultimately make the hiring decision. You can sit in and participate, certainly, but put a more social person in charge.

Decide how much time you want to spend interviewing each candidate. Prepare an agenda. If the interview is going to last more than an hour, plan a break or two. Know whether you want potential coworkers to take the candidate to lunch. This can be a nice way for your employees to get a personal feel for the candidate and for the candidate to learn more about the personal interactions within your company.

Don't Ask Applicants for Social Media Passwords

Some employers ask applicants to provide their Facebook or other social media site passwords during job interviews. Employers claim that they need to make sure the applicant's posts are in keeping with the company's image or security requirements. However, employees and their advocates have decried this practice as a clear violation of privacy rights. After all, people who take steps to keep their social networking private most likely would be quite surprised to face a demand like this at a job interview.

In response to publicity about this interview phenomenon, about half of the states have passed legislation to ban this practice. Maryland was the first, prohibiting employers from requesting or requiring passwords to social media sites. A large number of states have followed suit. Facebook has also weighed in by making password requests a violation of the site's code of conduct.

When you call the candidate to arrange the interview, explain who will attend, the agenda, and any special circumstances or instructions (for example, mention whether the candidate will be expected to bring anything along or take a skills test, or should wear any special attire).

Send the candidate a confirming email with the time and the place for the interview, the name of the person to ask for upon arrival, a copy of the agenda, and the names and positions of the people who will participate in the interview.

Relate to the Candidate

As the interviewer, your chief job is to put the candidate at ease. When the candidate arrives, shake hands warmly and offer a beverage. Make pleasant conversation before the official interview starts. Was the candidate able to find the office easily? Has the day warmed up yet? Point out different areas of the office as you walk with the candidate to the interview location. If appropriate, introduce the candidate to people whom you meet along the way.

Conduct the Interview

Start the interview by reviewing the candidate's qualifications and skills. As a courtesy, ask if you can take notes during the interview, and offer the candidate a notepad and pen to do the same.

> **CAUTION**
> **When taking notes, write down only job-related comments.** If the candidate ever decides to sue you for discriminatory hiring practices, your notes could become evidence. The last thing you want are notes of a nonprofessional kind, such as "pretty" or "too macho" or "speaks with an accent." Write down only those comments that you'd feel comfortable having a judge review. The same warning goes for doodles.

Listen actively. When appropriate, make comments to encourage the candidate to continue speaking. Make eye contact and ask follow-up questions to show you have been listening.

Before ending the interview, give the candidate the opportunity to ask questions. What a candidate chooses to ask can be as revealing as the answers you've gotten. In responding, be honest and professional. Be positive about the job and the workplace, but don't lie or embellish the truth. Tell the candidate what happens next: how much longer you will be conducting interviews; when, or under what circumstances you'll call references; and when you expect to make a decision. Thank the candidate for coming and walk them to the door.

Thorough Checking Protects You Even If a Bad Apple Slips By

The main reason to check out a prospective hire is to turn up information that will eliminate an unsuitable candidate. But what if you routinely and dutifully perform the checks, but the employee you hire turns out to be a danger to others? As we say in the law, every dog has a first bite, and you could be the unfortunate employer that hires that dog.

Having performed a reasonable check will help shield you from liability in such a situation. Remember, you're liable only if you have acted carelessly. If your background investigation of your new employee gave no hint of probable misbehavior, you couldn't reasonably have anticipated it, and chances are that a judge or jury won't hold you responsible. In short, you must be careful, not clairvoyant. But this protection will apply only if you have, indeed, done a reasonable job of learning about your new hire's past.

Investigate the Candidates

Once you've settled on the handful of candidates whom you want to consider for the position, the next big step is to do a little digging into the candidates' pasts. Even if you're convinced that one person stands out from the rest, there are important legal reasons to do your homework here. There are two primary ways of obtaining information about candidates: contacting references and conducting background checks.

Legal Reasons to Investigate

From a legal standpoint, it's critical to investigate any potential hire. If you're among the convinced, skip ahead to read about how to conduct your investigations. But if you need convincing, bear with us for a short course on what can happen to an employer that unwittingly hires someone who causes major trouble because it failed to look into the applicant's background.

A person who is injured by your employee can potentially sue you for failing to take reasonable care in selecting workers, using one of two legal theories: negligent hiring or negligent retention (or both). Negligent hiring occurs when an employer fails to use ordinary caution, under the circumstances, in selecting employees; negligent retention happens when an employer carelessly retains an employee who a reasonable person would know has caused, or is likely to cause, a problem. These legal theories can be used against you even when your worker's misdeeds have nothing to do with the job the worker was hired to do. In fact, these theories often are used to hold an employer responsible for a worker's violent criminal acts on the job, such as rape, murder, or robbery.

You are responsible under these theories only if you acted carelessly: that is, if you knew or should've known that an applicant or employee was unfit for the job, or a danger to others, yet you did nothing about it. The following are a few situations in which employers have had to pay up:

- A pizza company hired a delivery driver without looking into his criminal past, which included a sexual assault conviction and an arrest for stalking a woman he met while delivering pizza for another company. After he raped a customer, he was sent to jail for 25 years, and the pizza franchise was successfully sued by his victim for many thousands of dollars.

- A car rental company hired a man who later raped a coworker. Had the company verified his résumé claims, it would have discovered that he was in prison for robbery during the years he claimed to be in high school and college. The company was liable to the coworker.

- A furniture company hired a delivery-man without requiring him to fill out an application or performing a background check. The employee assaulted a female customer in her home with a knife. The company was liable to the customer for negligent hiring.

The clear legal trend is to allow injured third parties to sue employers for hiring or keeping on a dangerous worker. What can you do to stay out of trouble? Here are a few tips:

- **Gather information.** Verify information on résumés; look for criminal convictions and check driving records when appropriate, based on the requirements of the job. These simple steps will weed out many dangerous workers and help you show that you weren't careless in your hiring practices.

- **Use special care in hiring workers who will have a lot of public contact.** You are more likely to be found responsible for a worker's actions if the job involves working with the public. Workers who go to a customer's home (such as to make deliveries, perform home repairs, or manage apartment buildings); workers who deal with children, vulnerable adults, or the elderly; and workers whose jobs give them access to weapons (for example, security guards) all require more careful screening.

- **Root out problem employees immediately.** Under the theory of negligent retention, you can be responsible for keeping a worker on after you learn (or should have been aware) that the worker posed a potential danger. If an employee makes violent threats against customers, brought an unauthorized weapon to work, or racked up a few moving violations, you have to take immediate action.

Contact References

In some ways, interviewing references is like interviewing candidates: Know what you want to ask in advance, ask closed questions to obtain factual information, and ask behavioral questions to elicit softer information. In one key way, however, interviewing references is entirely unlike interviewing candidates: Candidates want to talk to you; references often don't.

Many companies now have a strict policy of verifying only factual information when contacted about a former employee (typically, they'll give you only dates of employment and positions held). They are afraid of being sued by the candidate for defamation, and it's simpler to have a bright-line policy than to follow the law on a case-by-case basis.

A wise employer will anticipate a "name, rank, and serial number" response from most references and will prepare in advance to get around it. The way to do so is to require candidates to provide you with references and tell them that they won't be hired if their former employers refuse to speak to you. Have your candidates sign a release, which gives former employers permission to talk freely to you.

Although you should contact the references that the candidate provided, don't limit your checking to those people. Contact former employers even if they aren't listed as references. If you can, avoid talking to the human resources manager at the candidate's former company. Instead, talk to people who had direct, one-on-one experience working with, working for, or supervising the candidate.

When you talk to a reference, explain that you have a release signed by the candidate. Offer to email or fax it over. Be courteous and professional. Don't get gossipy about the candidate; you have no idea what sort of relationship the two had, and you can't be sure your words won't get back to the candidate. Don't ask any questions that violate the law. If you can't ask a candidate something, then you can't ask it of a reference, either. Don't say anything to the reference that you wouldn't want a judge and jury to hear.

In addition to verifying factual information and learning about the reference's opinion of the candidate, try to verify some of what the candidate said during the interview. You can even quote the candidate: "Albert told me that he solved a computer networking problem last year. Do you remember that event? Can you explain to me what happened?"

Document carefully everything the reference says. Too often, people jot down notes of a reference check in the margins of a résumé. Take legible notes that you, and others, will be able to read later.

Conduct a Background Check

Depending on what sort of position you're hiring for, you might want to check into various aspects of the applicant's history. A background check can be as extensive or as minimal as needed. Sometimes, it's enough to verify educational information. Other times, you'll want to check credit reports and criminal records.

You don't have the right to dig into all of an applicant's or employee's personal affairs, though. Workers have a right to privacy in certain personal matters, a right they can enforce by suing if you pry too deeply. To avoid crossing this line, keep these tips in mind:

- **Make sure your inquiries are related to the job.** If you decide to do a background check, stick to researching information that's relevant to the position. For example, if you're hiring a security guard who will carry a weapon and be responsible for large amounts of cash, you might reasonably check for past criminal convictions. If you're hiring temporary holiday help for the shipping department, however, a criminal background check is probably unnecessary.
- **Ask for consent.** You are on safest legal ground if you ask the applicant, in writing, to consent to your background check. Explain clearly what you plan to check and how you'll gather information. This gives people the opportunity to take themselves out of the running if there are things in their past they want to keep private. It also prevents later claims of invasion of privacy. If an applicant refuses to consent to a reasonable request for information, you may

legally decide not to hire that person on that basis.

- **Be reasonable.** Employers can get in legal trouble if they engage in background check overkill. You don't need to perform an extensive background check on every applicant. Even if you check, you probably won't need to get into excessive detail. If you find yourself questioning neighbors, ordering credit reports, and performing exhaustive searches of public records every time you hire a clerk or a counterperson, you need to scale it back.

Complying With the Fair Credit Reporting Act

If you hire an outside person or company to handle any aspect of a background check, then you must comply with the federal Fair Credit Reporting Act (FCRA). Despite its name, the FCRA does not apply just to pulling credit reports on applicants. You'll also have to meet the FCRA's requirements, for example, if you order a background check from a consumer reporting agency or hire a private investigator to look into an applicant's past.

Under the FCRA, you must get an applicant's written consent before reviewing that person's credit report or asking a third party to perform any part of a background check. If you decide not to hire the applicant based on what the report shows, you must follow certain procedures to notify the applicant and give the applicant a copy of the report. If you conduct background checks entirely in house, however, you don't need to follow these rules.

RESOURCE

Want more information about the FCRA? The Federal Trade Commission publishes a useful guide, "Using Consumer Reports: What Employers Need to Know (www.ftc.gov/business-guidance/resources/using-consumer-reports-what-employers-need-know). You can also find a chapter devoted to employer responsibilities under the FCRA in *The Essential Guide to Federal Employment Laws*, by Sachi Clements (Nolo).

Rules for Specific Types of Records

To gather, request, or use certain types of information, you must follow special rules:

- **School records.** Under federal law and the law of some states, educational records—including transcripts, recommendations, and financial information—are confidential. Because of these laws, most schools won't release records without the consent of the student. And some schools will release records only to the student.
- **Credit reports.** Some states have even more stringent rules limiting the use of credit reports, and some prohibit employers from considering credit history in hiring.
- **Bankruptcies.** Federal law prohibits employers from discriminating against employees who file for bankruptcy. This

means you can't take a negative job action (like a demotion or transfer) against a worker who declares bankruptcy. Courts currently disagree over whether this law also applies to job applicants. Some states also prohibit employers from discriminating on the basis of bankruptcy. In situations such as this, when the law is in flux, it's best to play it safe. Don't discriminate against applicants based on bankruptcy declarations.

- **Criminal records.** Because arrest and incarceration rates are significantly higher for African Americans and Latinos, a blanket policy of excluding anyone with a criminal record could have a discriminatory effect. The EEOC has said that employers can avoid liability by considering each applicant's history individually, taking into consideration how serious the offense was, how long ago it occurred, and the nature of the job (including how much supervision the employee will have). In addition to this limitation, some state laws restrict whether, and to what extent, a private employer may ask about or consider an applicant's criminal history in making hiring decisions. You should consult with a lawyer or do further research on the law of your state before digging into an applicant's criminal past. At the end of this chapter, you can find a chart summarizing state laws regarding criminal history and employment.

- **Workers' compensation records.** An employer may consider the information contained in the public record from a workers' compensation appeal as a basis for rejecting an applicant only if the injury in question might interfere with the applicant's or worker's ability to perform required duties. However, if the worker's injury amounts to a disability under the Americans with Disabilities Act or ADA (42 U.S.C. §§ 12101 and following), you must make sure not to discriminate in hiring and offer reasonable accommodation, if requested.
- **Other medical records.** Under the ADA, employers may ask about an applicant's ability to perform specific job duties, but they may not request an applicant's medical records.
- **Records of military service.** Members and former members of the armed forces have a right to privacy in their service records. These records may be released only under limited circumstances, and consent is generally required. However, the military may disclose name, rank, pay grade, duty assignments, awards, and duty status without the member's consent.
- **Driving records.** An employer should check the driving record of an applicant whose job will require large amounts of driving (delivery persons, bus drivers, and child care providers, for example). Although these records usually aren't confidential, some states restrict the in-

formation that will be released or require the driver's consent. Check with your state's department of motor vehicles for information on the relevant law.

> CAUTION
> **Don't discriminate against unemployed people.** In recent years, some employers have made headlines for refusing to hire anyone who is out of work. In response, a few states and cities have outlawed this practice. And, the EEOC has heard testimony from employee advocates, who argue that a policy like this could have a disparate impact on protected groups with higher unemployment rates, including African Americans, Native Americans, Latinos, and older women. The bottom line is that this type of policy invites unwanted scrutiny.

Pick the Best Candidate

Now that you have carefully screened, interviewed, and investigated applicants for your open position, picking the best candidate should be a cakewalk, right? Not quite. There are still a few pitfalls as you make this final decision:

- **Beware of your gut instincts.** We're not saying ignore them entirely, but these feelings can be based on biases that are more troublesome than helpful. For example, if you find yourself drawn toward someone who is like you, reminds you of your daughter, or is attractive, you might not be choosing the right applicant. If your instincts include illegal biases (for example, disliking someone based on race), you'll be risking a discrimination lawsuit.

- **Don't be sidetracked.** Too often, employers get stars in their eyes about a candidate's one or two exceptional skills and ignore everything the person can't do. Refer to your job analysis from the beginning of the hiring process and use it to find someone with as many of those skills and qualifications as possible.

Don't abandon your criteria just because you like someone. You're engaged in this process to find a new employee, not to make a new friend. Too often, however, the hiring process comes down to whom the employer likes the most. Unfortunately, liking someone isn't going to help much a few months down the line when that person can't perform the job. Of course, liking someone can be one of the qualities that you consider; it just can't be the only quality. If you really don't like an applicant, that's a perfectly legitimate reason not to extend a job offer.

In the end, how should you make your hiring decision? Hire based on job-related criteria; only hire someone who has the needed skills and qualifications. Whether someone will be easy or difficult to work with is a job-related factor, as is whether you think the person will fit into your company culture. Just take care that you don't let illegal biases enter into these considerations.

Evaluate In-House Candidates Like the Others

Hiring a candidate from within your company can be a winning situation for everyone involved. The candidate gets rewarded for valuable service to your company and gets a fresh challenge. You get a known quantity with a proven ability to fit in and do good work. Coworkers get the satisfaction of knowing that hard work is rewarded in the company. What could be better?

This rosy picture will quickly become grim if you don't put this candidate through the same screening process that you would use for outside candidates. If you let your affection cloud your judgment as to whether the candidate really has the necessary qualifications and skills, you run the risk of hiring someone who isn't qualified for the job. Such a mistake can turn a valued employee into a problem employee.

Workplace Policies

Many employers create employee problems inadvertently, by failing to think through their employment practices and workplace rules, much less communicate that information to workers and managers.

Throughout this book, we've suggested personnel policies and forms that will help you handle current problems and avoid future trouble, including:

- an offer letter that clearly explains the at-will nature of the job, to protect you from claims that you entered into an employment contract (Chapter 2)
- a performance evaluation form that gives you a structured way to track— and give feedback about—an employee's performance (Chapter 3)
- a progressive discipline policy that gives employees notice of what's going wrong and the chance to improve (Chapter 4)
- a complaint policy that allows you to learn about problems and take action before they fester (Chapter 5), and
- an internal grievance process that helps you and employees resolve concerns or disputes.

These policies will be valuable allies in your efforts to stay out of trouble. However, many businesses will want (and need) more than a handful of written policies. They'll want a handbook that explains the rules of the workplace.

Smaller businesses often get along fine without any written employment policies. But at some point, especially as your company grows, a handbook that clearly sets out your policies makes good business sense. Although compiling the policies will take some effort, you'll save on time, headaches, and possibly legal fees in the long run.

RESOURCE
Create an employee handbook with a little help from Nolo. *Create Your Own Employee Handbook,* by Sachi Clements, provides all the help you'll need to make an employee handbook that works for your company. Packed with forms, sample policies, and modifications you can use to tailor the policies to your business, this resource allows you to cut and paste policies drafted by legal experts into an employee handbook.

Using an Employee Handbook

Some problem employees just can't be turned around. The best personnel policies in the world aren't going to transform the serial sexual harasser, the thief, or the utter incompetent into employee of the month.

However, many problem employees are made, not born. Employers help create them by following sloppy personnel habits. Lack of planning, poor communication (or none at all), treating workers inconsistently, and failing to document important decisions can lead even well-meaning employers straight into employee disasters.

The strategies we've described in this book will help you avoid these traps. And an employee handbook can serve as your roadmap to stay on the right path, by helping you:

- crystallize and evaluate your employment practices
- communicate with employees

- manage your workforce (and your managers), and
- protect your business from lawsuits.

Evaluate Your Personnel Practices

Many employers create personnel practices haphazardly, deciding each issue as it comes up rather than taking the time to think through their workplace rules. Without a clear set of rules to apply to each situation, however, you run the risk of acting inconsistently. Because your supervisors won't have clear guidelines to follow, they will manage employee problems according to their own rules or whims. What's more, you have virtually guaranteed a communication breakdown. If you don't have a clear sense of your rules, you won't be able to communicate them to your workers, and your workers certainly won't be able to follow them.

The process of creating a handbook will force you to think about every aspect of your relationship with your employees. And after you've laid those policies and habits on the table, you'll have an opportunity to evaluate their legality and value. Perhaps some changes are in order. If you've been inconsistent in your dealings with employees, you can decide on a single set of rules to guide your actions in the future.

Communicate With Your Employees

An employee handbook tells workers what your company expects from them and what they can expect from the company.

"What time do I have to be at work?" "Does my employer provide health insurance?" "How do I complain about my supervisor's sexual advances?" A well-drafted handbook will answer all of these questions and many more.

In addition to relaying basic information about benefits, hours, and pay, your employee handbook imparts your company's culture, values, and history. When was your company founded? Why do you think it is successful? What attitude do you want your employees to take toward their jobs and customers? This information helps your employees feel like part of a team, one that takes pride in its work and its history.

You can also include important performance and conduct rules in your handbook, such as policies on appropriate workplace behavior, performance evaluations, and progressive discipline. This information lets employees know that they will be held accountable, rewarded for good performance and disciplined for bad.

Let Everyone Know the Rules

Workers aren't mind readers. Although you might know what your practices and policies are, without a handbook, employees, managers, and supervisors have no place to turn for this information. This creates an environment ripe for trouble, both legal and practical.

An employee handbook promotes positive employee relations by ensuring that all employees are treated consistently and fairly. It will also save you time: You won't have to explain all of your workplace policies and procedures to every new employee. And it prevents misunderstandings, confusion, and complaints, by giving everyone in your workplace the same essential resource. If there is ever any doubt or dispute about a particular policy, you can simply open the document and take a look. You don't need to have long, agonizing discussions or try to reinvent the wheel.

Protect Your Company From Lawsuits

Just having a handbook available can help you comply with the law and cut your risk of lawsuits:

- Some laws require that employers communicate certain information to their employees. The handbook gives you a convenient place to put this material.
- Even if you aren't required to give information to your employees, there are times when you can protect yourself by providing it. For example, a well-crafted sexual harassment complaint policy can serve as a defense should someone ever sue you.
- Your policies can affirm your commitment to equal employment opportunity laws. This is one step toward creating a tolerant and discrimination-free workplace, which most employers are legally obligated to do.

- In certain situations, your company will be responsible for the actions of its employees and supervisors who violate the law, even if the company didn't condone, or even know about, the illegal conduct. You can cut down the risk of unlawful behavior by providing guidance and prohibitions in your handbook.

Preserve Your At-Will Employment Rights

One very important reason to have an employee handbook is to protect your legal right to terminate employees at will. As explained in detail in Chapter 2, unless you've entered into a contract with an employee promising something else, your relationship with that employee is automatically at will: You can terminate the employment relationship at any time for any reason that is not illegal.

Even when you haven't given your employee a written contract, you can inadvertently destroy your right to terminate at will by creating an *implied* contract with your employees not to fire them unless you have a legitimate business reason. Including an at-will provision in your employee handbook—and making sure that none of your policies promise continued employment—can help you fight off implied contract claims.

Policy Topics

Effective employee handbooks vary widely in size, style, and content. Some large corporations produce handbooks that come in multiple volumes and cover every conceivable aspect of the business. Smaller companies might have a more limited handbook that covers only the basics (and might more properly be called an "employee pamphlet").

No matter how extensive your handbook, it should incorporate the culture and values of your company.

> ! **CAUTION**
> **A handbook is a legal document.** Although an employee handbook can help you avoid problems, it can also land you in legal hot water if you're not careful. Before you distribute a handbook to your workers, you must run it past an attorney to make sure that your proposed policies don't violate the law, that you've included all legally required information, and that you haven't made any promises that an employee's lawyer might interpret as a contract.

Information About Your Company

A welcoming statement is a nice way to start your handbook. It gives new employees a positive feeling about the company and explains why you think it is special. In this opening section, you can also include a mission statement, a company history, biographies of the company's founders, and an organizational chart.

This information will help assimilate new employees into your company culture and lets them share in its goals and spirit. A handbook that makes new employees feel that they belong to a hard-working team really helps get the employment relationship off on the right foot and fosters positive attitudes about your company.

Your At-Will Policy Statement and Employee Acknowledgment

These are must-have policies: an airtight at-will provision and a form for employees to sign acknowledging their at-will status. In your at-will provision, explain that employment is at will; that employees are free to quit at any time, for any reason; and that the company is free to terminate employment, at any time and for any reason. Make clear that nothing in the handbook constitutes an employment contract or a promise of continued employment.

You should also state that no one has the authority to alter an employee's at-will status or make an agreement to the contrary, except the person named in the policy (such as the company president or CEO). The purpose of this language is to fend off claims that a manager's casual statement created an implied contract, while leaving your options open to enter into a contract that alters at-will employment if you choose to do so.

The savviest employers also ask their employees to sign a handbook acknowledgment form indicating that they've received a copy of the handbook and understand and agree to the at-will provision.

CAUTION
The National Labor Relations Board is showing interest in at-will policies and acknowledgments. In 2012, the National Labor Relations Board (NLRB) issued several decisions and opinion memos on at-will handbook provisions. The NLRB was concerned that requiring an employee to agree that at-will status could never be changed might discourage employees from joining together, in a union or otherwise, to improve the terms and conditions of their employment. (This right to act jointly applies to all employees, whether or not a company has a union.) Thus far, the NLRB has approved of policies that give the employer the right to change at-will status and that don't require employees to agree that at-will status can never be changed. At the time this book went to press, this issue was still a political hot potato; you should have an attorney double-check your at-will policy language to make sure it can be enforced.

Hiring and New Employee Information

Here's where you can explain any rules or policies you follow when hiring workers, including job posting, antidiscrimination practices, referral bonuses, employment of relatives (nepotism), hiring from within, and any testing requirements you impose on applicants. As explained above, careful hiring practices are your first defense against problem employees.

You can also explain the rules for new employees. For example, if you provide orientation programs to bring new workers into the company fold, you can describe them here.

Wages and Hours

Pay and hours form the basic exchange of the employment relationship: You pay for your workers' time. Realistically, pay is what your workers care most about, and hours are probably among your primary concerns. You can avoid a lot of problems by making your expectations abundantly clear.

Explain your pay policies, including your rules on overtime, compensatory time, show-up or on-call time, payroll deductions, and wage garnishments. If you have policies on expense reimbursements and pay advances, include those here as well. And you can let your workers know when they will be paid.

You can also describe your work hours here: your usual hours of operation, meal and rest breaks, shift schedules, attendance policies, flextime or other flexible scheduling arrangements, and rules on time cards or other ways of keeping track of hours. Laying out these rules clearly will help you avoid absenteeism and attendance problems (or give you the tools you need to handle them when they crop up).

Benefits

Explain the benefits you offer employees, such as health insurance, dental and vision coverage, life insurance, disability insurance, pensions or other retirement plans, profit-sharing plans, and so on. You probably won't want to go into all of the details about every plan, but you can explain who's eligible for coverage, what each plan offers in a nutshell, and whether employees will be expected to pick up part of the cost. These policies should refer your employees to someone who can give them detailed materials on your benefits programs and answer any questions. This will show your employees that you are concerned about their well-being beyond the workplace, which can help you retain high-quality employees.

Larger employers—those with at least 50 full-time employees (those working at least 30 hours a week) or the equivalent in part-time employees—are subject to the Affordable Care Act, also known as Obamacare. These employers must offer full-time employees health care coverage that meets certain quality and affordability requirements, or face a penalty (this is called the "employer mandate"). Since it was passed, the Affordable Care Act has faced legal challenges, including to the employer mandate. If your company is large enough to be covered and you have questions, talk to an employment lawyer to find out current requirements.

Company Property

What property do you make available to employees: company cars? telephones? computers? In this section, you can explain your rules for use of this equipment. Tell employees whether they can use company equipment for personal reasons and under what circumstances. This will avoid future misunderstandings and pave the way for you to discipline employees who take advantage.

> **TIP**
>
> **All employers need cyber policies.** Many employers have faced the unpleasant prospect of having to read employee email looking for evidence of wrongdoing, such as harassment or theft of trade secrets. These forays are necessary to protect your company, but they run the risk of violating employees' privacy rights. To protect yourself, adopt a policy explaining that the computer and email system is company property and that the company reserves the right to read employee emails at any time.

Time Off

If you offer your employees vacation days, sick leave, personal days, or paid time off, you can explain your policies here. You can also describe any parental leave, pregnancy leave, disability leave, or bereavement leave you offer. And if you have policies regarding leave for military service, jury duty, and voting (all of which might be required under federal law and the laws of your state), explain them here. Putting these policies in writing helps prevent employee abuse and ensures that managers won't play favorites when employees request time off.

If you are covered by the Family and Medical Leave Act (FMLA) and you provide your employees with a handbook or other written materials explaining your benefits, you are legally required to include information on the FMLA, including an explanation of employee rights and responsibilities under the law.

Workplace Conduct and Behavior

Here, you can describe your standards of conduct, such as rules on employee dress; prohibitions on horseplay, conflicts of interest, and unprofessional behavior; and policies about bringing children (or pets) to work. You can also explain your performance evaluation system. If you've decided to adopt a progressive discipline policy, you can describe it in this section of your handbook, too.

Health, Safety, and Security

Most employers benefit from adopting a clear policy explaining the safety rules for the workplace (for example, that hardhats or hairnets are required, or that open-toed shoes or jewelry are prohibited). Your safety policy should also tell workers what to do in case of an accident. You can also include policies on

workplace security (for example, rules on visitors in the workplace, setting the building alarm, working after hours, or dealing with workplace security guards), workplace violence, emergency preparedness, drug and alcohol use, and smoking. These policies will lay the groundwork for disciplining employees who endanger themselves or others.

Discrimination and Harassment

Your company should have a policy prohibiting discrimination and harassment (you can put this information all in one policy or adopt separate policies). Explain the types of discrimination and harassment that are prohibited, what employees should do if they have been harassed or discriminated against, and what the company will do in response. Explain that managers are responsible for reporting discrimination or harassment and that retaliation is prohibited.

You should also have a separate complaint policy; see Chapter 5 for details and sample policy language.

Confidential Company Information

In this section, you can describe company policies on trade secrets, proprietary information, and conflicts of interest. Almost every company has some confidential information: a customer list, a recipe or formula, a process for doing a task, or other company know-how. To make sure that your employees don't reveal this information unnecessarily, you can adopt a policy explaining what information is confidential and how you expect employees to treat it. You can also explain what you consider a conflict of interest, such as working for a competitor, using the company's resources for a personal business, or owning an interest in a competitor.

Remote Work

If you have employees working from home, you should have a policy explaining the rules for telecommuters, including which types of workers are eligible for remote work, expectations for attendance and schedules, what expenses the company will pay, and cybersecurity issues for those working from home.

Termination

In this section, explain your procedures for handling departing employees. You might include policies on exit interviews, final paychecks, continuation of benefits and insurance coverage, returning company property, and references. These policies will tell employees what they can expect when they leave the company to avoid the types of misunderstandings and unrealistic expectations that can lead to bad feelings (and fuel revenge-inspired lawsuits). ●

Hiring a Lawyer

Even the most conscientious employer occasionally needs help from a lawyer. Although you can handle many employment problems on your own, some will require legal expertise. Certain employment laws are highly technical, rapidly changing, or difficult to figure out. Courts and government agencies issue new opinions interpreting these laws all the time, sometimes completely overturning what everyone thought the law meant.

Consider also that lawsuits by former employees—especially by workers who claim that they suffered discrimination, harassment, or retaliation—can end in huge monetary awards against employers. In such a case, an employer can save money by seeking legal advice at the first sign of trouble, rather than waiting to be served with a lawsuit.

This chapter describes:

- how and when to seek help from a lawyer
- some of the trickier employment issues that might require legal assistance
- what you can DIY to lower your legal bills
- how to find and work with a lawyer
- how lawyers charge for their services, and
- how to fire your lawyer if things aren't working out.

Other Sources of Legal Information

Lawyers aren't the only source of legal information for enterprising employers. Federal agencies—including the Equal Employment Opportunity Commission (EEOC), the Department of Labor (DOL), the Department of Justice (DOJ), and the Internal Revenue Service (IRS)—offer many publications at little or no cost that explain federal laws and regulations affecting employers. You can find these materials on the agencies' websites (listed in Appendix B).

Similarly, many state agencies provide helpful materials on their websites or in print. State departments of labor and state fair employment offices can assist you in understanding a variety of state labor laws and antidiscrimination laws. You can find these agencies listed at www.nolo.com/FEPA.

Also, some professional and trade organizations or local business groups occasionally hold seminars, educational programs, or trainings that explain employment laws and regulations. Check with your local professional group, chamber of commerce, Small Business Administration office, community college, or trade organization to find out if these programs are available in your area (often listed on an organization's website or in its newsletter).

Keep in mind, too, that other professionals can help you with specific workplace issues for less than you would have to pay a lawyer. An accountant, workplace consultant, or professional HR trainer might meet your needs.

When to Hire a Lawyer

You don't need to talk to a lawyer every time you evaluate, discipline, or even fire a worker. After all, lawyers don't come cheap. In certain situations, however, money spent on legal advice is a sound investment. A lawyer can review your policies, contracts, and other employment documents to make sure that they'll stand up in court. And you can protect yourself from future lawsuits—and save time and money—by getting legal advice before taking risky action against a problem employee. Finally, you should definitely get legal help when faced with a lawsuit or other adversarial proceeding.

Reviewing Documents

A lawyer can review and troubleshoot any employment-related agreements you routinely use with workers, such as employment contracts, severance agreements, and releases. A lawyer can check your contracts to make sure they contain all the necessary legal terms and will be enforced by a court. If you've included any language that might cause problems later, or if you've gone beyond what the law requires of you, a lawyer can also draw these issues to your attention. And a lawyer can give you advice about when to use these contracts. For example, you might not want to give severance to every departing employee or enter into an employment contract with every new worker. A lawyer

can help you figure out what makes sense for your business and its employees.

You can also ask a lawyer to give your employee handbook or personnel policies a thorough legal review. First and foremost, a lawyer can make sure your policies don't violate any laws, such as those governing overtime pay, family leave, final paychecks, or occupational safety and health. A lawyer can also check for any language that might create an implied employment contract. And a lawyer might advise you about additional policies to consider.

Advice on Employment Decisions

If you're worried that an employee might sue, you should consider getting legal advice before firing the employee for misconduct, performance problems, or other bad behavior. A lawyer can tell you not only whether terminating the worker will be legal, but also what steps you can take to minimize the risk of a lawsuit.

Consider asking a lawyer to review your decision to fire in any of these situations:

- The worker has a written or oral employment contract restricting your right to fire.
- Your policies and statements might create an implied contract.
- The employee is due to vest benefits, stock options, or retirement money soon (such that firing the employee could lead to a bad-faith claim).

- The worker recently filed a complaint or claim with a government agency, or complained to you, of illegal or unethical activity.
- The employee recently filed a complaint of discrimination or harassment.
- Firing the employee would dramatically change your workplace demographics.
- The worker recently revealed membership in a protected class (for example, the worker is pregnant, has a disability, or practices a particular religion).
- You're concerned about the worker's potential for violence, vandalism, theft, or sabotage.
- The worker has access to your company's high-level trade secrets or competitive information.
- You are firing the worker for excessive absenteeism and are concerned that the absences or leave might be covered by the Family and Medical Leave Act or the Americans with Disabilities Act.
- The employee denies committing the acts that were the basis for the firing, even after an investigation.
- The employee has hired a lawyer.

You might also want to seek legal advice before taking employment actions short of termination. For example, a lawyer can help

Your Insurance Company Might Foot the Bill

Your business's insurance company might pay for a lawyer to defend you in a lawsuit, as well as pay any damages awarded (or settlement negotiated). Here are three types of policies that might apply:

- **Commercial general liability (CGL) insurance.** This policy protects your company when someone sues. However, many CGL policies exclude employment-related claims by employees, either expressly or by denying coverage for "intentional acts," defined by the insurance industry to include many types of discrimination, harassment, and other wrongful termination claims.
- **Directors and officers (D&O) insurance.** D&O insurance covers a company's directors and officers for lawsuits by third

parties, including employees. Many of these policies also fall short because they provide personal coverage only for the individuals named in the policy, not the company itself. This exclusion leaves employers uninsured for most employment claims.

- **Employment practices liability insurance (EPLI).** These policies are intended to fill in the gaps left by the more traditional policies by covering most employment-related litigation. The terms and definitions of these policies can vary widely. Some will pay for "risk management" assistance as well, such as the cost of having an attorney review employment policies, applications, handbooks, and procedures for dealing with complaints.

plan a thorough and legal investigation, decide on appropriate disciplinary action, or explain the extent of your obligations in accommodating a worker's disability. If money is tight, however, spend your legal budget getting advice on those issues that could cause the most trouble. You don't need a lawyer's help with every workplace investigation, for example, but it's well worth considering if a number of workers are accused of serious misconduct, such as harassing female employees.

Representation in Legal or Administrative Proceedings

If a current or former employee sues you, hire a lawyer right away. Employment lawsuits can be complex. You have to take certain actions immediately to make sure that your rights are protected and to preserve evidence that might be used in court. The time limits for taking action are short: Many courts require you to file a formal, legal response to a lawsuit within just a few weeks.

Sometimes a current or former worker initiates some kind of adversarial process short of a lawsuit. For example, an employee might file an administrative complaint of discrimination, retaliation, or harassment with the Equal Employment Opportunity Commission or a similar state agency. Or, a former employee might file a wage and hour complaint with the Department of Labor.

In these situations, you should at least consult a lawyer, if not hire one. It's also wise to contact your insurance broker and ask if your policies cover administrative proceedings. Although some employers can and do handle administrative matters on their own, most could benefit from legal advice on evaluating the strength of the employee's claim, preparing a response for the agency or administrative board, dealing with agency investigations or requests for information, and presenting evidence at a hearing. A lawyer can advise you of your rights and what to expect as the process continues.

If you have the money and the claim seems serious, you can also hire a lawyer to represent you in these proceedings. It might be worth paying for legal representation in any of the following situations:

- The employee raises serious claims that could result in a significant monetary award. If the worker alleges that severe harassment, discrimination, or retaliation took place, for example, it's risky to fight the claim on your own.
- Other employees or former employees have made similar allegations, either to the agency or within the workplace. An agency will be more likely to investigate closely—and more likely to find in the employee's favor—if other workers have come forward.

An Accused Employee Might Need a Separate Lawyer

Believe it or not, you might actually have to pay for two lawyers to handle a single employment problem. This can happen if both the company and an individual employee or manager are accused of wrongdoing. For example, if a former employee claims that a manager sexually harassed her or that a coworker assaulted her in the workplace, you and your accused employee might need separate lawyers.

The reason? A lawyer can't represent more than one client if the joint representation creates a conflict of interest: a situation in which the interests of the company and the interests of the individual employee are at odds. In the examples given above, the company might want to blame the accused employee (for example, by arguing that even though the employee engaged in this misconduct, it wasn't something for which the company should be held responsible). Obviously, if the accused employee wants to argue that he didn't do it, the two defenses will conflict. (In some situations, the lawyer may represent both the company and the employee, if both provide written consent. However, the employee might not agree to this.)

In these situations, you might have to not only find a separate lawyer for your employee, but pay the lawyer's bill as well. Some states handle this issue by requiring employers to "indemnify"—reimburse—their employees for any employment-related expenses, including the cost of defending against a lawsuit. Ask your lawyer about your state's rules.

- The worker intends to file a lawsuit. In this situation, the employee might simply be using the administrative proceeding to gather evidence to support a court case.
- The employee has hired a lawyer.

How to Find a Good Lawyer

We can't overestimate the importance of choosing the right lawyer to help you with employment-related legal issues. An experienced, skilled lawyer can help you make careful employment decisions, defend you in legal disputes with your employees, and even prevent legal problems before they start by advising you on your company's employment policies and practices. A lousy lawyer might do none of this, but charge you exorbitantly nonetheless. The sad truth is that legal advice is expensive regardless of its quality. Get your money's worth by hiring the right lawyer for your company.

Getting Leads

Your first step in finding the right lawyer is to get recommendations from other people and organizations. Remember to ask for referrals to lawyers who specialize in employment law. Because most lawyers specialize in one or two areas of law, a lawyer who skillfully handles divorces, bankruptcies, or trademark disputes won't do you much good in dealing with employees. Consider also why you need legal help. If you are facing a lawsuit, you will need help from a litigator: a lawyer who regularly handles lawsuits all the way through trial and is comfortable in a courtroom. If you need someone to review your personnel policies or a severance agreement, litigation experience isn't absolutely necessary.

You can get leads from many sources, including:

- **Business associates.** Other employers could be your best source of leads. Talk to the people in your community who own or operate excellent businesses. Ask for the names of their lawyers and whether they are satisfied with their lawyers' work.
- **Friends and relatives.** You might know someone who was recently involved in an employment dispute. Even if your acquaintance was suing an employer, find out whether they had a good lawyer. A lawyer who represents only employees (as many do) can probably refer you to respectable lawyers who work with employers.
- **Lawyers.** If you have a regular lawyer you use for estate planning, tax advice, or other legal issues, ask whether that person knows any employment lawyers.

- **Trade and business organizations.** If you belong to a professional group, ask other members for legal recommendations. Local groups that support the rights of business owners, such as the chamber of commerce, might also know of good employment lawyers.
- **Professionals outside your field.** People who provide services to the business community—such as bankers, accountants, insurance agents, or real estate brokers—might also give you leads.
- **Articles and newsletters.** Some employment lawyers write articles for trade magazines or newspapers. Track down these authors and find out whether they are taking on new clients or can refer you to other employment lawyers they respect.
- **Online lawyer directories.** Two sites that are part of the Nolo family, Lawyers.com and Avvo.com, provide excellent and free lawyer directories. These allow you to search by location and area of law, and list detailed information about and reviews of lawyers.

Comparison Shopping

Once you have some leads, do a little research. Check online reviews, Google the lawyers to look for relevant news articles or their own publications or blogs, and read their biographical sketches on www.martindale.com. With enough sleuthing, you should be able to get a picture of each lawyer's skills, personality, and reputation.

Don't Hire a Lawyer Sight Unseen

No matter how positive your initial conversation with a lawyer or how glowing the referral, it's never a good idea to hire a lawyer without meeting face to face. You have to assess the lawyer's demeanor and professionalism, how the lawyer interacts with you, and the many other intangibles that go into a solid working relationship. And few lawyers will take on a case—particularly one that might turn into a lawsuit—without meeting the client.

Next, call the lawyers on your list. Some take these calls directly; others have staff that screen calls from potential clients. A lawyer or screening person will usually ask basic questions about why you need a lawyer and the names of the parties involved. Often, these questions are geared toward making sure that your case is a good fit for the lawyer and that there wouldn't be any conflict for the attorney to talk further with you.

Preparing to Meet the Lawyer

Before your first meeting, organize your thoughts. Prepare for the lawyer an outline that contains all the key facts necessary to evaluate your problem.

Write down, in chronological order, the main events and conversations leading to the dispute. A page or two of notes should suffice. Also jot down the names and telephone numbers of any important witnesses the lawyer might need to interview.

Gather any documents the lawyer should review—an employment contract, employee handbook, offer letter, severance agreement, sexual harassment policy, or investigation notes, for example—and make copies to bring with you. Some lawyers will ask you to send the documents to them ahead of time so they can do any necessary legal research before the meeting.

Questions to Ask Your Sources

If you get a lead from someone who has actually worked with the recommended lawyer, find out what they liked about the lawyer and why. Ask how the legal problem turned out: Was the lawyer successful? Ask about the lawyer's legal abilities, communication skills, and billing practices. Here are additional questions to consider:

- Did the lawyer respond promptly to your telephone calls and emails?
- Did the lawyer keep you informed of developments in your lawsuit or other legal dispute?
- Were your legal bills properly itemized and in line with the costs the lawyer estimated for you at the outset?
- Did the lawyer oversee your case personally, or hand it off to a less experienced lawyer in the same firm?
- Did the lawyer respect your feelings about how your legal dispute should be handled?
- Did the lawyer deliver as promised?

Speaking With the Lawyer

When you meet with a lawyer, explain your legal problem and ask for the lawyer's advice about what to do next. Ask any questions you might have about your situation. Also, ask about the lawyer's background, experience, and billing practices. As you talk, consider not only the legal advice you receive, but also your impression of the lawyer's communication skills and style. Does the lawyer listen well? Are you getting answers to your questions? Do you feel comfortable talking honestly to the lawyer? Can you understand what the lawyer is talking about? Particularly if you're facing a lawsuit, these issues will only become more important as you move forward.

Whenever you talk privately to a lawyer about your legal matters, that conversation is subject to a legal "privilege," which means no one can force you or the lawyer to disclose what either of you said. This is true even before you actually hire the lawyer and even if you decide, ultimately, not to hire the lawyer at all.

This means that when you interview lawyers to decide whether you want them to represent you, you can freely discuss the facts of your situation, warts and all. The lawyer's advice will only be as good as the information you reveal. If you hold back important facts because you think they make you look bad or weaken your claims, you won't receive a candid assessment of your situation or sound advice about how to avoid further trouble.

You Might Have to Pay for a Consultation

Most lawyers require potential clients to pay a consultation fee for meeting to discuss legal concerns and the possibility of working together. If a lawyer charges such a fee, ask what you will get for your money. Ordinarily, you can expect a consultation fee to cover time the lawyer spends reviewing documents important to your case, doing research, and meeting with you. Find out if there's a flat fee or if the lawyer charges hourly. If you find the right lawyer and can afford it, this will be money well spent.

Legal Fees

Many disputes arise between lawyers and their clients about fees. (Given how much lawyers charge for their time, this isn't surprising.) Your best protection against problems over attorneys' fees is to work out a fee agreement before the lawyer you hire starts any legal work.

Have a frank discussion about fees and costs. Ask how the lawyer charges (by the hour or in some other manner), what the hourly rate is, and what the total legal bill will likely be. Tell the lawyer how much you're willing to spend. Although it's rare, a lawyer might sometimes agree to charge a lower fee, change the fee structure (for example, accept some payment in free services or products your company makes or in stock options), or otherwise accommodate your needs.

How Lawyers Charge for Their Time

There are four basic ways that lawyers charge for their services, depending on the type and amount of legal help needed:

- **Hourly.** Most employers will pay their lawyer an hourly fee, a set rate of anywhere from $150 to $500 or more per hour of legal work.
- **Flat fee.** For discrete tasks that are fairly straightforward, a lawyer might charge a set amount for the whole job. For example, a lawyer might draft a severance agreement or an employment contract for $2,000.
- **Retainer.** Larger companies might be able to hire a lawyer for a flat annual fee, called a "retainer," which covers any and all routine legal business during the year. If you run into extraordinary legal problems (a lawsuit, for example), you will usually have to pay more.
- **Contingency fee.** A lawyer who takes a percentage of the amount won for you in settlement or trial is charging a "contingency fee." This usually isn't an option for employers, who, in most lawsuits, won't be collecting any money from their current or former employee. However, if you're suing a former

employee for money—for misappropriating trade secrets, for example—and the employee is rich enough to pony up if you win, a lawyer might consider taking on at least that part of the work on a contingency fee basis.

Paying for Costs

In many cases, you'll be paying for more than just the lawyer's time. You might also have to pay what are called "legal costs": the expenses the lawyer incurs handling your legal work. If you're seeking legal advice to review contracts or help make an employment decision, you'll probably face minimal costs, perhaps just the price of copying documents and postage. However, if you're involved in a lawsuit, your costs will be substantial. You'll have to pay for depositions, expert witnesses, private investigators, court fees, and exhibits. Ask your lawyer ahead of time for a description and estimate of the costs you might have to pay.

> **TIP**
> **Don't pay for costs that are actually part of the lawyer's own operating expenses or overhead.** If you get billed for something the lawyer didn't have to pay for (using the law firm's conference room, for example) or something that the lawyer must have in order to stay in business (local phone service or internet, for example), question the charge.

Lawyers charge their clients for costs in several different ways. Some require clients to deposit a sum of money to be used to pay costs as they accrue. Others bill clients monthly for costs. Yet others bill clients when their legal work is finished. Find out which of these methods your lawyer plans to use.

Getting It in Writing

Once you've hammered out the details, put your fee agreement into writing. Make sure the written agreement covers the hourly billing rate or other charges, how often you'll be billed, whether you'll be required to deposit money in advance, how costs are billed, when the lawyer will be paid, and other relevant information. If the lawyer will delegate some of your legal work to a less experienced lawyer, paralegal, or secretary, that work should be billed at a lower hourly rate, which should be indicated in the written fee agreement.

Working With Your Lawyer

Your lawyer's job is to protect and enforce your company's legal rights. This might include reviewing important documents, providing legal representation in court, helping with difficult employment decisions, or keeping you out of lawsuits. Remember, however, that although your lawyer has the legal expertise, it's your business and reputation that are on the line. To get the best representation possible, you must work well with your lawyer and ensure that your interests are being safeguarded. Start by following these tips:

- **Be honest.** Tell your lawyer all the facts that relate to your legal problem. Thus armed, your lawyer can figure out how best to prevent legal trouble and meet your needs.

- **Keep in touch.** Stay in regular contact with your lawyer to find out what's going on in your dispute. Keep your lawyer apprised of any planned vacations or other lengthy absences, in case your presence will be required at upcoming legal proceedings.

- **Keep track of important documents and deadlines.** Keep a file that includes all important documents relating to your legal dispute. This will allow you to discuss your case with your lawyer intelligently and efficiently, even over the phone. Make a note of any important deadlines.

- **Do your own research.** By learning as much as you can about the laws and court decisions that apply to your dispute, you'll be able to monitor your lawyer's work, make informed decisions about settlement offers, and maybe even keep yourself out of legal trouble the next time around.

- **Check billing statements.** Every bill you receive from your lawyer should list the costs and fees incurred that month. If you have questions or don't agree with all the charges, talk to your lawyer. Most states require a certain amount of detail in a lawyer's billing statements, so ask for more information if you need it.

Ways to Keep Legal Bills Low

If your lawyer is billing by the hour, the devil is in the details. Most lawyers bill in increments as small as 1/10th of an hour (six minutes). Even if you use less than that time, however, you will get billed for the full six minutes. And any time the lawyer spends on you or your case—talking on the phone, responding to emails, reviewing documents, or doing research—is billable. With this in mind, you can take a few steps to minimize your legal bills.

Before picking up the phone to talk to your lawyer, think about the purpose of your call. Do you need documents, scheduling information, or other routine assistance? Maybe the lawyer's secretary can take care of it (for free). Do you have questions you need to ask? Write them down ahead of time, so you don't have to call back and get billed for a second conversation. Be pleasant, but keep chitchat to a minimum.

If you can provide information or ask simple questions by email or whatever electronic messaging system your lawyer prefers, that's even more time-efficient.

Firing a Lawyer

You have the right to change lawyers for any reason, at any time (although you might have to get a judge's permission to switch if you are on the eve of, or in the midst of, trial; see below).

When to Make the Change

Changing lawyers—especially in the middle of a lawsuit—will take time and money. Your new lawyer will have to get up to speed on your legal affairs, and you'll have to spend time explaining your situation and developing a working relationship. Despite these drawbacks, it can make sense to switch lawyers in any of these serious circumstances:

- Your dispute becomes a lawsuit, and your lawyer lacks litigation experience.
- You and your lawyer can't agree on important strategic decisions. You're unlikely to agree on everything, but if you find yourself butting heads frequently over significant legal matters, think about finding a lawyer who is more attuned to your wishes.
- You and your lawyer consistently disagree about fee and cost issues. Some discomfort over lawyers' high fees is inevitable. But if you keep getting billed for expenses that you think are unfair, and your lawyer can't or won't explain the logic behind them, consider going elsewhere.

- Your lawyer fails to stay in touch. Sometimes a lawyer will be unable to take your phone call right away or will need to postpone a meeting. But if your lawyer drops out of sight or stops returning your calls, it might be time for a change.
- You can't get along with your lawyer. Personality clashes happen. If things reach a point where you can't stand each other, switching lawyers might be the only way to keep the legal matter on track.
- You lose confidence in your lawyer. Perhaps your lawyer has done something truly upsetting—lied outright, missed an important court deadline, or misplaced crucial documents. Or you might be unimpressed with your lawyer's skills or advice. Any time you lose confidence in your lawyer's abilities, competence, or ethics, you should find another lawyer.

How to Fire Your Lawyer

The first thing to do is tell your lawyer—in writing—that you're taking your business elsewhere. Ask your now-former lawyer to send your client file and related materials to your new lawyer. Your new lawyer should also send your former lawyer a letter saying that the new lawyer is taking over the case.

If a lawsuit has already been filed, you'll have to file a court document, usually called a "Substitution of Attorneys" or "Substitution of Counsel." This officially informs the court, the other parties, and their lawyers of the switch. Your new lawyer can prepare this form. If you are in or about to start a trial, the judge will have to approve the change. The judge will consider, among other things, whether your opponent will be unfairly affected by any delay that your change in lawyers might cause.

If you're changing lawyers because of deceptive, unethical, or otherwise illegal behavior, consider taking action. Call the local or state bar association for guidance on what types of lawyer misconduct are prohibited and how to file a complaint.

Using the Downloadable Forms

This book comes with interactive files that you can access online at:

www.nolo.com/back-of-book/PROBM.html

You can open, edit, print, and save these RTF (Rich Text Format) form files with most word processing programs such as Microsoft *Word*, Windows *WordPad*, and recent versions of *WordPerfect*. On a Mac, you can use Apple *TextEdit* or Apple *Pages*. You can also work with the forms through a word processing app such as Google Docs (www.docs.google.com).

Editing RTFs

Here are some general instructions about editing RTF forms in your word processing program. Refer to the book's instructions and examples for help about what should go in each blank. Items you can edit include:

- **Underlines.** Underlines indicate where to enter information. After filling in the needed text, delete the underline.
- **Bracketed and italicized text.** Bracketed and italicized text indicates instructions. Be sure to remove all instructional text before you finalize your document.
- **Signature lines.** Signature lines should appear on a page with at least some text from the document itself.

Every word processing program uses different commands to open, format, save, and print documents, so refer to your software's help documents for assistance using your program. Nolo cannot provide technical support for questions about how to use your computer or your software.

CAUTION
In accordance with U.S. copyright laws, the forms and audio files provided by this book are for your personal use only.

List of Forms

The following files are available for download at: **www.nolo.com/back-of-book/PROBM.html**

Form Title	File Name
Performance Log	Performance Log.rtf
Performance Evaluation	Performance Evaluation.rtf
Employee Disciplinary Notice	Employee Disciplinary Notice.rtf
Progressive Discipline Policy	Progressive Discipline Policy.rtf
Company Complaint Policy	Company Complaint Policy.rtf
Termination Risk Assessment	Termination Risk Assessment.rtf
Checklist of Considerations Before Firing an Employee	Checklist of Considerations Before Firing.rtf
Termination Meeting Checklist	Termination Meeting Checklist.rtf

State and Federal Laws

Federal Agencies That Enforce Workplace Laws

U.S. Equal Employment Opportunity Commission
131 M Street, NE
Washington, D.C. 20507
Phone: 1-800-669-4000
www.eeoc.gov

U.S. Department of Labor
200 Constitution Avenue, NW
Washington, D.C. 20210
Phone: 1-866-4-USA-DOL (866-487-2365)
www.dol.gov

U.S. Department of Justice
950 Pennsylvania Avenue, NW
Washington, D.C. 20530
Phone: 202-514-2000
www.justice.gov

Federal Fair Employment Laws

Title VII of the Civil Rights Act of 1964 (commonly referred to as "Title VII")

Legal citation:
42 U.S.C. §§ 2000e and following

Covered employers:
- private employers with 15 or more employees
- state governments and their agencies with 15 or more employees
- local governments and their agencies with 15 or more employees
- the federal government and its agencies (regardless of size)
- employment agencies (regardless of size)
- labor unions that operate a hiring hall or have 15 or more members

Prohibited conduct:
Title VII prohibits employers from discriminating against applicants and employees on the basis of race, color, religion, sex (including pregnancy, sexual orientation, and gender identity), and national origin (including membership in a Native American tribe).

Title VII also prohibits harassment based on any of the protected characteristics listed above.

Title VII also prohibits an employer from retaliating against someone who asserts his or her rights under Title VII.

Title VII's prohibition against discrimination applies to all terms, conditions, and privileges of employment.

Enforcing agency:
The U.S. Equal Employment Opportunity Commission

The Age Discrimination in Employment Act (commonly referred to as the "ADEA")

Legal citation:
29 U.S.C. §§ 621 et seq.

Covered employers:
- private employers with 20 or more employees
- the federal government and its agencies (regardless of size)
- state and local governments and their agencies (regardless of size)
- employment agencies (regardless of size)
- labor unions that operate a hiring hall or have 15 or more members

Prohibited conduct:
The ADEA prohibits discrimination against employees who are age 40 or older. The ADEA also prohibits harassment of those employees based on their age. The ADEA also prohibits employers from retaliating

against employees who assert their rights under the ADEA.

The ADEA's prohibition against discrimination applies to all terms, conditions, and privileges of employment.

Enforcing agency:

The U.S. Equal Employment Opportunity Commission

The Equal Pay Act

Legal citation:

29 U.S.C. § 206(d)

Covered employers:

- virtually all private employers (regardless of the number of employees)
- the federal government and its agencies
- state governments and their agencies
- local governments and their agencies
- employment agencies
- labor unions

Prohibited conduct:

Employers cannot pay different wages to men and women who do substantially equal work.

Enforcing agency:

The U.S. Equal Employment Opportunity Commission

The Immigration Reform and Control Act of 1986 (commonly referred to as "IRCA")

Legal citation:

8 U.S.C. § 1324

Covered employers:

- private employers with four or more employees
- the federal government and its agencies
- state governments and their agencies
- local governments and their agencies
- employment agencies
- labor unions

Prohibited conduct:

The IRCA prohibits employers from discriminating against applicants or employees on the basis of their citizenship or national origin. The IRCA's prohibition against discrimination applies to all terms, conditions, and privileges of employment.

The IRCA also makes it illegal for employers to knowingly hire or retain in employment people who are not authorized to work in the United States. It also requires employers to keep records that verify that their employees are authorized to work in the United States.

The Americans with Disabilities Act (commonly referred to as the "ADA")

Legal citation:

42 U.S.C. §§ 12101–12213

Covered employers:

- private employers with 15 or more employees
- state and local governments and their agencies with 15 or more employees
- employment agencies
- labor unions

Prohibited conduct:

The ADA prohibits employers from discriminating against a qualified individual who has a disability, who has a history of a disability, or who is perceived to have a disability, in any aspect of employment.

The ADA also prohibits employers from refusing to hire someone or discriminating against someone because that person is related to or associates with someone with a disability.

The ADA also prohibits harassment of the people described above.

The ADA prohibits retaliation against people who assert their rights under the ADA.

Enforcing agencies:

The U.S. Equal Employment Opportunity Commission and the U.S. Department of Justice

State Laws Prohibiting Discrimination in Employment

The following chart is a state-by-state comparison of factors that private employers may not use as the basis for any employment decisions. In legal parlance, the groups that have these factors are called "protected classes."

Keep in mind that this is only a synopsis and that each state has its own way of interpreting who is or is not a member of a protected class. In addition, many of the laws in this chart apply only to employers with a minimum number of employees, such as five or more.

For details about your state laws, contact your state fair employment agency. (Contact information can be found at www.nolo.com/FEPA.) Where no special agency has been designated to enforce antidiscrimination laws, your state's labor department or the closest office of the federal Equal Employment Opportunity Commission should direct you to the right agency that can give you information about fair employment laws in your state. You can find contact information for your state's labor department at www.dol.gov/whd/contacts/state_of.htm.

This list only describes state laws. Your city or county might have its own set of fair employment ordinances. To learn more, contact someone within your local government, such as your county clerk's office. Also, local offices of the Small Business Administration or the chamber of commerce can be good sources for information about local laws.

State Laws Prohibiting Discrimination in Employment

Alabama

Ala. Code §§ 25-1-20, 25-1-21, 25-1-30

Law applies to employers with: 20 or more employees

Private employers may not make employment decisions based on:

- Age (40 and older)
- Refusal to provide pay history

Alaska

Alaska Stat. §§ 18.80.220, 18.80.300, 23.10.490, 39.20.520, 47.30.865

Law applies to employers with: One or more employees

Private employers may not make employment decisions based on:

- Age
- Ancestry or national origin
- Physical or mental disability
- Gender
- Marital status (includes changes in status)
- Pregnancy, childbirth, and related medical conditions (accommodations required; includes parenthood)
- Race or color
- Religion or creed
- Mental illness
- Refusal to attend employer-sponsored meetings or listen to employer communications concerning religious or political matters

Arizona

Ariz. Rev. Stat. §§ 36-506, 36-2813, 41-1461, 41-1463, 41-1465

Law applies to employers with: 15 or more employees; one or more (sexual harassment only)

Private employers may not make employment decisions based on:

- Age (40 and older)
- Ancestry or national origin

- Physical or mental disability
- AIDS/HIV
- Pregnancy, childbirth, and related medical conditions
- Gender
- Race or color
- Religion or creed
- Genetic testing information
- Certified medical marijuana use

Arkansas

Ark. Code §§ 11-4-601, 11-5-116, 11-5-403, 16-123-102, 16-123-107; Ark. Const. Amendment 98, § 3

Law applies to employers with: Nine or more employees

Private employers may not make employment decisions based on:

- Ancestry or national origin
- Physical, mental, or sensory disability
- Gender
- Pregnancy, childbirth, and related medical conditions (accommodations required)
- Race or color
- Religion or creed
- Genetic testing information
- Medical marijuana use
- Natural, protective, or cultural hairstyles

California

Cal. Gov't Code §§ 12920, 12926, 12926.1, 12940, 12941, 12945, 12945.7, 12945.8, 12954; Cal. Lab. Code §§ 432.3, 1033, 1101

Law applies to employers with: Five or more employees

Private employers may not make employment decisions based on:

- Age (40 and older)
- Ancestry or national origin
- Physical or mental disability

State Laws Prohibiting Discrimination in Employment (continued)

- AIDS/HIV
- Gender
- Marital status
- Pregnancy, childbirth, and related medical conditions (including breastfeeding and other accommodations)
- Race or color (including hair texture and protective hairstyles)
- Religion or creed
- Sexual orientation
- Genetic testing information
- Gender identity, gender expression
- Medical condition
- Political activities or affiliations
- Status as victim of domestic violence, sexual assault, or stalking
- Military and veteran status
- Salary history, unless voluntarily disclosed
- Reproductive health decision-making
- Use of bereavement leave
- Status as victim of violence or crime
- Off-duty cannabis use
- Lack of driver's license (applicants only)

Colorado

Colo. Rev. Stat. §§ 6-1-1701 and following, 24-34-301, 24-34-401, 24-34-402, 24-34-402.3, 24-34-402.5, 27-65-117; 3 Colo. Code Regs. §§ 708-1:60.1, 708-1:80.6

Law applies to employers with: One or more employees; 25 or more employees (in cases regarding marital status involving a coworker)

Private employers may not make employment decisions based on:

- Age (40 and older)
- Ancestry or national origin
- Physical, mental, or learning disability
- AIDS/HIV
- Gender
- Marital status (includes marriage to a coworker or plans to marry a coworker)

- Pregnancy, childbirth, and related medical conditions (accommodations required)
- Race or color (including hairstyles and hair length)
- Religion or creed
- Sexual orientation (including perceived sexual orientation)
- Lawful conduct outside of work
- Mental illness
- Transgender status
- Wage differential based on sex, or salary history
- Domestic abuse or stalking victimization
- Gender identity
- Gender expression (including the individual's chosen name
- Colorado law also prohibits discrimination on the basis of protected categories resulting from the use of an artificial intelligence system.

Connecticut

Conn. Gen. Stat. §§ 21a-408p, 31-40s, 31-40z, 31-51i, 31-51m, 31-51ss, 46a-51, 46a-60, 46a-80a, 46a-80d, 46a-81c

Law applies to employers with: One or more employees

Private employers may not make employment decisions based on:

- Age
- Ancestry or national origin
- Past or present physical, mental, learning, or intellectual disability
- Gender
- Marital status (includes civil unions)
- Pregnancy, childbirth, and related medical conditions (accommodations required)
- Race or color
- Religion or creed
- Sexual orientation (includes having a history of or being identified with a preference)
- Genetic testing information

State Laws Prohibiting Discrimination in Employment (continued)

- Gender identity or expression
- Salary history, unless voluntarily disclosed
- Arrests or convictions that have been erased, pardoned, or rehabilitated
- Status as victim of domestic violence, stalking, or sexual assault
- Status as a veteran
- Ethnic traits historically associated with race (hairstyle, protective hairstyles, headwraps, etc.)
- Medical marijuana use
- Whistle-blowers
- Off-duty tobacco use
- Status as a victim of sexual assault or of trafficking in persons

Delaware

Del. Code tit. 16, § 4905A; tit. 19, §§ 710, 711, 711A, 724, 1703

Law applies to employers with: Four or more employees; one or more (whistle-blowers)

Private employers may not make employment decisions based on:

- Age (40 and older)
- Ancestry or national origin
- Physical or mental disability
- AIDS/HIV
- Gender
- Marital status
- Pregnancy, childbirth, and related medical conditions (includes breastfeeding; accommodations required)
- Race or color (including hair texture and protective hairstyles)
- Religion or creed
- Sexual orientation
- Genetic testing information
- Gender identity
- Salary history
- Status as victim of domestic violence, sexual offense, or stalking

- Family responsibilities
- Reproductive health decisions
- Medical marijuana use
- Whistle-blowers
- Housing status

District of Columbia

D.C. Code §§ 2-1401.02, 2-1401.05, 2-1402.11, 2-1402.82, 7-1703.03, 32-531.08, 32-951.02, 32-1362

Law applies to employers with: One or more employees

Private employers may not make employment decisions based on:

- Age (18 and older)
- Ancestry or national origin
- Physical or mental disability
- Gender (includes reproductive health decisions)
- Marital status (includes domestic partnership)
- Pregnancy, childbirth, and related medical conditions (includes parenthood and breast-feeding; accommodations required)
- Race or color
- Religion or creed
- Sexual orientation
- Genetic testing information
- Enrollment in vocational, professional, or college education
- Family duties
- Personal appearance
- Political affiliation
- Gender identity or expression
- Status as unemployed
- Tobacco use
- Credit information
- Victim of domestic violence, sexual offense, or stalking
- Medical or recreational marijuana use
- Homeless status

State Laws Prohibiting Discrimination in Employment (continued)

Florida

Fla. Stat. §§ 104.081, 381.00316, 448.07, 448.075, 760.01, 760.02, 760.10, 760.50, 790.251

Law applies to employers with: 15 or more employees (except as noted below)

Private employers may not make employment decisions based on:

- Age
- Ancestry or national origin
- "Handicap"
- AIDS/HIV
- Gender
- Marital status
- Pregnancy, childbirth, and related medical conditions
- Race or color
- Religion or creed
- Sickle cell trait (applies to all firms or private entities)
- Voting or not voting
- Knowledge or belief of a person's vaccination or COVID-19 postinfection recovery status or failure to take a COVID-19 test (applies to all business entities)
- Wage discrimination based on sex (employers with two or more employees)
- Exercising the constitutional right to keep and bear arms or for exercising the right of self-defense as long as a firearm is never exhibited on company property for any reason other than lawful defensive purposes

Georgia

Ga. Code §§ 34-1-2, 34-5-1, 34-5-2, 34-5-3, 34-6A-1 and following

Law applies to employers with: 15 or more employees (disability); ten or more employees (gender; domestic and agricultural employees not protected); one or more employees (age)

Private employers may not make employment decisions based on:

- Age (40-70)
- Physical, mental, or learning disability
- Gender (wage discrimination only)
- Pregnancy, childbirth, and related medical conditions (accommodations only)

Hawaii

Haw. Rev. Stat. §§ 378-1 and following; Haw. Admin. Rules §§ 12-46-107, 12-46-182

Law applies to employers with: One or more employees

Private employers may not make employment decisions based on:

- Age
- Ancestry or national origin
- Physical or mental disability
- AIDS/HIV
- Gender
- Marital status
- Pregnancy, childbirth, and related medical conditions (includes breastfeeding; accommodations required)
- Race or color
- Religion or creed
- Sexual orientation
- Genetic testing information
- Arrest and court record (unless there is a conviction directly related to job)
- Salary history, unless voluntarily disclosed
- Credit history or credit report, unless the information in the individual's credit history or credit report directly relates to a bona fide occupational qualification
- Gender identity and gender expression
- Status as a victim of domestic or sexual violence (if employer has knowledge or is notified of this status)
- Reproductive health decisions

State Laws Prohibiting Discrimination in Employment (continued)

Idaho

Idaho Code §§ 39-8303, 44-1701 to 44-1704, 67-5902, 67-5909, 67-5910

Law applies to employers with: Five or more employees

Private employers may not make employment decisions based on:

- Age (40 and older)
- Ancestry or national origin
- Physical or mental disability
- Gender
- Pregnancy, childbirth, and related medical conditions
- Race or color
- Religion or creed
- Genetic testing information

Illinois

410 Ill. Comp. Stat. §§ 513/25, 130/50; 775 Ill. Comp. Stat. §§ 5/1-102, 5/1-103, 5/2-101, 5/2-102, 5/2-103, 5/2-103.1, 5/2-109, 45/10; 820 Ill. Comp. Stat. §§ 55/5, 57/15, 105/4, 112/10, 140/5.5, 180/30; Ill. Admin. Code tit. 56, § 5210.110

Law applies to employers with: One or more employees

Private employers may not make employment decisions based on:

- Age (40 and older)
- Ancestry or national origin
- Physical or mental disability
- Gender
- Marital status
- Pregnancy, childbirth, and related medical conditions (accommodations required)
- Race or color (including hair texture, "protective hairstyles," and traits historically associated with race)
- Religion or creed
- Sexual orientation
- Genetic testing information
- Citizenship or work-authorization status
- Military status
- Unfavorable military discharge
- Gender identity
- Arrest or conviction record
- Genetic information
- Order of protection status
- Lack of permanent mailing address or having a mailing address of a shelter or social service provider
- Salary history
- Medical marijuana use
- Association with a disabled person
- Use of lawful products off the premises during nonworking and non-call hours
- Arrest or conviction record
- Victims of criminal or domestic violence
- Reproductive health decisions
- Status as a family caregiver
- Refusal to attend meetings or listen to communications concerning employer's opinion on religious or political matters
- Exercising a right under, complaining under, instituting a procedure under, or testifying about a proceeding under the One Day Rest In Seven Act

Indiana

Ind. Code §§ 22-2-14-2, 22-5-4-1, 22-9-1-2, 22-9-2-1, 22-9-2-2, 22-9-5-1 and following, 22-9-10-9, 22-9-12-1 and following, 35-38-9-10

Law applies to employers with: Six or more employees; one or more employees (age only); 15 or more employees (disability and pregnancy accommodations only)

State Laws Prohibiting Discrimination in Employment (continued)

Private employers may not make employment decisions based on:
- Age (40 to 75)
- Ancestry or national origin
- Physical or mental disability (15 or more employees)
- Gender
- Pregnancy, childbirth, and related medical conditions (accommodations only)
- Race or color
- Religion or creed
- Status as a veteran
- Off-duty tobacco use
- Sealed or expunged arrest or conviction record

Iowa

Iowa Code §§ 29A.43, 216.2, 216.6, 216.6A, 729.4, 729.6

Law applies to employers with: Four or more employees

Private employers may not make employment decisions based on:
- Age (18 and older)
- Ancestry or national origin
- Physical or mental disability
- AIDS/HIV
- Gender
- Pregnancy, childbirth, and related medical conditions (accommodations required)
- Race or color
- Religion or creed
- Sexual orientation
- Genetic testing information
- Wage discrimination
- Military status

Kansas

Kan. Stat. §§ 44-1002, 44-1009, 44-1112, 44-1113, 44-1125, 44-1126, 65-6002(e)

Law applies to employers with: Four or more employees

Private employers may not make employment decisions based on:
- Age (40 and older)
- Ancestry or national origin
- Physical or mental disability
- AIDS/HIV
- Gender
- Pregnancy, childbirth, and related medical conditions (accommodations required)
- Race or color
- Religion or creed
- Genetic testing information
- Military service or status

Kentucky

Ky. Rev. Stat. §§ 207.130, 207.135, 207.150, 342.197, 344.010, 344.030, 344.040

Law applies to employers with: Eight or more employees

Private employers may not make employment decisions based on:
- Age (40 and older)
- Ancestry or national origin
- Physical or mental disability
- AIDS/HIV
- Gender
- Pregnancy, childbirth, and related medical conditions (accommodations required)
- Race or color
- Religion or creed
- Occupational pneumoconiosis with no respiratory impairment resulting from exposure to coal dust
- Off-duty tobacco use

Louisiana

La. Rev. Stat. §§ 23:301–23:368; 23:966

Law applies to employers with: 20 or more employees; 25 or more employees (pregnancy, childbirth, and related medical condition only)

State Laws Prohibiting Discrimination in Employment (continued)

Private employers may not make employment decisions based on:
- Age (40 and older)
- Ancestry or national origin
- Physical or mental disability
- Gender
- Pregnancy, childbirth, and related medical conditions (applies to employers with more than 25 employees; accommodations may be required)
- Race or color
- Religion or creed
- Genetic testing information
- Sickle cell trait
- Being a smoker or nonsmoker
- Natural, protective, or cultural hairstyles
- Military status

Maine

Me. Rev. Stat. tit. 5, §§ 4552, 4553, 4553-A, 4571 to 4577, 19302; tit. 22, § 2430-C; tit. 26, §§ 597, 628, 833; tit. 39-A, § 353

Law applies to employers with: One or more employees

Private employers may not make employment decisions based on:
- Age
- Ancestry or national origin
- Physical or mental disability
- AIDS/HIV
- Gender
- Pregnancy, childbirth, and related medical conditions (accommodations may be required)
- Race or color
- Religion or creed
- Sexual orientation (includes perceived sexual orientation)
- Genetic testing information
- Actual or perceived gender identity or expression
- Past workers' compensation claim

- Salary history, unless voluntarily disclosed, or past whistle-blowing
- Medical support notice for child
- Genetic predisposition
- Familial status, including adult family members dependent for care
- Medical marijuana use
- Off-duty tobacco use
- Employee received an order of protection
- Familial status
- Traits historically associated with race, including hair texture and protective hairstyles

Maryland

Md. Code (State Government) §§ 20-101, 20-601 to 20-609; Md. Code (Lab. & Empl.) §§ 3-304.2, 3-1002, 3-1407; Md. Code (Crim. Proc.) § 10-306; Md. Code Regs. § 14.03.02.02

Law applies to employers with: 15 or more employees/contractors; one or more employees/contractors (harassment only)

Private employers may not make employment decisions based on:
- Age
- Ancestry or national origin
- Physical or mental disability
- AIDS/HIV
- Gender
- Marital status
- Pregnancy, childbirth, and related medical conditions (accommodations required)
- Race or color (including hair texture and cultural and/or protective hairstyles)
- Religion or creed
- Sexual orientation
- Genetic testing information
- Civil Air Patrol membership
- Gender identity
- Organ donation

State Laws Prohibiting Discrimination in Employment (continued)

- Wage history
- Genetic identity
- Criminal record
- Military status

Massachusetts

Mass. Gen. Laws ch. 4, § 7; ch. 149, §§ 24A, 105A; ch. 151B, §§ 1, 4; 804 Code Mass. Regs 3.01

Law applies to employers with: Six or more employees

Private employers may not make employment decisions based on:

- Age (40 and older)
- Ancestry or national origin
- Physical or mental disability
- Gender
- Marital status
- Pregnancy, childbirth, and related medical conditions (includes breastfeeding; accommodations required)
- Race or color (including hair texture, type, and length; protective hairstyles; and traits historically associated with race)
- Religion or creed
- Sexual orientation
- Genetic testing information
- Military service
- Salary history
- Arrest record
- Gender identity
- Status as a veteran
- Sealed or expunged criminal record

Michigan

Mich. Comp. Laws §§ 37.1103, 37.1201, 37.1202, 37.2103, 37.2201, 37.2202, 37.2205a, 408.921, 750.556

Law applies to employers with: One or more employees

Private employers may not make employment decisions based on:

- Age
- Ancestry or national origin
- Physical or mental disability
- AIDS/HIV
- Gender
- Marital status
- Pregnancy, childbirth, the termination of a pregnancy, and related medical conditions
- Race or color (including traits historically associated with race, including hair texture and protective hairstyles)
- Religion or creed
- Genetic testing information
- Civil Air Patrol membership
- Height or weight
- Misdemeanor arrest record
- Sexual orientation
- Gender identity or expression

Minnesota

Minn. Stat. §§ 181.172, 181.531, 181.81, 181.932, 181.939, 181.941, 181.945, 181.9456, 181.956, 181.964, 181.974, 192.34, 342.57, 363A.03, 363A.08

Law applies to employers with: One or more employees; 15 or more employees (pregnancy and childbirth accommodations)

Private employers may not make employment decisions based on:

- Age (18 to 70)
- Ancestry or national origin
- Physical, sensory, or mental disability
- Gender
- Marital status
- Pregnancy, childbirth, and related medical conditions (including breastfeeding; accommodations required)

State Laws Prohibiting Discrimination in Employment (continued)

- Race or color (includes traits historically associated with race, including hair texture and hairstyles)
- Religion or creed
- Sexual orientation (includes perceived sexual orientation)
- Genetic testing information
- Gender identity
- Member of local commission
- Receiving public assistance
- Familial status (protects parents or guardians living with a minor child)
- Medical marijuana use
- Whistle-blowers
- Receiving public assistance
- Refusal to provide wage history
- Military status
- Good faith reports of legal violations or harmful provision of substandard health care, participation in investigations or hearings, refusal to comply with employer's illegal order, and disclosure of information to governmental bodies
- Minnesota law also prohibits employers from retaliating against employees who assert any of various rights.

Mississippi

Miss. Code §§ 33-1-15, 71-7-33, 71-17-5

Law applies to employers with: One or more employees; five or more (gender-based wage discrimination)

Private employers may not make employment decisions based on:

- Gender (wage discrimination only)
- Military status
- Off-duty smoking or tobacco use
- No other protected categories unless employer receives public funding

Missouri

Mo. Rev. Stat. §§ 41.730, 191.665, 213.010, 213.055, 290.145, 375.1306

Law applies to employers with: Six or more employees

Private employers may not make employment decisions based on:

- Age (40 to 70)
- Ancestry or national origin
- Physical or mental disability
- AIDS/HIV
- Gender
- Race or color
- Religion or creed
- Genetic testing information
- Off-duty use of alcohol or tobacco
- Military status

Montana

Mont. Code §§ 39-2-307, 39-2-313, 49-2-101, 49-2-303, 49-2-310, 49-2-312; 2025 Mt. HB 667

Law applies to employers with: One or more employees

Private employers may not make employment decisions based on:

- Age
- Ancestry or national origin
- Physical or mental disability
- Gender
- Marital status
- Pregnancy, childbirth, and related medical conditions
- Race or color
- Religion or creed
- Legal use of marijuana during non-work hours
- A legal expression of free speech on social media
- Seeking election or appointment to a city, county, or state public office
- Vaccination status or having an immunity passport

State Laws Prohibiting Discrimination in Employment (continued)

Nebraska

Neb. Rev. Stat. §§ 20-168, 48-236, 48-1001 to 48-1010, 48-1102, 48-1104, 48-1107.02

Law applies to employers with: 15 or more employees; 20 or more employees (age only)

Private employers may not make employment decisions based on:

- Age (40 and over) (applies to employers with 20 or more employees)
- Ancestry or national origin
- Physical or mental disability
- AIDS/HIV
- Gender
- Marital status
- Pregnancy, childbirth, and related medical conditions (accommodations required)
- Race or color
- Religion or creed
- Genetic testing information (applies to all employers)
- Hair texture and protective hairstyles
- Military or veteran status

Nevada

Nev. Rev. Stat. §§ 412.606, 608.0193, 608.0198, 613.133, 613.223, 613.310 and following, 613.4353 and following, 613.570

Law applies to employers with: 15 or more employees

Private employers may not make employment decisions based on:

- Age (40 and over)
- Ancestry or national origin
- Physical or mental disability
- AIDS/HIV
- Gender
- Pregnancy, childbirth, and related medical conditions (including breastfeeding; accommodations required)
- Race or color (and traits historically associated with race, including hair texture)

- Religion or creed
- Sexual orientation (includes perceived sexual orientation)
- Genetic testing information
- Use of service animal
- Gender identity or expression
- Opposing unlawful employment practices
- Credit report or credit information (with some exceptions)
- Requesting leave or reasonable accommodation due to status as victim of domestic violence or sexual assault against themself or a family member (applies to all employers)
- Payment history
- Protective hairstyles
- Medical marijuana (including reasonable accommodation) and recreational marijuana use
- Membership in the Nevada National Guard

New Hampshire

N.H. Rev. Stat. §§ 110-B:65, 141-H:3, 275:37-a, 275:37-e, 275:71, 354-A:2, 354-A:6, 354-A:7

Law applies to employers with: Six or more employees

Private employers may not make employment decisions based on:

- Age
- Ancestry or national origin
- Physical or mental disability
- Gender
- Marital status
- Pregnancy, childbirth, and related medical conditions
- Race or color
- Religion or creed
- Sexual orientation
- Genetic testing information
- Victims of domestic violence, harassment, sexual assault, or stalking

State Laws Prohibiting Discrimination in Employment (continued)

- Gender identity
- Membership in the national guard
- Off-duty use of tobacco products
- Protective hairstyles

New Jersey

N.J. Stat. §§ 10:5-1, 10:5-3.1, 10:5-4, 10:5-4.1, 10:5-5, 10:5-12, 10:5-29.1, 24:6I-52, 34:6B-1, 43:21-49

Law applies to employers with: One or more employees

Private employers may not make employment decisions based on:

- Age (18 to 70)
- Ancestry or national origin
- Past or present physical or mental disability
- AIDS/HIV
- Gender
- Marital status (includes civil union or domestic partnership status)
- Pregnancy, childbirth, and related medical conditions (includes breastfeeding; accommodations required)
- Race or color (and traits historically associated with race, including hair texture and protective hairstyles)
- Religion or creed
- Sexual orientation (includes affectional orientation and perceived sexual orientation)
- Genetic testing information
- Atypical hereditary cellular or blood trait
- Military service
- Accompanied by service or guide dog
- Gender identity
- Unemployed status
- Liability for service in the U.S. Armed Forces
- Familial status
- Salary history (job applicants)
- Testing positive for recreational and/or medical marijuana use

New Mexico

N.M. Stat. §§ 20-4-6, 24-21-4, 28-1-2, 28-1-7, 50-4A-4, 50-11-3; N.M. Admin. Code § 9.1.1

Law applies to employers with: Four or more employees; 50 or more employees (marital status); one or more (smoking)

Private employers may not make employment decisions based on:

- Age (40 and older)
- Ancestry or national origin
- Physical or mental disability
- Gender
- Marital status (applies to employers with 50 or more employees)
- Pregnancy, childbirth, and related medical conditions (accommodations required)
- Race or color
- Religion or creed
- Sexual orientation (includes perceived sexual orientation)
- Genetic testing information
- Gender identity
- Serious medical condition
- Domestic abuse leave
- Cultural or religious headdresses
- "Protective hairstyles" and traits historically associated with race such as hair texture or length
- Membership in the national guard
- Being a tobacco smoker or nonsmoker
- Military status

New York

N.Y. Exec. Law §§ 292, 296; N.Y. Lab. Law §§ 201-d, 203-e, 215; N.Y. Pub. Health Law § 3369

Law applies to employers with: One or more employees

Private employers may not make employment decisions based on:

- Age (18 and older)

State Laws Prohibiting Discrimination in Employment (continued)

- Ancestry or national origin
- Physical or mental disability
- Gender
- Marital status
- Pregnancy, childbirth, and related medical conditions (accommodations required)
- Race or color (including traits historically associated with race, such as hair texture and protective hairstyles)
- Religion or creed
- Sexual orientation (includes perceived sexual orientation)
- Genetic testing information
- Lawful recreational activities when not at work
- Military status or service
- Observance of Sabbath
- Political activities
- Use of service dog
- Arrest or criminal accusation
- Domestic violence victim status
- Familial status
- Reproductive health decision-making
- Gender identity and transgender status
- Medical marijuana
- Whistle-blowers
- Citizenship or immigration status
- Certain sealed conviction records
- Domestic violence victim status
- Refusal to attend meetings, listen to speeches, or view communications concerning religious or political matters

North Carolina

N.C. Gen. Stat. §§ 95-28.1, 95-28.1A, 95-28.2, 127B-11, 130A-148, 143-422.2, 143B-1033, 168A-5

Law applies to employers with: 15 or more employees

Private employers may not make employment decisions based on:

- Age
- Ancestry or national origin
- Physical or mental disability
- AIDS/HIV
- Gender
- Race or color
- Religion or creed
- Genetic testing information
- Military status or service
- Sickle cell or hemoglobin C trait
- Lawful use of lawful products off site and off duty
- Membership in the North Carolina Wing-Civil Air Patrol

North Dakota

N.D. Cent. Code §§ 14-02.4-02, 14-02.4-03, 34-01-17, 37-29-02, 37-29-03, 62.1-02-13

Law applies to employers with: One or more employees

Private employers may not make employment decisions based on:

- Age (40 and older)
- Ancestry or national origin
- Physical or mental disability
- Gender
- Marital status
- Pregnancy, childbirth, and related medical conditions (accommodations required)
- Race or color
- Religion or creed
- Lawful conduct outside of work
- Receiving public assistance
- Keeping and bearing arms (as long as firearm is never exhibited on company property except for lawful defensive purposes)
- Status as a volunteer emergency responder

State Laws Prohibiting Discrimination in Employment (continued)

Ohio

Ohio Rev. Code §§ 4111.17, 4112.01, 4112.02, 5906.01 and following

Law applies to employers with: Four or more employees

Private employers may not make employment decisions based on:

- Age (40 and older)
- Ancestry or national origin
- Physical, mental, or learning disability
- AIDS/HIV
- Gender
- Pregnancy, childbirth, and related medical conditions
- Race or color
- Religion or creed
- Military status
- Caring for a sibling, child, parent, or spouse injured while in the armed services

Oklahoma

Okla. Stat. tit. 10A tit. § 1-2-101; tit. 25, §§ 1301, 1302; tit. 36, § 3614.2; tit. 40, § 500; tit. 44, § 208; 63 Okl.St. §§ 1-728, 425, 427.8

Law applies to employers with: One or more employees

Private employers may not make employment decisions based on:

- Age (40 and older)
- Ancestry or national origin
- Physical or mental disability
- Gender
- Pregnancy, childbirth, and related medical conditions (except abortions where the woman is not in "imminent danger of death")
- Race or color
- Religion or creed
- Genetic testing information
- Military service

- Being a tobacco smoker or nonsmoker or using tobacco off duty
- Reporting child abuse or neglect
- Medical marijuana

Oregon

Or. Rev. Stat. §§ 25.337, 659.785, 659A.030, 659A.112 and following, 659A.290, 659A.303, 659A.314, 659A.315, 659A.320, 659A.347, 659A.357

Law applies to employers with: One or more employees; six or more employees (disability and pregnancy, childbirth, and related medical condition accommodations)

Private employers may not make employment decisions based on:

- Age (18 and older)
- Ancestry or national origin
- Physical or mental disability (applies to employers with six or more employees)
- Gender
- Marital status
- Pregnancy, childbirth, and related medical conditions (accommodations required)
- Race or color (including traits historically associated with race, such as hair texture and protective hairstyles)
- Religion or creed
- Sexual orientation
- Genetic testing information
- Parent who has medical support order imposed by court
- Domestic violence victim status
- Refusal to attend an employer-sponsored meeting with the primary purpose of communicating the employer's opinion on religious or political matters
- Credit history
- Whistle-blowers
- Off-duty use of tobacco products
- Salary history, unless voluntarily disclosed
- Gender identity

State Laws Prohibiting Discrimination in Employment (continued)

- Expunged juvenile record
- Requiring a valid driver's license from a current or prospective employee unless legally required for an essential job function or legitimate business purpose
- Status as a victim of domestic violence, harassment, sexual assault, stalking, or bias
- Employee's service or scheduled service as appointed member of state board or commission
- Salary history, unless voluntarily disclosed.

Pennsylvania

35 Pa. Cons. Stat. § 10231.2103; 43 Pa. Cons. Stat. §§ 954 to 955

Law applies to employers with: Four or more employees

Private employers may not make employment decisions based on:

- Age (40 to 70)
- Ancestry or national origin
- Physical or mental disability
- Gender
- Pregnancy, childbirth, and related medical conditions
- Race or color
- Religion or creed
- GED rather than high school diploma
- Use of service animal
- Relationship or association with a person with a disability
- Medical marijuana

Rhode Island

R.I. Gen. Laws §§ 12-28-10, 21-28.6-4, 23-6.3-11, 28-5-6, 28-5-7, 28-6-18, 28-6.7-1, 34-37.1-3

Law applies to employers with: Four or more employees; one or more employees (gender-based wage discrimination only)

Private employers may not make employment decisions based on:

- Age (40 and older)
- Ancestry or national origin
- Physical or mental disability
- AIDS/HIV
- Gender
- Pregnancy, childbirth, and related medical conditions (includes breastfeeding and menopause-related conditions; accommodations required)
- Race or color (includes traits historically associated with race, including, but not limited to hair texture and protective hairstyles)
- Religion or creed
- Sexual orientation (includes perceived sexual orientation)
- Genetic testing information
- Domestic abuse victim
- Gender identity or expression
- Homelessness
- Medical marijuana

South Carolina

S.C. Code §§ 1-13-30, 1-13-80, 41-1-85

Law applies to employers with: 15 or more employees; one or more (off-duty tobacco use)

Private employers may not make employment decisions based on:

- Age (40 and older)
- Ancestry or national origin
- Physical or mental disability
- AIDS/HIV
- Gender
- Pregnancy, childbirth, and related medical conditions (accommodations required)
- Race or color
- Religion or creed
- Off-duty tobacco use

State Laws Prohibiting Discrimination in Employment (continued)

South Dakota

S.D. Codified Laws §§ 20-13-1, 20-13-10, 60-2-20, 60-4-11, 60-12-15, 62-1-17

Law applies to employers with: One or more employees

Private employers may not make employment decisions based on:

- Ancestry or national origin
- Physical or mental disability
- Gender
- Race or color
- Religion or creed
- Genetic testing information
- Preexisting injury
- Off-duty use of tobacco products

Tennessee

Tenn. Code §§ 4-21-102, 4-21-401 and following, 8-50-103, 50-1-304, 50-1-307, 50-1-313, 50-2-201, 50-2-202, 50-10-103, 58-1-604

Law applies to employers with: Eight or more employees; one or more employees (gender-based wage discrimination and hairstyle discrimination)

Private employers may not make employment decisions based on:

- Age (40 and older)
- Ancestry or national origin
- Physical, mental, or visual disability
- Gender
- Pregnancy, childbirth, and related medical conditions (accommodations required for employers with 15 or more employees; see statutes)
- Race or color
- Religion or creed
- Use of guide dog
- Volunteer rescue squad worker or firefighter responding to an emergency
- Hairstyles belonging to an employee's ethnic group (including braids, locs, and twists)

- Whistle-blowers
- Off-duty tobacco use
- Membership in the Tennessee National Guard

Texas

Tex. Lab. Code §§ 21.002, 21.051, 21.101, 21.106, 21.1095, 21.402; Tex. Fam. Code § 261.110

Law applies to employers with: 15 or more employees; one or more employees for sexual harassment; 20 or more employees for age discrimination

Private employers may not make employment decisions based on:

- Age (40 and older)
- Ancestry or national origin
- Physical or mental disability
- Gender
- Pregnancy, childbirth, and related medical conditions (accommodations required)
- Race or color (including hair texture or a protective hairstyle historically associated with race)
- Religion or creed
- Genetic testing information
- Reporting child abuse or neglect

Utah

Utah Code §§ 13-60-204, 34A-5-102, 34A-5-106, 34A-5-113, 71A-8-105

Law applies to employers with: 15 or more employees (except as noted below)

Private employers may not make employment decisions based on:

- Age (40 and older)
- Ancestry or national origin
- Physical or mental disability
- AIDS/HIV
- Gender
- Pregnancy, childbirth, and related medical conditions (includes breastfeeding; accommodations required)

State Laws Prohibiting Discrimination in Employment (continued)

- Race or color
- Religion or creed
- Sexual orientation
- Genetic testing information (all employers)
- Gender identity
- Status as a member of a reserve component of the armed forces of the United States
- Immunity status (all employers)

Vermont

Vt. Stat. tit. 18, § 9333; tit. 21, §§ 305, 495, 495d, 495i, 495m, 495o

Law applies to employers with: One or more employees

Private employers may not make employment decisions based on:
- Age (18 and older)
- Ancestry or national origin
- Physical, mental, or emotional disability
- AIDS/HIV
- Gender
- Pregnancy, childbirth, and related medical conditions (accommodations required)
- Race or color
- Religion or creed
- Sexual orientation
- Genetic testing information
- Gender identity
- Salary history
- Place of birth
- Credit report or credit history
- Status as crime victim
- Protective hairstyles
- Declining to attend employer-sponsored meetings or listen to employer communications concerning religious or political matters

Virginia

Va. Code §§ 2.2-3900, 2.2-3901, 2.2-3905, 19.2-389.3, 40.1-27.4, 40.1-28.6, 40.1-28.7:1, 40.1-33.11, 51.5-41

Law applies to employers with: 15 or more employees (or one or more domestic workers); six or more employees (or one or more domestic workers) for unlawful discharge and disabilities; and six or more but fewer than 20 employees for unlawful discharge based on age

Private employers may not make employment decisions based on:
- Age (40 and older)
- Ancestry or national origin
- Physical or mental disability
- AIDS/HIV
- Gender
- Marital status
- Pregnancy, childbirth, and related medical conditions (accommodations required)
- Race or color (including traits historically associated with race, such as hair texture, hair type, and protective hairstyles)
- Religion or creed
- Sexual orientation
- Genetic testing information
- Military or veteran status
- Gender identity
- Lawful use of cannabis oil
- Taking organ donation leave
- Arrest or conviction for marijuana possession (will not apply after July 1, 2026)

Washington

Wash. Rev. Code §§ 38.40.110, 43.10.005 (repealed effective 1/1/2027), 49.44.090, 49.44.180, 49.44.240, 49.44.250, 49.58.020, 49.58.040, 49.60.030, 49.60.040, 49.60.172, 49.60.180, 49.60.210, 49.76.120; Wash. Admin. Code § 162-30-020; 2025 Wa. SB 5217 (effective 1/1/2027)

Law applies to employers with: UNTIL JANUARY 1, 2027: 8 or more employees; 1 or more employees (gender-based wage discrimination only); 15 or more employees (pregnancy and childbirth accommodations)

State Laws Prohibiting Discrimination in Employment (continued)

ON AND AFTER JANUARY 1, 2027: 8 or more employees; 1 or more employees (gender-based wage discrimination and pregnancy and childbirth accommodations)

Private employers may not make employment decisions based on:
- Age (40 and older)
- Ancestry or national origin
- Physical, mental, or sensory disability
- AIDS/HIV
- Gender
- Marital status
- Pregnancy, childbirth, and related medical conditions (including breastfeeding; accommodations required)
- Race or color (including traits historically associated with race, such as hair texture and protective hairstyles)
- Religion or creed
- Sexual orientation
- Genetic testing information
- Hepatitis C infection
- Member of state militia
- Use of a trained service animal by a person with a disability
- Gender identity
- Salary history
- Whistle-blowers
- Domestic violence, sexual assault, stalking, or hate crime (effective 1/1/2026) victim
- Immigration status
- Refusal to attend meetings or listen to communications concerning employer's opinion on religious or political matters
- Off-duty marijuana use (applicants only)

West Virginia

W. Va. Code §§ 15-1K-4, 16-3-4b, 16-3C-3, 16A-15-4, 16B-17-3, 16B-17-9, 16B-19-2, 21-3-19, 21-5B-1, 21-5B-3

Law applies to employers with: 12 or more employees; one or more employees (gender-based wage discrimination only)

Private employers may not make employment decisions based on:
- Age (40 and older)
- Ancestry or national origin
- Physical or mental disability, blindness
- AIDS/HIV
- Gender
- Pregnancy, childbirth, and related medical conditions (accommodations required)
- Race or color
- Religion or creed
- Off-duty use of tobacco products
- Membership in the Civil Air Patrol (for employers with 16 or more employees)
- Medical marijuana
- Religious objection to COVID-19 vaccination

Wisconsin

Wis. Stat. §§ 111.32 and following

Law applies to employers with: One or more employees

Private employers may not make employment decisions based on:
- Age (40 and older)
- Ancestry or national origin
- Physical or mental disability
- Gender
- Marital status
- Pregnancy, childbirth, and related medical conditions
- Race or color
- Religion or creed
- Sexual orientation (includes having a history of or being identified with a preference)
- Genetic testing information

State Laws Prohibiting Discrimination in Employment (continued)

- Arrest or conviction record
- Military service
- Declining to attend a meeting or to participate in any communication about religious matters or political matters
- Use or nonuse of lawful products off duty and off site

Wyoming

Wyo. Stat. §§ 19-11-104, 27-9-102, 27-9-105

Law applies to employers with: Two or more employees

Private employers may not make employment decisions based on:
- Age (40 and older)
- Ancestry or national origin
- Disability
- Gender
- Pregnancy, childbirth, and related medical conditions
- Race or color
- Religion or creed
- Military service or status
- Off-duty tobacco use

State Family and Medical Leave Laws

Alabama

Ala. Code § 25-1-61

Family and medical leave: Employers with 50 or more employees must provide 12 weeks of unpaid leave for the birth or adoption of a child during the first year after the child's birth or adoption. Employees are eligible if they have worked for the employer for at least 12 months and have worked at least 1,250 hours in the previous year.

Alaska

Alaska Stat. §§ 23.10.066 and following

Family and medical leave: Employees can use paid sick leave to attend to their own or a family member's mental or physical illness, injury, or health condition; for medical diagnosis, care, or treatment; or for preventative medical care.

Domestic violence: Paid sick leave can be used for absences due to domestic violence, sexual assault, or stalking, including to allow the employee or a family member to obtain medical or psychological attention, for relocation, to take steps to secure an existing home, or for legal services or proceedings.

Paid sick leave: Employers must provide at least one hour of paid sick leave for every 30 hours worked. Employers with at least 15 employees may place a cap on accrual and use of 56 hours per year. Smaller employers may impose a cap on accrual and use of 40 hours per year. Paid sick leave shall carry over to the following year, subject to the yearly caps.

Arizona

Ariz. Rev. Stat. §§ 13-4439, 23-371 and following

Domestic violence: Paid sick leave may also be used to allow employee to obtain (for self or family member) or do any of the following when needed: (1) medical care (including counseling) to recover from physical or psychological injury or disability caused by domestic violence, sexual violence, abuse, or stalking; (2) services from domestic violence,

sexual violence, or victim services organization; (3) legal services; or (4) relocate or take steps to secure existing home. Employers with 50 or more employees must give unpaid leave to all crime victims to attend certain legal proceedings.

Paid sick leave: All employers must provide one hour paid sick time for every 30 hours worked. Employers with 15 or more employees may cap accrual and use at 40 hours per year; employers with fewer than 15 employees may cap accrual and use at 24 hours per year. Sick leave may be used for the employee's illness, to care for an ill family member, to seek assistance relating to domestic violence, or due to the closure of the employee's work or a child's school due to a public health emergency.

Arkansas

Ark. Code §§ 9-9-105, 11-3-205

Family and medical leave: Employers that allow employees to take leave for the birth of a child must give the same leave to employees adopting a child no older than 18 (does not apply to step-parent or foster parent adoptions).

Organ and bone marrow donation: Private employers must provide up to 90 days of unpaid leave for organ or bone marrow donation to employees who are not eligible for FMLA leave.

California

Cal. Gov't. Code §§ 12945, 12945.2, 12945.6, 12945.7, 12945.8; Cal. Lab. Code §§ 245.5, 246, 246.5, 1508 to 1513; Cal. Unemp. Ins. Code §§ 2601 and following, 3300 and following

Family and medical leave: Employers with five or more employees must provide up to 12 weeks of leave each year to care for child, parent, parent-in-law, grandparent, grandchild, sibling, spouse, domestic partner, or designated person with serious health condition; for employee's own serious illness; to bond with new child; or for qualifying exigency related to

State Family and Medical Leave Laws (continued)

active military duty of employee or spouse, domestic partner, child, or parent. Employees are eligible if they have worked for the employer for more than 12 months and have worked 1,250 hours in the previous year (or meet special eligibility requirements for certain employees of air carriers). Employers with at least five employees must provide up to five days of bereavement leave to an employee whose immediate family member has died. Such leave is unpaid and must be taken within three months of the death. Employees may use paid sick days or vacation days for bereavement purposes.

Pregnancy disability leave: Employers with five or more employees must provide up to four months of pregnancy disability leave to employees who are unable to work due to pregnancy or childbirth. This time is in addition to 12 weeks of bonding leave under state family leave law. Employers with five or more employees must provide up to five days of reproductive loss leave following a failed adoption or surrogacy, miscarriage, stillbirth, or unsuccessful assisted reproduction, capped at 20 days per 12 months.

School activities: Employers with 25 or more employees must provide up to 40 hours per year, but not more than eight hours per calendar month, to enroll a child in a school or a licensed child care provider or to participate in activities related to the school or licensed child care provider.

Domestic violence: Employers with 25 or more employees must provide employees who are victims of domestic violence, stalking, sexual assault, or certain other crimes with a reasonable amount of time off to obtain medical treatment, counseling, or mental health services; take safety measures; or deal with other issues related to the crime.

Organ and bone marrow donation: Employers with 15 or more employees must provide paid leave for organ donation (up to 30 days in one-year period) or bone marrow donation (up to five days within one-year period), plus additional unpaid leave for organ donation (up to 30 days). As condition of initial leave, employer may require employee to use accrued sick leave, vacation time, or paid time off (up to two weeks for organ donation or five days for bone marrow donation).

Paid sick leave: All employers must provide employees with one hour of sick leave for every 30 hours worked. Employers may cap sick leave at 40 hours per year. Employees are eligible if they have worked at least 30 days for the employer. Employees may use sick leave for their own illnesses, to care for an ill family member or designated person, or to deal with the effects of domestic violence.

Paid family leave: Employees may receive up to eight weeks of paid family leave benefits from the state disability insurance program when taking leave to bond with a new child; to care for a seriously ill family member; or for qualifying exigencies related to covered active military duty or the employee or the employee's spouse, domestic partner, child, or parent.

Temporary Disability Insurance: Employees may receive up to 52 weeks of short-term disability from the state when unable to work due to disability (including pregnancy).

Colorado

Colo. Rev. Stat. §§ 8-13.3-203, 8-13.3-401 to 8-13.3-418, 8-13.3-501 to 8-13.3-524, 19-5-211, 24-34-402.7

Family and medical leave: Employers that offer leave for the birth of a child must give the same leave for adoption (doesn't apply to stepparent adoption).

Colorado employees are entitled to FMLA leave to care for a seriously ill domestic partner or partner in civil union.

Domestic violence: Employees who are victims of domestic violence, sexual assault, or harassment (or have family members who are victims) may use accrued paid sick leave to seek medical attention,

State Family and Medical Leave Laws (continued)

obtain victim services or counseling, relocate, or seek legal services related to such violence or harassment. In addition, employers with 50 or more employees must provide up to three days' paid or unpaid leave per year to seek restraining order, obtain medical care or counseling, relocate, or seek legal assistance relating to domestic violence, sexual assault, or stalking. Employees are eligible for this leave if they have worked for the employer for one year.

Paid sick leave: Private and state/local public employers must provide at least one hour paid sick for every 30 hours worked, beginning on first day of employment. Employees may use sick leave for their own illnesses, to care for ill family member, to grieve or deal with financial and legal matters that arise after the death of a family member, when public health emergency closes place of business (or closes schools, and employees need to care for children), to deal with effects of domestic violence, when inclement weather or another unexpected occurrence results in the closure of a family member's school or place of care (and the employee needs to care for them), or when the employee needs to evacuate their residence due to inclement weather or other unexpected occurrence. Employees may roll over up to 48 hours' accrued sick leave to next year. During public health emergencies, employers must also supplement accrued paid sick leave as necessary to ensure that full-time employees may take at least 80 hours of leave for certain reasons related to emergency.

Paid family and medical leave: Covered employees allowed up to 12 weeks of paid family or medical leave per 12-month period to care for seriously ill family member, for their own serious health condition, to bond with new child, or for reasons related to domestic violence, sexual assault, or stalking suffered by employee or employee's family member. Four additional weeks permitted for complications related to pregnancy or childbirth.

Connecticut

Conn. Gen. Stat. §§ 31-49e to 31-49t; 31-51kk to 31-51qq; 31-51ss; 31-57r to 31-57t; 46a-60

Family and medical leave: Employees entitled to total of 12 weeks of paid leave during any 12-month period for childbirth, adoption, the employee's serious health condition, a family member's serious health condition, or a qualifying exigency arising out of a family member's active duty in the military; employee may take additional two weeks for serious, incapacitating health condition during pregnancy. Employee may take up to 26 weeks of unpaid leave in a 12-month period for a family member who is a current member of the armed forces and is undergoing medical treatment for a serious illness or injury. Employees are eligible if they worked for the employer at least three months immediately before request for leave.

Pregnancy disability leave: Employers with at least one employee must provide a reasonable amount of leave to employees who are unable to work due to pregnancy.

Domestic violence: Employers with three or more employees must allow employee who is victim of family violence or sexual assault to take paid or unpaid leave when necessary to seek medical treatment/counseling, obtain victim services, relocate, or participate in legal proceeding related to the violence. Employers may limit unpaid leave to 12 days in calendar year. Employers with at least one employee must give reasonable leave of absence to employee to seek treatment/counseling for injuries caused by domestic violence, including for a family member who is the victim of domestic violence; to seek victim services, including for a family member; to relocate; or to obtain legal services.

Organ and bone marrow donation: Employees may also take leave to serve as organ or bone marrow donor, subject to same eligibility requirements and time limits as any other family and medical leave.

State Family and Medical Leave Laws (continued)

Paid sick leave: Employers with 25 or more employees must provide employees with one hour of paid sick leave for every 30 hours worked, but may cap accrual at 40 hours per year. (Starting January 1, 2026, employers with at least 11 employees must provide such leave; and starting January 1, 2027, the law expands to cover all employers.) Employees may use leave for their own illness, injury, or health condition, or to care for an affected family member (defined broadly), or to deal with a business or school closure due to a public health emergency. Employees can use such leave starting on the 120th calendar day of employment.

Delaware

Del. Code tit. 19, §§ 3701 and following

Family and medical leave: Starting January 1, 2026, employers with at least 25 eligible employees must provide paid parental leave of up to 12 weeks per 12-month period; and up to six weeks per 24-month period to care for a family members or one's own serious health condition or for a qualifying military exigency. Employees are limited to 12 weeks of total, combined leave per year. Employers with between 10 and 24 eligible employees are subject only to the parental leave provisions. Benefits are paid through the state's Paid Family and Medical Leave program and funded by employer and employee contributions that began on January 1, 2025.

District of Columbia

D.C. Code §§ 32-501 and following; 32-521.01 and following; 32-531.01 and following; 32-541.01 and following

Family and medical leave: Employers with 20 or more employees must provide up to 16 weeks in a 24-month period for the birth of a child, adoption, foster care, placement of a child with the employee for whom the employee permanently assumes and discharges parental responsibility, or to care for family member with a serious health condition. Employees may take an additional 16 weeks in a 24-month period for their own serious health conditions. Employees must have worked for the employer for at least 12 months consecutively or non-consecutively over the previous seven years and worked at least 1,000 hours in the year before the start of leave.

School activities: All employers must provide up to 24 hours of unpaid leave per year for an employee to attend a child's school activities.

Domestic violence: Paid sick leave may also be used for employee or family member who is a victim of stalking, domestic violence, or abuse to get medical attention, get services, seek counseling, relocate, take legal action, or take steps to enhance health and safety.

Paid sick leave: All employers must provide paid sick leave for employees to use for their own illness or to care for a family member. Amount of paid leave ranges from three days to seven days per year, depending on size of the employer. Sick leave may be used for the employee's illness, to care for an ill family member, or to deal with the effects of stalking, domestic violence, or abuse against the employee or a family member.

Paid family leave: Employees may receive paid family leave benefits from the district when taking leave for their own serious health conditions (12 weeks), for prenatal medical care (two weeks), to bond with a new child (12 weeks), or to care for a family member with a serious health condition (12 weeks). Employee generally cannot exceed 12 weeks of paid leave per 12-month period, although an individual who takes prenatal leave and parental leave can take up to 14 weeks.

Florida

Fla. Stat. § 741.313

Domestic violence: Employers with at least 50 employees must provide up to three days of unpaid leave each year to employees who are the

State Family and Medical Leave Laws (continued)

victims of domestic violence or sexual abuse or whose family members are victims. Employees are eligible if they have worked for the employer for at least three months.

Georgia

Ga. Code § 34-1-10

Family and medical leave: No requirement to provide sick leave, but employers with 25 or more employees that choose to do so must allow up to five days each year to be used to care for a sick immediate family member.

Hawaii

Haw. Rev. Stat. §§ 378-1; 378-71 to 378-74; 392-23; 398-1 to 398-11; 398A-3; Haw. Code R. 12-46-108

Family and medical leave: Employers with 100 or more employees must provide up to four weeks of unpaid leave each year for the birth of a child or adoption, or to care for family member with a serious health condition. (If employer provides paid sick leave, up to ten days may be used for these purposes.) Employees are eligible if they have worked for the employer for six months.

Pregnancy disability leave: All employers must provide a reasonable period of time off for disability resulting from pregnancy, childbirth, or a related condition.

Domestic violence: All employers must provide domestic violence leave. Employers with 50 or more employees must allow up to 30 days' unpaid leave per year for employee who is a victim of domestic or sexual violence or if employee's minor child is a victim. Employer with 49 or fewer employees must allow up to five days' leave.

Organ and bone marrow donation: Employers with 50 or more employees must provide up to seven days of unpaid leave for bone marrow donation and 30 days' unpaid leave for organ donation.

Temporary disability insurance: Eligible employees who are temporarily unable to work because of illness or injury (including pregnancy) may collect up to 26 weeks of benefits through the state disability insurance program.

Illinois

820 Ill. Comp. Stat. §§ 147/1 and following; 149/1 and following; 154/1 and following; 156/1 and following; 180/1 and following; 192/1 and following

Family and medical leave: Employers with 50 or more employees must allow eligible employees to take up to 10 days of unpaid bereavement leave upon the death of a covered family member, or for fertility-related issues including miscarriage, failed IVF, failed adoption or surrogacy, or stillbirth. Employees can receive up to six weeks of such leave in the event of two deaths over a 12-month period. All employers must provide unpaid leave of up to ten days if a family or household member is killed in a violent crime. Employers with at least 250 employees must offer up to 12 weeks of unpaid leave to employees who experience the loss of a child through suicide or homicide; employers with between 50 and 249 employees must provide 6 weeks.

School activities: Employers with 50 or more employees must provide eight hours per year, but not more than four hours in a day, for employees to participate in a child's school activities. Employees are eligible if they have worked for the employer at least half time for six months and have no paid leave available.

Domestic violence: All employers must provide unpaid leave each year to an employee who is a victim of domestic violence, sexual violence, gender violence, or any other crime of violence, or whose family or household member is a victim. Employers with 50 or more employees must provide 12 weeks of leave; employers with 15 to 49 employees must provide eight weeks of leave; and employers with 14 or fewer employees must provide four weeks of leave.

State Family and Medical Leave Laws (continued)

Organ and bone marrow donation: Employers with more than 50 employees must provide one hour of paid leave every 56 days for the purpose of blood donation; and up to 10 days of paid leave per 12-month period for organ donation.

Paid leave: Illinois employees are entitled to earn up to 40 hours of paid leave in a 12-month period, usable for any purpose and accrued at the rate of one hour of leave per 40 hours worked.

Indiana

Ind. Code §§ 22-2-20-1 to 22-2-20-9

School activities: Employers can't take adverse action against an employee who is absent because of attending a child's truancy attendance conference or case conference committee meeting. Adverse action can be taken if the employee attends more than one of these conferences in the calendar year, if the employee is gone longer than was reasonably necessary, or if the employee doesn't give the employer 5 days' advance notice of the conference. The employee is not entitled to pay for the time absent.

Iowa

Iowa Code § 216.6

Pregnancy disability leave: Employers with four or more employees must provide eight weeks of leave for disability due to pregnancy, childbirth, or related conditions.

Kentucky

Ky. Rev. Stat. § 337.015

Family and medical leave: All employers must provide up to six weeks of leave to employees adopting a child under ten years old. If employer provides more than six weeks to employees following birth of a child, the same amount of leave must be offered to adoptive parents.

Louisiana

La. Rev. Stat. §§ 23:341 to 23:342; 23:1015 and following; 40:1263.4

Pregnancy disability leave: Employers with 25 or more employees must provide a reasonable period of time off for disability due to pregnancy and childbirth, not to exceed six weeks for normal pregnancies or four months for more disabling pregnancies.

School activities: All employers must provide 16 hours of leave each year to attend a child's school or day care activities.

Organ and bone marrow donation: Employers with 20 or more employees must provide 40 hours of paid leave each year for employees to donate bone marrow. Employees are eligible if they work at least 20 hours per week.

Maine

Me. Rev. Stat. tit. 26, §§ 637, 843 and following, 850, 850-a and following

Family and medical leave: Employers with 15 or more employees at one location must provide 10 weeks of leave in a 2-year period for the birth of a child, adoption (for child 16 or younger), the employee's serious health condition, a family member's serious health condition, organ donation, or the death or serious health condition of a family member incurred while on active military duty. Employees are eligible if they have worked for the employer for at least one year.

Domestic violence: All employers must provide reasonable and necessary leave to an employee who is the victim of domestic violence, sexual assault, or stalking, or whose parent, spouse, or child is a victim. Leave may be used to prepare for and attend court, for medical treatment, and for other necessary services.

State Family and Medical Leave Laws (continued)

Organ and bone marrow donation: Employees may also take leave to serve as organ donor, subject to same eligibility requirements and time limits as any other family and medical leave.

Paid leave: Employers with more than 10 employees must allow employees to earn up to 40 hours paid leave annually; paid leave accrues at 1 hour for every 40 hours worked. The accrued and unearned paid leave from the previous year must be available for use in the year of employment immediately following, and won't count to reduce the total amount of hours the employee is entitled to earn in the current year.

Paid family and medical leave: Starting January 1, 2026, eligible employees (regardless of employer size) are entitled to up to 12 weeks of paid time off per 12-month period to care for a family member with a serious health condition; to bond with a child after birth, fostering, or adoption; to care for their own medical needs; to deal with a military exigency; or to keep safe following a sexual assault.

Maryland

Md. Code Lab. & Empl., §§ 3-801 to 3-803, 3-1201 to 3-1211, 3-1301 to 3-1311, 3-1401 to 3-1409,8.3-101 to 8.3-1001

Family and medical leave: Employers that have 15 to 49 employees AND aren't covered under the federal FMLA for the current calendar year must provide up to 6 weeks of unpaid parental leave for child's birth, adoption, or foster placement. Employees are eligible if they have worked for the employer for at least 12 months and worked at least 1,250 hours in the last year. Employers with at least 15 employees must provide the same leave for adoption as allowed for the birth of a child. Such employers must also allow employees to use paid leave as bereavement leave upon the death of a spouse, child, or parent.

Organ and bone marrow donation: Employers with 15 or more employees must provide unpaid leave for organ donation (up to 60 business days

in a 1-year period) or bone marrow donation (up to 30 days within a 1-year period). Employees are eligible if they have worked for the employer for at least 12 months and have worked at least 1,250 hours in the previous year.

Paid sick leave: Employers with 15 or more employees must provide sick leave; smaller employers must provide unpaid sick leave. Employees accrue 1 hour of sick leave for every 30 hours worked. However, employers may cap accrual at 40 hours per year and use at 64 hours per year. Employees may use sick leave for their own illnesses, to care for an ill family member, for preventative medical care for the employee or a family member, for maternity or paternity leave, or to deal with the effects of domestic violence.

Paid family and medical leave: Starting July 1, 2026, eligible employees (regardless of employer size) are entitled to up to 12 weeks of paid time off per 12-month period to deal with one's own or a family member's serious health condition; to welcome a new child through birth, adoption, or foster care; or to handle a military exigency. An additional 12 weeks may be available to qualifying employees. Employees must have worked in Maryland for at least 680 hours in the 12 months preceding their leave request. Benefits are paid through a state insurance program.

Massachusetts

Mass. Gen. Laws ch. 149, §§ 52D, 52E, 105D, 148C; ch. 151B, § 1(5); ch. 175M, §§ 1 to 11

Family and medical leave: Employers with six or more employees must provide eight weeks of unpaid leave to employees for the birth of a child or the adoption of a minor. Employees are eligible once they have completed their initial probationary period of employment, as long as it doesn't exceed three months.

Employers with 50 or more employees must provide 24 hours of leave each year to take a minor child or relative who is 60 or older to medical or dental

State Family and Medical Leave Laws (continued)

appointment (combined with school activities leave). Employees must meet the same eligibility requirements of the FMLA.

School activities: Employers with 50 or more employees must provide 24 hours of leave each year for an employee to attend a child's school activities (combined with family and medical leave for medical appointments). Employees must meet the same eligibility requirements of the FMLA.

Domestic violence: Employers with 50 or more employees must provide 15 days of unpaid leave in a 12-month period if the employee, or the employee's family member, is a victim of abusive behavior. Leave may be used to seek medical attention or counseling, obtain a protective order from a court, attend child custody proceedings, and other related purposes. Employees must meet the same eligibility requirements of the FMLA.

Paid sick leave: All employers must provide one hour of sick leave for every 30 hours worked, although employers may cap annual accrual at 40 hours. Employers with 11 or more employees must provide paid time off; employers with ten or fewer employees may provide unpaid time off. Employees may use leave for their own illnesses, for spouse's or one's own reproductive loss, to care for an ill family member, or domestic violence reasons.

Paid family and medical leave: Eligible employees, former employees (within 26 weeks from separation), and some self-employed individuals are eligible to receive paid benefits when taking up to 20 weeks of medical leave for their own serious health condition; up to 12 weeks of family leave to care for a family member with a serious health condition, to bond with a new child, or because of an emergency related to a family member's active duty in the military; or up to 26 weeks to care for a family member who is a covered servicemember. Benefits are not paid during first seven days of leave, but individuals may use accrued sick/vacation pay during that time.

Michigan
Mich. Comp. Laws §§ 408.961 and following

Paid sick leave: Employees accrue 1 hour of paid sick time per 30 hours worked. Employers with fewer than 10 employees must allow up to 40 hours of paid sick leave to be earned and used per year, and up to 32 hours unpaid. All other employers must allow up to 72 hours of earned sick time to be accrued and used per year. An employer may require a new hire to wait until the 120th calendar day after starting employment before using accrued earned sick time. Employees may use sick leave for their own illnesses or preventative care; a family member's illness or preventative care; to deal with the effects of domestic violence or sexual assault; for meetings at a child's school or place of care related to child's health or disability; or due to the closure of the employee's workplace or a child's school due to a public health emergency.

Minnesota
Minn. Stat. §§ 181.940 and following, 268B.001 and following

Family and medical leave: Employers must provide 12 weeks of leave for the birth of a child or adoption. Employees may also use accrued sick leave to care for an ill family member.

School activities: All employers must provide 16 hours in a 12-month period to attend a child's activities related to child care, preschool, or special education.

Domestic violence: Employers must allow accrued sick leave to be used to seek assistance due to sexual assault, domestic violence, harassment, or stalking.

Organ and bone marrow donation: Employers with 20 or more employees must provide 40 hours of paid leave each year to donate bone marrow. Employees are eligible if they work at least 20 hours per week.

State Family and Medical Leave Laws (continued)

Paid sick and safe leave: All employers must provide one hour of paid sick and safe time for every 30 hours worked. Employers may cap sick and safe leave at 48 hours per year. Employees are eligible if they work at least 80 hours per year for the employer. Employees may use sick and safe time for their own illnesses; to care for an ill family member; for preventative medical care for the employee or a family member; for bereavement purposes; to deal with the effects of domestic violence, sexual assault, or stalking; when inclement weather or public emergency results in the closure of the employee's workplace, or a family member's school or place of care (and the employee needs to care for them); or when a health authority or a health care professional determines that the employee or a family member is at risk of infecting others with a communicable disease.

Paid family and medical leave: Starting January 1, 2026, employees are entitled to 12 to 20 weeks per year of partial wage replacement through a state program for the following reasons: one's own serious health condition; caring for a family member with a serious health condition; bonding with a new child; safety leave; or a qualifying military exigency.

Missouri

Mo. Rev. Stat. §§ 285.625, 285.630

Domestic violence: Employers with 20 to 49 employees must offer one week of leave per year if employee is victim of domestic or sexual violence, or if employee has family or household member who is victim of such violence. If employer has 50 or more employees, employee receives two weeks.

Montana

Mont. Code §§ 49-2-310, 49-2-311

Pregnancy disability leave: All employers must provide a reasonable leave of absence for pregnancy disability and childbirth.

Nebraska

Neb. Rev. Stat. §§ 48-234, 48-3803

Family and medical leave: Employers that allow employees to take leave for the birth of a child must give the same leave for adoption of a child no older than eight, or a child no older than 18 if the child has special needs (does not apply to stepparent or foster parent adoptions).

Paid leave: All employees begin accruing paid sick time after 80 hours of employment. It accrues at the rate of 1 hour of paid sick time for every 30 hours worked. Accrued paid sick time is carried over to the following year, or an employer can pay an employee for unused paid sick time.

Nevada

Nev. Rev. Stat. §§ 200.366, 392.920, 392.4577, 608.0197, 608.0198, 613.4383

Pregnancy disability leave: Employers that provide sick or disability leave to employees with other medical conditions must provide the same leave for pregnancy, miscarriage, childbirth, and related medical conditions.

School activities: Employers with 50 or more employees must provide employees with a child in public school 4 hours of leave per school year to attend parent-teacher conferences, school-related activities during regular school hours, school-sponsored events, or to volunteer or be involved at the school. All employers may not fire or threaten to fire a parent, guardian, or custodian for attending a school conference or responding to a child's emergency.

Domestic violence: All employers must provide 160 hours of unpaid leave within 12 months of an incident of domestic violence or sexual assault for the following purposes: to seek medical treatment, to obtain counseling, to participate in court proceedings, or to create a safety plan. Employees are eligible if they have worked for at least 90 days and if

State Family and Medical Leave Laws (continued)

they are victims of domestic violence or have a family member who is a victim.

Paid leave: Employers with at least 50 employees must provide employees with at least .01923 hours of paid leave for each hour worked; employers may limit use or carryover of accrued paid leave to 40 hours per year.

New Hampshire

N.H. Rev. Stat. § 354-A:7(VI)

Pregnancy disability leave: Employers with six or more employees must provide temporary disability leave for pregnancy, childbirth, or a related medical condition.

New Jersey

N.J. Stat. §§ 34:11B-1 and following, 34:11C-1 and following, 34:11D-1 and following, 43:21-25 and following

Family and medical leave: Employers with 30 or more employees must provide 12 weeks of leave (or 24 weeks' reduced leave schedule) in any 24-month period to care for a family member with a serious health condition; to care for a new child; to care for a child at home because a school or child care center has closed during a public health emergency; or to quarantine or care for a family member in quarantine during an epidemic. Employees are eligible if they have worked for at least one year and at least 1,000 hours in the previous 12 months.

Domestic violence: Employers with 25 or more employees must provide 20 unpaid days in one 12-month period for employee who is (or whose family member is) a victim of domestic violence or a sexually violent offense. Employees are eligible if they have worked for at least one year and worked at least 1,000 hours in the last 12 months.

Paid sick leave: All employers must provide paid sick leave to their employees. Employees accrue one hour of paid sick leave for every 30 hours worked.

However, employers may cap accrual and use at 40 hours per year. Employees may use sick leave for their own illnesses, to care for an ill family member, or for preventative medical care for themselves or a family member; to attend a child's school meeting or other events; to deal with the effects of domestic violence; or, due to a public health emergency, when the employee is unable to work because the workplace or a child's school or care center has closed, the employee is in quarantine, or the employee must care for a family member in quarantine.

Paid individual temporary disability leave: Employees may receive temporary disability benefits from the state for up to 26 weeks when they are unable to work because of their own disability (including disability resulting from bone/organ donation or exposure to a communicable disease during a public health emergency) or because they are victims of domestic or sexual violence.

Paid family temporary disability leave: Employees may receive up to 12 weeks of temporary disability benefits from the state to care for a seriously ill family member, assist a family member who has been a victim of domestic or sexual violence, bond with a new child, or care for a family member in quarantine due to exposure to a communicable disease during a public health emergency.

New Mexico

N.M. Stat. §§ 50-4A-1 and following; N.M. Stat. §§ 50-17-1 and following

Domestic violence: Employees can use paid sick leave for reasons related to domestic abuse, sexual assault, or stalking suffered by employee or family member. All employers must provide intermittent leave for up to 14 days each calendar year, but no more than eight hours in one day, to obtain an order of protection or other judicial relief from domestic abuse, to meet with law enforcement officials, to consult with attorneys or district

State Family and Medical Leave Laws (continued)

attorneys' victim advocates, or to attend court proceedings related to the domestic abuse of an employee or an employee's family member.

Paid sick leave: Employers with at least one employee must provide employees one hour of paid sick leave for every 30 hours worked, up to a maximum of 64 hours per year, to use for employees' or family members' medical care.

New York

N.Y. Lab. Law §§ 196-b, 201-c, 202-a; N.Y. Workers' Comp. Law §§ 200 and following

Family and medical leave: Employers that allow employees to take leave for the birth of a child must provide the same leave to employees adopting a child of preschool age or younger (or no older than 18 if disabled).

Pregnancy disability leave: Employers must provide 20 hours of paid prenatal personal leave during any 52-week calendar period. Leave may be taken for health care services including physical examinations, medical procedures, monitoring and testing, and pregnancy-related discussions with a health care provider. Unused leave is lost.

Organ and bone marrow donation: Employers with 20 or more employees at one site must provide 24 hours' leave to donate bone marrow. Employees are eligible if they work at least 20 hours per week.

Paid sick leave: Employers with five or more employees (or net income over $1 million) must provide employees with paid sick leave: up to 40 hours per year for employers with five to 99 employees, or up to 56 hours per year for employers with at least 100 employees.

Paid temporary disability leave: Employees who have worked for a covered employer for at least four consecutive weeks may receive benefits from the state for up to 26 weeks while unable to work due to disability (including pregnancy).

Paid family leave: Employees may receive benefits from the state when taking leave to care for a family member with a serious health condition, to bond with a new child, or for qualifying exigency arising out of a family member's call to active duty in the military. Paid family leave is limited to 12 weeks within any 52-week period.

North Carolina

N.C. Gen. Stat. §§ 50B-5.5, 95-28.3

School activities: All employers must give employees four hours of leave per year to parents or guardians of school-aged children to participate in school activities.

Domestic violence: All employers must provide reasonable time off to obtain or attempt to obtain relief from domestic violence and sexual assault.

Oregon

Or. Rev. Stat. §§ 657B.005 and following, 659A.029, 659A.150 and following, 659A.190 and following, 659A.270 and following, 659A.312, 653.601 and following

Family and medical leave: Employers with 25 or more employees must provide 12 weeks off per year for the birth or adoption of a child (parental leave), the employee's serious health condition, to care for a family member with a serious health condition, to care for a child (under the age of 18 or substantially limited with a physical or mental impairment) with an illness or injury that requires home care (sick child leave), or to deal with the death of a family member (bereavement leave). Employees may take two additional weeks of leave to handle the legal aspects of foster child placement or adoption. Bereavement leave is capped at two weeks. Employees can take 12 weeks of parental leave and an additional 12 weeks for sick child leave. Employees are eligible if they have worked 25 or more hours per week for at least 180 days (except parental leave, which only requires that the employee has worked 180 days).

State Family and Medical Leave Laws (continued)

Pregnancy disability leave: Employers with 25 or more employees must provide 12 weeks off per year for pregnancy disability or for prenatal care. This is in addition to 12 weeks for parental leave and 12 weeks for sick child leave. Employees are eligible if they have worked 25 or more hours per week for at least 180 days.

Domestic violence: Employers with six or more employees must provide reasonable leave to employee who is victim of, or whose minor child is a victim of, domestic violence, harassment, sexual assault, or stalking. Leave may be used to seek legal treatment, medical services, counseling, or to relocate or secure existing home. Employers with six or more employees must provide unpaid leave for victims of crime to attend certain legal proceedings. Employees are eligible if they have worked an average of 25 hours per week for at least 180 days.

Organ and bone marrow donation: All employers must allow the employee to use accrued leave or must provide the employee with 40 hours of unpaid leave, whichever is less, to donate bone marrow. Employees are eligible if they work at least 20 hours per week. Also, for purposes of family leave, a serious health condition includes a period required for donation of a body part, organ, or tissue.

Paid sick leave: All employers must provide one hour of sick leave for every 30 hours worked, although employers may cap accrual and use at 40 hours per year. Up to 40 hours of accrued leave must carry over to the next year. Employers with ten or more employees must provide paid time off; employers with nine or fewer employees may provide unpaid time off. Employees may use leave for their own illnesses, to care for an ill family member, to deal with domestic violence issues, to donate blood, or for any purpose described under the "Family and medical leave" section.

Paid family and medical leave: Eligible employees (as well as self-employed workers who have elected coverage and contributed to the insurance fund) will be entitled to benefits from a state insurance fund for leave due to employee's own serious health condition, to care for family member with serious health condition, or to care for and bond with new child.

Pennsylvania

35 Pa. Stat. Ann. §§ 6130.1 to 6130.9

Organ and bone marrow donation: Employers with 50 or more employees must provide FMLA-eligible employees with up to 12 weeks per year for organ donation, or to care for family member undergoing organ donation surgery; leave runs concurrently with FMLA leave.

Rhode Island

R.I. Gen. Laws §§ 28-41-34 to 28-41-42; 28-48-1 and following; 28-57-1 and following

Family and medical leave: Employers with 50 or more employees must provide 13 weeks of leave in a 2-year period for the birth of a child, adoption of child up to 16 years old, the employee's serious health condition, or to care for family member with serious health condition. Employees must have worked an average of 30 or more hours a week for at least 12 consecutive months.

School activities: Employers with 50 or more employees must provide up to 10 hours a year to attend a child's school conferences or other activities.

Organ and bone marrow donation: Employees are eligible for temporary caregiver benefits for participating as a bone marrow transplant donor or a living organ donor.

Paid sick leave: Employers with 18 or more employees must provide 1 hour of paid sick leave for every

State Family and Medical Leave Laws (continued)

35 hours worked, up to a maximum of 40 hours. Employers with fewer than 18 employees must provide the same amount of unpaid sick leave. Sick leave may be used for the employee's own illness, to care for an ill family member, for reasons relating to domestic violence, or due to the closure of the employee's work or a child's school due to a public health emergency.

Paid family leave: Employees who take time off to bond with a new child or care for a family member with a serious health condition may receive up to 12 weeks of temporary caregiver benefits from the state per year.

Temporary disability insurance: Employees who are unable to work due to illness, injury, or pregnancy may collect up to 30 weeks of benefits from the state through its short-term disability insurance program (temporary caregiver benefits are counted against the 30 weeks).

South Carolina

S.C. Code § 44-43-80

Organ and bone marrow donation: Employers with 20 or more employees in the state at one site may—but are not required to—allow employees to take up to 40 hours' paid leave per year to donate bone marrow. Employees are eligible if they work at least 20 hours per week.

Tennessee

Tenn. Code § 4-21-408

Family and medical leave: Employers with 100 or more employees must provide up to four months of unpaid leave for pregnancy, childbirth, nursing, and adoption. Employees must give three months' notice unless a medical emergency requires the leave to begin sooner. Employees are eligible if they have worked full-time for the employer for 12 consecutive months.

Texas

Tex. Lab. Code § 21.0595

Family and medical leave: Employers with 15 or more employees that provide leave to care for a sick child must also allow leave to care for a sick foster child.

Vermont

Vt. Stat. tit. 21, §§ 471 and following, 481 and following

Family and medical leave: Employers with 10 or more employees must provide unpaid leave for parental leave (pregnancy, recovery from childbirth or miscarriage, birth and to care for child within one year after the birth, and initial placement of adopted or foster child/care for child within one year of adoption or foster placement), bereavement leave, safe leave (see "Domestic violence" entry), and leave for a qualifying exigency (related to active duty service in the U.S. Armed Forces). Employers with 15 or more employees must also provide unpaid leave for family leave (the employee's serious health conditions or to care for family member with a serious health condition). Employees may take up to 12 weeks each year for any of these purposes. Employees are also entitled to take an additional four hours of unpaid leave in any 30-day period, but not more than 24 hours per year, to take a family member to a medical, dental, or professional well-care appointment or respond to a family member's medical emergency. Employees are eligible if they have worked an average of 30 hours per week for one year (or meet the service requirement in 29 C.F.R. § 825.801 regarding airline flight crew employees).

School activities: Employees are entitled to 4 hours of unpaid leave in a 30-day period, but not more than 24 hours per year, to participate in a child's school activities (combined with leave to take a family member to medical appointments). Employees are eligible if they have worked an average of 30 hours per week for one year.

State Family and Medical Leave Laws (continued)

Domestic violence: Unpaid leave for alleged victims of crime, including domestic violence and sexual assault, to attend certain legal proceedings. Also, employees are eligible for the unpaid "safe leave": a leave of absence because the employee or their family member has been the victim of domestic violence, sexual assault, or stalking.

Paid sick leave: All employers must provide at least one hour of paid sick leave for every 52 hours worked. Employers may cap accrual at 40 hours per year. Employees are eligible if they have worked for a covered employer for an average of 18 hours per week for at least 20 weeks. Employees may use sick leave for their own illnesses, to care for an ill family member, for preventative medical care for themselves or a family member, to arrange long-term care for a family member, to deal with the effects of domestic violence on themselves or a family member, or to care for a family member when a school or business is closed due to a public health emergency.

Virginia

Va. Code § 40.1-33.7 and following

Organ and bone marrow donation: Employers with 50 or more employees must provide unpaid leave for organ donation (up to 60 business days in a 12-month period) or bone marrow donation (up to 30 days within a 12-month period). Employees are eligible if, as of the date that the requested organ donation leave begins, they will have been employed by the employer for at least 12 months and worked 1,250 hours in the previous 12 months.

Washington

Wash. Rev. Code §§ 49.12.265 and following; 49.12.350 and following; 49.46.200 and following; 49.76.010 and following; 50A.05.005 and following; Wash. Admin. Code 162-30-020

Pregnancy disability leave: Employers with eight or more employees must provide leave for the period of time when an employee is temporarily disabled due to pregnancy or childbirth. This is in addition to any leave available under federal FMLA and state family and medical leave laws.

Domestic violence: All employers must provide reasonable leave from work to employees who are victims of domestic violence, sexual assault, stalking, or hate crimes—or whose family member is a victim—to prepare for and attend court, for medical treatment, and for other necessary services.

Paid sick leave: All employers must provide one hour of paid sick leave for every 40 hours worked. No annual cap on accrual, but employees may only carry over 40 hours of accrued leave from year to year. Employees may use sick leave for their own illness, the illness of a family member, the closure of a child's school or day care due to a public health or other declared emergency, to prepare for or participate in their own (or a family member's) immigration proceeding, and to seek services relating to domestic violence.

Paid family and medical leave: Eligible employees (who have worked at least 820 hours during previous 12 months for any Washington employers) are entitled to benefits from state insurance program when taking medical leave due to employee's own serious health condition or family leave to care for family member with serious health condition, to bond with new child, or to deal with urgent need due to family member's active military duty. Paid family or medical leave is limited to 12 weeks in 52-week period, plus two additional weeks for employee's pregnancy-related incapacitating health condition. Employees may use paid family leave during the seven calendar days following the death of a child. Combined family and medical leave may not exceed total of 16 weeks in 52-week period (or 18 weeks if it includes employee's pregnancy-related condition).

State Family and Medical Leave Laws (continued)

Wisconsin

Wis. Stat. §§ 103.10, 103.11

Family and medical leave: Employers with 50 or more employees must provide six weeks of leave per 12-month period for pregnancy, childbirth, and to bond with a baby arriving by birth or adoption. These employers must provide an additional two weeks off each year for the employee's own serious health condition and an additional two weeks each year to care for a family member with a serious health condition. Employees are eligible if they have worked for at least one year and have worked 1,000 hours in the preceding 12 months.

Organ and bone marrow donation: Employers with at least 50 permanent employees must provide up to six weeks of unpaid leave in a 12-month period for organ or bone marrow donation. Employees must have worked for the employer for at least 52 consecutive weeks and at least 1,000 hours during the preceding 52 weeks.

State Health Insurance Continuation Laws

Alabama

Ala. Code § 27-55-3(a)(4)

Special situations: 18 months for subjects of domestic abuse who have lost coverage they had under abuser's insurance and who do not qualify for COBRA.

Arizona

Ariz. Rev. Stat. §§ 20-1377, 20-1408, 20-2330

Employers affected: All employers that offer group disability insurance. Under § 20-2330, employers that offer group health insurance and have one to 19 employees.

Eligible employees: Employees covered under an employer's health benefits plan for at least three months before a qualifying event.

Length of coverage for employee: 18 months.

Length of coverage for dependents: 18 months, plus an additional 11 months for dependents with disabilities.

Insurer must either continue coverage for dependents or convert to individual policy upon death or divorce of covered employee. Coverage must be the same unless the insured chooses a lesser plan.

Qualifying event: Death of an employee; change in marital status; any other reason stated in policy (other than failure to pay premium).

Under § 20-2330, voluntary or involuntary termination of employment other than for gross misconduct; reduction of hours required to qualify for coverage under group plan; divorce or separation; employee's death or eligibility for Medicare; dependent child ceases to qualify as dependent under group plan; retired employees or their spouses or dependent children lose coverage within a year before or after employer files for bankruptcy.

Time employer has to notify employee: No provisions for employer. Insurance policy must include notice of conversion privilege. Clerk of court must provide notice to anyone filing for divorce that dependent spouse is entitled to convert health insurance coverage.

Under § 20-2330, 30 days after the qualifying event.

Time employee has to apply: 31 days after termination of existing coverage.

Under § 20-2330, 60 days after date of employer's notice.

Arkansas

Ark. Code §§ 23-86-114–23-86-116

Employers affected: All employers that offer group health insurance.

Eligible employees: Employees continuously insured for previous three months.

Length of coverage for employee: 120 days.

Length of coverage for dependents: 120 days.

Qualifying event: Termination of employment; change in insured's marital status. Employer may—but is not required to—continue benefits on death of employee.

Time employee has to apply: Ten days.

California

Cal. Health & Safety Code §§ 1366.20 to 1366.29, 1373.6, 1373.621; Cal. Ins. Code §§ 10128.50 to 10128.59

Employers affected: Employers that offer group health insurance and have two to 19 employees.

Eligible employees: All covered employees are eligible.

Length of coverage for employee: 36 months.

Length of coverage for dependents: 36 months.

Qualifying event: Termination of employment; reduction in hours; death of employee; change in marital status; loss of dependent status; covered employee's eligibility for Medicare (for dependents only).

Time employer has to notify employee: 14 days.

Time employee has to apply: 60 days.

Special situations: Employee who is at least 60 years old and has worked for employer for previous five

State Health Insurance Continuation Laws (continued)

years may continue benefits for self and spouse beyond COBRA or Cal-COBRA limits (also applies to COBRA employers). Employee who began receiving COBRA coverage on or after January 1, 2003, and whose COBRA coverage is for less than 36 months may use Cal-COBRA to bring total coverage up to 36 months.

Colorado

Colo. Rev. Stat. § 10-16-108

Employers affected: All employers that offer group health insurance.

Eligible employees: Employees continuously insured for previous six months.

Length of coverage for employee: 18 months.

Length of coverage for dependents: 18 months.

Qualifying event: Termination of employment; reduction in hours; death of employee; change in marital status.

Time employer has to notify employee: Within ten days (by postmark or employee's signature on notice) after termination of employment.

Time employee has to apply: 30 days after termination; 60 days if employer fails to give notice.

Connecticut

Conn. Gen. Stat. § 38a-512a

Employers affected: All employers that offer group health insurance.

Eligible employees: All covered employees are eligible.

Length of coverage for employee: 30 months.

Length of coverage for dependents: 30 months; 36 months in case of employee's death, divorce, or loss of dependent status.

Qualifying event: Layoff; reduction in hours; termination of employment; death of employee; change in marital status; loss of dependent status.

Delaware

18 Del. Code § 3571F

Employers affected: Employers that offer group health insurance and have one to 19 employees.

Eligible employees: Employees continuously insured for previous three months.

Length of coverage for employee: Nine months.

Length of coverage for dependents: Nine months.

Qualifying event: Employee's death; termination of employment; divorce or legal separation; employee's eligibility for Medicare; loss of dependent status.

Time employer has to notify employee: Within 30 days of the qualifying event.

Time employee has to apply: 30 days.

District of Columbia

D.C. Code §§ 32-731 to 32-732

Employers affected: Employers with fewer than 20 employees.

Eligible employees: All covered employees are eligible.

Length of coverage for employee: Three months.

Length of coverage for dependents: Three months.

Qualifying event: Any reason employee or dependent becomes ineligible for coverage, except employee's termination for gross misconduct.

Time employer has to notify employee: Within 15 days of termination of coverage.

Time employee has to apply: 45 days after termination of coverage.

Florida

Fla. Stat. § 627.6692

Employers affected: Employers with fewer than 20 employees.

Eligible employees: Full-time (25 or more hours per week) employees covered by employer's health insurance plan.

State Health Insurance Continuation Laws (continued)

Length of coverage for employee: 18 months.

Length of coverage for dependents: 18 months.

Qualifying event: Termination of employment (other than for gross misconduct); reduction in hours; employee's death; change in marital status; employee's eligibility for Medicare; loss of dependent status; loss of coverage within one year of employer's bankruptcy.

Time employer has to notify employee: Carrier notifies within 14 days of learning of qualifying event (beneficiary has 63 days to notify carrier of qualifying event).

Time employee has to apply: 30 days from receipt of carrier's notice.

Georgia

Ga. Code §§ 33-24-21.1 to 33-24-21.2

Employers affected: All employers that offer group health insurance.

Eligible employees: Employees continuously insured for previous six months.

Length of coverage for employee: Three months plus any part of the month remaining at termination.

Length of coverage for dependents: Three months plus any part of the month remaining at termination.

Qualifying event: Termination of employment (except for cause).

Special situations: Employee, spouse, or former spouse who is 60 years old and who has been covered for previous six months may continue coverage until eligible for Medicare. (Applies to companies with more than 20 employees; does not apply when employee quits for reasons other than health.)

Hawaii

Haw. Rev. Stat. §§ 393-11, 393-15

Employers affected: All employers required to offer health insurance (those paying a regular employee a monthly wage at least 86.67 times state hourly minimum—about $1,387 as of 1/1/2026).

Length of coverage for employee: If employee is hospitalized or prevented from working by sickness, employer must pay insurance premiums for three months or for as long as employer continues to pay wages, whichever is longer.

Qualifying event: Employee is hospitalized or prevented by sickness from working.

Idaho

Idaho Code § 41-2213

Employers affected: All employers that offer group disability insurance.

Eligible employees: Employees or dependents who are totally disabled at the time the policy ends. (Applies to policies that provide benefits for loss of time during periods of hospitalization, benefits for hospital or medical expenses, or benefits for dismemberment.)

Length of coverage for employee: Must provide a reasonable extension of coverage (in the case of medical and hospital expenses, a reasonable extension is at least 12 months).

Length of coverage for dependents: Must provide a reasonable extension of coverage (in the case of medical and hospital expenses, a reasonable extension is at least 12 months).

Illinois

215 Ill. Comp. Stat. §§ 5/367e, 5/367.2, 5/367.2-5

Employers affected: All employers that offer group health insurance.

Eligible employees: Employees continuously insured for previous three months.

Length of coverage for employee: 12 months.

Length of coverage for dependents: Upon death or divorce, two years' coverage for spouse under 55 and eligible dependents who were on employee's plan. A dependent child who has reached plan age limit or who was not already covered by plan, is also entitled to two years' continuation coverage.

State Health Insurance Continuation Laws (continued)

Qualifying event: Termination of employment; reduction in hours; death of employee; divorce.

Time employer has to notify employee: Ten days.

Time employee has to apply: 30 days after termination or reduction in hours or receiving notice from employer, whichever is later, but not more than 60 days from termination or reduction in hours.

Iowa

Iowa Code §§ 509B.1 to 509B.5

Employers affected: All employers that offer group health insurance.

Eligible employees: Employees continuously insured for previous three months.

Length of coverage for employee: Nine months.

Length of coverage for dependents: Nine months.

Qualifying event: Any reason employee or dependent becomes ineligible for coverage.

Time employer has to notify employee: Ten days after termination of coverage.

Time employee has to apply: Ten days after termination of coverage or receiving notice from employer, whichever is later, but not more than 31 days from termination of coverage.

Kansas

Kan. Stat. § 40-2209(i)

Employers affected: All employers that offer group health insurance.

Eligible employees: Employees continuously insured for previous three months.

Length of coverage for employee: 18 months.

Length of coverage for dependents: 18 months.

Qualifying event: Any reason employee or dependent becomes ineligible for coverage.

Time employer has to notify employee: Reasonable notice.

Time employee has to apply: 31 days after termination of coverage.

Kentucky

Ky. Rev. Stat. § 304.18-110

Employers affected: All employers that offer group health insurance.

Eligible employees: Employees continuously insured for previous three months.

Length of coverage for employee: 18 months.

Length of coverage for dependents: 18 months.

Qualifying event: Any reason employee or dependent becomes ineligible for coverage.

Time employer has to notify employee: Employer must notify insurer as soon as employee's coverage ends; insurer then notifies employee.

Time employee has to apply: 31 days from receipt of insurer's notice, but not more than 90 days after termination of group coverage.

Louisiana

La. Rev. Stat. §§ 22:1045, 22:1046

Employers affected: All employers that offer group health insurance and have fewer than 20 employees.

Eligible employees: Employees continuously insured for previous three months.

Length of coverage for employee: 12 months.

Length of coverage for dependents: 12 months.

Qualifying event: Termination of employment; death of insured; divorce.

Time employee has to apply: By the end of the month following the month in which the qualifying event occurred.

Special situations: Surviving spouse who is 50 or older may have coverage until remarriage or eligibility for Medicare or other insurance.

Maine

Me. Rev. Stat. tit. 24-A, § 2809-A

Employers affected: All employers that offer group health insurance and are not subject to COBRA.

State Health Insurance Continuation Laws (continued)

Eligible employees: Employees employed for at least six months.

Length of coverage for employee: 12 months.

Length of coverage for dependents: 12 months.

Qualifying event: Temporary layoff; permanent layoff if employee is eligible for federal premium assistance for laid-off employees who continue coverage; loss of employment because of a work-related injury or disease.

Time employee has to apply: 31 days from termination of coverage.

Maryland

Md. Code Ins. §§ 15-407 to 15-409

Employers affected: All employers that offer group health insurance.

Eligible employees: Employees continuously insured for previous three months.

Length of coverage for employee: 18 months.

Length of coverage for dependents: 18 months.

Qualifying event: Termination of employment; death of employee; change in marital status.

Time employer has to notify employee: Must notify insurer within 14 days of receiving employee's continuation request.

Time employee has to apply: 45 days from termination of coverage. Employee begins application process by requesting an election of continuation notification form from employer.

Massachusetts

Mass. Gen. Laws ch. 175, §§ 110G, 110I; ch. 176J, § 9

Employers affected: All employers that offer group health insurance and have fewer than 20 employees.

Eligible employees: All covered employees are eligible.

Length of coverage for employee: 18 months; 29 months if disabled.

Length of coverage for dependents: 18 months upon termination or reduction in hours; 29 months if disabled; 36 months upon divorce, death of employee, employee's eligibility for Medicare, or employer's bankruptcy.

Qualifying event: Involuntary layoff; death of insured employee; change in marital status.

Time employer has to notify employee: Carrier must notify beneficiary within 14 days of learning of qualifying event.

Time employee has to apply: 60 days.

Special situations: Termination due to plant closing: 90 days' coverage for employee and dependents, at the same payment terms as before closing.

Minnesota

Minn. Stat. §§ 62A.17, 62A.20, 62A.21, 62A.148

Employers affected: All employers that offer group health insurance and have two or more employees.

Eligible employees: All covered employees are eligible.

Length of coverage for employee: 18 months; indefinitely if employee becomes totally disabled while employed.

Length of coverage for dependents: 18 months for current spouse or child after termination of employment; divorced or widowed spouse can continue until eligible for Medicare or other group health insurance. Upon divorce or death of employee, dependent children can continue until they no longer qualify as dependents under plan.

Qualifying event: Termination of employment; reduction in hours.

Time employer has to notify employee: Within 14 days of termination of coverage.

Time employee has to apply: 60 days from termination of coverage or receipt of employer's notice, whichever is later.

State Health Insurance Continuation Laws (continued)

Mississippi

Miss. Code § 83-9-51

Employers affected: All employers that offer group health insurance and have fewer than 20 employees.

Eligible employees: Employees continuously insured for previous three months.

Length of coverage for employee: 12 months.

Length of coverage for dependents: 12 months.

Qualifying event: Termination of employment; divorce; employee's death; employee's eligibility for Medicare; loss of dependent status.

Time employer has to notify employee: Insurer must notify former or deceased employee's dependent child or divorced spouse of option to continue insurance within 14 days of their becoming ineligible for coverage on employee's policy.

Time employee has to apply: Employee must apply and submit payment before group coverage ends; dependents or former spouse must elect continuation coverage within 30 days of receiving insurer's notice.

Missouri

Mo. Rev. Stat. § 376.428

Employers affected: All employers that offer group health insurance and are not subject to COBRA.

Eligible employees: All employees.

Length of coverage for employee: 18 months.

Length of coverage for dependents: 18 months if eligible due to termination or reduction in hours; 36 months if eligible due to death or divorce.

Qualifying event: Termination of employment; death of employee; divorce; reduction in hours; employee's eligibility for Medicare; loss of dependent status.

Time employer has to notify employee: Same rules as COBRA.

Time employee has to apply: Same rules as COBRA.

Montana

Mont. Code §§ 33-22-506 to 33-22-507

Employers affected: All employers that offer group disability insurance.

Eligible employees: All employees.

Length of coverage for employee: One year (with employer's consent).

Qualifying event: Reduction in hours.

Special situations: Insurer may not discontinue benefits to child with a disability after child exceeds age limit for dependent status.

Nebraska

Neb. Rev. Stat. §§ 44-1640 and following, 44-7406

Employers affected: Employers not subject to federal COBRA laws.

Eligible employees: All covered employees.

Length of coverage for employee: Six months.

Length of coverage for dependents: One year upon death of insured employee. Subjects of domestic abuse who have lost coverage under abuser's plan and who do not qualify for COBRA may have 18 months' coverage (applies to all employers).

Qualifying event: Involuntary termination of employment (layoff due to labor dispute not considered involuntary).

Time employer has to notify employee: Within ten days of termination of employment; must send notice by certified mail.

Time employee has to apply: Ten days from receipt of employer's notice.

Nevada

Nev. Rev. Stat. § 689B.0345

Employers affected: All employers that offer group health insurance.

Eligible employees: Employees who are on unpaid leave due to total disability.

State Health Insurance Continuation Laws (continued)

Length of coverage for employee: 12 months.
Length of coverage for dependents: 12 months.

New Hampshire
N.H. Rev. Stat. § 415:18

Employers affected: All employers that offer group health insurance.

Eligible employees: All insured employees are eligible.

Length of coverage for employee: 18 months; 29 months if disabled at termination or during first 60 days of continuation coverage.

Length of coverage for dependents: 18 months; 29 months if disabled at termination or during first 60 days of continuation coverage; 36 months upon death of employee, divorce or legal separation, loss of dependent status, or employee's eligibility for Medicare.

Qualifying event: Any reason employee or dependent becomes ineligible for coverage.

Time employer has to notify employee: Carrier must notify beneficiary within 30 days of receiving notice of loss of coverage.

Time employee has to apply: Within 45 days of receipt of notice.

Special situations: Layoff or termination due to strike: six months' coverage with option to extend for an additional 12 months. Surviving, divorced, or legally separated spouse who is 55 or older may continue benefits available until eligible for Medicare or other employer-based group insurance.

New Jersey
N.J. Stat. §§ 17B:27-51.12, 17B:27A-27

Employers affected: Employers with two to 50 employees.

Eligible employees: Employed full time (25 or more hours).

Length of coverage for employee: 18 months; 29 months if disabled at termination or during first 60 days of continuation coverage.

Length of coverage for dependents: 18 months; 36 months upon death of employee, divorce or legal separation, loss of dependent status, or employee's eligibility for Medicare.

Qualifying event: Termination of employment; reduction in hours; change in marital status; death.

Time employer has to notify employee: At time of qualifying event.

Time employee has to apply: Within 30 days of qualifying event.

Special benefits: Coverage must be identical to that offered to current employees.

Special situations: Total disability: Employee who has been insured for previous three months and employee's dependents entitled to continuation coverage that includes all benefits offered by group policy (applies to all employers).

New Mexico
N.M. Stat. § 59A-18-16

Employers affected: All employers that offer group health insurance.

Eligible employees: All insured employees are eligible.

Length of coverage for employee: Six months.

Length of coverage for dependents: Six months for termination of employment. May continue group coverage or convert to individual policies upon death of covered employee or divorce or legal separation.

Qualifying event: Termination of employment.

Time employer has to notify employee: Insurer or employer must give written notice at time of termination.

Time employee has to apply: 30 days after receiving notice.

State Health Insurance Continuation Laws (continued)

New York

N.Y. Ins. Law § 3221(m)

Employers affected: All employers that offer group health insurance.

Eligible employees: All covered employees are eligible.

Length of coverage for employee: 36 months.

Length of coverage for dependents: 36 months.

Qualifying event: Termination of employment; death of employee; divorce or legal separation; loss of dependent status; employee's eligibility for Medicare.

Time employee has to apply: 60 days after termination or receipt of notice, whichever is later.

North Carolina

N.C. Gen. Stat. §§ 58-53-5 to 58-53-40

Employers affected: All employers that offer group health insurance.

Eligible employees: Employees continuously insured for previous three months.

Length of coverage for employee: 18 months.

Length of coverage for dependents: 18 months.

Qualifying event: Termination of employment.

Time employer has to notify employee: Employer has option of notifying employee as part of the exit process.

Time employee has to apply: 60 days.

North Dakota

N.D. Cent. Code §§ 26.1-36-23, 26.1-36-23.1

Employers affected: All employers that offer group health insurance.

Eligible employees: Employees continuously insured for previous three months.

Length of coverage for employee: 39 weeks.

Length of coverage for dependents: 39 weeks; 36 months if required by divorce or annulment decree.

Qualifying event: Termination of employment; change in marital status, if divorce or annulment decree requires employee to continue coverage.

Time employee has to apply: Within ten days of termination or of receiving notice of continuation rights, whichever is later, but not more than 31 days from termination.

Ohio

Ohio Rev. Code §§ 1751.53, 3923.38

Employers affected: All employers that offer group health insurance.

Eligible employees: Employees continuously insured for previous three months who were involuntarily terminated for reasons other than gross misconduct on the part of the employee.

Length of coverage for employee: 12 months.

Length of coverage for dependents: 12 months.

Qualifying event: Involuntary termination of employment.

Time employer has to notify employee: At termination of employment.

Time employee has to apply: Whichever is earlier: 31 days after coverage terminates; ten days after coverage terminates if employer notified employee of continuation rights prior to termination; ten days after employer notified employee of continuation rights, if notice was given after coverage terminated.

Oklahoma

Okla. Stat. tit. 36, § 4509

Employers affected: All employers that offer group health insurance.

Eligible employees: Employees insured for at least six months. (All other employees and their dependents entitled to 30 days' continuation coverage.)

State Health Insurance Continuation Laws (continued)

Length of coverage for employee: 63 days for basic coverage; six months for major medical at the same premium rate prior to termination of coverage (only for losses or conditions that began while group policy in effect).

Length of coverage for dependents: 63 days for basic coverage; six months for major medical at the same premium rate prior to termination of coverage (only for losses or conditions that began while group policy in effect).

Qualifying event: Any reason coverage terminates (except employment termination for gross misconduct).

Time employer has to notify employee: Carrier must notify employee in writing within 30 days of receiving notice of termination of employee's coverage.

Time employee has to apply: 31 days after receipt of notice.

Special benefits: Includes maternity care for pregnancy begun while group policy was in effect.

Oregon

Or. Rev. Stat. §§ 743B.343 to 743B.347

Employers affected: Employers not subject to federal COBRA laws.

Eligible employees: Employees continuously insured for previous three months.

Length of coverage for employee: Nine months.

Length of coverage for dependents: Nine months.

Qualifying event: Termination of employment; reduction in hours; employee's eligibility for Medicare; loss of dependent status; termination of membership in group covered by policy; death of employee.

Time employer has to notify employee: Ten days after qualifying event.

Time employee has to apply: Within the time limit determined by the insurer, which must be at least ten days after the qualifying event or employee's receipt of notice, whichever is later.

Special situations: Surviving, divorced, or legally separated spouse who is 55 or older and dependent children entitled to continuation coverage until spouse remarries or is eligible for other coverage. Must include dental, vision, or prescription drug benefits if they were offered in original plan (applies to employers with 20 or more employees).

Pennsylvania

40 Pa. Stat. § 764j

Employers affected: Employers that offer group health insurance and have two to 19 employees.

Eligible employees: Employees continuously insured for at least three months.

Length of coverage for employee: Nine months.

Length of coverage for dependents: Nine months.

Qualifying event: Termination of employment; reduction in hours; death of employee; change in marital status; employee's eligibility for Medicare; loss of dependent status; employer's bankruptcy.

Time employer has to notify employee: 30 days after qualifying event.

Time employee has to apply: 30 days after receiving notice.

Rhode Island

R.I. Gen. Laws §§ 27-19.1-1, 27-20.4-1 to 27-20.4-2

Employers affected: All employers that offer group health insurance.

Eligible employees: All insured employees are eligible.

Length of coverage for employee: 18 months (but not longer than continuous employment). Cannot be required to pay more than one month premium at a time.

Length of coverage for dependents: 18 months (but not longer than continuous employment). Cannot be required to pay more than one month premium at a time.

State Health Insurance Continuation Laws (continued)

Qualifying event: Involuntary termination of employment; death of employee; change in marital status; permanent reduction in workforce; employer's going out of business.

Time employer has to notify employee: Employers must post a conspicuous notice of employee continuation rights.

Time employee has to apply: 30 days from termination of coverage.

Special situations: If right to receiving continuing health insurance is stated in the divorce judgment, divorced spouse has right to continue coverage as long as employee remains covered or until divorced spouse remarries or becomes eligible for other group insurance.

South Carolina

S.C. Code § 38-71-770

Employers affected: All employers that offer group health insurance.

Eligible employees: Employees continuously insured for previous six months.

Length of coverage for employee: Six months (in addition to part of month remaining at termination).

Length of coverage for dependents: Six months (in addition to part of month remaining at termination).

Qualifying event: Any reason employee or dependent becomes ineligible for coverage.

Time employer has to notify employee: At time of termination, employer must clearly and meaningfully advise employee of continuation rights.

South Dakota

S.D. Codified Laws §§ 58-18-7.5, 58-18-7.12, 58-18C-1

Employers affected: All employers that offer group health insurance.

Eligible employees: All covered employees.

Length of coverage for employee: 18 months; 29 months if disabled at termination or during first 60 days of continuation coverage.

Length of coverage for dependents: 18 months; 29 months if disabled at termination or during first 60 days of continuation coverage; 36 months upon death of employee, divorce or legal separation, loss of dependent status, employee's eligibility for Medicare.

Qualifying event: Termination of employment; death of employee; divorce or legal separation; loss of dependent status; employee's eligibility for Medicare.

Special situations: When employer goes out of business: 12 months' continuation coverage available to all employees. Employer must notify employees within ten days of termination of benefits; employees must apply within 60 days of receipt of employer's notice or within 90 days of termination of benefits if no notice given.

Texas

Tex. Ins. Code §§ 1251.252 to 1251.255; 1251.301 to 1251.310

Employers affected: All employers that offer group health insurance.

Eligible employees: Employees continuously insured for previous three months.

Length of coverage for employee: Nine months; for employees eligible for COBRA, six months after COBRA coverage ends.

Length of coverage for dependents: Nine months; for employees eligible for COBRA, six months after COBRA coverage ends. Three years for dependents with coverage due to the death or retirement of employee or severance of the family relationship.

Qualifying event: Termination of employment (except for cause); employee leaves for health reasons; severance of family relationship; retirement or death of employee.

State Health Insurance Continuation Laws (continued)

Time employee has to apply: 60 days from termination of coverage or receiving notice of continuation rights from employer or insurer, whichever is later. Must give notice within 15 days of severance of family relationship. Within 60 days of death or retirement of family member or severance of family relationship, dependent must give notice of intent to continue coverage.

Utah

Utah Code § 31A-22-722

Employers affected: All employers that offer group health insurance.

Eligible employees: Employees continuously insured for previous three months.

Length of coverage for employee: 12 months.

Length of coverage for dependents: 12 months.

Qualifying event: Termination of employment; retirement; death; divorce or legal separation; reduction in hours; sabbatical; leave of absence; disability; loss of dependent status.

Time employer has to notify employee: In writing within 30 days of termination of coverage.

Time employee has to apply: Within 60 days of qualifying event.

Vermont

Vt. Stat. tit. 8, §§ 4047A, 4047B, 4047C

Employers affected: All employers that offer group health insurance.

Eligible employees: All covered employees are eligible.

Length of coverage for employee: 18 months.

Length of coverage for dependents: 18 months.

Qualifying event: Termination of employment; reduction in hours; death of employee; change of marital status; loss of dependent status.

Time employer has to notify employee: Within 30 days of qualifying event.

Time employee has to apply: Within 60 days of receiving notice following the occurrence of a qualifying event.

Virginia

Va. Code §§ 38.2-3541 to 38.2-3542

Employers affected: Employers not subject to federal COBRA laws.

Eligible employees: Employees continuously insured for previous three months.

Length of coverage for employee: 12 months.

Length of coverage for dependents: 12 months.

Qualifying event: Any reason employee or dependent becomes ineligible for coverage, except employee's termination for gross misconduct.

Time employer has to notify employee: 14 days from termination of coverage.

Time employee has to apply: Within 31 days of receiving notice of eligibility, but no more than 60 days following termination.

Special situations: Employee may convert to an individual policy instead of applying for continuation coverage (must apply within 31 days of termination of coverage).

Washington

Wash. Rev. Code § 48.21.075

Employers affected: All employers that offer disability insurance.

Eligible employees: Insured employees on strike.

Length of coverage for employee: Six months if employee goes on strike.

Length of coverage for dependents: Six months if employee goes on strike.

Qualifying event: If employee goes on strike.

Special situations: All employers have option of offering continued group health benefits.

State Health Insurance Continuation Laws (continued)

West Virginia

*W. Va. Code §§ 33-16-2, 33-16-3(e); W. Va. Code R. §
114-93-3*

Employers affected: Employers providing insurance
for between two and 20 employees.

Eligible employees: All employees are eligible.

Length of coverage for employee: 18 months in
case of involuntary layoff.

Qualifying event: Involuntary layoff.

Time employer has to notify employee: Carrier
must notify beneficiaries within 15 days of receiving
notice from beneficiary of intent to apply.

Time employee has to apply: 20 days to send
notice of intention to apply; 30 days to apply after
receiving election and premium notice.

Wisconsin

Wis. Stat. § 632.897

Employers affected: All employers that offer group
health insurance.

Eligible employees: Employees continuously
insured for previous three months.

Length of coverage for employee: 18 months
(or longer at insurer's option).

Length of coverage for dependents: 18 months
(or longer at insurer's option).

Qualifying event: Any reason employee or
dependent becomes ineligible for coverage (except
employment termination due to misconduct).

Time employer has to notify employee: Five days
from termination of coverage.

Time employee has to apply: 30 days after
receiving employer's notice.

Wyoming

Wyo. Stat. § 26-19-113

Employers affected: Employers not subject to
federal COBRA laws.

Eligible employees: Employees continuously
insured for previous three months.

Length of coverage for employee: 12 months.

Length of coverage for dependents: 12 months.

Time employee has to apply: 31 days from
termination of coverage.

State Laws on Information From Former Employers

Alaska

Alaska Stat. § 09.65.160

Information that may be disclosed: Job performance.

Who may request or receive information: Prospective employer; former or current employee.

Employer immune from liability unless: Employer knowingly or intentionally discloses information that is false or misleading, that violates an employee's civil rights, or is rendered in malice.

Arizona

Ariz. Rev. Stat. § 23-1361

Information that may be disclosed: Job performance; reasons for termination; performance evaluation; professional conduct.

Who may request or receive information: Prospective employer; former or current employee.

Copy to employee required: Copy of disclosures must be sent to employee's last known address.

Employer immune from liability: Employer with fewer than 100 employees who provides only information listed above; employer with at least 100 employees who has a regular practice of providing information listed above upon request of a prospective employer.

Employer immune from liability unless: Information is intentionally misleading; employer provided information knowing it was false or not caring if it was true or false.

Arkansas

Ark. Code § 11-3-204

Information that may be disclosed: Dates and duration of employment; current pay rate and pay history; job description and job duties; last written performance evaluation; attendance information; results of drug or alcohol tests administered within one year before the request; threats of violence, harassing acts, or threatening conduct toward another

employee or related to the workplace; a substantiated allegation of sexual abuse or sexual harassment by the employee, or the resignation by a former employee during a pending investigation of an allegation of sexual abuse or sexual harassment against the former employee; the reasons for termination, including whether it was voluntary or involuntary; whether the employee is eligible for rehire.

Who may request or receive information: Prospective employer (employee must provide written consent); former or current employee.

Employer immune from liability unless: Employer disclosed information knowing it was false or not caring if it was true or false; information was provided with the intent to discriminate or retaliate against an employee for exercising a federal or state right or for acting in accordance with the public policy of the state.

Other provisions: Employee consent required before employer can release information. Consent must follow required format and must be signed and dated. If the employee secures new employment for six months or more, the consent is no longer valid. If the employee secures new employment, but works there for less than six months, the consent is valid for another six months.

California

Cal. Civ. Code § 47(c); Cal. Lab. Code §§ 1053, 1055

Information that may be disclosed: Job performance; reasons for termination or separation; knowledge, qualifications, skills, or abilities based upon credible evidence; eligibility for rehire.

Who may request or receive information: Prospective employer.

Employer required to write letter: Public utilities companies only.

Employer immune from liability unless: Information was known to be false or was disclosed with reckless disregard for its truth or falsity.

State Laws on Information From Former Employers (continued)

Colorado

Colo. Rev. Stat. § 8-2-114

Information that may be disclosed: Job history; job performance, including work-related skills, abilities, and habits; reasons for separation; eligibility for rehire.

Who may request or receive information: Prospective employer; former or current employee.

Copy to employee required: Upon request, a copy must be sent to employee's last known address. Employee may obtain a copy in person at the employer's place of business during normal business hours. Employer may charge reproduction costs if multiple copies are required.

Employer immune from liability unless: Information disclosed was false, and employer knew or reasonably should have known it was false.

Connecticut

Conn. Gen. Stat. § 31-51

Information that may be disclosed: "Truthful statement of any facts."

Who may request or receive information: Prospective employer; former or current employee.

Delaware

Del. Code tit. 19, §§ 708 to 709

Information that may be disclosed: All employers: job performance; performance evaluation or opinion; work-related characteristics; violations of law. Health or child care employers: job description and duties; length of employment; nature of separation from employment; substantiated incidents of abuse, neglect, violence, or threats of violence; disciplinary actions.

Who may request or receive information: Prospective employer (child or health care employers must provide signed statement from prospective applicant authorizing former employer to release information).

Employer required to write letter: Letter required for employment in health care and child care facili-

ties; letter must follow required format; employer must have written consent from employee; employer must send letter within 10 business days of receiving request.

Employer immune from liability unless: Information was known to be false, was deliberately misleading, or was disclosed without caring whether it was true; information was confidential or disclosed in violation of a nondisclosure agreement.

Florida

Fla. Stat. §§ 435.10, 655.51, 768.095

Information that may be disclosed: Employers that require background checks: reasons for termination or separation; disciplinary matters. Banks and financial institutions: violation of an industry-related law or regulation, which has been reported to appropriate enforcing authority.

Who may request or receive information: Prospective employer; former or current employee.

Employer required to write letter: Only employers that require background checks.

Employer immune from liability unless: Information is known to be false or is disclosed without caring whether it is true; disclosure violates employee's civil rights.

Georgia

Ga. Code § 34-1-4

Information that may be disclosed: Job performance; violations of state law; ability (or lack of ability) to perform job duties.

Who may request or receive information: Prospective employer; former or current employee.

Employer immune from liability unless: Information was disclosed in violation of a nondisclosure agreement; information was confidential according to federal, state, or local law or regulations; employer didn't act in good faith in disclosing information.

State Laws on Information From Former Employers (continued)

Hawaii

Haw. Rev. Stat. § 663-1.95

Information that may be disclosed: Job performance.

Who may request or receive information: Prospective employer.

Employer immune from liability unless: Information disclosed was knowingly false or misleading.

Idaho

Idaho Code § 44-201(2)

Information that may be disclosed: Job performance; performance evaluation or opinion; professional conduct.

Employer immune from liability unless: Information is deliberately misleading, known to be false, or provided with reckless disregard for its truth or falsity.

Illinois

745 Ill. Comp. Stat. 46/10, 820 Ill. Comp. Stat. 112/10

Information that may be disclosed: Job performance.

Who may request or receive information: Prospective employer.

Employer immune from liability: Information is truthful, or employer believed, in good faith, that it was.

Employer immune from liability unless: Information is knowingly false or in violation of a civil right.

Other provisions: It is unlawful for an employer to seek the wage or salary history, including benefits or other compensation, of a job applicant from any current or former employer.

Indiana

Ind. Code §§ 22-5-3-1(b),(c), 22-6-3-1

Information that may be disclosed: Information about a current or former employee.

Who may request or receive information: Former or current employee (must be in writing).

Copy to employee required: Prospective employer must provide copy of any written communications from current or former employers that may affect hiring decision. Prospective employers must make request in writing within 30 days of applying for employment.

Employer required to write letter: If employee is discharged or quits, employer must, upon employee's written request, issue employee a letter stating whether employee was discharged or quit. Requirement not applicable to employers that don't require written recommendations or applications showing qualifications or experience for employment.

Employer immune from liability unless: Information was known to be false.

Iowa

Iowa Code § 91B.2

Information that may be disclosed: Work-related information.

Who may request or receive information: Prospective employer; former or current employee.

Employer immune from liability unless: Information violates employee's civil rights; information is not relevant to inquiry being made; information is knowingly provided to a person who has no legitimate interest in receiving it; information is provided maliciously; information is provided with no good-faith belief that it is true.

Kansas

Kan. Stat. §§ 44-119a, 44-808(3)

Information that may be disclosed: Does not have to be in writing: dates of employment; pay level; wage history; job description and duties. May be in writing: performance evaluation or opinion (written evaluation conducted prior to employee's separation); reasons for termination or separation.

Who may request or receive information: Prospective employer (written request required for performance evaluation and reasons for termination or separation); former or current employee (request must be in writing).

State Laws on Information From Former Employers (continued)

Copy to employee required: Employee must be given copy of performance evaluations and reasons for separation upon request.

Employer required to write letter: Must give former employee a service letter stating the length of employment, job classification, and rate of pay, upon written request.

Employer immune from liability: Employer who provides information as it is specified in the law.

Kentucky

Ky. Rev. Stat. § 411.225

Information that may be disclosed: Job performance; performance evaluation; professional conduct.

Who may request or receive information: Prospective employer; former or current employee.

Employer immune from liability unless: Employer knows information is false or provides it with reckless disregard as to its truth or falsity; information is intentionally misleading; providing the information is an illegal discriminatory act under state law.

Louisiana

La. Rev. Stat. § 23:291

Information that may be disclosed: Accurate information on reasons for employee's separation and employee's job performance, including: attendance; attitude; awards; demotions; job duties; effort; evaluations; knowledge; skills; promotions; disciplinary actions.

Who may request or receive information: Prospective employer; former or current employee.

Employer immune from liability: Under certain conditions if employer has conducted a background check.

Employer immune from liability unless: Information is knowingly false and deliberately misleading.

Maine

Me. Rev. Stat. tit. 26, §§ 598, 630

Information that may be disclosed: Job performance; work record.

Who may request or receive information: Prospective employer.

Employer required to write letter: Must provide a discharged employee with a written statement of the reasons for termination within 15 days of receiving employee's written request.

Employer immune from liability unless: Employer knowingly discloses false or deliberately misleading information with malicious intent.

Maryland

Md. Code Cts. & Jud. Proc. § 5-423

Information that may be disclosed: Job performance; reasons for termination or separation; information disclosed in a report or other document required by law or regulation.

Who may request or receive information: Prospective employer; former or current employee; federal, state, or industry regulatory authority.

Employer immune from liability unless: Employer intended to harm or defame employee; employer intentionally disclosed false information, or disclosed without caring if it was false.

Massachusetts

Mass. Gen. Laws ch. 111, § 72L 1/2

Information that may be disclosed: Applies only to hospitals, convalescent or nursing homes, home health agencies, and hospice programs: reasons for termination or separation; length of employment, pay level, and history.

Employer immune from liability unless: Information disclosed was false, and employer knew it was false.

State Laws on Information From Former Employers (continued)

Michigan

Mich. Comp. Laws §§ 423.452, 423.506–423.507

Information that may be disclosed: Job performance information that is documented in personnel file.

Who may request or receive information: Prospective employer; former or current employee.

Employer immune from liability unless: Employer knew that information was false or misleading; employer disclosed information without caring if it was true or false; disclosure was specifically prohibited by a state or federal statute.

Other provisions: Employer may not disclose any disciplinary action or letter of reprimand that is more than four years old to a third party (with exceptions, to do with certain sorts of legal actions and licensing or termination of law enforcement officers). Employer must notify employee by first class mail on or before the day of disclosure of disciplinary records (does not apply if employee waived notification in a signed job application with another employer).

Minnesota

Minn. Stat. §§ 181.933, 181.967

Information that may be disclosed: Dates of employment; compensation history; job description and job duties; any education and training provided by the employer; any acts of violence, harassment, theft, or illegal conduct documented in the employee's personnel records that led to the employee's discipline or resignation, along with the employee's written response, if any (this information may be disclosed only in writing). If employee provides written authorization, employer may also disclose: written evaluations, along with the employee's written response (if any); written warnings and other disciplinary actions that took place within five years of the employee's authorization, along with the employee's written response (if any), and written reasons for the employee's separation from employment.

Who may request or receive information: Prospective employer; former or current employee.

Copy to employee required: Employer who provides written evaluations, written warnings, written reasons for employee's separation, or information on acts of violence, harassment, theft, or illegal conduct must send a copy to the employee's last known address.

Employer required to write letter: Must provide a written statement of the reasons for termination within ten working days of receiving employee's request; employee must make request in writing within 15 working days of being discharged.

Employer immune from liability: Employer that provides information allowed by law may be sued only if the information was false and defamatory, and the employer knew or should have known that the information was false and acted with malicious intent to injure the employee; employer can't be sued for libel, slander, or defamation for sending employee written statement of reasons for termination.

Missouri

Mo. Rev. Stat. §§ 290.140, 290.152

Information that may be disclosed: Reasons for termination or separation; length of employment, pay level, and history; job description and duties.

Who may request or receive information: Prospective employer (request must be in writing).

Copy to employee required: Employer must send copy to employee's last known address; employee may request copy of letter up to one year after it was sent to prospective employer.

Employer required to write letter: Only employers with seven or more employees, and employees with at least 90 days of service; must state the nature and length of employment and reason, if any, for separation; employee must make request by certified mail within one year after separation; employer must reply within 45 days of receiving request.

State Laws on Information From Former Employers (continued)

Employer immune from liability unless: Information provided was false, and employer either knew it was false or provided it with reckless disregard as to its truth or falsity. Employer is protected from liability only if it provides information in writing.

Other provisions: All information disclosed must be in writing and must be consistent with service letter.

Montana

Mont. Code §§ 39-2-801, 39-2-802

Information that may be disclosed: Reasons for termination or separation.

Who may request or receive information: Prospective employer.

Employer required to write letter: Must give discharged employee a written statement of reasons for discharge, upon request; if employer doesn't respond to request within a reasonable time, may not disclose reasons to another person.

Nebraska

Neb. Rev. Stat. § 48-201

Information that may be disclosed: With written consent from the current or former employee: (i) date and duration of employment; (ii) pay rate and wage history; (iii) job description and duties; (iv) most recent written performance evaluation; (v) attendance information; (vi) most recent year's results of drug or alcohol tests; (vii) threats of violence, harassing acts, or threatening behavior related to the workplace or directed at another employee; (viii) whether the employee was voluntarily or involuntarily separated from employment and the reasons; and (ix) whether the employee is eligible for rehire.

Who may request or receive information: Any current or former employee, agent, or representative authorized to provide information.

Employer immune from liability unless: Employer discriminated or retaliated against an employee who was exercising a federal or state statutory right or taking an action encouraged by state public policy.

Nevada

Nev. Rev. Stat. §§ 41.755, 613.210(4)

Information that may be disclosed: The employee's ability to perform the job; the employee's diligence, skill, or reliability in carrying out the job's duties; or any illegal act or wrong the employee committed.

Who may request or receive information: Former or current employee.

Employer required to write letter: Must provide a written statement listing reasons for separation and any meritorious service employee may have performed, upon request of an employee who leaves or is discharged; statement not required unless employee has worked for at least 60 days; employee entitled to only one statement.

Employer immune from liability unless: Employer acted with malice or ill will; employer disclosed information that the employer believed was inaccurate or had no reasonable grounds to believe was accurate; employer recklessly or intentionally disclosed inaccurate information; employer intentionally disclosed misleading information; employer disclosed information in violation of federal or state law or in violation of an agreement with the employee.

New Mexico

N.M. Stat. § 50-12-1

Information that may be disclosed: Job performance.

Who may request or receive information: No person specified ("when requested to provide a reference...").

Employer immune from liability unless: Information disclosed was known to be false or was deliberately misleading; disclosure was made with malicious intent or violated former employee's civil rights.

State Laws on Information From Former Employers (continued)

North Carolina

N.C. Gen. Stat. § 1-539.12

Information that may be disclosed: Job performance or history; reasons for termination or separation; suitability for reemployment; job-related skills, abilities, or traits.

Who may request or receive information: Prospective employer; former or current employee.

Employer immune from liability unless: Information disclosed was false, and employer knew or reasonably should have known it was false.

North Dakota

N.D. Cent. Code § 34-02-18

Information that may be disclosed: Job performance; length of employment, pay level, and wage history; job description and duties.

Who may request or receive information: Prospective employer.

Employer immune from liability unless: Employer that provides information only on employee's length of employment, pay level, wage history, and job description and duties is immune unless providing the information violated a nondisclosure agreement or other legal confidentiality requirement; employer that provides information on job performance may also be sued if the information was knowingly false, deliberately misleading, provided with reckless disregard as to its truth or falsity or provided with a malicious purpose.

Ohio

Ohio Rev. Code § 4113.71

Information that may be disclosed: Job performance.

Who may request or receive information: Prospective employer; former or current employee.

Employer immune from liability unless: Disclosed information knowing that it was false or with the deliberate intent to mislead the prospective employer or another person; information was disclosed in bad faith or with a malicious purpose; disclosure constitutes an unlawful or discriminatory practice.

Oklahoma

Okla. Stat. tit. 40, §§ 61, 171

Information that may be disclosed: Job performance.

Who may request or receive information: Prospective employer (must have consent of employee); former or current employee.

Employer required to write letter: Law applies only to public service corporations and contractors who work for them; upon request from employee, must provide letter that states length of employment, nature of work, and reasons employee quit or was discharged; letter must follow prescribed format for paper and signature.

Employer immune from liability unless: Information was false, and employer knew it was false, acted maliciously, or acted with reckless disregard as to its truth or falsity.

Oregon

Or. Rev. Stat. § 30.178

Information that may be disclosed: Job performance.

Who may request or receive information: Prospective employer; former or current employee.

Employer immune from liability unless: Information was knowingly false or deliberately misleading; information was disclosed with malicious intent; disclosure violated a civil right of the former employee.

Pennsylvania

42 Pa. Cons. Stat. § 8340.1

Information that may be disclosed: Job performance.

Who may request or receive information: Prospective employer; former or current employee.

State Laws on Information From Former Employers (continued)

Employer immune from liability unless: Employer knew the information was false or should have known it was false, had the employer exercised due diligence; provided information that was deliberately misleading; provided information that was false with reckless disregard as to whether it was true or false; or violated the employee's contract, statutory, common law, or civil rights.

Rhode Island

R.I. Gen. Laws § 28-6.4-1(c)

Information that may be disclosed: Job performance.

Who may request or receive information: Prospective employer; former or current employee.

Employer immune from liability unless: Information was knowingly false or deliberately misleading; information was in violation of current or former employee's civil rights under the employment discrimination laws in effect at time of disclosure; information was disclosed for a malicious purpose.

South Carolina

S.C. Code § 41-1-65

Information that may be disclosed: Length of employment, pay level, and wage history; the employee's written performance evaluations; official personnel documents that state the reasons for the employee's termination; whether the employment relationship was terminated voluntarily or involuntarily, and the reasons for that termination; and information about the employee's job performance, including attendance, attitudes, awards, demotions, duties, effort, evaluation, knowledge, skills, promotions, and disciplinary actions.

Who may request or receive information: Prospective employer (written request required for all information except dates of employment and wage history); former or current employee.

Copy to employee required: Employee must be allowed access to any written information sent to prospective employer.

Employer immune from liability unless: Employer knowingly or recklessly releases or discloses false information.

Other provisions: All disclosures other than length of employment, pay level, and wage history must be in writing for employer to be entitled to immunity.

South Dakota

S.D. Codified Laws § 60-4-12

Information that may be disclosed: Job performance (must be in writing).

Who may request or receive information: Prospective employer (request must be in writing); former or current employee (request must be in writing).

Copy to employee required: Upon employee's written request.

Employer immune from liability unless: Employer knowingly, intentionally, or carelessly disclosed false or deliberately misleading information; information is subject to a nondisclosure agreement or is confidential according to federal or state law.

Tennessee

Tenn. Code § 50-1-105

Information that may be disclosed: Job performance.

Who may request or receive information: Prospective employer; former or current employee.

Employer immune from liability unless: Information is knowingly false, deliberately misleading, or disclosed for malicious reasons; employer disclosed information regardless of whether it was false or defamatory; disclosure is in violation of employee's civil rights according to current employment discrimination laws.

State Laws on Information From Former Employers (continued)

Texas

Tex. Lab. Code §§ 52.031(d), 103.001 to 103.004; Tex. Civ. Stat. Art. 5196

Information that may be disclosed: Reasons for termination or separation (must be in writing); job performance; attendance, attitudes, effort, knowledge, behavior, and skills.

Who may request or receive information: Prospective employer; former or current employee.

Copy to employee required: Within ten days of receiving employee's request, employer must send copy of written disclosure or true statement of verbal disclosure, along with names of people to whom information was given. Employer may not disclose reasons for employee's discharge to any other person without sending employee a copy, unless employee specifically requests disclosure.

Employer required to write letter: Employee must make request in writing; employer must respond within ten days of receiving employee's request; discharged employee must be given a written statement of reasons for termination; employee who quits must be given a written statement that includes all job titles and dates, states that separation was voluntary, and indicates whether employee's performance was satisfactory; employee entitled to another copy of statement if original is lost or unavailable.

Employer immune from liability unless: Employer knew the information was false (this means that the employer had information about the employee demonstrating the falsity of the reference); the employer disclosed the information in reckless disregard for its truth or falsity; or the employer disclosed the information maliciously.

Utah

Utah Code § 34-42-1

Information that may be disclosed: Job performance.

Who may request or receive information: Prospective employer; former or current employee.

Employer immune from liability unless: There is clear and convincing evidence that employer disclosed information with the intent to mislead, knowing it was false, or not caring if it was true or false.

Virginia

Va. Code § 8.01-46.1

Information that may be disclosed: The employee's professional conduct, including the ethical standards governing the employee's profession or the standards of conduct imposed by the employer; the employee's job performance, including ability, attendance, awards, demotions, duties, effort, evaluations, knowledge, skills, promotions, productivity, and discipline; and the reasons for the employee's separation from employment.

Who may request or receive information: Prospective employer.

Employer immune from liability unless: Employer disclosed information deliberately intending to mislead, knowing it was false, or not caring if it was true or false.

Washington

Wash. Rev. Code §§ 4.24.730, 49.12.250; Wash. Admin. Code § 296-126-050

Information that may be disclosed: The employee's ability to perform the job; the employee's diligence, skill, or reliability in performing the job's duties; and any illegal or wrongful act the employee committed relating to the job.

Who may request or receive information: Prospective employer.

Copy to employee required: Employer must keep written records of all prospective employers to whom it has provided reference information for at least two years; employee has the right to inspect these records on request.

State Laws on Information From Former Employers (continued)

Employer required to write letter: Within 21 calendar days of receiving written request, employer must give former employee a signed statement indicating the effective date of discharge, whether the employer had a reason for the discharge, and if so, the reasons.

Employer immune from liability unless: Employer provided information with the intent to mislead, knowing it was false, or with reckless disregard for its truth or falsity.

West Virginia

W.Va. Code § 55-7-18a

Information that may be disclosed: Employer may provide job-related information that might reasonably be considered adverse about an employee and information for the purpose of evaluating the employee's suitability for employment, including: education; training; experience; qualifications; conduct; job performance. Information must be provided in writing.

Who may request or receive information: Prospective employer.

Copy to employee required: Employee must receive copy of information provided to prospective employers. If employer provides incorrect information, it must, on employee's request, provide corrected information to every prospective employer that received the incorrect information.

Employer immune from liability unless: Employee can prove, by clear and convincing evidence, that employer provided information knowing that it was false, with reckless disregard for its truth or falsity, with the intent to mislead, with a malicious purpose, or in violation of the law or a nondisclosure agreement.

Wisconsin

Wis. Stat. §§ 134.02(2)(a), 895.487

Information that may be disclosed: Job performance; qualifications; any statement employer and employee have negotiated as part of an agreement to end the employment relationship.

Who may request or receive information: Prospective employer; former or current employee.

Employer immune from liability unless: Employer knowingly provided false information in the reference; employer made the reference maliciously; reference was in violation of employee's civil rights.

Wyoming

Wyo. Stat. § 27-1-113

Information that may be disclosed: Job performance.

Who may request or receive information: Prospective employer.

Employer immune from liability unless: Information was knowingly false or deliberately misleading; information was disclosed for a malicious purpose.

State Laws That Control Final Paychecks

Alabama

Unused vacation pay due: Only if agreed to by employer or required by company policy or practice.

Alaska

Alaska Stat. § 23.05.140(b)

Paycheck due when employee is fired: Within three working days after termination.

Paycheck due when employee quits: Next regular payday at least three days after employee gives notice.

Unused vacation pay due: Only if agreed to by employer or required by company policy or practice.

Arizona

Ariz. Rev. Stat. §§ 23-350, 23-353

Paycheck due when employee is fired: Next payday or within seven working days, whichever is sooner.

Paycheck due when employee quits: Next regular payday or by mail at employee's request.

Unused vacation pay due: No provision.

Arkansas

Ark. Code § 11-4-405

Paycheck due when employee is fired: Next regular payday.

Paycheck due when employee quits: No provision.

Unused vacation pay due: Only if agreed to by employer or required by company policy or practice.

California

Cal. Lab. Code §§ 201 to 202, 227.3

Paycheck due when employee is fired: Immediately.

Paycheck due when employee quits: Immediately if employee has given 72 hours' notice; otherwise, within 72 hours.

Unused vacation pay due: Yes.

Special employment situations: Motion picture business: next payday. Oil drilling industry: within 24 hours (excluding weekends & holidays) of

termination. Seasonal agricultural workers: within 72 hours of termination.

Colorado

Colo. Rev. Stat. §§ 8-4-101, 8-4-109

Paycheck due when employee is fired: Immediately (within six hours of start of next workday, if payroll unit is closed; 24 hours if unit is off-site). When paycheck is not due immediately, employer may make the check available at the worksite, the employer's local office, or the employee's last-known mailing address.

Paycheck due when employee quits: Next payday.

Unused vacation pay due: Yes.

Connecticut

Conn. Gen. Stat. §§ 31-71c, 31-76k

Paycheck due when employee is fired: Next business day after discharge.

Paycheck due when employee quits: Next payday.

Unused vacation pay due: Only if policy or collective bargaining agreement requires payment on termination.

Delaware

Del. Code tit. 19, §§ 1103, 1109

Paycheck due when employee is fired: Next payday or within three business days, whichever is later.

Paycheck due when employee quits: Next payday or within three business days, whichever is later.

Unused vacation pay due: Only if required by employer policy or agreement, in which case vacation must be paid within 30 days after it becomes due.

District of Columbia

D.C. Code §§ 32-1301, 32-1303

Paycheck due when employee is fired: Next business day unless employee handles money, in which case employer has four days.

State Laws That Control Final Paychecks (continued)

Paycheck due when employee quits: Next payday or seven days after quitting, whichever is sooner.

Unused vacation pay due: Yes, unless there is an agreement to the contrary.

Hawaii
Haw. Rev. Stat. § 388-3

Paycheck due when employee is fired: Immediately, or next business day if timing or conditions prevent immediate payment.

Paycheck due when employee quits: Next payday, or immediately if employee gives one pay period's notice.

Unused vacation pay due: Only if agreed to by employer or required by company policy or practice.

Idaho
Idaho Code §§ 45-606

Paycheck due when employee is fired: Next payday or within 10 days (excluding weekends & holidays), whichever is sooner. If employee makes written request for earlier payment, within 48 hours of receipt of request (excluding weekends & holidays).

Paycheck due when employee quits: Next payday or within 10 days (excluding weekends & holidays), whichever is sooner. If employee makes written request for earlier payment, within 48 hours of receipt of request (excluding weekends & holidays).

Unused vacation pay due: Only if agreed to by employer or required by company policy or practice.

Illinois
820 Ill. Comp. Stat. § 115/5

Paycheck due when employee is fired: At time of separation if possible, but no later than next payday. Employer must comply with employee's written request to mail final paycheck.

Paycheck due when employee quits: At time of separation if possible, but no later than next payday. Employer must comply with employee's written request to mail final paycheck.

Unused vacation pay due: Yes.

Indiana
Ind. Code §§ 22-2-5-1, 22-2-9-1, 22-2-9-2

Paycheck due when employee is fired: Next payday.

Paycheck due when employee quits: Next payday. (If employee has not left address, (1) ten business days after employee demands wages or (2) when employee provides address where check may be mailed.)

Unused vacation pay due: If employer agrees to vacation pay, absent an agreement to the contrary, employer must pay out accrued unused vacation upon termination.

Special employment situations: Does not apply to railroad employees.

Iowa
Iowa Code §§ 91A.2(7)(b), 91A.4

Paycheck due when employee is fired: Next payday.

Paycheck due when employee quits: Next payday.

Unused vacation pay due: Yes.

Special employment situations: If employee is owed commission, employer has 30 days to pay.

Kansas
Kan. Stat. § 44-315

Paycheck due when employee is fired: Next payday.

Paycheck due when employee quits: Next payday.

Unused vacation pay due: Only if required by employer's policies or practice.

Kentucky
Ky. Rev. Stat. §§ 337.010, 337.055

Paycheck due when employee is fired: Next payday or within 14 days, whichever is later.

Paycheck due when employee quits: Next payday or within 14 days, whichever is later.

Unused vacation pay due: Yes.

State Laws That Control Final Paychecks (continued)

Louisiana

La. Rev. Stat. § 23:631

Paycheck due when employee is fired: Next payday or within 15 days, whichever is earlier.

Paycheck due when employee quits: Next payday or within 15 days, whichever is earlier.

Unused vacation pay due: Yes.

Maine

Me. Rev. Stat. tit. 26, § 626

Paycheck due when employee is fired: Next payday or within 14 days, whichever is earlier.

Paycheck due when employee quits: Next payday or within 14 days, whichever is earlier.

Unused vacation pay due: Yes, unless employer has ten or fewer employees.

Special employment situations: Employer must pay employees all wages due within two weeks of the sale of a business.

Maryland

Md. Code [Lab. & Empl.], § 3-505

Paycheck due when employee is fired: Next scheduled payday.

Paycheck due when employee quits: Next scheduled payday.

Unused vacation pay due: Yes, unless employer has written policy to the contrary.

Massachusetts

Mass. Gen. Laws ch. 149, § 148

Paycheck due when employee is fired: Day of discharge.

Paycheck due when employee quits: Next payday. If no scheduled payday, then following Saturday.

Unused vacation pay due: Yes.

Michigan

Mich. Comp. Laws §§ 408.471 to 408.475; Mich. Admin. Code § 408.9007

Paycheck due when employee is fired: Next payday.

Paycheck due when employee quits: Next payday.

Unused vacation pay due: Only if required by written policy or contract.

Special employment situations: Hand-harvesters of crops: within one working day of termination.

Minnesota

Minn. Stat. §§ 181.13, 181.14, 181.74, 181.145

Paycheck due when employee is fired: Within 24 hours.

Paycheck due when employee quits: Next regular payday. If next payday is less than five days after employee's last day, employer may delay payment until payday after that. But in no event may payment exceed 20 days from employee's last day.

Unused vacation pay due: Only if required by written policy or contract.

Special employment situations: If employee was responsible for collecting or handling money or property, employer has ten days after termination or resignation to audit and adjust employee accounts before making payment.

Commissions must be paid to sales employees within three days if employee is fired or quits with at least five days' notice. Otherwise, commissions must be paid within six days.

Migrant agricultural workers who resign: within three days.

Mississippi

Unused vacation pay due: Only if required by written policy or contract.

State Laws That Control Final Paychecks (continued)

Missouri

Mo. Rev. Stat. § 290.110

Paycheck due when employee is fired: Day of discharge.

Paycheck due when employee quits: No provision.

Unused vacation pay due: Only if required by agreement.

Special employment situations: Requirements do not apply if employee is paid primarily based on commission and an audit is necessary or customary to determine the amount due.

Montana

Mont. Code § 39-3-205

Paycheck due when employee is fired: Immediately if fired for cause or laid off (unless there is a written policy extending time to earlier of next payday or 15 days).

Paycheck due when employee quits: Next payday or within 15 days, whichever comes first.

Unused vacation pay due: Only if required by policy.

Nebraska

Neb. Rev. Stat. §§ 48-1229 to 48-1230.01

Paycheck due when employee is fired: Next payday or within two weeks, whichever is earlier.

Paycheck due when employee quits: Next payday or within two weeks, whichever is earlier.

Unused vacation pay due: Yes.

Special employment situations: Commissions due on next payday following receipt.

Nevada

Nev. Rev. Stat. §§ 608.020, 608.030

Paycheck due when employee is fired: Immediately.

Paycheck due when employee quits: Next payday or within seven days, whichever is earlier.

Unused vacation pay due: Only if required by policy.

New Hampshire

N.H. Rev. Stat. §§ 275:43(V), 275:44

Paycheck due when employee is fired: Within 72 hours. If laid off, next payday.

Paycheck due when employee quits: Next payday, or within 72 hours if employee gives one pay period's notice.

Unused vacation pay due: Only if required by policy.

New Jersey

N.J. Stat. § 34:11-4.3

Paycheck due when employee is fired: Next payday.

Paycheck due when employee quits: Next payday.

Unused vacation pay due: Only if required by policy.

New Mexico

N.M. Stat. §§ 50-4-4, 50-4-5

Paycheck due when employee is fired: Within five days. Ten days for commission- or piece-based workers.

Paycheck due when employee quits: Next payday.

Unused vacation pay due: Only if required by policy.

Special employment situations: If paid by task or commission, ten days after discharge.

New York

N.Y. Lab. Law §§ 191(3), 198-c(2)

Paycheck due when employee is fired: Next payday.

Paycheck due when employee quits: Next payday.

Unused vacation pay due: Only if required by policy.

North Carolina

N.C. Gen. Stat. §§ 95-25.7, 95-25.12

Paycheck due when employee is fired: Next payday.

Paycheck due when employee quits: Next payday.

Unused vacation pay due: Only if required by policy.

State Laws That Control Final Paychecks (continued)

Special employment situations: If paid by commission or bonus, on next payday after amount calculated.

North Dakota

N.D. Cent. Code §§ 34-14-03, 34-14-09.2; N.D. Admin. Code § 46-02-07-02(12)

Paycheck due when employee is fired: Next payday.

Paycheck due when employee quits: Next payday.

Unused vacation pay due: Yes. However, if an employer provides written notice at the time of hire, employer need not pay out vacation that has been awarded, but not yet earned. And, if an employee quits with less than five days' notice, employer may withhold accrued vacation, as long as the employer gave written notice of the limitation at the time of hire and the employee was employed for less than one year.

Ohio

Ohio Rev. Code § 4113.15

Paycheck due when employee is fired: First of month for wages earned in first half of prior month; 15th of month for wages earned in second half of prior month.

Paycheck due when employee quits: First of month for wages earned in first half of prior month; 15th of month for wages earned in second half of prior month.

Unused vacation pay due: Yes, if company has policy or practice of making such payments.

Oklahoma

Okla. Stat. tit. 40, §§ 165.1(4), 165.3

Paycheck due when employee is fired: Next payday.

Paycheck due when employee quits: Next payday.

Unused vacation pay due: Yes.

Oregon

Or. Rev. Stat. §§ 652.140, 652.145

Paycheck due when employee is fired: End of first business day after termination.

Paycheck due when employee quits: Immediately, with 48 hours' notice (excluding weekends & holidays); without notice, within five business days or next payday, whichever comes first (must be within five days if employee submits time records to determine wages due).

Unused vacation pay due: Only if required by policy.

Special employment situations: Seasonal farmworkers: fired or quitting with 48 hours' notice, immediately; quitting without notice, within 48 hours or next payday, whichever comes first. If the termination occurs at the end of harvest season, the employer is a farmworker camp operator, and the farmworker is provided housing at no cost until wages are paid, employer must pay by noon on the day after termination.

Pennsylvania

43 Pa. Stat. §§ 260.2a, 260.5

Paycheck due when employee is fired: Next payday.

Paycheck due when employee quits: Next payday.

Unused vacation pay due: Only if required by policy or contract.

Rhode Island

R.I. Gen. Laws § 28-14-4

Paycheck due when employee is fired: Next payday. Paycheck is due within 24 hours if employer liquidates, merges, or disposes of the business, or moves it out of state.

Paycheck due when employee quits: Next payday.

Unused vacation pay due: Yes, if employee has worked for one full year and the company has verbally or in writing awarded vacation.

State Laws That Control Final Paychecks (continued)

South Carolina
S.C. Code §§ 41-10-10(2), 41-10-50

Paycheck due when employee is fired: Within 48 hours or next payday, but not more than 30 days.

Paycheck due when employee quits: Within 48 hours or next payday, but not more than 30 days.

Unused vacation pay due: Only if required by policy or contract.

South Dakota
S.D. Codified Laws §§ 60-11-10, 60-11-11, 60-11-14

Paycheck due when employee is fired: Next payday (or until employee returns employer's property).

Paycheck due when employee quits: Next payday (or until employee returns employer's property).

Unused vacation pay due: No.

Tennessee
Tenn. Code § 50-2-103

Paycheck due when employee is fired: Next payday or within 21 days, whichever is later.

Paycheck due when employee quits: Next payday or within 21 days, whichever is later.

Unused vacation pay due: Only if required by policy or contract.

Special employment situations: Applies to employers with five or more employees.

Texas
Tex. Lab. Code §§ 61.001, 61.014

Paycheck due when employee is fired: Within six days.

Paycheck due when employee quits: Next payday.

Unused vacation pay due: Only if required by policy or contract.

Utah
Utah Code § 34-28-5; Utah Admin. Code § 610-3-4

Paycheck due when employee is fired: Within 24 hours.

Paycheck due when employee quits: Next payday.

Unused vacation pay due: Only if required by policy or contract.

Special employment situations: Requirements do not apply to commission-based portion of sales employees' earnings if audit is necessary to determine the amount due.

Vermont
Vt. Stat. tit. 21, § 342(b)

Paycheck due when employee is fired: Within 72 hours.

Paycheck due when employee quits: Next regular payday or next Friday, if there is no regular payday.

Unused vacation pay due: Only if required by policy or contract.

Virginia
Va. Code § 40.1-29(A)

Paycheck due when employee is fired: Next payday.

Paycheck due when employee quits: Next payday.

Unused vacation pay due: Only if agreed to in a written statement.

Special employment situations: Requirements apply to all employers operating a business or engaging individuals to perform domestic service.

Washington
Wash. Rev. Code § 49.48.010

Paycheck due when employee is fired: End of pay period.

Paycheck due when employee quits: End of pay period.

Unused vacation pay due: Only if required by policy or contract.

State Laws That Control Final Paychecks (continued)

West Virginia
W. Va. Code §§ 21-5-1, 21-5-4

Paycheck due when employee is fired: Next regular payday (minus withheld amount for replacement cost of employer's unreturned property).

Paycheck due when employee quits: Next regular payday (minus withheld amount for replacement cost of employer's unreturned property).

Unused vacation pay due: Only if required by policy or contract.

Wisconsin
Wis. Stat. §§ 109.01(3), 109.03

Paycheck due when employee is fired: Next payday or within one month, whichever is earlier. If termination is due to merger, relocation, or liquidation of business, within 24 hours.

Paycheck due when employee quits: Next payday.

Unused vacation pay due: Only if required by policy or contract.

Special employment situations: Does not apply to managers, executives, or sales agents working on commission basis.

Wyoming
Wyo. Stat. §§ 27-4-104, 27-4-501, 27-4-507(c)

Paycheck due when employee is fired: Next regular payday.

Paycheck due when employee quits: Next regular payday.

Unused vacation pay due: No, if employer's policies state that vacation is forfeited upon termination of employment and the employee acknowledged the policy in writing.

Special employment situations: Requirements do not apply to commissioned sales employees if audit is necessary to determine the amount due.

State Laws on Employee Arrest and Conviction Records

The following chart summarizes state laws and regulations on whether an employer can get access to an employee's or prospective employee's past arrests or convictions. It includes citations to statutes and agency websites, as available.

Many states allow or require private sector employers to run background checks on workers, particularly in fields like child care, elder care, home health care, private schools, private security, and the investment industry. Criminal background checks usually consist of sending the applicant's name (and sometimes fingerprints) to the state police or to the FBI. State law may forbid hiring people with certain kinds of prior convictions, depending on the kind of job or license involved.

Federal law allows the states to establish procedures for requesting a nationwide background check to find out if a person has been "convicted of a crime that bears upon the [person's] fitness to have responsibility for the safety and well-being of children, the elderly, or individuals with disabilities." (42 U.S.C.A. § 5119a(a)(1).)

If your state isn't listed in this chart, then it doesn't have a *general statute* on whether private sector employers can find out about arrests or convictions. There might be a law about your particular industry, though.

It's always a good idea to consult your state's nondiscrimination enforcement agency or labor department to see what kinds of questions you can ask. The agency guidelines are designed to help employers comply with state and federal law. For further information, contact your state's agency.

Alabama

Ala. Code §§ 15-27-1, 15-27-6

Rights of employees and applicants: Need not disclose expunged records on employment application.

Arizona

Ariz. Rev. Stat. §§ 13-905, 41-1093.04, 41-1093.08

Rights of employees and applicants: In an application for an occupational license, an agency may not consider any arrest that was not followed by a conviction; conviction that has been sealed, dismissed, expunged, or pardoned; juvenile adjudication; or nonviolent misdemeanor. An occupational license cannot be denied, suspended, or revoked based on a prior criminal offense unless the offense is substantially related to the occupation, or it poses a reasonable threat to public health and safety. An occupational license cannot be denied solely on the basis of a criminal conviction if the individual has obtained a Certificate of Second Chance.

Agency guidelines for preemployment inquiries: Office of the Attorney General, Guide to Preemployment Inquiries, at www.azag.gov/office/publications/pre-employment-inquiries.

Arkansas

Ark. Code §§ 16-90-1417, 17-1-103

Rights of employees and applicants: In application for occupational license, agency may not consider convictions that have been annulled, expunged, or pardoned; arrests not followed by convictions; or nonviolent misdemeanors. Applicant may deny the existence of sealed criminal records and may state that underlying conduct never occurred.

California

Cal. Lab. Code §§ 432.7, 432.8; Cal. Gov't Code § 12952, Cal. Penal Code § 1000.4, Cal. Code Regs. tit. 2 § 11017.1

Rules for employers: Employers with five or more employees may not ask about or consider an applicant's criminal history (or criminal history of existing employee applying for a different position) until after making a conditional offer of employment. Once making a conditional offer, an

376 | DEALING WITH PROBLEM EMPLOYEES

State Laws on Employee Arrest and Conviction Records (continued)

employer may consider the applicant's conviction records. But before rejecting the applicant based on such records, the employer must conduct an individualized assessment (considering numerous factors set out by law) as to whether the conviction has a direct and adverse relationship with the specific duties of the job.

All employers may not seek or consider the following at any time: arrests that did not lead to conviction (unless the applicant is awaiting trial); participation in or referral to pretrial or post-trial diversion program; convictions that have been judicially sealed, dismissed, or expunged; convictions for which the person has received a full pardon or certificate of rehabilitation; non-felony convictions for marijuana possession that are more than two years old; or juvenile criminal history, including arrests, detentions, processings, adjudications, and court dispositions that occurred while applicant was subject to the juvenile court system.

Rights of employees and applicants: When an employer with five or more employees decides to reject an applicant based on a conviction record, the applicant is entitled to written notice. The applicant must be given at least five days to challenge the accuracy of the criminal record or provide mitigating evidence. The employer must take this evidence into account before making a final decision. If the final decision is a rejection, the applicant is entitled to written notice.

Applicant who completed a pretrial diversion program—with limited exceptions—need not disclose the underlying offense, and the record of the arrest can't be used to deny employment without the applicant's consent.

Agency guidelines for preemployment inquiries: Civil Rights Department, "Fair Chance Act: Criminal History and Employment," at www.calcivilrights. ca.gov/wp-content/uploads/sites/32/2022/11/ Fair-Chance-Act-FAQ_ENG.pdf.

Colorado

Colo. Rev. Stat. §§ 8-2-130, 8-3-108(1)(m), 19-2.5-108, 24-72-702(4), 24-72-703(2)(d)(l)

Rules for employers: Employers cannot state in help wanted ads and/or applications that applicants with criminal histories "need not apply," or ask about criminal histories on initial applications—except for positions requiring those disclosures. May not ask an applicant to disclose records of civil or military disobedience, unless the incident resulted in a guilty plea or conviction. May not ask about information contained in juvenile records or sealed criminal records. May not ask about expunged records where employee was arrested due to mistaken identity.

Rights of employees and applicants: Need not disclose any information in a sealed criminal record; may answer questions about sealed arrests or convictions as though they never occurred. Need not disclose information in an expunged record relating to arrest due to mistaken identity.

Agency guidelines for preemployment inquiries: Department of Labor and Employment, "Hiring & Screening: What Employers Must Disclose, & Information They Must Not Ask or Use" at https://cdle. colorado.gov. Search for "Hiring & Screening Laws."

Connecticut

Conn. Gen. Stat. §§ 46a-79, 46a-80, 31-51i

Rules for employers: Employer may not ask about criminal records in an initial employment application, unless required to by law or the position requires a security or fidelity bond. If exception applies and employment application form contains question concerning criminal history, it must include a notice in clear and conspicuous language that (1) the applicant is not required to disclose the existence of any arrest, criminal charge, or conviction, the records of which have been erased; (2) defines what criminal records are subject to erasure; and (3) any person whose criminal records have

State Laws on Employee Arrest and Conviction Records (continued)

been erased will be treated as if never arrested or convicted and may swear so under oath. Employers may not discriminate against applicants or employees on the basis of arrests or convictions that have been erased or for which an employee or applicant has received a provisional pardon or certificate of rehabilitation. Employer may not disclose information about a job applicant's criminal history except to members of the personnel department or, if there is no personnel department, person(s) in charge of hiring or conducting the interview.

Rights of employees and applicants: Employee may file a complaint with the Labor Commissioner if employer asks about criminal records on employment application. May not be asked to disclose information about a criminal record that has been erased; may answer any question as though arrest or conviction never took place.

Special situations: Applicants may not be denied a license, permit, registration, or other authorization to engage in a particular trade solely on the basis of a criminal conviction, unless the agency determines that the applicant isn't suitable based on: the nature of the crime and its relationship to the job; any rehabilitation the person has completed; and how long it has been since the conviction. A consumer reporting agency that issues a consumer report that is used or is expected to be used for employment purposes and that includes in such report criminal matters of public record concerning the consumer shall provide the consumer who is the subject of the consumer report (1) notice that the consumer reporting agency is reporting criminal matters of public record, and (2) the name and address of the person to whom such consumer report is being issued.

Delaware

Del. Code tit. 11, §§ 4372, 4376

Rights of employees and applicants: Do not have to disclose an arrest or conviction record that has been expunged.

District of Columbia

D.C. Code § 32-1342

Rules for employers: Employers with 11 or more employees: May not ask about or require an applicant to disclose any arrest or criminal accusation that is not pending or that did not lead to a conviction. May not ask about or require an applicant to disclose a conviction until after a conditional offer of employment is made. Employer may only withdraw conditional offer based on a legitimate business reason. Employers need not comply for certain positions, including those working with minors and vulnerable adults.

Rights of employees and applicants: If employer withdraws conditional offer based on criminal history, applicant has the right to request within 30 days: all records collected by the employer, including criminal records, and a notice of the applicant's right to file an administrative complaint with the Office of Human Rights.

Florida

Fla. Stat. §§ 112.011, 768.096, 943.0585, 943.059

Rules for employers: Employers need not conduct criminal background checks. However, employers are legally presumed not to have been negligent in hiring if they conduct a background investigation before hiring employees, including a criminal records check. If the employer conducted such a check and did not discover any information reasonably demonstrating that the employee was unfit for the job (or for employment in general), the employer is entitled to a presumption that it did not act negligently.

Rights of employees and applicants: May not be disqualified to practice or pursue any occupation or profession that requires a license, permit, or certificate because of a prior conviction, unless it was for a felony or first-degree misdemeanor and is directly related to the regulatory standards for that line of work. Employee whose criminal record

State Laws on Employee Arrest and Conviction Records (continued)

is expunged or sealed may deny the existence of the arrest, except when seeking employment in certain occupations or obtaining certain licenses.

Georgia

Ga. Code §§ 35-3-34, 35-3-34.1, 35-3-37, 42-8-62, 42-8-63, 42-8-63.1

Rules for employers: In order to obtain a criminal record from the state Crime Information Center, employer must supply the individual's fingerprints or signed consent. Employer will not be provided with records of arrests, charges, and sentences for first-time offenders where the individual was exonerated. Where, pursuant to Georgia's First Offender Statute, the charges were dismissed without an adjudication of guilt, the discharge may not be used to disqualify candidates except for specific occupations. If an adverse employment decision is made on the basis of the records provided, employer must disclose all information in the record to the employee or applicant and tell how it affected the decision.

Rights of employees and applicants: Probation for a first offense is not a conviction and an individual may not be disqualified for employment once probation is completed, except for certain occupations.

Hawaii

Haw. Rev. Stat. §§ 378-2, 378-2.5, 831-3.2

Rules for employers: Arrest records: It is a violation of law for any employer to refuse to hire, to discharge, or to discriminate in terms of compensation, conditions, or privileges of employment because of a person's arrest or court record. Convictions: May inquire into a conviction only after making a conditional offer of employment, may withdraw offer if conviction has a rational relation to job. May not examine felony convictions over seven years old, or misdemeanors over five years old.

Rights of employees and applicants: If an arrest or conviction has been expunged, may state that no

record exists and may respond to questions as a person with no record would respond.

Agency guidelines for preemployment inquiries: Hawaii Civil Rights Commission, "Pre-Employment Inquiries (Application Forms and Job Interviews)" at https://labor.hawaii.gov/hcrc/publications/#employment.

Idaho

Agency guidelines for preemployment inquiries: Idaho Department of Labor, "A Guide to Lawful Applications and Interviews" at www.idahofalls idaho.gov/DocumentCenter/View/448/Idaho-Interview-Guide-PDF. Using (criminal) records as an absolute bar to employment can have an adverse impact on some protected groups.

Illinois

775 Ill. Comp. Stat. §§ 5/2-103, 103.1, 20 Ill. Comp. Stat. 2630/12, 820 Ill. Comp. Stat. 75/15

Rules for employers: It is a civil rights violation to ask an applicant about arrests or criminal records that have been expunged or sealed, or to use the fact of an arrest or an expunged or sealed record as a basis for refusing to hire or renew employment. An employer may use other means to find out if person actually engaged in conduct leading to arrest. Job applications must clearly state that the applicant is not required to provide information about sealed or expunged records of convictions or arrest. An employer taking an adverse action in hiring or regarding an individuals current employment due to a criminal conviction must show that the conviction has a substantial relationship to the criminal offense or that granting employment or continued employment would result in an unreasonable risk to the safety and welfare of the public. Employer must notify applicant/employee about the action and the right to pursue charges under the IL Human Rights Act. Except in limited situations, employer may not ask about

State Laws on Employee Arrest and Conviction Records (continued)

criminal history or criminal records until the applicant is selected for an interview, or if there is none, until a conditional offer of employment has been made.

Agency guidelines for preemployment inquiries: Illinois Department of Human Rights, "Conviction Record Protection - Frequently Asked Questions" at https://dhr.illinois.gov/conviction-record-protection-frequently-asked-questions.html.

Indiana

Ind. Code § 35-38-9-10

Rules for employers: Employer may ask about criminal record only in terms that exclude expunged convictions or arrests. It is unlawful discrimination to refuse to employ someone based on a sealed or expunged arrest or conviction record. Information about expunged convictions is not admissible evidence in negligent hiring lawsuit against employer who relied on expungement order in deciding to hire the employee.

Rights of employees and applicants: May answer any question as though expunged arrest or conviction never occurred. May not be discriminated against on the basis of a conviction or arrest that has been expunged or sealed.

Special situations: Sealed or expunged arrest or conviction record may not be used to refuse to grant or renew a license, permit, or certificate necessary to engage in any activity, occupation, or profession.

Iowa

Agency guidelines for preemployment inquiries: Iowa Workforce Development, "Successful Interview Guide," at https://workforce.iowa.gov/media/1296/download?inline.

Kansas

Kan. Stat. §§ 12-4516, 22-4710

Rules for employers: Cannot require an employee to inspect or challenge a criminal record in order to obtain a copy of the record to qualify for employment, but may require an applicant to sign a release to allow employer to obtain record to determine fitness for employment. Employers can require access to criminal records for specific businesses. Employer is not liable for making hiring or contracting decision based on applicant's criminal record, as long as it reasonably bears on applicant's trustworthiness or the safety or well-being of customers or other employees.

Rights of employees and applicants: Need not disclose expunged records on employment application except for sensitive positions enumerated in Kan. Stat. § 12-4516(i)(2)(A)-(K).

Agency guidelines for preemployment inquiries: Kansas Human Rights Commission, "Guidelines on Equal Employment Practices: Preventing Discrimination in Hiring," at www.khrc.net/hiring.html.

Kentucky

Ky. Rev. Stat. §§ 431.073, 431.076, 431.078

Rights of employees and applicants: Need not disclose expunged records on employment application.

Louisiana

La. Rev. Stat. §§ 23:291.2, 37:2950

Rights of employees and applicants: Employer may not consider arrest record or charge that was not followed by conviction in hiring decisions.

Rights of employees and applicants: Prior conviction cannot be used as a sole basis to deny an occupational or professional license, unless conviction directly relates to the license being sought.

Maine

Me. Rev. Stat. tit. 5, § 5301; Me. Rev. Stat. tit. 15 §§ 2265, 2266; Me. Rev. Stat. tit. 26 § 600-A

Rules for employers: Employer may not inquire into criminal history in employment application, but can make such inquiries during interview or once

State Laws on Employee Arrest and Conviction Records (continued)

employer has determined applicant is otherwise qualified for the position.

Rights of employees and applicants: Need not give any information to employer about sealed record. A conviction is not an automatic bar to obtaining an occupational or professional license. Only convictions that directly relate to the profession or occupation, that include dishonesty or false statements, that are subject to imprisonment for more than 1 year, or that involve sexual misconduct on the part of a licensee may be considered.

Agency guidelines for preemployment inquiries: The Maine Human Rights Commission, "PreEmployment Inquiry Guide," at www.maine.gov/mhrc/laws-guidance/employment/pre-employment.

Maryland

Md. Code Crim. Proc. §§ 10-109, 10-301, 10-306; Md. Code Lab. & Empl. § 3-1503; Md. Regs. Code § 09.01.10.02

Rules for employers: May not inquire about criminal charges that have been expunged or criminal records that have been shielded under the Maryland Second Chance Act. May not use a refusal to disclose information as sole basis for not hiring an applicant. Employers with at least 15 employees may not require applicant to disclose criminal record or accusations before first in-person interview.

Rights of employees and applicants: Need not refer to or give any information about an expunged charge or shielded record. A professional or occupational license may not be refused or revoked simply because of a conviction—agency must consider the nature of the crime and its relation to the occupation or profession; the conviction's relevance to the applicant's fitness and qualifications; when conviction occurred and other convictions, if any; and the applicant's behavior before and after conviction.

Agency guidelines for preemployment inquiries: DLLR, "Ban the Box Labor and Employment Article § 3-1501 Frequently Asked Questions," at www.dllr. state.md.us/labor/wages/esscrimscreen.shtml.

Massachusetts

Mass. Gen. Laws ch. 6, § 171A; ch. 151B, § 4; ch. 276, § 100A; Code Mass. Regs. tit. 804, § 3.02

Rules for employers: Unless federal or state law disqualifies applicants with certain convictions from holding position, may not ask about criminal record information of any kind on initial written application. If job application has a question about prior arrests or convictions, it must include a formulated statement (that appears in the statute) that states that an applicant with a sealed or expunged record is entitled to answer, "No record." May not ask about arrests that did not result in conviction. May not ask about first-time convictions for drunkenness, simple assault, speeding, minor traffic violations, affray, or disturbing the peace; may not ask about misdemeanor convictions three or more years old unless applicant has another conviction within the last three years.

Rights of employees and applicants: If criminal record is sealed, may answer "No record" to any inquiry about past arrests or convictions.

Special situations: Employer must give applicant a copy of criminal record before asking about it. Employer must give applicant a copy of record after making adverse job decision (if it didn't already provide the record). Additional rules apply to employers that conduct five or more criminal background checks per year.

Agency guidelines for preemployment inquiries: Massachusetts Commission Against Discrimination, "Criminal Record Discrimination in the Workplace," at www.mass.gov/info-details/criminal-record-discrimination-in-the-workplace.

State Laws on Employee Arrest and Conviction Records (continued)

Michigan

Mich. Comp. Laws § 37.2205a

Rules for employers: May not request information on any misdemeanor arrests or charges that did not result in conviction. May ask about felony arrests and misdemeanor or felony convictions.

Rights of employees and applicants: Employees or applicants are not making a false statement if they fail to disclose information they have a civil right to withhold.

Agency guidelines for preemployment inquiries: Michigan Department of Civil Rights, "Pre-Employment Inquiry Guide," at www.michigan.gov/documents/mdcr/Preemploymentguide62012_388403_7.pdf.

Minnesota

Minn. Stat. §§ 181.981, 364.01 to 364.03

Rules for employers: Employers may not ask, consider, or require applicants to disclose criminal record or history until selected for an interview or, if there is no interview, until a conditional offer of employment is made. However, employer may notify applicants that particular criminal records will disqualify applicants from holding particular jobs.

Rights of employees and applicants: No one can be disqualified from pursuing or practicing an occupation that requires a license, unless the crime directly relates to the occupation. Agency may consider the nature and seriousness of the crime and its relation to the applicant's fitness for the occupation. Even if the crime does relate to the occupation, a person who provides evidence of rehabilitation and present fitness cannot be disqualified.

Special situations: Employee's criminal record is not admissible in any civil lawsuit against the employer based on the employee's actions if: the lawsuit is based on the employer's compliance with the state's "ban the box" law; the employee's record was sealed, expunged, or pardoned prior to the actions; the employee's record consists only of arrests or charges that did not lead to conviction; or the employee's job duties did not create any greater risk of harm than being employed in general or interacting with the public outside of work.

Agency guidelines for preemployment inquiries: Minnesota Department of Human Rights, "Criminal Background Checks" at https://mn.gov/mdhr/employers/criminal-background.

Mississippi

Miss. Code § 99-19-71

Rules for employers: Employer may ask applicant if expunction order has been issued regarding the applicant.

Rights of employees and applicants: Applicant need not disclose expunged arrest or conviction when responding to inquiries.

Missouri

Mo. Rev. Stat. §§ 314.200, 610.140

Rights of employees and applicants: May answer "no" to employer's inquiry about criminal record if such record has been expunged unless employer is legally required to exclude applicants with certain criminal convictions from employment. No one may be denied a license for a profession or occupation primarily on the basis that a prior conviction negates the person's good moral character, if the applicant has been released from incarceration by pardon, parole, or otherwise, or the applicant is on probation with no evidence of violations. The conviction may be considered, but the licensing board must also consider the crime's relation to the license, the date of conviction, the applicant's conduct since the conviction, and other evidence of the applicant's character.

State Laws on Employee Arrest and Conviction Records (continued)

Montana

Mont. Admin. R. § 24.9.1406

Rules for employers: Employer should not ask questions about arrests at any point in the hiring process. Employers may ask about convictions, however.

Nebraska

Neb. Rev. Stat. § 29-3523

Rules for employers: May not obtain access to information regarding arrests after one year if no charges are filed by prosecutor decision; after two years if no charges are filed as a result of completed diversion; or after three years if charges were filed but were dismissed by the court. May not ask about sealed records in an employment application.

Rights of employees and applicants: As to sealed records, employee may respond as if the offense never occurred.

Nevada

Nev. Rev. Stat. §§ 176A.850, 179.285, 179.301, 179A.100(3)

Rules for employers: Unless applicant consents, employer may obtain only records of convictions or incidents for which the applicant or employee is currently within the criminal justice system, including parole or probation.

Rights of employees and applicants: Employees may not be required to disclose sealed convictions, or convictions for which they were honorably discharged from probation (except to a gaming establishment or state employer).

Agency guidelines for preemployment inquiries: Nevada Equal Rights Commission, "Nevada Pre-Employment Guide," at https://cms.detr.nv.gov/content/media/pre_employment_guiderev2.pdf.

New Hampshire

N.H. Rev. Stat. § 651:5(X)

Rules for employers: May ask about a previous criminal record only if question substantially follows this wording, "Have you ever been arrested for or convicted of a crime that has not been annulled by a court?"

Agency guidelines for preemployment inquiries: New Hampshire Commission for Human Rights, "Guide to Pre-Employment Inquiries," at https://www.humanrights.nh.gov/sites/g/files/ehbemt911/files/inline-documents/guide-to-preemployment-inquiries.pdf.

New Jersey

N.J. Stat. §§ 2C:52-27, 5:5-34.1, 5:12-89, 5:12-91, 34:6B-11 to 34:6B-21; N.J. Admin. Code § 13:59-1.6

Rules for employers: Employers with 15 or more employees may not publish a job advertisement that states that applicants who have been arrested or convicted will not be considered for the position. These employers also may not ask applicants about criminal history until after an interview has been conducted. These employers also may not refuse to hire an applicant based on a criminal record that has been expunged or erased through executive pardon. If criminal history may be used to disqualify individual from position, applicant must be given notice and opportunity to challenge the accuracy of the criminal record. Employers may not require an applicant to disclose or take adverse action based solely on any arrest, charge, or conviction for marijuana-related offenses unless the position is for law enforcement, corrections, or similar employers.

Rights of employees and applicants: May deny the occurrence of any arrest, conviction, or other proceedings related to a criminal record that has been expunged, with limited exceptions.

Special situations: There are specific rules for casino employees, longshoremen and related occupations, horse racing, and other gaming industry jobs.

State Laws on Employee Arrest and Conviction Records (continued)

New Mexico

N.M. Stat. §§ 28-2-1 to 28-2-4, 29-3A-7

Rules for employers: May not inquire into applicants' criminal history on initial employment application.

Rights of employees and applicants: Applicants generally not required to disclose criminal record information that has been sealed or expunged. Occupational license shall not be denied solely on the basis of a previous arrest or conviction, unless conviction is related to the position in question and consistent with business necessity.

New York

N.Y. Correct. Law §§ 750 to 754; N.Y. Exec. Law § 296(15), (16)

Rules for employers: It is unlawful discrimination to ask about any arrests or charges that did not result in conviction, unless they are currently pending. Employers also may not ask about sealed convictions or youthful offender adjudications. Employers with ten or more employees may not deny employment based on a conviction unless it relates directly to the job or would be an "unreasonable" risk to property or to public or individual safety. Employer must consider eight factors listed in statute. If employer considers these factors and makes a reasonable, good-faith decision to hire or retain employee, there's a rebuttable presumption that evidence of the employee's criminal history should be excluded in any subsequent lawsuit for negligent hiring or retention.

Rights of employees and applicants: Upon request, applicant must be given, within 30 days, a written statement of the reasons why employment was denied. An individual required or requested to provide information in violation of this subdivision may respond as if the arrest, criminal accusation, or disposition of such arrest or criminal accusation did not occur. May not be asked about criminal records that are sealed, and may respond to any inquiry as though the conduct did not occur.

Agency guidelines for preemployment inquiries: New York State Human Rights Law (NYSHRL) prohibits employers from discriminating on the basis of criminal conviction history: https://dhr.ny.gov/system/files/documents/2024/05/hrl.pdf.

North Carolina

N.C. Gen. Stat. §§ 15A-146, 15A-153, 93B-8.1

Rules for employers: May not ask applicants about expunged arrests, charges, or convictions.

Rights of employees and applicants: Person whose arrest or charge was expunged may omit expunged entries in response to questions. Occupational license may not be denied on the basis of a criminal conviction unless conviction is directly related to duties and responsibilities for the licensed occupation or crime was violent or sexual in nature. Applicant has right to provide evidence of inaccuracy in record, mitigation, or rehabilitation.

North Dakota

N.D. Cent. Code § 12-60-16.6

Rules for employers: May obtain records of arrests (adults only) occurring in the past three years or of convictions, provided the information has not been purged or sealed.

Agency guidelines for preemployment inquiries: North Dakota Department of Labor and Human Rights, "Employment Applications and Interviews," at www.nd.gov/labor/sites/www/files/documents/Brochures/Employment%20Applications%20%26%20Interviews.pdf.

Ohio

Ohio Rev. Code §§ 2151.357, 2925.14, 2925.141, 2953.34

Rules for employers: May inquire only into convictions or bail forfeitures that have not been sealed or expunged, unless question has a direct and substantial relationship to job.

State Laws on Employee Arrest and Conviction Records (continued)

Rights of employees and applicants: May not be asked about arrest records that are sealed or expunged; may respond to inquiry as though arrest did not occur. Arrest or misdemeanor conviction for marijuana need not be reported in any application for employment.

Oklahoma

Okla. Stat. tit. 22, § 19(J)

Rules for employers: May not inquire into any criminal record that has been expunged.

Rights of employees and applicants: If record is expunged, may state that no criminal action ever occurred. May not be denied employment solely for refusing to disclose sealed criminal record information.

Oregon

Or. Rev. Stat. §§ 181A.230, 181A.240, 181A.245, 659A.030, 659A.360

Rules for employers: Employer may not ask about criminal convictions on an employment application. Employer may ask about criminal convictions only after an initial interview or after a conditional offer of employment has been made. Employer may request information from state police department about convictions and arrests in the past year that have not resulted in dismissal or acquittal. Before making request, employer must notify employee or applicant; when submitting request, must tell department when and how person was notified. May not discriminate against an applicant or current employee on the basis of an expunged juvenile record unless there is a "bona fide occupational qualification."

Rights of employees and applicants: Before state police department releases any criminal record information, it must notify employee or applicant and provide a copy of all information that will be sent to employer. Notice must include protections under federal civil rights law and the procedure for challenging information in the record. Record may not be released until 14 days after notice is sent.

Agency guidelines for preemployment inquiries: Oregon Bureau of Labor & Industries, "Hiring discrimination and 'Ban the Box,'" at www.oregon.gov/boli/workers/Pages/hiring-discrimination.aspx.

Pennsylvania

18 Pa. Cons. Stat. §§ 9122.5, 9125

Rules for employers: May consider felony and misdemeanor convictions only if they relate to person's suitability for the job. Expunged criminal records may not be used for employment purposes.

Rights of employees and applicants: Must be informed in writing if refusal to hire is based on criminal record information.

Rhode Island

R.I. Gen. Laws §§ 12-1.3-4, 13-8.2-1 to 13-8.2-8, 28-5-7(7)

Rules for employers: It is unlawful to include on an application form or to ask as part of an interview if the applicant has ever been arrested or charged with any crime. Application form may not include questions about arrests, charges, or convictions, except questions about convictions for specific offenses that would legally disqualify the applicant for the position under federal or state law, or would preclude bonding (if bonding is required for the position). May ask about convictions during the first interview or later.

Rights of employees and applicants: Do not have to disclose any conviction that has been expunged. As to sealed records for arrests due to mistaken identity, employee may respond as if the offense never occurred.

Special situations: Those convicted of crimes may apply to the parole board for a Certificate of Recovery and Re-Entry, stating that the holder has achieved certain rehabilitation goals. Parole board will consider applications for a certificate one year or more after conviction of a misdemeanor, or

State Laws on Employee Arrest and Conviction Records (continued)

three years or more after conviction of a nonviolent felony. Although the purpose of this certificate is to assist the holder in reentering society, employers are not liable for denying employment based on prior conviction(s), even if the applicant holds a certificate.

South Carolina

S.C. Code § 40-1-140

Rights of employees and applicants: Applicant may not be denied professional or occupational license based solely on a prior criminal conviction, unless it relates directly to the profession or occupation. Applicant must be given a hearing prior to denial based on criminal history, and applicant must receive written grounds for denial and opportunity to appeal.

South Dakota

Agency guidelines for preemployment inquiries: South Dakota Division of Human Rights, "Pre-Employment Inquiry Guide," at https://dlr.sd.gov/human_rights/publications/preemployment.pdf suggests that an employer shouldn't ask or check into arrests or convictions if they are not substantially related to the job.

Texas

Tex. Crim. Proc. Code § 55A.401; Tex. Fam. Code § 58.261

Rights of employees and applicants: Employee may deny the occurrence of any arrest that has been expunged. An employee whose juvenile records have been sealed is not required to disclose in a job application that the employee was the subject of a juvenile court proceeding.

Utah

Utah Code §§ 34-52-301, 53-10-108

Rights of employees and applicants: Applicant for a job with a private employer may answer a question related to an expunged criminal record or juvenile delinquency record as though they never occurred.

Vermont

13 Vt. Stat. §§ 7606 to 7607; 21 Vt. Stat. § 495j

Rules for employers: May not ask about criminal history on an employment application, except for specific offenses that would disqualify the applicant for the position under state or federal law. Employer may ask about criminal history during an interview or once the applicant has been deemed qualified for the position.

Rights of employees and applicants: Need not disclose arrests or convictions that have been expunged or sealed.

Virginia

Va. Code §§ 19.2-389.3 (to be repealed effective July 1, 2026), 19.2-392.4 (and Va. Code §§ 19.2-392.5 and 19.2-392.15 as of July 1, 2026)

Rules for employers: UNTIL JULY 1, 2026: May not require an applicant to disclose information about any arrest, criminal charge, conviction, or civil offense that has been expunged, nor any record of arrest, criminal charge or conviction for possession of marijuana unless the position is for law enforcement, school boards or similar "sensitive" employers. Employers may inquire as to criminal history during or after an interview of a prospective employee.

ON AND AFTER JULY 1, 2026: May not require an applicant to disclose information about any arrest, criminal charge, conviction, or civil offense that has been expunged or sealed unless the position is for law enforcement, school boards, or similar "sensitive" employers.

Rights of employees and applicants: UNTIL JULY 1, 2026: Need not refer to any arrest or criminal charge that has been expunged if asked about criminal record or civil offenses.

ON AND AFTER JULY 1, 2026: Need not refer to any arrest or criminal charge that has been expunged if asked about criminal record or civil offenses. Also, if the employee has an arrest, charge, or conviction

State Laws on Employee Arrest and Conviction Records (continued)

that was sealed, the employee can deny the sealed record or not disclose it unless they are applying for employment with any state police office or another position for which the code requires disclosure of sealed records.

Washington

Wash. Rev. Code §§ 9.96.060(3), 9.96A.020, 43.43.815, 49.94.010; Wash. Admin. Code § 162-12-140

Rules for employers: An employer may not ask about, seek, or consider an applicant's criminal history until after it has determined that the applicant is "otherwise qualified" for the job and makes an offer of employment conditioned on obtaining the applicant's criminal record. At a minimum, the employer must first determine that the applicant meets the basic criteria of the job. After that, employers may seek out criminal history, subject to the limitations below.

An employer that obtains a conviction record must notify the applicant within 30 days of receiving it and must allow the employee to examine it. And, according to the Human Rights Commission, employers with eight or more employees must consider certain information before rejecting an applicant based on criminal history. With respect to arrest records, these employers must ask whether the charges are still pending, have been dismissed, or led to conviction that would adversely affect job performance and whether the arrest occurred in the last 10 years. These employers may make an employment decision based on a conviction record, but only if the conviction or the applicant's release from prison occurred within the last 10 years and the crime reasonably relates to the job duties.

Rights of employees and applicants: If a conviction record is cleared or vacated, may answer questions as though the conviction never occurred. A person convicted of a felony cannot be refused an occupational license unless the conviction is less than 10 years old and the felony relates specifically to the occupation or business.

Agency guidelines for preemployment inquiries: Washington Human Rights Commission, "Preemployment inquiry guide," at https://apps.leg. wa.gov/WAC/default.aspx?cite=162-12.

West Virginia

W. Va. Code §§ 49-4-723, 61-11-25

Rules for employers: Employers may not discriminate on the basis of juvenile criminal records that have been expunged.

Rights of employees and applicants: As to expunged records, employee may respond as if offense never occurred.

Wisconsin

Wis. Stat. §§ 111.31, 111.335

Rules for employers: It is a violation of state civil rights law to discriminate against an employee on the basis of a prior arrest or conviction record. Arrest records: May not ask about arrests unless there are pending charges. May not reject applicant unless pending charges are substantially related to the job or would preclude required bonding. Convictions: May not ask about convictions unless charges substantially relate to job or would preclude required bonding.

Special situations: Employers are entitled to obtain complete criminal record information for positions that require bonding and for burglar alarm installers.

Agency guidelines for preemployment inquiries: Wisconsin Department of Workforce Development, Equal Rights Division, Civil Rights Bureau, "Fair Hiring and Avoiding Discriminatory Interview Questions," at https://dwd.wisconsin.gov/er/civil-rights/discrimination/interviewquestions.htm.

Wyoming

Wyo. Stat. § 7-13-1401

Rights of employees and applicants: If an arrest or charge has been expunged, may respond to questions as if arrest or charge never occurred.

State OSHA Laws and Offices

If a state has a health and safety law that meets or exceeds federal OSHA standards, the state can take over enforcement of the standards from federal administrators. This means that all inspections and enforcement actions will be handled by your state OSHA rather than its federal counterpart.

So far 21 states and Puerto Rico have been approved for such enforcement regarding private employers: Alaska, Arizona, California, Hawaii, Indiana, Iowa, Kentucky, Maryland, Michigan, Minnesota, Nevada, New Mexico, North Carolina, Oregon, South Carolina, Tennessee, Utah, Vermont, Virginia, Washington, and Wyoming. You can find an up-to-date list, along with contact information, at www.osha.gov/stateplans.

Connecticut, Illinois, Maine, Massachusetts, New Jersey, and New York also have OSHA-type laws, but they only apply to government employees. Other states are considering passing OSHA laws—and some of the above states are considering amending the coverage and content of existing laws.

If your business is located in a state that has an OSHA law, contact your state agency for a copy of the safety and health standards that are relevant to your business. State standards may be more strict than federal standards, and the requirements for posting notices might be different.

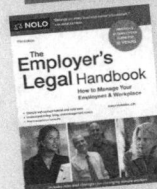

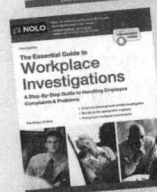

On Nolo.com you'll also find:

Books & Software

Nolo publishes hundreds of great books and software programs for consumers and
business owners. Order a copy, or download an ebook version instantly, at Nolo.com.

Online Forms

You can quickly and easily make a will or living trust, form an LLC or corporation,
or make hundreds of other forms—online.

Free Legal Information

Thousands of articles answer common questions about everyday legal issues,
including wills, bankruptcy, small business formation, divorce, patents,
employment, and much more.

Plain-English Legal Dictionary

Stumped by jargon? Look it up in America's most up-to-date source for definitions
of legal terms, free at Nolo.com.

Lawyer Directory

Nolo's consumer-friendly lawyer directory provides in-depth profiles of lawyers all
over America. You'll find information you need to choose the right lawyer.

PROBM13